Worlds Seen and Imagined

To Adlai

With hopes of doing more with you in Chicago.

William McKeen

Worlds Seen and

Japanese Screens from The Idemitsu Museum of Arts

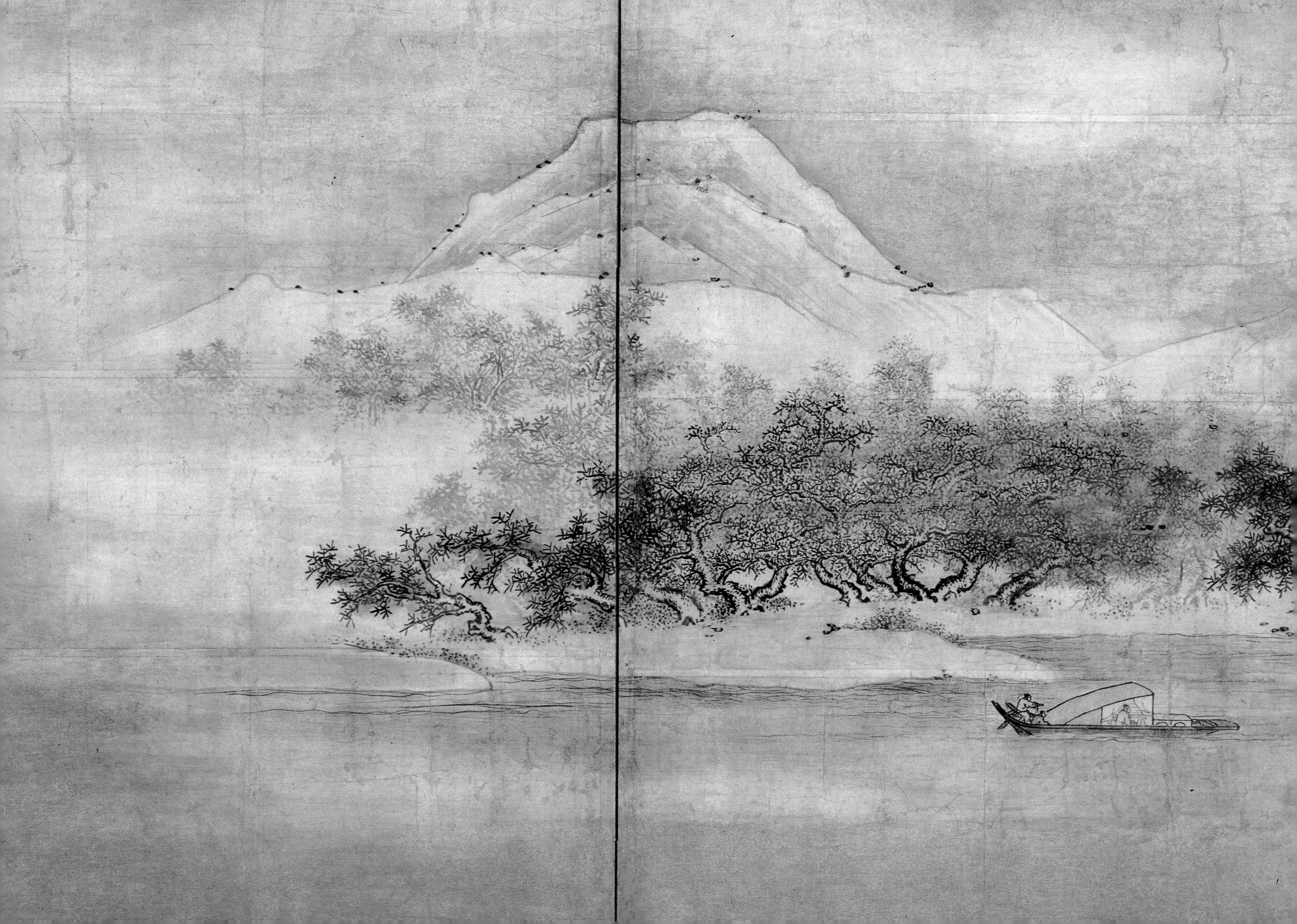

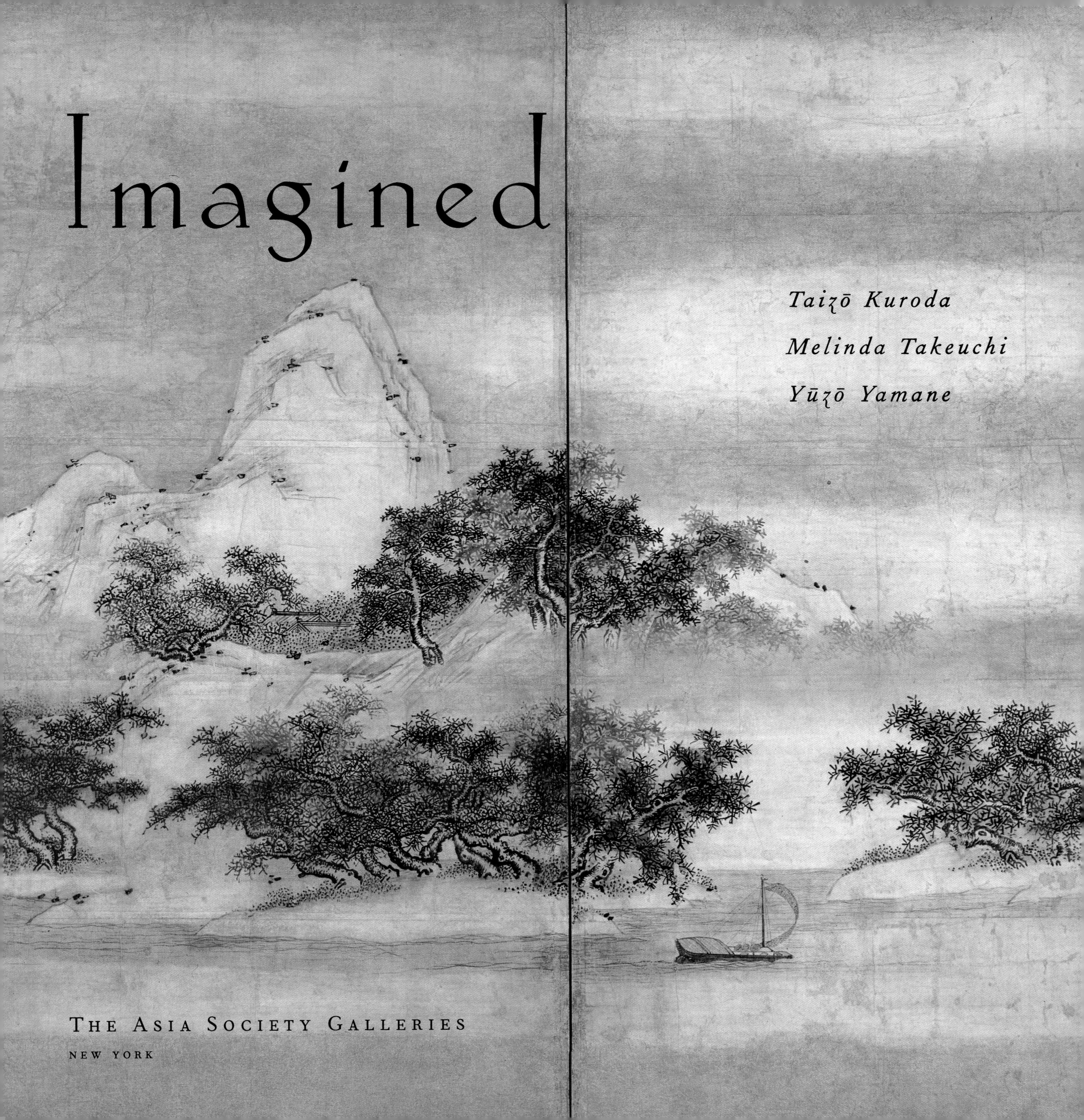

Imagined

Taizō Kuroda

Melinda Takeuchi

Yūzō Yamane

THE ASIA SOCIETY GALLERIES

NEW YORK

Worlds Seen and Imagined:
Japanese Screens from The Idemitsu Museum of Arts
is co-organized by The Asia Society Galleries
and The Idemitsu Museum of Arts. It is made possible, in part, by grants
from the National Endowment for the Arts, Idemitsu Kosan Co., Ltd.,
The Blanchette Hooker Rockefeller Fund, The Japan Foundation,
and the Mary Livingston Griggs and Mary Griggs Burke Foundation.
Additional support for the exhibition and galleries education program is provided
by the Friends of The Asia Society Galleries, The Starr Foundation,
the Arthur Ross Foundation, Charles E. Culpeper Foundation,
and The New York Times Company Foundation.
The exhibition is also supported by an indemnity from
the Federal Council on the Arts and the Humanities.

EXHIBITION ITINERARY
The Asia Society Galleries, New York
October 18–December 31, 1995

The Art Institute of Chicago
February 18–April 30, 1996

PUBLISHED BY
The Asia Society Galleries
725 Park Avenue
New York, New York 10021-5088

AND

Abbeville Press Publishers
488 Madison Avenue
New York, New York 10022

ISBN: 0-87848-081-1 (paper; The Asia Society Galleries)
ISBN: 0-7892-0081-3 (cloth; Abbeville)

Library of Congress Cataloging-in-Publication Data
can be found on page 168.

JACKET
Trees and Plants of the Four Seasons, details, cat. no. 2

TITLE PAGE
Winter Landscape, detail, cat. no. 18

THIS PAGE
Whose Sleeves? (Tagasode), detail, cat. no. 24

Note to the Reader

In the narrative, modern Japanese names are given with the surname last. References to historical figures throughout the book follow traditional Japanese usage, surname first, and citations in the notes and bibliography follow the source. Dimensions of screens comprise painting and hardware.

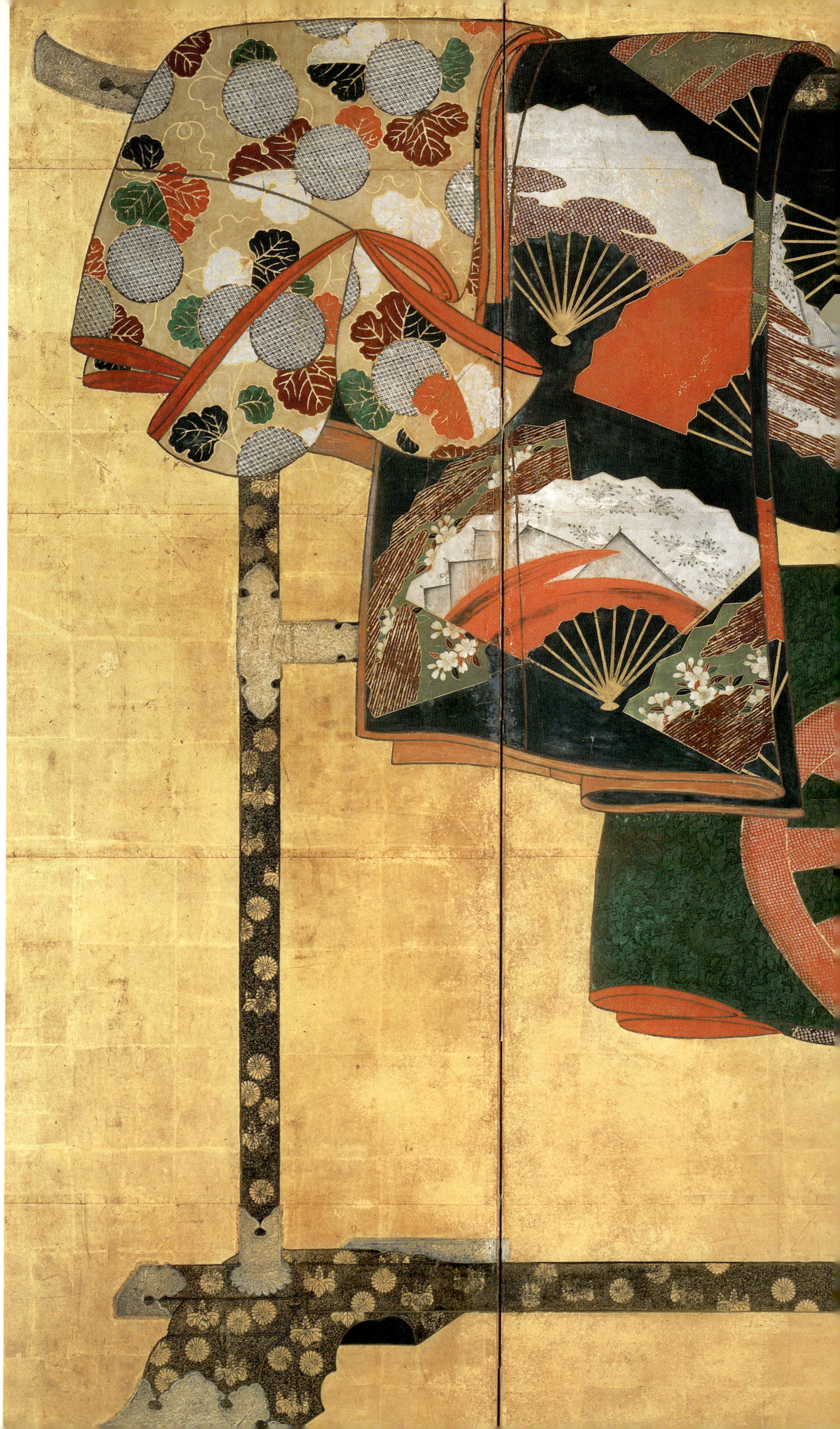

Contents

Foreword 6
Vishakha N. Desai

Preface 7
Shōsuke Idemitsu

Acknowledgments 8
Denise Patry Leidy

10 SCREEN PAINTINGS OF THE MUROMACHI PERIOD: THE MIXING OF CHINESE AND JAPANESE STYLES
Yūzō Yamane, translated by Sarah E. Thompson

30 THE GOLDEN LINK: PLACE, POETRY, AND PARADISE IN A MEDIEVAL JAPANESE DESIGN
Melinda Takeuchi

54 FIGURATIVE SCREEN PAINTING IN THE LATE MOMOYAMA AND EARLY EDO PERIODS—INTRODUCING A RECENTLY DISCOVERED WORK OF THE KANO SCHOOL
Taizō Kuroda, translated by Laurie Berman

71 CATALOGUE OF THE EXHIBITION
Taizō Kuroda and Matthew McKelway

Glossary 160

Map of Japan 163

Bibliography 164

Index of Artists and Works in the Exhibition 167

Foreword

Worlds Seen and Imagined: Japanese Screens from The Idemitsu Museum of Arts has been in the making since 1990 when we and our colleagues at the Idemitsu Museum began to discuss the possibility of an exchange of exhibitions. By the time The Asia Society's loan exhibition of selected masterpieces from the Mr. and Mrs. John D. Rockefeller 3rd Collection of Asian Art opened in Tokyo in 1992, the idea of bringing an exhibition of screens from The Idemitsu Museum of Arts to the United States was firmly established.

Although Japanese screens are universally admired for their striking format and exquisite painting, very few exhibitions have been devoted exclusively to the art of the folding screen. The fifty-seven screens, most of which are in pairs, in *Worlds Seen and Imagined* were selected to help illuminate the diversity of screen painting from the fifteenth through the early nineteenth century. The large majority date from the sixteenth and seventeenth centuries, generally regarded as the golden age of Japanese screen painting. The formative Muromachi period is represented by rare early examples of indigenous styles (*Yamato-e*), including one from the fifteenth century, and examples of Chinese-style ink painting (*Kanga*). Well-known masters in the exhibition include Kano Motonobu and several subsequent heads of the Kano lineage as well as Hasegawa Tōhaku, Ogata Kōrin, Yosa Buson, and Sakai Hōitsu.

As the title of the exhibition implies, the works represent observed realities—of Kyoto and Tokyo, of historic events—and imagined designs in which elements of nature such as birds, flowers, trees, and waterfalls are used to create bold, sometimes abstract, patterns. This carefully selected group of images from the extensive holdings of The Idemitsu Museum of Arts provides a rare view of the development and the dazzling variety of Japanese screens. There are screens with spare ink washes that stretch across vast surfaces as well as images with ornate gold fields and vivid color schemes that fill the available space.

The Idemitsu Museum of Arts is world famous for its exquisite collection of ceramics and other three-dimensional objects from China and Japan. Exhibitions of masterpieces of Ming porcelain and selections from the entire collection have traveled to the United States in the past fifteen years. Being relatively new, the museum's holdings of Japanese screens are not as well known outside Japan. Among Japanese art specialists and connoisseurs, however, the Idemitsu Museum's collecting in the field of Japanese screens, under the leadership of Yūzō Yamane, is considered one of the most exciting developments in the Japanese art field in recent years.

The building of the collection has coincided with a period of profound change in Japanese art scholarship, and the screens have supported this shift in fundamental views by providing new evidence of the relationship between the indigenous style and the Chinese style in later Japanese painting. Essays in this catalogue by Professor Yamane, Taizō Kuroda, and Melinda Takeuchi attest to important aspects of new scholarship. Two deal with issues of early Yamato-e style screens, an area of interest only in the last few years, and the third introduces a newly discovered Kanga screen and attributes it to an artist whose oeuvre is under scrutiny.

In addition to being an important special exhibition of Japanese screens, *Worlds Seen and Imagined: Japanese Screens from The Idemitsu Museum of Arts* celebrates the thirty-fifth anniversary of the sister-city relationship between Tokyo and New York. It marks the special ties between The Idemitsu Museum of Arts and The Asia Society Galleries, private museums with superb collections of Asian art in the respective cities. The connection between the two institutions predates the planning for the exchange of exhibitions, for it began with a special bond established between the Rockefeller and Idemitsu families in the 1950s. Indeed, it was Mr. Shōsuke Idemitsu, the son of Sazō Idemitsu and the museum's present director, who proposed that this special relationship be celebrated by the mounting of traveling exhibitions from our respective collections. We are indebted to him for his sustained support of this joint venture.

I would like to extend a special note of gratitude to the patrons and supporters of this project, without whom the exhibition, publication, and public programs would not be possible.

The director of The Art Institute of Chicago, James N. Wood, was an early and enthusiastic advocate of having the exhibition there, and we are delighted that it will be seen by the visitors to The Art Institute. Through its travel and this catalogue, we hope that *Worlds Seen and Imagined: Japanese Screens from The Idemitsu Museum of Arts* will make a lasting contribution to the understanding of one of the most important and unique forms of Japanese art.

Vishakha N. Desai
Director of the Galleries
Vice President for Program Coordination
The Asia Society

Preface

The Idemitsu Museum of Arts is proud to present *Worlds Seen and Imagined: Japanese Screens from The Idemitsu Museum of Arts* at The Asia Society Galleries in New York and The Art Institute of Chicago. This is a follow-up to the highly acclaimed exhibition *Treasures of Asian Art from The Mr. and Mrs. John D. Rockefeller 3rd Collection, The Asia Society, New York*, held at The Idemitsu Museum of Arts in Tokyo and Osaka in 1992, for which we are grateful to The Asia Society.

The Japanese folding screen, or *byōbu*, was used in traditional architecture as interior decoration either free-standing within rooms or on walls and was a quick way to create new spatial configurations through the division of space. Behind folding screens, gatherings were held under various pretexts and by many groups, including nobility of high rank as well as common citizens. Information in the worlds of politics, literature, and war was also transmitted behind folding screens. Thus the folding screen was a witness to the past. Moreover, its wide surfaces, decorated with multicolored paintings of flowers, birds, and other subjects, provided a vivid depiction of the changing seasons as well as creating a space for the enjoyment of pictures.

In the realm of Japanese painting where small sizes are the norm, the breadth of folding screens gave Japanese artists the chance to work on a larger scale and the freedom to display their personal genius and ability. The result was the development of a great many styles. An extremely high level of excellence was reached in Muromachi period folding screens, in both painting and workmanship. This achievement reflected the era's flourishing trade and the high value placed on folding screens as gifts from the Japanese *daimyō* to the Chinese emperor. By including a wide variety of screens from the Muromachi period to the latter half of the Edo period, this exhibition makes it possible to view the dynamism of large-scale Japanese painting across five hundred years.

It is my hope that through this exhibition, more American viewers will be introduced to this particular aspect of Japanese culture.

In closing I would like to express my gratitude to directors Vishakha N. Desai of The Asia Society Galleries and James N. Wood of The Art Institute of Chicago and to all the many people whose cooperation helped make this exhibition possible.

Shōsuke Idemitsu
Chairman and Director
The Idemitsu Museum of Arts

Acknowledgments

This exhibition and catalogue featuring important folding screens from the collection of The Idemitsu Museum of Arts are the result of a long-standing collaboration between the staffs of the Idemitsu Museum and The Asia Society Galleries. Our first joint venture, an exhibition of works from across Asia in The Asia Society's Rockefeller collection, traveled to both the Tokyo and Osaka branches of the Idemitsu Museum in 1992. The exhibition *Worlds Seen and Imagined: Japanese Screens from The Idemitsu Museum of Arts*, which will be presented in New York and Chicago, focuses on the art of the Japanese screen, particularly examples from the fifteenth through the seventeenth century. Many represent types of paintings that are not prevalent in American collections. Their consistently high quality will provide American audiences with a breathtaking introduction to an important Japanese art form and to some of the newer scholarship that informs the study of this material.

The leadership of Tarō Nakao, deputy director, and Tadanori Yuba, chief curator, of The Idemitsu Museum of Arts was invaluable in organizing this exhibition. The definition of its scope and the choice of objects were undertaken by the curatorial team of Yūzō Yamane, trustee, and Taizō Kuroda, deputy chief curator. These two scholars have played important roles in the development of the screen collection at the Idemitsu Museum and in current Japanese scholarship on this material. Some of the results of their research are detailed in their essays as well as in the catalogue entries written by Mr. Kuroda and Matthew McKelway. As the exhibition curator, Mr. Kuroda coordinated the innumerable tasks entailed in organizing an international loan exhibition and catalogue. Hirokazu Yatsunami, curator, and Masao Matsushita, registrar, again proved invaluable in working out many curatorial and logistical details. Susumu Wakisaka photographed all the screens in the collection that appear in this catalogue. The professionalism of all our colleagues at the Idemitsu Museum has made it a true pleasure to work closely with them once again.

Melinda Takeuchi of Stanford University wrote the third essay, which contains much information not published before in English, and she consulted on a number of issues that arose during the preparation of the catalogue. Miyeko Murase of Columbia University and Yoshiaki Shimizu of Princeton University, members of the Advisory Committee of The Asia Society Galleries, reviewed the checklist and provided curatorial advice as the exhibition evolved.

We are indebted to many individuals and institutions that have contributed to various aspects of this project; these include Ai Kono, Traditional Culture Division, Cultural Properties Protection Department, Agency for Cultural Affairs; Maribeth Graybill, Swarthmore College; Norikazu Kumano and Michiko Ito, Itsuo Museum; Steven Little and Dorothy Schroeder, The Art Institute of Chicago; Yutaka Mino; Ann Morse and Karen L. Otis, Museum of Fine Arts, Boston; Mikki Nishimura; a private collector, Osaka; Keizo Saji and Satoru Sakakibara, Suntory Museum of Art; Hiroyuki Suzuki, Tokyo National Research Institute of Cultural Properties; Mary Burke and Stephanie S. Wada, The Mary and Jackson Burke Collection; Gen Watanabe; Alice Whelihan, National Endowment for the Arts; Ms. Yamamoto, Ishiyama Temple; and Ann Yonemura, Freer Gallery of Art and Arthur M. Sackler Gallery, Smithsonian Institution.

As always, director Vishakha Desai and I had the good fortune to work with superb colleagues on the presentation of this exhibition. Amy V. McEwen, registrar, has once again smoothly handled all of the logistics involved in the planning, transport, and insurance of the exhibition, while Tucker Nichols, a new and welcome addition to the team as a Galleries associate, undertook the supervision of the installation. The perfectionism of Galleries associate Merantine Hens-Nolan is reflected both in her work on the catalogue and in her supervision of the graphics for the exhibition. Nancy Blume, tour coordinator, deserves thanks for developing education programs to accompany the exhibition, and Nancy and our docents are due special gratitude for making the material available and interesting to many diverse audiences. Nicolas G. Schidlovsky's work in fundraising, Heather Steliga Chen's development of a publicity campaign, and the programming efforts of Linden Chubin and Ann Kirkup contributed in many ways to the success of this project. In addition, we are all indebted to the organizational skills of Mirza Burgos, assistant to the director, and Alexandra Johnson, administrative assistant.

The elegant design of the installation in New York is the work of David Harvey, exhibition designer, and Zack H. Zanolli, lighting designer, and we are grateful to them and their colleagues for their fine work.

Joseph N. Newland, the Galleries' publications manager, served as the project director for the handsome and informative catalogue that accompanies this exhibition. Joseph and editor Jacolyn A. Mott are to be thanked for their diligent work in adapting the material in this book for American audiences; the entire text has benefitted from Jackie's care. We are also grateful to Sarah E. Thompson, translator of Professor Yamane's essay, and to Laurie Berman, translator of Mr. Kuroda's, for their special combination of linguistic skill and art historical knowledge. Graphic designer Sandy Bell brought vision and great sensitivity to the design of this graceful book. Valuable contributions were made by typographers Richard and Beth Decena of Chelsea Arts and by all of those involved in the separations and printing, especially Hiroshi Kurosawa and Hiroyuki Nakao, at Nissha.

Denise Patry Leidy
Curator
The Asia Society Galleries

YŪZŌ YAMANE

Screen Paintings of the Muromachi Period: The Mixing of Chinese and Japanese Styles

WHEN WE SPEAK OF PAINTING OF THE MUROMACHI period (1392–1573), we generally think of ink paintings: hanging scrolls of landscapes or figures in the style of such artists as Shūbun and Sesshū. We imagine an austere realm of unworldliness and elegant simplicity, closely related to the Zen sect and the tea ceremony. It is in dramatic contrast to the subsequent Momoyama period, which marked the full flowering of gorgeous and colorful gold paintings on folding screens (*byōbu*, hereafter called simply "screens") and sliding-door panels (*fusuma*, hereafter "sliding panels," dividers that made up most of the walls of a room in traditional Japanese architecture).

Certainly the differences between Muromachi painting and that of the Momoyama period (1573–1615), if viewed in this way, strike us as extremely distinct: "Muromachi ink painting" versus "Momoyama screens." In the same fashion, the characteristic difference between the painting of the Heian and Kamakura periods (794–1185 and 1185–1333, respectively) and that of the Muromachi period tends to be perceived as a movement from illustrated narrative handscrolls in the courtly style toward Muromachi ink painting, from an aesthetic of elegance and charm to one of simplicity and austerity.

In the past, most brief histories of Japanese art interpreted the development of painting in more or less this way: through the Heian and Kamakura periods, Japanese painting consisted mainly of Buddhist paintings, portraits, and narrative picture scrolls (*emaki*). Then, from the late Kamakura to the Nanbokuchō period (1336–1392), numerous Chinese paintings of the Song dynasty (960–1279) and the Yuan dynasty (1260–1368) were imported into Japan in connection with the Zen sect and were treasured as "Chinese objects" (*karamono*). Strongly influenced by these imported works, a new style later known as *Kanga* ("Chinese painting"), centering on ink painting and generally depicting Chinese subjects, rose to sudden prominence in Japan. During the Muromachi period, according to this conventional explanation, Kanga flourished under the patronage of the shogunate, and there was a decline in traditional *Yamato-e* ("Japanese painting," pictures of native subjects, usually portraiture or narrative, typically done in a colorful and detailed style). Even when discussed in more depth, these two branches of Muromachi painting are usually described separately, with about seventy percent of the attention devoted to Kanga, primarily ink hanging scrolls, and about thirty percent to Yamato-e, primarily narrative handscrolls.

Opposite:
Trees and Plants of the Four Seasons, detail from right screen
Muromachi period, about 1500
Pair of six-panel screens
Important Cultural Property
CATALOGUE NO. 2

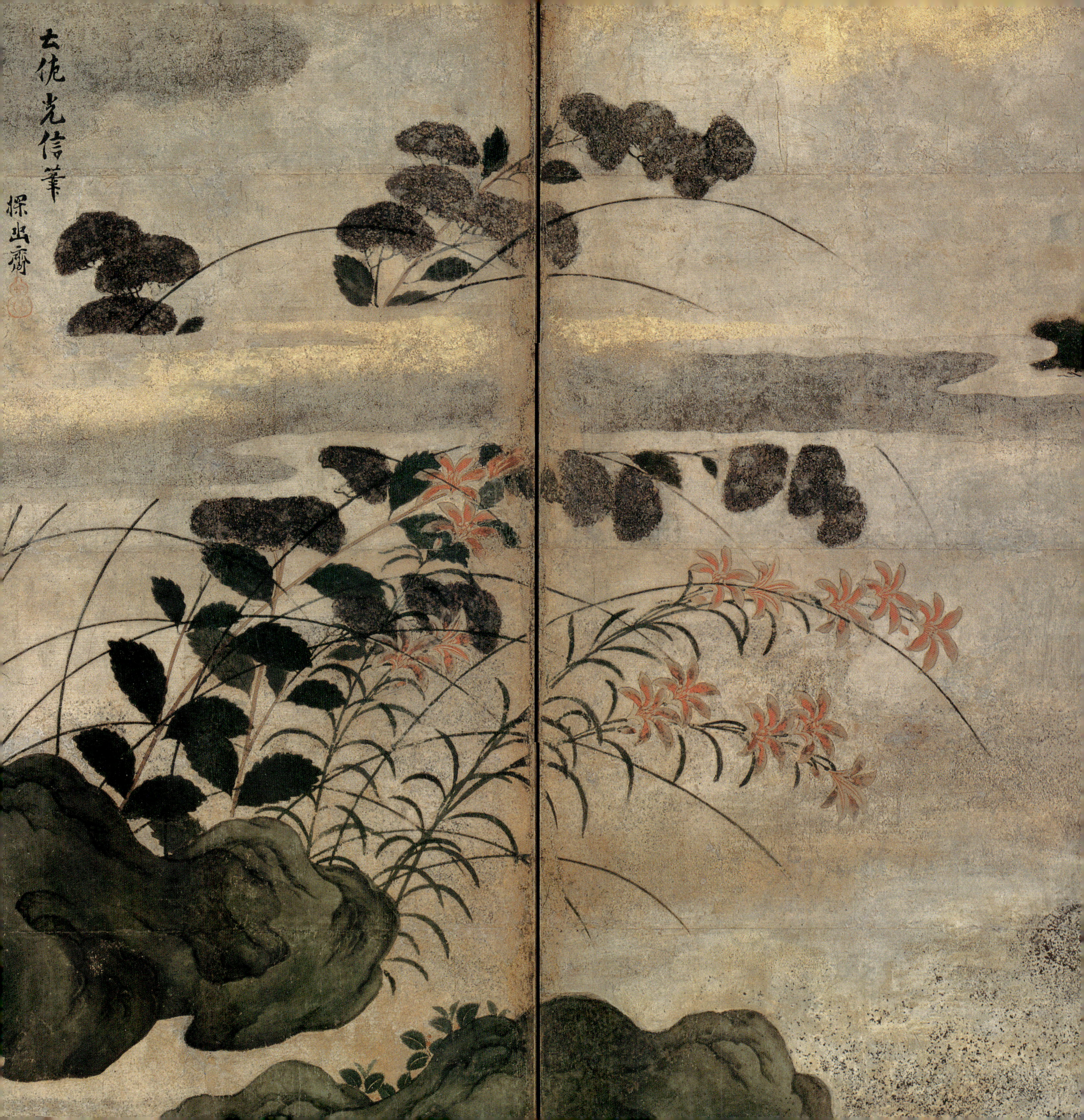

土佐光信筆
探幽齋

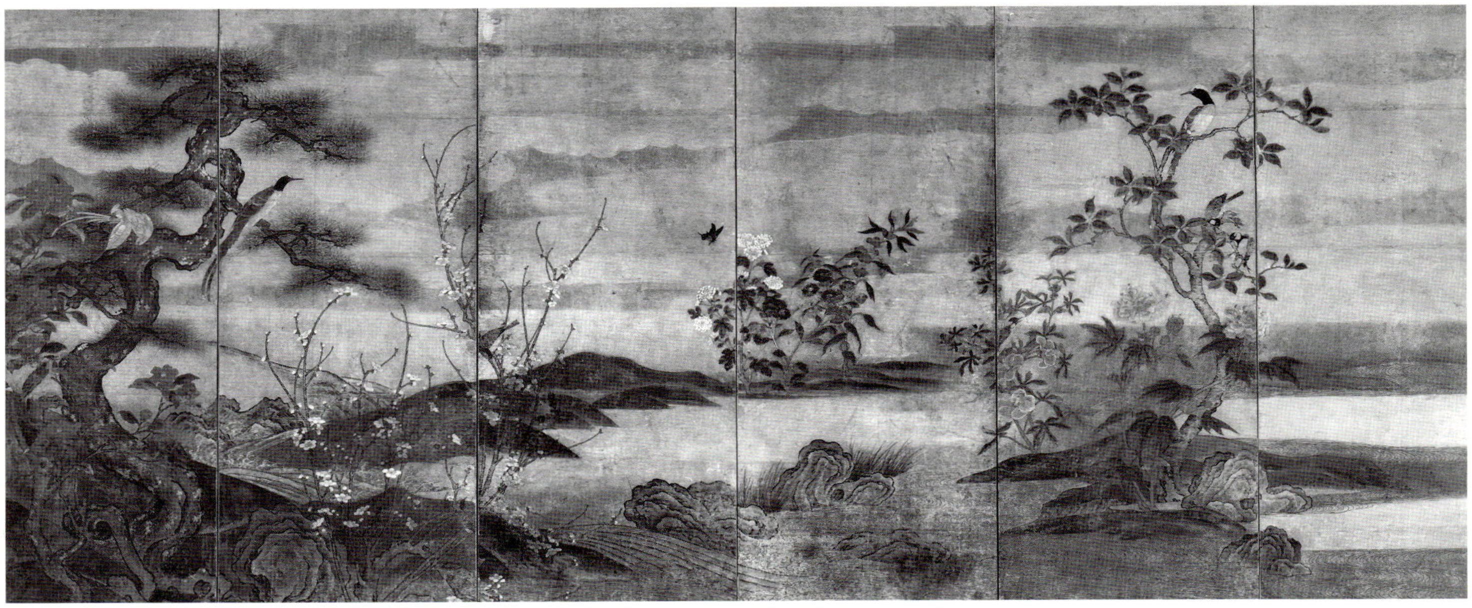

FIGURE 1

Flowers and Birds of the Four Seasons
Muromachi period, 15th century
Pair of six-panel screens
Color on paper
Each, 59 x 142½ in. (150.0 x 361.8 cm)
Suntory Museum of Art, Tokyo

It is as if we were to deal with the painting of the Meiji period (1868–1912) by allotting seventy percent of the discussion to the style known as "Western painting" (*Yōga*, i.e., European style, mainly oils), with its obvious differences from the painting styles of the preceding Edo period, and only thirty percent to its counterpart, "Japanese painting" (*Nihonga*), which continued all the painting styles of the Edo period. But the true history of painting does not alter so abruptly from one period to the next.

The standard prewar explanation for the development of painting from the Muromachi to the Momoyama period was as follows: the newly arisen Kano school absorbed the techniques and subject matter of the conservative Tosa school of Yamato-e, established a style that fused Chinese and Japanese elements, and thereby created the gorgeous screen and sliding-panel paintings (*shōbyōga*) that conformed so well to the heroism and love of gold of the Momoyama period. This explanation was supported to some extent by historical evidence. Certainly there was a trend in the arts of tea ceremony and flower arrangement during the late Muromachi period that was expressed by the motto "It is essential to blur the boundaries between what is Chinese and what is Japanese"; and the Kano school, patronized by the powerful warlords Oda Nobunaga (1534–1582) and Toyotomi Hideyoshi (1536–1598), did indeed dominate the world of painting. The prewar theory did not address the problems raised by the works themselves, however, in terms of the basis for the hypothesized fusion of Chinese and Japanese styles and the motivation for it. In particular, the process by which the new style developed was not clearly explained. The difficulty was that, at the time, the Yamato-e screen and sliding-panel paintings of the Muromachi period were unknown.

In the postwar period, scholars seeking the origin of the gold screen and sliding-panel paintings of the Momoyama period began to pay attention to representations of early paintings in these formats depicted in the narrative picture scrolls of the Kamakura, Nanbokuchō, and Muromachi periods. Using these historical materials, they developed the theory that, in the residences of the time, screen and sliding-panel paintings in the traditional Yamato-e style were joined by examples in the new ink painting style and that the two styles co-existed and mutually influenced each other. The emphasis on the existence during this period of large-scale screen and sliding-panel paintings in addition to handscrolls and hanging scrolls was an epoch-making hypothesis. There was still some question, however, as to the value of the illustrated scrolls as historical documents—that is, how accurately did depictions of screen and sliding-panel paintings in the scrolls represent contemporary reality? The question remained unresolved because there were

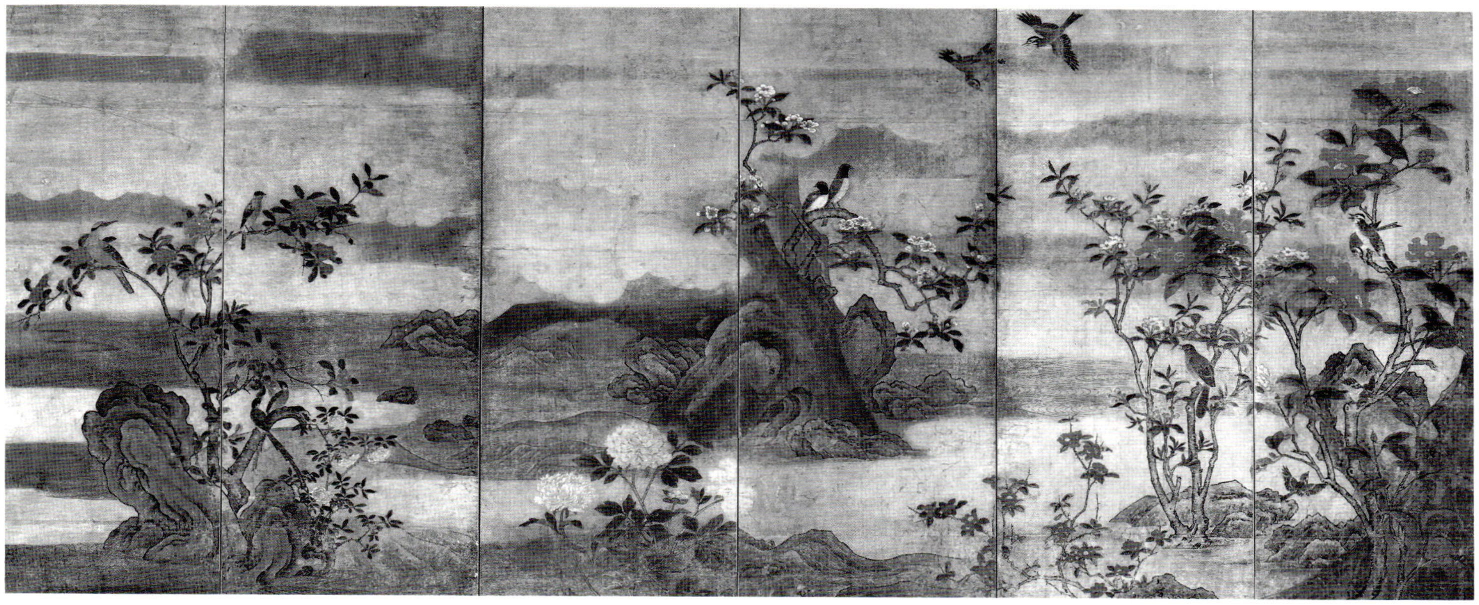

very few extant screen or sliding-panel paintings of the fourteenth or even the fifteenth century. Screen paintings in ink were known from the late fifteenth century on, and there were surviving examples of ink sliding-panel paintings dating from about 1500 at Shinjuan and Daisenin, subtemples of Daitokuji in Kyoto. However, no buildings of this period with Yamato-e sliding-panel paintings survived; and only two or three scattered examples of Yamato-e screens were known, all dating from the mid-sixteenth century, the end of the Muromachi period. Furthermore, although historical records indicated that a number of gold screens were sent out by the shogunate as official gifts to China and Korea during the fifteenth century, no examples of these exported screens had survived.

In 1951 the screens *Pine Trees on a Shore* (private collection), unmistakably a Yamato-e work of the late fifteenth century, were introduced to the scholarly world.[1] The charm of their bold composition and colorful use of gold and silver immediately drew attention to Yamato-e screens of the Muromachi period. Meanwhile, architectural historians had been conducting research into the construction of shogunal residences. Their findings suggested that, in addition to the rooms decorated with sliding-panel paintings in ink (Kanga), there might also have been rooms with sliding-panel paintings in Yamato-e style.

As if in response to the eager investigations of scholars, additional Yamato-e screens considered to date from the Muromachi period came to light. Among them were *Pine Trees on a Shore* (Tokyo National Museum) and *Flowers and Birds of the Four Seasons* (fig. 1). In 1969 the Kyoto National Museum held a ground-breaking exhibition, *Shōbyōga of the Medieval Period*, which pushed screen and sliding-panel paintings to the fore. Works in these formats served as an element linking Muromachi and Momoyama painting. The exhibition included more than forty Kanga works—both folding screens and sliding panels—but only ten or so Yamato-e screens. Many picture scrolls containing depictions of screen and sliding-panel paintings were included as reference material. Ten years later, the Osaka Municipal Museum organized an exhibition limited to screens—*Screen Paintings of the Medieval Period*—at which the ratio of Kanga to Yamato-e was just seven to three. The mutual relationship between Yamato-e screens and paintings in other formats was beginning to be confirmed.

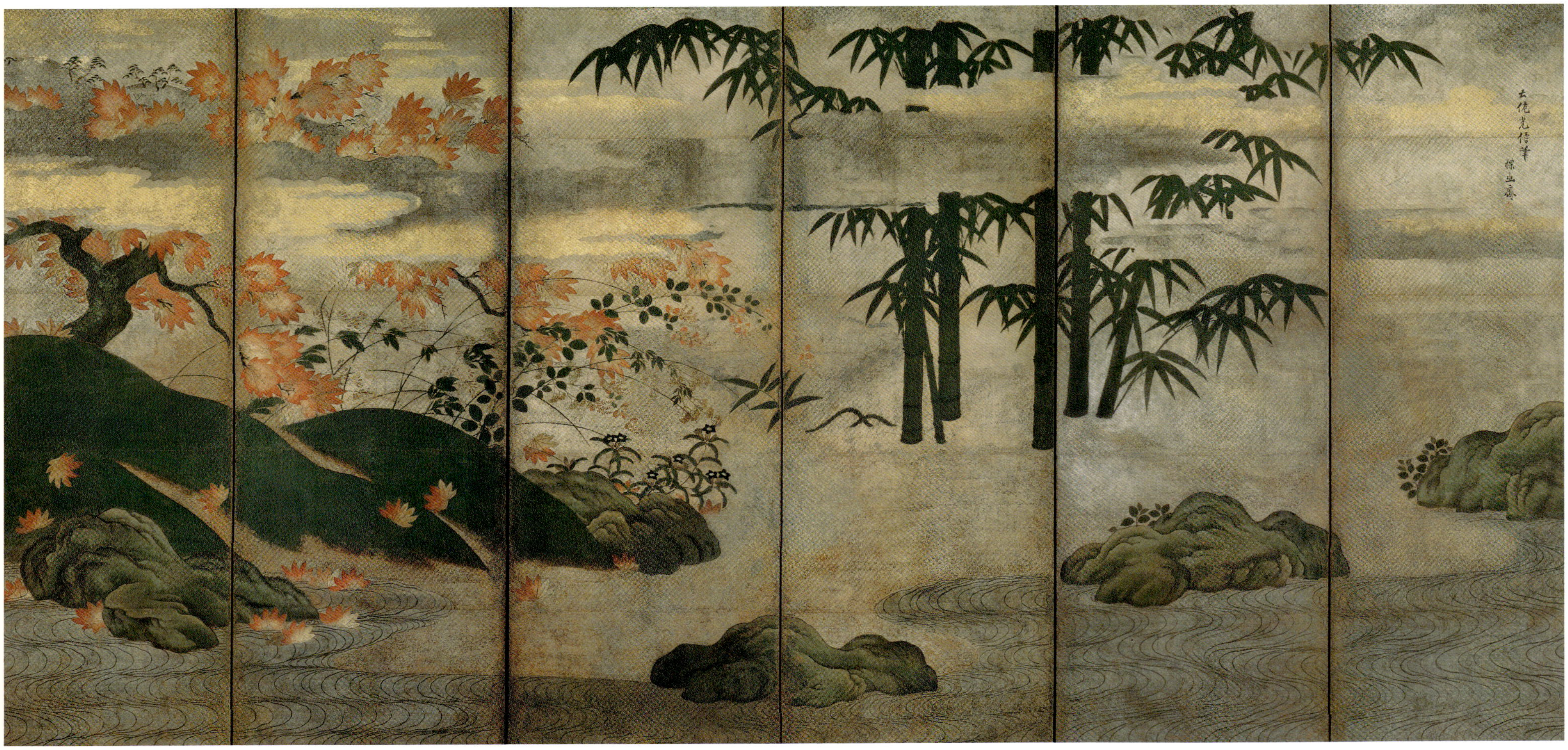

FIGURE 2

Trees and Plants of the Four Seasons
Muromachi period, about 1500
Pair of six-panel screens
Important Cultural Property
CATALOGUE NO. 2

The 1989 exhibition *Screen Paintings of the Muromachi Period* at the Tokyo National Museum, for which this essay was originally prepared,[2] actually included more screens in Yamato-e than Kanga style. Over forty Yamato-e works were displayed, including several masterpieces that had been discovered only during the preceding decade, such as *Flowers and Birds of the Four Seasons with the Sun and the Moon* (cat. no. 1) and *Trees and Plants of the Four Seasons* (fig. 2; cat. no. 2). Among the paintings exhibited in 1989 were numerous works previously unknown to most Japanese scholars because either they had gone out of Japan during the immediate postwar period or they had not been published (and there were more unpublished examples of Yamato-e than of Kanga). Because the date of Yamato-e screens usually cannot be determined by any method other than stylistic analysis, it is possible that some works of the late sixteenth century, the early Momoyama period, were inadvertently included among the Muromachi screens. With the addition of gold screens by artists of the Kano school and others dating from the late Muromachi to the early Momoyama period, the number of fifteenth and sixteenth century works came to nearly a hundred pairs of screens. The exhibition included as reference material Yamato-e fans of the Muromachi period (originally intended to be pasted on screens), of which a large number had been recently discovered. The method of display was innovative: Yamato-e and Kanga screens were shown in the same room to facilitate comparisons.

The study of screen paintings produced during the fourteenth, fifteenth, and sixteenth centuries reveals that painting styles developed not intermittently but consistently, in keeping with the changing times. Accordingly, the following overview of Muromachi painting begins with the mixing of Chinese and Japanese styles and links it to the fusion of the two styles that occurred during the Momoyama period.

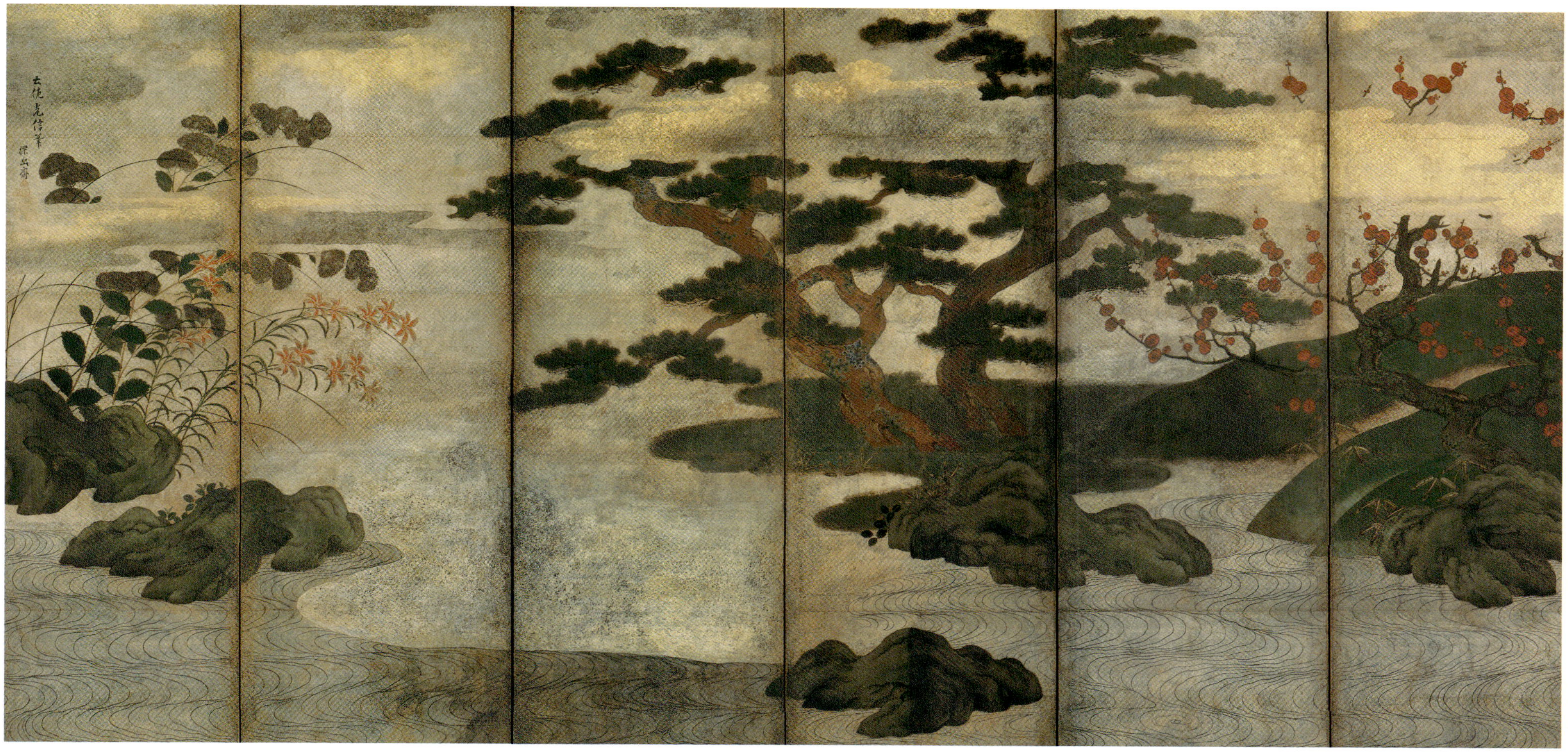

The Mixing of Chinese and Japanese Styles in Interior Decoration

The *shoin* style of residential architecture came into existence in the Muromachi period, during the first half of the fifteenth century. It developed from the earlier *shinden* style and was defined, among other characteristics, by the addition of the *oshiita* (a low platform for the display of decorative objects, forerunner of the *tokonoma* alcove with a built-in platform), staggered shelves (*chigaidana*), and a windowed alcove with a built-in writing desk (*tsukeshoin*, sometimes simply called *shoin*). The origins of the shoin style are profoundly related to the desire to enjoy in daily life the precious objects imported from China. At the time, the greatest number of Chinese masterpieces were owned by the Ashikaga shogunate;[3] and it was likewise the Ashikaga family that was able to build splendid palaces incorporating current architectural innovations. The shoin style made its first appearance in shogunal residences; and the methods of decorating these interiors with an assortment of Chinese objects (known as "decoration of the study" [*shoin-kazari*] or "decoration of the reception room" [*zashiki-kazari*]) were, naturally enough, recorded by the official cultural advisors (*dōbōshū*) of the shogun, such as Nōami (1397–1471) and Sōami (about 1455–1525).[4] It gradually became customary to unify the iconographic program of the sliding-panel paintings and the paintings attached to the surface of the fixed walls (collectively known as *shōheki-ga*) in each room. Thus the term "room paintings" (*zashiki-e*) was born.

Among the architectural works of the Ashikaga shoguns, the most famous extant buildings are the Golden Pavilion (at Rokuonji in Kyoto) of Yoshimitsu, the third shogun (1358–1408, r. 1368–1395), and the Silver Pavilion (at Jishōji in Kyoto; originally part of the Higashiyama Palace complex) of Yoshimasa, the eighth shogun (1436–1490, r. 1443–1473). Other important buildings of the time, such as the shogunal palaces, are known only through descriptions in documents. The most lavishly appointed was the Muromachi Palace, built in the time of Yoshinori, the sixth shogun (1394–1441, r. 1428–1441). In addition to the sleeping quarters (*shinden*) and the main living quarters (*tsune no gosho*), there were three meeting halls (*kaisho*, also sometimes translated "audience halls" or "banquet halls": rooms, suites of rooms, or buildings used for the formal reception of guests and for social events). They were built on the north and south sides of the garden: the South-facing Meeting Hall, the North-facing Meeting Hall and Fountain Pavilion (*izumidono*, a pavilion extending out over the water of the pond in the garden of the complex, similar to a *tsuridono*, "fishing pavilion"), and the New Meeting Hall. It is especially noteworthy that such a large number of meeting halls, intended to be used for private entertainments, were built at this time.

In the tenth month of 1437, the emperor GoHanazono made an official visit to Yoshinori's Muromachi Palace. Great interest has been aroused by the recent discovery of the manuscript handscroll of Nōami's *Record of the Decorations for the Imperial Visit to the Muromachi Palace* (*Muromachi-dono gyokō okazari ki*; Tokugawa Art Museum, Nagoya). It records the decoration of the three meeting halls on this occasion. The objects—all Chinese treasures, including twenty-three works of Song and Yuan dynasty painting—demonstrated the shogun's taste for precious Chinese objects. I would like to consider, however, the various locations in which, according to the document, these Chinese hanging scrolls were displayed. What kinds of paintings on the walls and sliding panels in each of the rooms formed the background against which the particular Chinese paintings specified in the record were hung? I feel that to emphasize the Chinese hanging scroll paintings in the alcoves and ignore the room paintings that surounded them is unbalanced. It is essential to grasp simultaneously the innovative aspect and the traditional aspect of the life of the period—its ideals, as well as their realization—in other words, both the outward face (*tatemae*) and the true intention (*honne*) so often spoken of in describing Japanese society.

The meeting hall developed from a combination of the Japanese style (*wayō*) and a room plan typical of the Chinese style (*karayō*), similar to the abbot's quarters in a Zen monastery. As a result, "the meeting hall was a blending of Chinese and Japanese elements, a world that unified Zen and the Pure Land [Buddhist] sects."[5] In this setting, one could enjoy traditional amusements such as "linked poetry" (*renga*), appreciate the novelty of decorative objects in the Chinese taste, or carry out tea ceremonies and tea competitions.

From the standpoint of its intended uses, the North-facing Meeting Hall and Fountain Pavilion in the Muromachi Palace must have been largely Japanese in style. Its various rooms were designated as the Six-mat Room, the Four-mat Room, the Three-mat Room, the Four-mat Tea Room, the North-facing Four-mat Room, the Sumiyoshi Tokonoma (during this period the term *tokonoma* could be used not only for the display alcove itself but also for a room containing such an alcove), the Brushwood Fence Room, and the Red Lacquer Tokonoma. Among these, at the very least the Sumiyoshi Tokonoma and the Brushwood Fence Room must have been decorated with Yamato-e paintings, to judge by their names. According to Sōami's *Record of Decorations (Okazari ki)* the so-called Ishiyama Room in Yoshimasa's later Higashiyama Palace had scenes of Ishiyama, Seta, and Ōtsu painted on its sliding panels. Clearly this was the popular Yamato-e theme of the Views of Ōmi (well-known scenic spots in the general vicinity of Kyoto). Likewise, the name of the Sumiyoshi Tokonoma in the Muromachi Palace suggests that the paintings decorating the room were views of Sumiyoshi, a site famous in classical Japanese poetry. If we accept this assumption as to the decor, then there is a strong probability that a group of four ink hanging scrolls by the thirteenth century Chinese Chan painter Muqi—of which only two survive, depicting the Tang poet Du Fu and the Northern Song monk Zhenghuangniu—recorded as having been displayed in this room on the occasion of the imperial visit were hung in a tokonoma alcove, on the walls of which were Yamato-e paintings of views of Sumiyoshi (given that walls inevitably had paintings on paper pasted to them). I consider this to be a kind of mixing of the Chinese and Japanese styles.

With regard to the Brushwood Fence Room, the Higashiyama Palace of Yoshimasa had a room of the same name, which has been identified as one with paintings of autumn grasses and flowers. We may surmise, therefore, that the room so-named in the Muromachi Palace also was decorated with Yamato-e paintings of autumn plants. This means that the Chinese diptych *Dove and Quail* by the Huizong emperor (1082–1135, r. 1101–1126) would have hung in a room filled with Yamato-e paintings of autumn plants.

In the New Meeting Hall, the largest of the three meeting halls in the Muromachi Palace, there were two main rooms equipped with the formal decorative features of display platform, staggered shelves, and built-in writing desk. They were known as the Hashidate Room and the Room of Small Birds. The former, like the Sumiyoshi Tokonoma discussed above, probably had Yamato-e paintings depicting a famous Japanese landscape, namely, the sand bar at Ama-no-hashidate. Thus the triptych *Bust of Budai, Boatman, and Fisherman* by Muqi, as well as the diptych *Dogs* by Li Di (about 1100–after 1197), would have been surrounded by Yamato-e landscapes of Ama-no-hashidate. The North-facing Four-mat Room in the New Meeting Hall, which is thought to have served as the shogun's living room, was designated as the Room of Farming in the Style of Liang Kai, which clearly indicates that the sliding panels were decorated with Kanga paintings of agricultural activities of the four seasons, modeled on a handscroll, *Farming and Weaving*, by Liang Kai (active early thirteenth century).[6] In this room was hung a single painting by Liang Kai, depicting Budai, a fat Chinese monk (J. Hotei), who was a popular subject in Zen painting.

In addition to the mixing of Chinese and Japanese styles that resulted from the hanging of imported Chinese paintings in rooms decorated with Yamato-e paintings, it is interesting to note that there is a mixing of the two styles in the room paintings themselves. Specifically, in the New Meeting Hall, the main reception room (*hare*, i.e., formal) had Yamato-e paintings of famous scenic spots (*meisho*), while the living quarters (*ke*, i.e., informal) had Chinese paintings of agricultural scenes in the style of Liang Kai. I would next like to discuss this mixing of Chinese and Japanese styles as it occurred in the interior paintings of Yoshimasa's Higashiyama Palace.

The Meeting Hall of the Higashiyama Palace was completed in 1487. The decorations of its rooms can be ascertained from the accounts in the *Onryōken Diary (Onryōken nichiroku)* and the *Record of Decorations*. The Ishiyama Room and Brushwood Fence Room would, as noted above, have had Yamato-e paintings of scenic spots and flowers and grasses, respectively. There were Kanga paintings in the Storage Room (*nando no ma*) and the Tea Ceremony Room (or Northern Five-mat Room). The former had flower-and-bird paintings in the style of Ma Yuan (about 1190–1225); the latter, landscapes in the manner of Xia Gui (about 1190–1225). Apparently, in the Higashiyama Palace, room decorations in the Yamato-e and Kanga styles co-existed within the same building. Furthermore, the Yamato-e style seems to have been used for the more important rooms. We can assume that this was generally the case in the meeting halls of shogunal residences. In the meeting halls of the residences of the nobility of the imperial court, who were the traditional patrons of Yamato-e, the proportion of rooms decorated with Yamato-e paintings would naturally have been much higher.

However, in the main living quarters (completed in 1483) of the Higashiyama Palace, all the rooms for which the nature of the decorative paintings can be determined were, atypically, in the Kanga style. Of the three reception rooms (*zashiki*) on the south side, the main one, known as the Eight Views Room, was decorated with sliding-panel paintings of the Eight Views of Xiao and Xiang, identified as the work of Kano Masanobu (1434–1530), the official painter to the shogunate. The second room, called the Farming Room, is thought to have contained paintings of agricultural scenes in the style of Liang Kai (like the room in the New Meeting Hall of the Muromachi Palace). On the north side of the building were private living quarters: among these seven rooms, the Sleeping Chamber had landscapes and figures in the style of Ma Yuan, the Northern Withdrawing Room (*kita no ochima*) had figure paintings in the style of Muqi, and the Waiting Room for Bath Attendants (*oyudono no ue*) had landscapes in the style of Yujian (active mid-thirteenth century). All of the rooms had interior paintings based on the ink-painting style. The subject matter and technique varied from room to room. All were most likely painted by Masanobu or his pupils, artists of the Kano school.

The Chinese nature of the decor of the main living quarters is unusual. It clearly reflects the preferences of the shogun Yoshimasa, who was thoroughly familiar with Chinese painting. These decorations are probably a special case; they resemble paintings that might be seen in a Zen temple. Viewed as a whole, however, the wall and sliding-panel paintings of the shogunal palaces are, as noted above, a combination of Chinese and Japanese styles, with Yamato-e and Kanga co-existing. The folding-screen paintings found in the shogunal residences were most likely the same kind of mixture. These circumstances provided a setting in which the two groups of official painters to the shogunate—namely, the Kanga painters represented by Kano school artists such as Masanobu and Motonobu (1476–1559) and the Yamato-e painters represented by Tosa school artists such as Hirochika (about 1439–1492) and Mitsunobu (1434–1525)—could come into contact, compete, and mutually influence each other.

Yamato-e Screens and Chinese Paintings

At the beginning of the *Scroll of Festivals (Sairei sōshi)*, a narrative picture scroll now in the Maeda Ikutokukai considered to be a work of the first half of the fifteenth century, there are depictions of a Fountain Pavilion and a Meeting Hall. The Fountain Pavilion contains staggered shelves decorated with Chinese objects, and on the adjacent walls and sliding panels are what appear to be Yamato-e paintings in color of such themes as Pine Trees on a Shore and Flowers and Birds, while inside the room are people preparing and serving tea. In the Meeting Hall, a built-in display platform runs the entire length of the right wall, facing the garden. Hanging against the colored wall paintings (probably Yamato-e, although damage to this area of the painting prevents a clear identification) are three hanging scrolls (probably Chinese works or Japanese Kanga). In the center of the display platform stands an incense burner, on either side of which are three small vases of either bronze or porcelain on trays. In the back of the room is a freestanding display platform lined with a number of small vases that appear to be Chinese. The damage to the picture makes them difficult to see, but each of these small vases holds a different variety of flowering pink. This picture appears to illustrate a festival custom in which each participant brought his own treasured Chinese vase for all to enjoy. It provides evidence that the style of interior decoration in the shogunal residences had now spread to other groups of Japanese society. The decorative objects are entirely Chinese, but we must not overlook the existence of Yamato-e room paintings behind and around them.

The *Record of Things Seen and Heard (Kanmon gyoki)*, the diary of Fushimi Prince Sadafusa (1372–1456), begins in the year 1416 and continues through the Eikyō era (1429–1440). Almost every year, Sadafusa recorded the celebration of Tanabata (the Festival of the Milky Way) for which large numbers of people gathered. Either the main living quarters or the sleeping quarters were used as a meeting hall. Guests brought Chinese treasures, such as vases of bronze, celadon, or blue-and-white porcelain, or imported paintings, and they enjoyed activities like the "arrangement of fifty vases of flowers." The "flower competition" (*hana-awase*) and "flower room" (*hana-zashiki*) that Sadafusa mentions seem to be recorded as well in an illustration in the *Scroll of Festivals*.

Of particular interest in Sadafusa's diary are the entries indicating that, for these occasions, various kinds of screens and hanging scrolls were brought from elsewhere. For example, two pairs of screens borrowed for the Tanabata celebration of 1432 were described as "Pines of the Four Seasons with gold burnishing" and "Sea, Boats, and Pine Trees" (the latter motif is generally known today as Pine Trees on a Shore, or *hamamatsu*). Both of these were Yamato-e screens, as were the screens recorded as borrowed in other years. In contrast, the hanging scrolls used for the Tanabata festival of 1435 were described as a "triptych of Chinese paintings." They could have been either Chinese imports or Kanga. Furthermore, there are notations such as "two pairs of screens were set up and seven scroll paintings were hung there" and "two pairs of screens were set up and nineteen Chinese scroll paintings were hung." It is unclear how these statements should be interpreted. If the screens were accordion-folded in the usual way, it would be impossible to display more than about fifteen scrolls on two pairs of screens, and the hanging scrolls would interfere with each other and be difficult to see. Also, the rooms of Sadafusa's residence, the Fushimi Palace, were (according to documentary evidence) not particularly large; if a sizable group of people were to gather in them, the only feasible way to display scroll paintings would be to unfold the screens completely, place them flat against the walls, and suspend the scrolls from the frieze rail of the wall above the screens, so that the scrolls would hang down over the screens. But why would Chinese-style paintings (whether imports or Kanga) be hung directly against Yamato-e screens, where they would obscure the paintings on the screens themselves? I believe this was owed to the fact that in the shogunal residences, as described in detail above, treasured Chinese paintings were often hung in rooms decorated in the Yamato-e style. The deliberate use of Yamato-e screens, borrowed specifically to provide backgrounds for the display of Chinese paintings, was the result of that influence. It could even be said to have been adopted by the court nobility (*kuge*) as the standard method of appreciating Chinese paintings. This ability to appreciate the new while continuing to esteem the traditional exemplifies the multilayered nature of Japanese culture.

The mixing of Chinese and Japanese styles produced by hanging Chinese-style paintings over Yamato-e screens was seen even in the Buddhist temples of Nara. According to *The Daijōin Miscellaneous Record of Temples and Shrines* (*Daijōin jisha zōjiki*, a collection of records, including the abbot's diary, kept at Daijōin, a subtemple of Kōfukuji in Nara), the Tanabata festival of 1475 was celebrated by a group of twenty-nine members of the nobility, including Ichijō Kaneyoshi, who had fled to Nara to escape the Ōnin War. They enjoyed such amusements as "one hundred vases of flowers" and "one hundred *waka* poems." A sketch of the hall in which the event was held shows seven pairs of screens set up flat (unfolded) in the interior of the large meeting hall. Vases of flowers are on tables in front of them, and scrolls are hung against the screens.[7] The screens are described as "gold screens" (*kimihyōfu*, i.e., *kinbyōbu*), which could mean either screens with gold paint or screens with gold leaf (see below); but in any case, they were certainly Yamato-e screens. The hanging scrolls are described only as "triptych" or "tetraptych," but to judge by the record of the Tanabata celebration in Sadafusa's diary, they were probably Chinese works or Kanga. In this case, as well, we see the mixing of Chinese and Japanese styles.

Types of Screens

In the *Collection for the Use of Priests (Sōyōshū)*, a sixteenth-century work on traditional etiquette included in the *Second Series of the Collection of Assembled Documents (Zoku gunsho ruiju)*, is a section entitled "On the placement of screens in the reception room." It states, "Ink paintings (*sumi-e*) may be considered higher, and colored paintings with burnishing (*shikiga migakitsuke*) may be placed lower; streams of assembled fans (*kumiōgi nagashi*) are higher, burnished paintings (*migakitsuke*) are lower." "Ink paintings" undoubtedly refers to Kanga, but the "colored paintings" cannot be automatically assumed to be Yamato-e, because there are surviving examples of Kanga-style works using color (either ink and slight color or ink and heavy color). "Burnished paintings" and "streams of fans," discussed below, may be tentatively assumed to be Yamato-e. The references to "higher" and "lower" are thought to indicate positions from front to back within a room. To judge by the wording of such statements as "ink paintings may be considered higher" and "burnished paintings are lower," ink paintings (Kanga) seem to have been more highly valued than burnished paintings (Yamato-e). It must be kept in mind, however, that this is the opinion of a priest.

Mon'ami on Flower Arrangement (Mon'ami kadensho), which continues the tradition of the *Record of Decorations* included in the *Collection of Assembled Documents*, says that "from the highest seat on down, [screens] should be set out in descending order according to this division": (1) gold burnishing, or *kimigakitsuke*, (2) streams of fans, or *ōginagashi*, (3) *shikishi*, (4) brushed-on powdered gold and silver pigments, or *deibiki*, (5) Yamato-e, (6) *usudame*, which probably means with "light colors," (7) ink painting, or *sumi-e*, and (8) a special category, *shirohari*, used to decorate a birthing room. (Categories 1, 2, and 7 are also mentioned in the *Collection for the Use of Priests*, but the order is different.)

Because *Mon'ami on Flower Arrangement* is a secular work, I take it as evidence that screen paintings were divided into these eight categories by most people at that time. Here, the screens with "gold burnishing" (part of the Yamato-e group) are placed in the first position at the high seat, while ink paintings (part of the Kanga group) are much lower, in seventh place. This may have been the general view of their relative value outside the Buddhist temples. Of the remaining five types, category 3, screens with shikishi (pieces of decorated paper used for calligraphy or paintings) pasted on them, and category 2, screens with fans pasted on them, can be regarded as Yamato-e. To judge by the order in which category 4, gold and silver pigments, is listed, it probably refers to screens that were conspicuous in their use of gold and silver pigments and more highly decorative than category 5, "Yamato-e." Category 6, usudame, is difficult to understand but probably means "light colors." Its juxtaposition with category 7, ink painting, suggests that usudame might refer to screens painted in ink with slight color added. Thus the colored paintings can be divided into deibiki, Yamato-e, and usudame. Category 8, shirohari, seems to have been a somewhat unusual type used specifically to decorate a room in which a birth took place. A work entitled *Record of the Lying-in Room (Sanjo no ki)*, in the *Collection of Assembled Documents*, says, "A style of screen painting, with pine, bamboo, crane, and tortoise depicted in mica. This is shirohari."

According to the above analysis, categories 1 through 5 and 8 can be considered to be varieties of Yamato-e, while categories 6 and 7 are Kanga. It appears that the Yamato-e category was more extensively subdivided and encompassed a greater number of varieties. Furthermore, the instructions indicating that the eight types of screens should be "set out in descending order" imply that the screens were valued in direct proportion to the degree of their decorativeness. Interestingly, the order of precedence is almost exactly the opposite for those categories given also in the *Collection for the Use of Priests*.[8]

With regard to the term *gold burnishing* (kimigakitsuke), an entry in the *Diary of the Ladies of the Waiting Room for Bath Attendants (Oyudono no ue no nikki)*, a journal kept by ladies-in-waiting in the Imperial Palace, states that "three pairs of kimigakitsuke screens came from a warrior clan [*buke*]" (1560, fifth month, sixth day). This indicates that, during the Muromachi period, such screens were used by assorted social classes. In this instance the term *kimigakitsuke* is spelled in Japanese phonetic script (*kana*), so its meaning is not certain; but the mention in Prince Sadafusa's diary of "one pair of screens: Pines of the Four Seasons, kimigakitsuke" (1432, seventh month, sixth day) gives the term in Chinese characters (*kanji*) that have the meaning "with gold burnishing." In *The Daijōin Miscellaneous Record of Temples and Shrines*, screens are described as being "gold-burnished" (*kimigakitsuke*) or "polished" (*togitsuke*; this term appears to have the same meaning as *kimigakitsuke*).

However, in the *Onryōken Diary*, only "gold screens" (*kinbyōbu* or *kinbyō*) are mentioned, and "gold burnishing" (*kimigakitsuke*) never appears. In documents such as *Records of Friendly Nations* (*Zenrin kokuhō ki*; a Japanese account of foreign affairs), the Chinese book of laws titled *Institutes of the Ming Dynasty (Da Ming hui dian)*, and the Korean *True Records of the Choson Dynasty (Choson wangjo sillok)*, the screens that were exported from Japan to China and Korea are variously described as "gold screens" (J. *kinbyōbu*), "gold-painted colored screens" (J. *tokin shōsai byōbu*), "gold-painted screens" (J. *tokin byōbu*), "gold-decorated screens"

(J. *kinshō byōbu*), "screens with gold ornament" (J. *sōkin byōbu*), and "screens with gold affixed" (J. *chōkin byōbu*).[9] Here again, "screens with gold burnishing" (J. *kimigakitsuke byōbu*) does not appear. If we assume that the gold-painted screens were painted with gold and silver pigments, they would belong to category 4 above (deibiki). But what is the relationship between the gold-burnished screens and other types—described as "gold-decorated," "with gold ornament," and "with gold affixed"? Researchers have suggested a variety of theories. It is essential, however, to base one's idea on the evidence of the actual surviving screens of the Muromachi period. I will discuss this matter in the following section, but my conclusion is that, in Japan during the Muromachi period, the types of screens described as "gold-decorated," "with gold ornament," and "with gold affixed" were collectively called "gold-burnished screens" (*kimigakitsuke byōbu*) or simply "gold screens" (*kinbyōbu*). The Japanese-Portuguese dictionary *Vocabulario da Lingoa de Iapam* (1603) defines *migaki* and *migakitsuke* as "to burnish. Also, to make something gold-colored by placing gold leaf over it." In short, "gold-burnished screens," that is, gold screens, were extremely important among the Yamato-e screens of the Muromachi period.

Let us next consider the examples in which arrangements of fans (paintings on paper in the shape of unfolded fans) or shikishi were affixed to screens. In Prince Sadafusa's diary, various references are made to screens with "streams of assembled fans with Genji pictures," beginning with the entry for the Tanabata festival of 1434, which mentions the borrowing of "palace screens [*dairi byōbu*], formerly belonging to the Retired Emperor: streams of fans with Genji pictures." The diary of Prince Sanjōnishi Sanetaka (1455–1537), the *Sanetaka kō ki*, includes such notations as "Genji fan painting screens" (1489) and "Hosokawa screens: streams of fan paintings of the *Tale of the Heike*" (1486). The prince's comment that "the stupendous spectacle amazes the eyes" suggests that the design of these screens of assembled fans enjoyed the highest critical favor. It is still unclear, however, whether these works consisted of illustrations of stories painted in fan shapes directly onto the surface of the screens in such a way that the fans appeared to be floating down a stream (the earliest surviving example is an early Edo period work of the school of Sōtatsu) or of separate fan paintings, either intended for this purpose or from fans that had actually been used, which were collected and pasted to the screens (many examples are noted in Muromachi documents).

The *Screens with Fan Paintings of the Tale of Genji and Other Subjects* (fig. 3) were created by gathering together used fans with Muromachi period illustrations from the *Tale of Genji*, adding some landscape scenes, and combining them with a background painting of a flowing stream that covered the entire surface of the screen and was appropriate to the concept of a "stream of fans." The stream was painted by an artist of the Momoyama period, probably Kaihō Yūshō (1533–1615), to judge by the style. In the same way, the pair of *Screens with Fan Paintings of the Tale of Genji* (Jōdōji, Hiroshima) gathers together used fan paintings, all illustrating the *Tale of Genji*, with a background painting of vines covering both screens. One of the oldest forms of background painting for these fan screens was a design of autumn flowers, as indicated by an entry for 1443 in the diary of a courtier: the *Kennaiki* by Madenokōji Tokifusa (1394–1457) describes a screen as having "a ground of autumn plants—grass with Rose of Sharon and clover—with fans attached over it." In an illustration in the first scroll of the *Pictures of Longing for Extinction (Bōki-e)*, dated 1482 (Nishihonganji, Kyoto), a pictorial biography of the monk Kakunyo (1270–1351), is what may possibly be a screen of scattered fans in which the fans are pasted onto a screen of the kind known as *sōkin* ("all gold"; see below), completely covered with gold leaf. The practice of collecting a number of small fan pictures to create a gorgeous gold screen must have been widely enjoyed.

Screens and sliding panels to which small paintings in the shikishi format have been affixed in the same manner as the fans, appear in historical documents as early as the middle of the thirteenth century. Some screen and

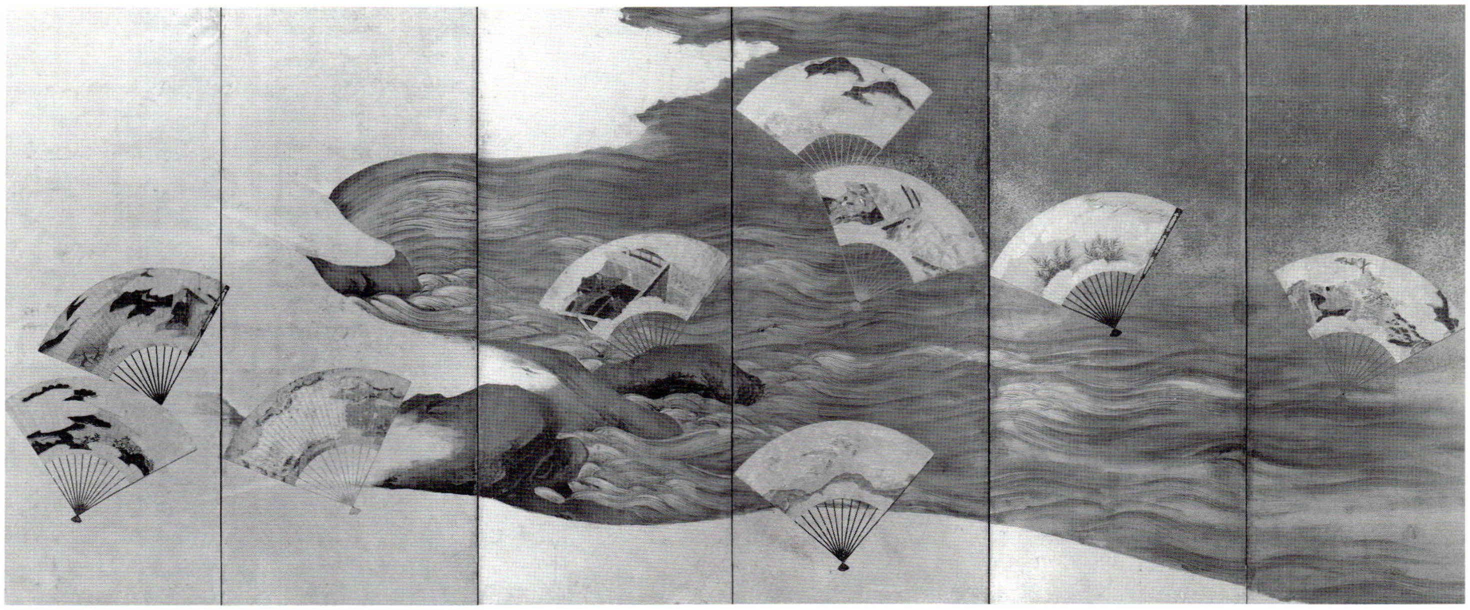

FIGURE 3

Screens with Fan Paintings of the Tale of Genji and Other Subjects
Muromachi period, 15th century
Pair of six-panel screens
Color and gold leaf on paper
Each, 57 x 135½ in. (144.7 x 344.0 cm)
The Idemitsu Museum of Arts

sliding-panel paintings of this type are also illustrated in narrative picture scrolls. There are, however, no surviving examples from the Muromachi period. The earliest extant works of this kind are the *Screens with Shikishi of Genji Pictures* by Tosa Ittoku (active early seventeenth century) in the Tokyo National Museum and the *Screens with Shikishi by Kōetsu* in the Ishikawa Prefectural Museum. These screens have painted backgrounds of grass or autumn plants; and it is thought that they, like the fan screens, continue a tradition dating from the Muromachi period.

During the Muromachi period, in addition to the Yamato-e works, many fans were made in the Kanga style either in ink or in color. They depicted landscapes, figures, or flower-and-bird subjects. Collections of poetry by contemporary Zen monks record many poems with the heading "written for a screen painting." They would have been written on fans that were pasted on screens. In such cases, the screens may well have been decorated with a background design of running water or autumn grasses like the designs of a "stream of fans" or "scattered fans" seen on the Yamato-e screens. This hypothesis is supported by the screen with *Genre Scenes of the Twelve Months in Kyoto* (Kōenji, Kyoto). There is also an example of a fan painting that has four still smaller fan paintings within it. The small paintings depict the Eight Views of Xiao and Xiang in ink, and are placed against a colored background painting of autumn grasses; poems by a Zen monk accompany them. The presence within a single fan painting of a Kanga depiction of the Eight Views and a Yamato-e rendition of autumn plants is an excellent example of the mixing of the two styles. Among the gold fans of the mid-Muromachi period, there are cases in which, although the subject matter is Chinese figures, the painting style appears to be Yamato-e (i.e., characterized by even lines, rounded shapes, fine details, and bright colors rather than the calligraphic brushwork typical of the Chinese style). There is also a number of flower-and-bird paintings for which the stylistic lineage is unclear—truly a blending of the Chinese and the Japanese.

On a larger scale than the screens of fans or shikishi are the screens known as *oshi-e bari byōbu* in which a single painting has been mounted on each panel of the screen. This type of work in the Yamato-e lineage is exemplified by the *Scenes from the Tale of the Heike* (Kanagawa Prefectural Museum). An example in the Kanga lineage is *Flowers, Birds, and Figures* by Tōshun (active 1506–1542) (private collection). The pair of screens with *Flowers, Birds, and Insects* in the Virginia Museum of Fine Arts, Richmond, represents a fine melding of the two styles.

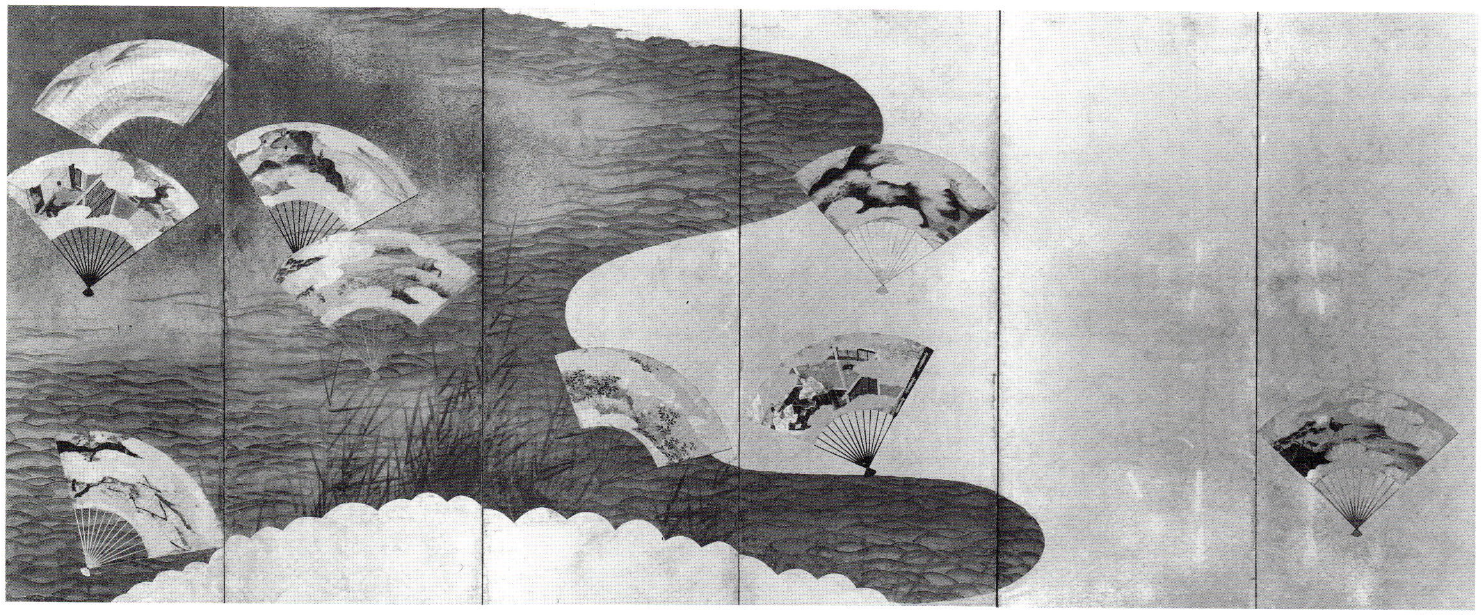

The Development of the Gold Screens

The body of presently known screen paintings can be broadly divided into Yamato-e style and Kanga style. Leaving aside for future study the individual characteristics of each of these lineages, I would like to consider here the use of gold in both styles: the differences in its handling and effect, and its development.

Let us begin with the question of gold pigment (*kin deibiki*). In my discussion of the types of screens, both those with gold burnishing (kimigakitsuke) and those with brushed-on powdered gold and silver pigments (deibiki) were placed in the Yamato-e group; but there are only a few known examples of these types. Among the numerous screens with Scenes in and around Kyoto (*rakuchū-rakugaizu*) made from the end of the Muromachi period to the beginning of the Edo period, the earliest example, in the National Museum of Japanese History, Tokyo, has only trails of gold mist. Unlike later examples, it does not have gold clouds. The painted streaks of gold mist give expansiveness to the scene and create a gentle mood. *Flowers and Birds of the Four Seasons* (fig. 1) is a Yamato-e work that shows the influence of Chinese flower-and-bird painting of the Yuan dynasty in the drawing of the subjects. Extending horizontally across the pair of six-panel screens is a great deal of gold pigment, resembling thin mist. It gives brightness to the relatively dark picture surface and connects the right and left sides of the composition. If this screen had been exported to Ming China, it would surely have been designated a "gold-painted colored screen" (*tokin shōsai byōbu*).

Although gold might seem foreign to the basic concept of ink painting, the use of mist rendered with gold pigment became, with time, increasingly conspicuous in the hanging scrolls with landscape paintings and poetic inscriptions (*shigajiku*) of the Muromachi period. A similar technique is apparent in ink screens, though in some cases the gold was added later. This use of gold may well have been influenced by the gold pigment in Yamato-e screens. Especially fine examples are the *Eight Views of Xiao and Xiang* attributed to Shūbun (active 1414–1463) (Kōsetsu Art Museum, Hyōgo) and *Gibbons at Play in Trees by a Cliff* by Terutada Shikibu (active early sixteenth century) (Kyoto National Museum).
In most cases, however, the gold merely adds a superficial decorativeness. The early sixteenth century *Pine Grove at Miho*, attributed to Nōami (Egawa Art Museum, Hyōgo), considered to be an early example of the Japanization of ink painting because of its subject matter and brilliant ink tones, has clouds or mist painted in gold pigment, visible upon careful examination, in the upper part of the composition. The shapes and drawing techniques of these clouds are similar to the underpaintings

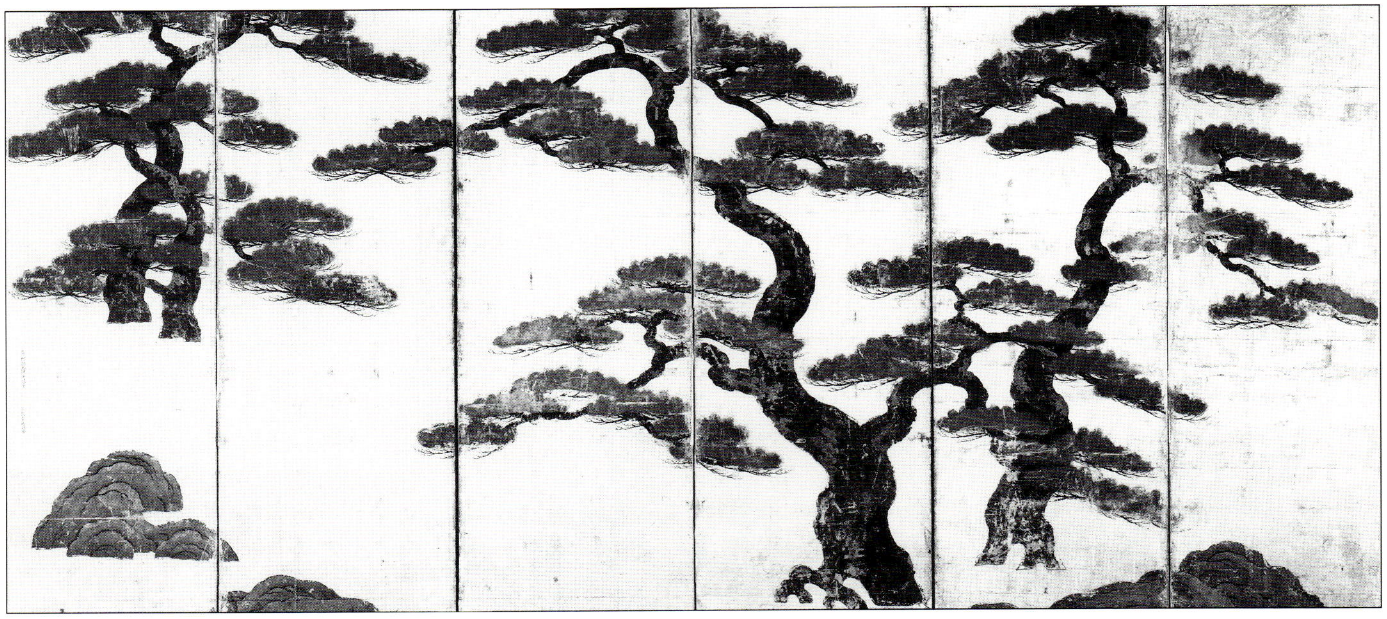

FIGURE 4

Pine Trees
Muromachi period, 16th century
Six-panel screen
Color and gold leaf on paper
60½ x 135¾ in. (153.3 x 345.0 cm)
Tokyo National Museum

in gold pigment found on decorated writing paper. This work deserves special mention as the earliest known example of the conscious adoption of a Yamato-e technique in ink painting.

Now we shall examine the so-called screens with gold burnishing noted in the Muromachi documents. As stated, I conclude that these kimigakitsuke screens were the gold screens of the Muromachi period. I believe this point is proven by the body of known Yamato-e screens dating from that time. Because there are conflicting scholarly theories, however, I shall begin with a consideration of some unusual gold screens.

As previously noted, the only terms used in documents of the Muromachi period are "gold screens" (kinbyōbu) and "screens with gold burnishing" (kimigakitsuke byōbu). There is, however, one exception. An entry for the year 1550 in volume 5 of the *Second Series of Accounts of the Ōnin War (Zoku Ōnin kōki,* in *Gaitei shiseki shūran*) mentions that at the funeral of Ashikaga Yoshiharu (1511–1550, r. 1521–1546) "a pair of all-gold [sōkin] screens" by Kano Motonobu provided a backdrop for the coffin. The book is not a scholarly work, but it seems likely that the "all-gold screens" were ones with gold leaf affixed to the entire surface. (Screens of this kind are still used for funeral ceremonies.)

The afore-mentioned illustration of a screen with fans pasted to it in the first scroll of the *Pictures of Longing for Extinction* is also relevant to the question of all-gold screens. It is possible that the custom of pasting fans to these screens was already practiced by the beginning of the fifteenth century; that such works were followed by screens in which a painting of, for example, autumn grasses was added to a gold-leaf ground to form a background for the fans; and that, finally, gold-leaf screens appeared that did not have fans pasted to them but instead had independent pictures painted directly on them.

The screen *Pine Trees* attributed to Tosa Mitsunobu (fig. 4) depicts two groups of pines, each with two trees, branches spread wide across the picture, with a few isolated rocks in the foreground, against a solid background of gold leaf. Of all the known Muromachi screens, it is one of the few that would probably be recognized by anyone as a "gold screen." Nevertheless, works of this kind were overlooked until recently because screens covered entirely with gold leaf were simply not thought to have existed in the Muromachi period (though they were frequently made during the early Edo period by Sōtatsu and his workshop). Whether or not we accept the attribution of this work to Mitsunobu, which appears on a separate accompanying document written by Tosa Mitsuoki (1617–1691), it is certainly a Yamato-e work of the early sixteenth century, when Mitsunobu was active.[10] To judge by the fact that even in the 1989 exhibition *Screen Paintings of the Muromachi Period* there were only a few other screens covered entirely in gold leaf (probably the type known in China and Korea as "affixed gold" [*chōkin*]), the Tokyo National Museum's *Pine Trees* screen seems to be a special case. The vast majority of Muromachi Yamato-e screens presently known are of the "gold-burnished" type (kimigakitsuke). Two recently discovered screens dating from this period, *Pine Tree* (cat. no. 3) and *Pine Trees and Chinese Black Pines* (cat. no. 7), are neither gold burnished nor entirely covered with gold leaf. Rather, large areas of the picture surfaces are covered with gold leaf; such discoveries will shed new light on the development of screens with solid gold leaf grounds.

Let us now consider a representative example of the gold-burnished type: *Pine Trees on a Shore* (Tokyo National Museum).[11] The first impression upon viewing this screen is one of amazement at the gold that shines so brightly and beautifully from more than half the picture surface. Gold areas include both the ground and the trailing mist and clouds. The second astonishing aspect of the painting is that no trace of the use of sheets of gold leaf can be found. The technique seems to have consisted of painting the surface with mica or a thick white pigment (*gofun*) similar to gesso, then sprinkling powdered gold or tiny particles of gold leaf over it, and polishing it. This method of gold burnishing had been used as far back as the Heian period, for example, in the decorated papers of the late twelfth century *Sutras Dedicated by the Taira Family (Heike nōkyō)* at the Itsukushima Shrine. An identical tradition was handed down in the decoration of lacquer, where it was known as *togidashi* (literally, "brought out by polishing").

These screens are thought to date from the mid-sixteenth century, near the end of the Muromachi period. The splendid pair of six-panel screens *Pine Trees on a Shore* (private collection),[12] in which we can almost hear the sound of the surf, are the work of nearly a century earlier. The trailing mist and clouds in the upper half of the picture appear to have been done with this same gold burnishing technique. A substantial quantity of powdered silver was also used; and the sea, which covers a large area, seems to have underpainting in mica. Because the silver and mica are tarnished, the full splendor of these kimigakitsuke screens may not be apparent. The same can be said of *Trees and Plants of the Four Seasons* (fig. 2; cat. no. 2), which dates from the latter half, perhaps the end, of the fifteenth century. In this picture, the astringent tone of the mica predominates; the trailing mist and clouds of gold and silver in the upper half of the composition are inconspicuous by comparison (fig. 5).

In short, from the fifteenth century to the sixteenth, the amount of gold used to decorate screens gradually increased, although people who expect "gold-burnished screens" to be spectacularly gorgeous might be disappointed. The *migakitsuke* technique, by which gold and silver were applied to the surface of a large painting, was reminiscent of the fine craftsmanship of *maki-e* lacquer (decoration by the sprinkling of metallic powders into damp lacquer). The painstaking use of migakitsuke must have been considered remarkable in other countries, where the screens were described as "gold-decorated" (*kinshō*) or "with gold ornament" (*sōkin*). Even in fifteenth-century Japan itself, the fact that Prince Sadafusa went to the trouble to borrow "one pair of screens: kimigakitsuke Pines of the Four Seasons" shows that such works were highly prized. The shapes and drawing techniques seen in the clouds and mist rendered in gold burnishing on such screens as *Pine Trees on a Shore* had already been used in the fourteenth-century *Narrative Scroll of the Biography of the Priest Rajū Sanzō (Rajū Sanzō den-e;* private collection). The techniques were then applied to large-scale screens.

The conspicuous use of gold in narrative handscrolls begins in the early fifteenth century with the second scroll of the Seiryōji version of the *Miraculous Legends of the Circulating Invocation to Amida Buddha (Yūzū nenbutsu engi)*, of 1414. In addition to the use of gold pigment on the ground and other areas, there are traces of the powdered-gold (migakitsuke) technique. Almost all

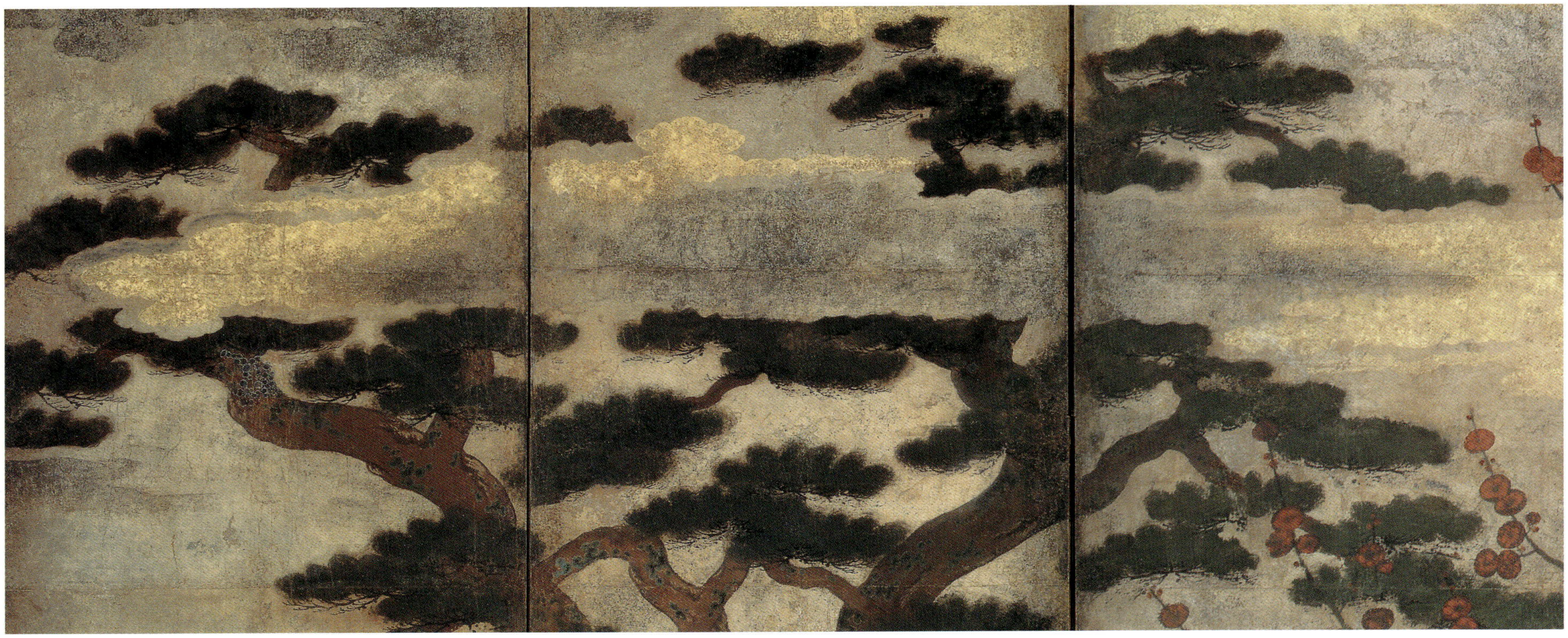

FIGURE 5

Trees and Plants of the Four Seasons, detail from right screen
CATALOGUE NO. 2

Yamato-e fan paintings of the fifteenth century, such as those in *Screens with Fan Paintings of the Tale of Genji and Other Subjects* (fig. 3) and in albums of fans (The Idemitsu Museum of Arts and Agency for Cultural Affairs, Tokyo, for example), make surprisingly copious use of gold mist and clouds. They would be readily identifiable as "gold fans." In each case, however, the gold is applied by gold burnishing rather than gold leaf. From the mid-sixteenth century on, there are indeed gold fans to which large sheets of gold leaf have been applied, but in many cases no trace of the gold leaf shows, perhaps because powdered-gold migakitsuke has been added over it (the fact that there is a base of gold leaf is proven by the damaged areas). The intention was probably to continue the tradition of gold burnishing. This may be the reason that the afore-mentioned *Pine Trees*, although covered entirely in gold leaf, does not show the sheets of gold leaf very clearly—and also the reason that it shines so beautifully. I have therefore grouped it with the gold-burnished screens.

In light of these observations I would like to note that the early Edo period painter Tawaraya Sōtatsu, who revived the tradition of Muromachi-style Yamato-e during the early seventeenth century, created works such as gold fans and the *Matsushima Screens* in the Freer Gallery of Art, Smithsonian Institution, Washington, D.C., that do not have the usual type of gold leaf (squares of approximately four inches [10 cm]). The gold surfaces (ground and mist) in the *Matsushima Screens* are all created by dense sprinkling of powdered gold or tiny pieces of gold leaf: that is, by the gold-burnishing technique.

A different method of gold burnishing can be seen in such works as *Landscape with the Sun and Moon* (Kongōji, Osaka). In this technique, the clouds and mist are formed by sprinkling small squares of gold and silver foil in various sizes (*kirihaku*), threads of metal foil (*noge*), and metal powder (*sunago*). The oldest known example is *Flowers and Birds of the Four Seasons with the Sun and the Moon* (fig. 6; cat. no. 1), thought to be a work of the first half of the fifteenth century. This technique has already been mentioned in connection with the decorated paper of the *Sutras Dedicated by the Taira Family* of the second half of the twelfth century. A painted cypress wood fan dating from the end of the fourteenth century (private collection), said to come from the Kumano Hayatama

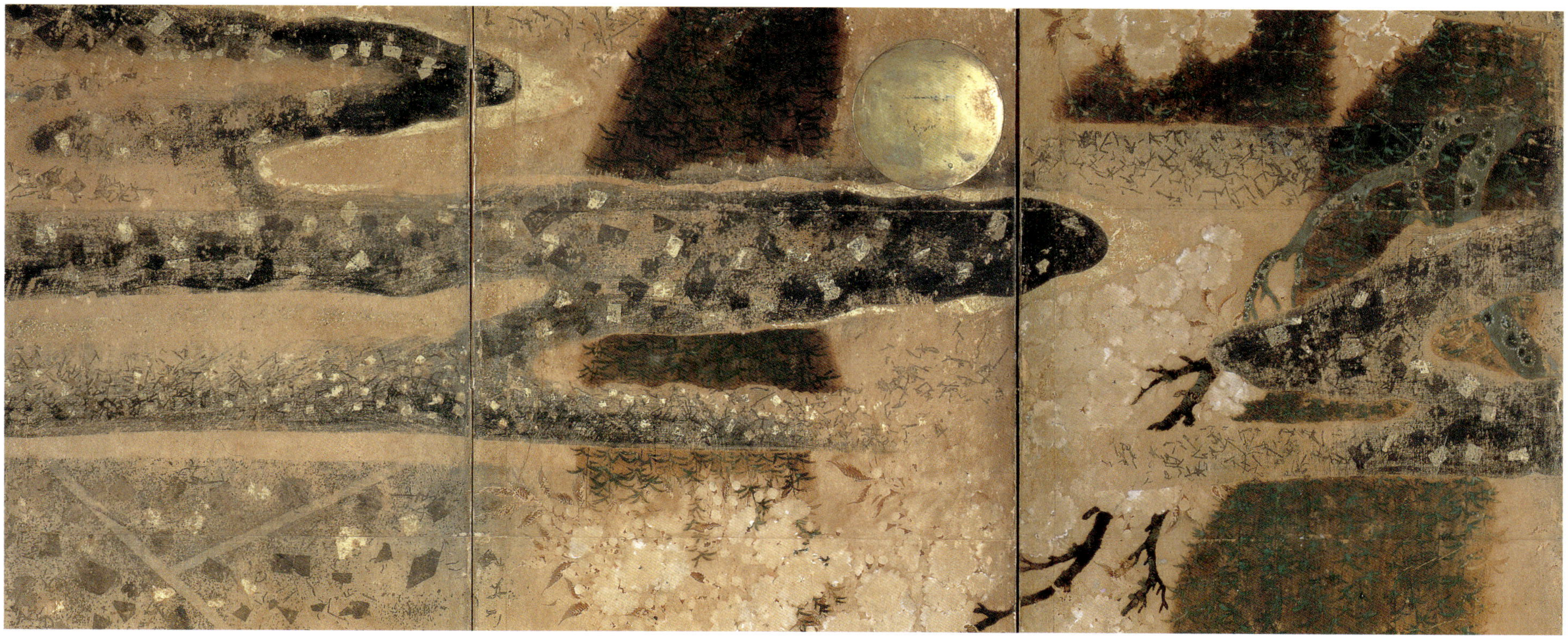

FIGURE 6

Flowers and Birds of the Four Seasons with the Sun and the Moon, detail from right screen
CATALOGUE NO. 1

Shrine, displays this method in a gorgeous effect. The same technique, on a large scale, was applied to screens (though it does not appear in the gold fans of the Muromachi period). However, in the case of this technique as well, the Muromachi screens maintained a refined beauty and did not lapse into gaudiness. At the end of the Muromachi period there are Yamato-e screens that, in addition to clouds and mist rendered by these two methods, have gold clouds made of attached gold leaf (see cat. nos. 4, 7).

Finally, I would like to discuss a major difference between the clouds and mist in the Yamato-e gold burnished screens and the gold clouds in the gold screens of the Kano school painters in the Kanga lineage. Up to this point I have spoken of "either mist or clouds" in gold burnishing because these forms are not clearly outlined (in some cases their edges are shaded with white or blue). Trailing easily across the painting and floating from foreground to background, they suggest the moist Japanese landscape and enhance the elegance of the flowers and birds. Whereas Yamato-e makes extensive use of gold and silver mist, Kano school gold screens, such as *Scenes in and around Kyoto* by Kano Eitoku (1543–1590) (Uesugi collection) and *Flowers, Birds, and Insects of the Four Seasons* (Agency for Cultural Affairs), have solid and palpable gold clouds made of large sheets of gold leaf and emphasized by very clear-cut outlines. Gold mist is not used at all. The colors, deep and intense, contrast strongly with the gold clouds, which are an important element in large-scale compositions.

A subdued quality reminiscent of the patina of old silver is inherent in the elegant decorativeness of Yamato-e gold burnished screens of the Muromachi period. Gold Kanga-style paintings of the Kano school project a more spectacular decorativeness by using gold leaf aggressively so that the edges of the sheets of gold show. In the next stage, gold leaf is applied not only for clouds but also for ground and even background space. This greatly increases the amount of gold and leads to the full flowering of the gorgeous Momoyama screen and sliding-panel paintings that blended the Chinese and Japanese styles.

In the early Momoyama period, at the end of the sixteenth century, works covered almost entirely in gold leaf appear—for example, the famous *Cypress Trees* attributed to Eitoku (Tokyo National Museum). Even in this case, however, the inclusion of gold cloud shapes reveals that this use of gold is an expansion of the gold clouds seen in earlier works. The Kano school painters, coming from the Kanga lineage, strove to depict flowers and birds in natural landscapes. Therefore, much as they exerted themselves to expand the clouds of gold and make their paintings decorative, they always retained streams and distant mountains within the picture. They were unable to separate their subjects from nature to the same extent seen in Yamato-e works, such as *Pine Trees* (fig. 4) in which only pines and rocks, with no indication of earth or water, appear against the solid gold background. Some of the room paintings by Kano artists of the Kan'ei era (1624–1644) of the early Edo period—such as the sliding panels at Nijō Castle, Kyoto, of 1625, and Tenkyūin, of about 1632—use a solid gold leaf background on all four sides of a room; but somewhere in the overall composition of each room there will always be the gold cloud shape, pointing to the source of the overall gold surface. These gold rooms were the most extreme examples of a trend in which the later Kano school under the leadership of Tan'yū (1602–1674) and Sansetsu (1589–1651) utilized the techniques of the gold Yamato-e screens of the Muromachi period (gold-burnished clouds and mist). During this same Kan'ei era, the overall gold leaf background of the Yamato-e *Pine Trees* (fig. 4) was revived with deliberate self-consciousness by Tawaraya Sōtatsu in gold screens such as *Court Dancing* (Daigoji, Kyoto) and *Wind and Thunder Gods* (Kenninji, Kyoto). Sōtatsu consciously employed the two techniques of Muromachi Yamato-e gold screens (gold burnishing and solid gold leaf backgrounds) but eschewed the swelling clouds of the Kano school screen and sliding-panel paintings that had flourished during the Momoyama period.

Within the Kanga lineage, Momoyama period artists such as Hasegawa Tōhaku (1539–1610) and Kaihō Yūshō (1533–1615) and their pupils utilized the heritage of Muromachi Yamato-e somewhat differently from the Kano school. Tōhaku, known for the wall and sliding-panel paintings *Maple Trees* in the Chishakuin, Kyoto, and the sliding-panel paintings *Willows and Autumn Plants* in the Sanbōin, Kyoto, also created the screens *Mount Fuji* (Kotohiragū Museum, Kyoto) and *Bamboo and Fence* (private collection). Yūshō painted gold screens of a different type, such as *Pine Trees on a Shore* and *Fishing Nets* (both, Imperial Household Agency, Tokyo). Clearly, the Kano school did not hold a monopoly on the fusion of Chinese and Japanese styles in Kanga. Tōhaku's masterpiece *Pine Trees in Mist* (Tokyo National Museum) is the most Japanese of ink paintings. Yūshō, too, created an ink painting rich in mood, *Landscape with a Pavilion* (MOA Museum of Art, Atami). In the Edo period, Sōtatsu produced ink paintings in a Japanese style exemplified by such works as *Lotus Pond and Waterfowl* (Kyoto National Museum).

I have attempted to show that the history of Japanese painting from the Muromachi to the Momoyama period did not change at one stroke from austere and high-minded beauty to splendor and spectacle. Rather, there was a gradual transformation from the misty silver beauty of the period of the "mixing of Chinese and Japanese styles" to the world of gold shining in the brilliant midday sun of the "fusion of Chinese and Japanese styles." Many problems still remain regarding the division of the various screens into Yamato-e and Kanga (here done provisionally for the sake of convenience) and the attribution and dating of individual works. In any case, it is my hope that the development of painting from Muromachi to Momoyama can be apprehended from a more comprehensive, concrete viewpoint based on the works themselves. Needless to say, it is essential for this purpose that additional examples of gold screens of every kind, dating from the late Muromachi to the early Momoyama, be brought to light.

NOTES

1. Tanaka Ichimatsu, "Hamamatsu zu byōbu," pp. 244–251.

2. Yamane Yūzō, "'Muromachi jidai no byōbue' gaikan—Wakan haigō no sekai" (Overview of the "Screen Paintings of the Muromachi Period" exhibition: The mixing of Chinese and Japanese styles), *Muromachi jidai no byōbue*, pp. 8–14.

3. *Gomotsu on'e mokuroku* (Catalogue of paintings in the official collection) compiled by Nōami.

4. Recorded, for example, in the *Kundaikan sōchōki* (Evaluation and ranking of Chinese artists and instructions for the proper display of their paintings), to which both Nōami and Sōami contributed, and the *Okazari ki* (Record of decorations) by Sōami.

5. Miyakami Shigetaka, "Kaisho kara chanoyu zashiki e" (From the meeting hall to the tearoom), in *Chadō shūkin* (Tea ceremony compendium) (Tokyo: Shogakkan, 1984), vol. 7, pp. 46–76.

6. The original scroll is no longer extant, but similar sliding-panel paintings have survived at Daisenin, Daitokuji, Kyoto.

7. Adachi Keiko, "Muromachi jidai ebyōbue kō," pp. 119–124.

8. During the Kamakura and Muromachi periods, Buddhist priests, especially those of the Zen sect, were keenly interested in China and its culture. They transmitted this appreciation of things Chinese to the shoguns and the elite classes.

9. Akazawa Eiji, "Jūgo seiki ni okeru kinbyōbu ni tsuite," pp. 567–579.

10. Murashige Yasushi, "Den Tosa Mitsunobu hitsu Matsu zu byōbu ni tsuite," pp. 30–41.

11. Reproduced in *The Triumph of Japanese Style*, pp. 24–25.

12. Reproduced in *Muromachi jidai byōbue*, pp. 42–45.

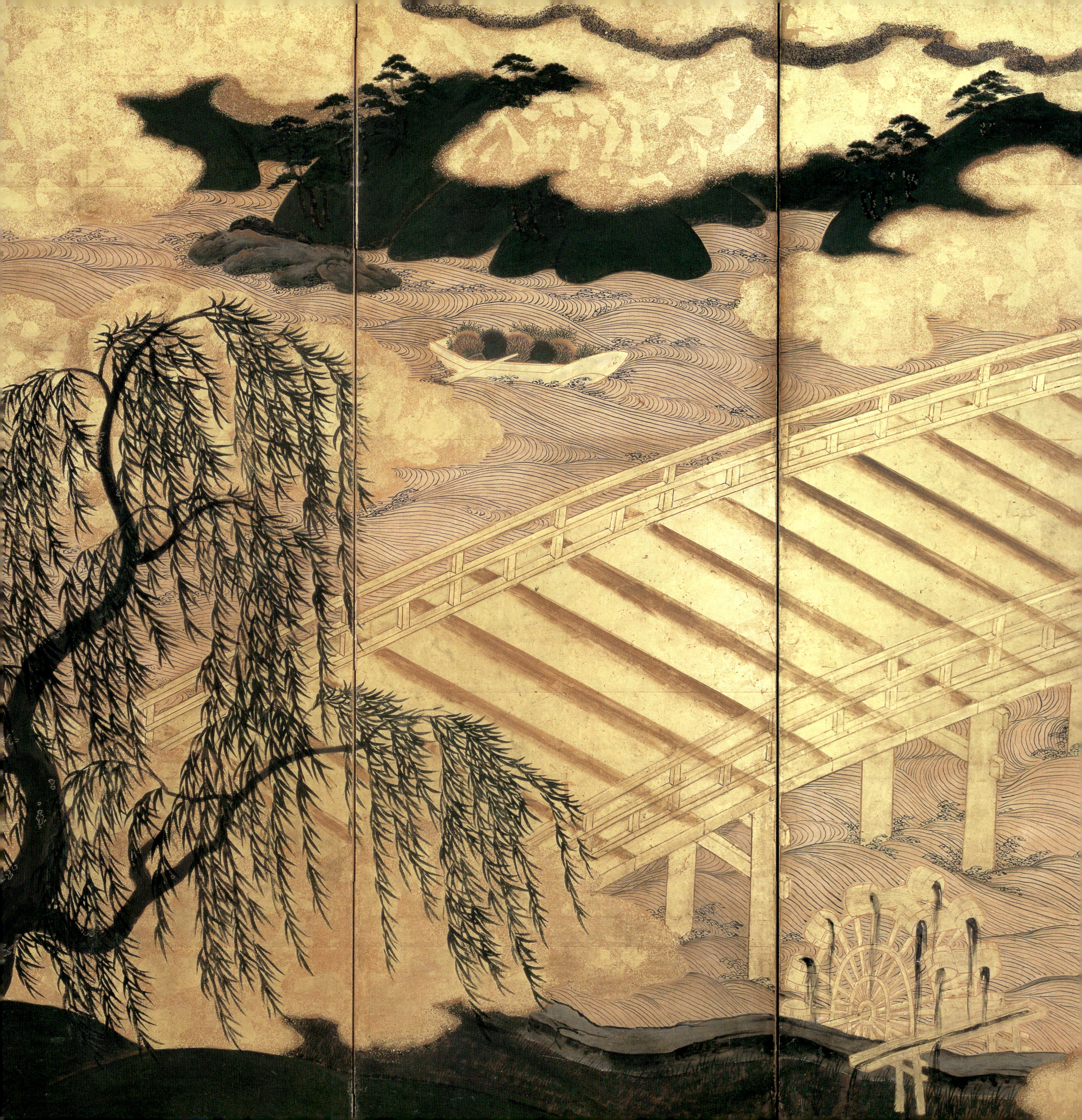

The Golden Link: Place, Poetry, and Paradise in a Medieval Japanese Design

Medieval Japanese screens in the so-called native style, or *Yamato-e*, combine the telegraphic language of symbols—that is, familiar images used by Japanese for centuries—with an abstract directness that speaks immediately to modern viewers. I have always felt an attraction to, even a kind of mystery emanating from, the compelling style born of this era's special marriage of cryptic symbol and graceful abstraction. Although one need not be conversant with the codes communicating nuances of meaning in this long, rich, inward-looking cultural tradition to recognize the power of these works, their designers had, nonetheless, specific messages in mind, even though these may not be immediately apprehensible. Because of the many difficulties in studying these paintings, medieval screens in the native style have received only a fraction of the scholarly attention devoted to the Chinese-style ink paintings of the same era.[1] The equation of Muromachi art with the Chinese style dies hard.[2]

The Idemitsu Museum of Arts possesses a spectacular collection of important Yamato-e screens of the Muromachi period (1392–1573), many of them displayed in America for the first time. Thus an excellent opportunity arises to consider some of the issues inherent in medieval Japanese screen painting by focusing on a single exceptional pair, the *Uji River* screens (fig. 1; cat. no. 8).

The screens are executed with ink—prominent in the elaborate line drawing of the waves—and thick pigment (primarily a fresh, matte malachite green) for the landforms and trees with touches of rust brown for the brushwood in the boats and bright accents on the waterbirds. The pillars, curved railings of the bridge, and the boats are outlined with subtle red lines, reminiscent of the technique in traditional Buddhist paintings. An opulent combination of shiny gold leaf (both solid and scattered irregularly), gold paint of a contrasting hue and reflectivity, and tiny variegated gold and silver particles produces an effect of shimmering, almost unworldly luxury.

A turbulent river tosses up delicate arabesques among its swells as it rushes across all twelve panels of the screens from left to right, the reverse of the direction from which East Asian painting is customarily "read." Passing under the arch of the gold-leafed bridge, the water billows and swirls around the pillars. Three boats laden with brushwood make an uncertain journey down the treacherous watercourse; they have no one on board to guide them to their destination.

In a sequence that starts from the opposite direction, five graceful willow trees mark the passing seasons. The willow at the extreme right-hand edge of the composition, its tender leaves just starting to bud, signifies spring. It directs the eye across the bridge towards the next willow, which brackets the left edge of the right

Opposite:
Uji River, detail from right screen
Muromachi to Momoyama period,
possibly mid-16th century
Pair of six-panel screens
CATALOGUE NO. 8

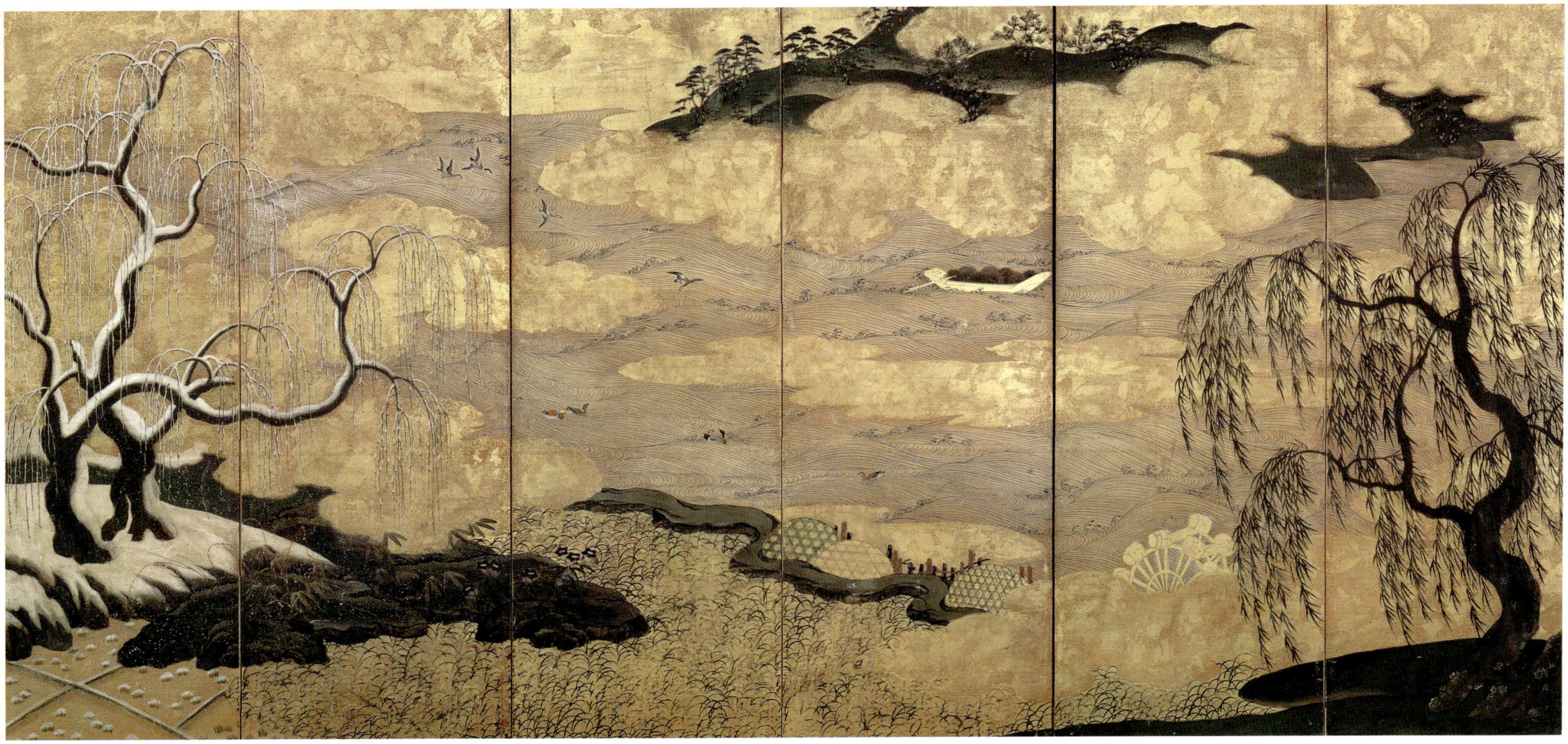

FIGURE 1

Uji River
Muromachi to Momoyama period,
possibly mid-16th century
Pair of six-panel screens
CATALOGUE NO. 8

screen. More developed, the foliage of the second willow waves pliantly in a summer breeze. A churning waterwheel decants water into flooded rice paddies, the reflective green fields being a conventional marker of summer. Picking up the composition at the right edge of the left screen, the third willow presides over fields bounteously laden with ripe ears of rice. The waterwheel here lies quiet, its job done. A path snakes between the paddies and the riverbank, which is marked by rock-filled baskets that prevent erosion and by vertical sticks indicating the presence of fish weirs. Chinese bellflowers, waving grasses, low-lying bamboos called *sasa*, and migrating birds enhance the autumnal mood. The sequence closes with intertwined, bare, snow-laden willows, which, together with the harvested paddies, dessicated reeds, and gentle snowfall, proclaim winter. On the opposite shore, rolling green hills peek out from scalloped clouds composed of gold paint overlaid with irregular pieces of gold foil in various sizes, including minute particles. Some clouds are outlined with silver dust, now tarnished. U-shaped fingers of mist, done in gold paint, complement the gold clouds.

The uniqueness and importance of these screens have attracted the attention of scholars for some thirty years. The first surviving opinion regarding their date and authorship appears on an anonymous label on their storage box attributing them to Tosa Mitsunobu (active 1469–1521). This is too early a date for them, but it was characteristic of connoisseurs beginning in the early Edo period (1615–1868) routinely to ascribe unknown works like these to that master (this suggests that by the seventeenth century, art-historical knowledge of medieval Yamato-e had become shaky, if indeed it had ever been systematic).[3] Modern published opinion on the dating of the *Uji River* screens ranges from late Muromachi through the Keicho era (1596–1615).[4] Because the design and execution are unique, there is little material for

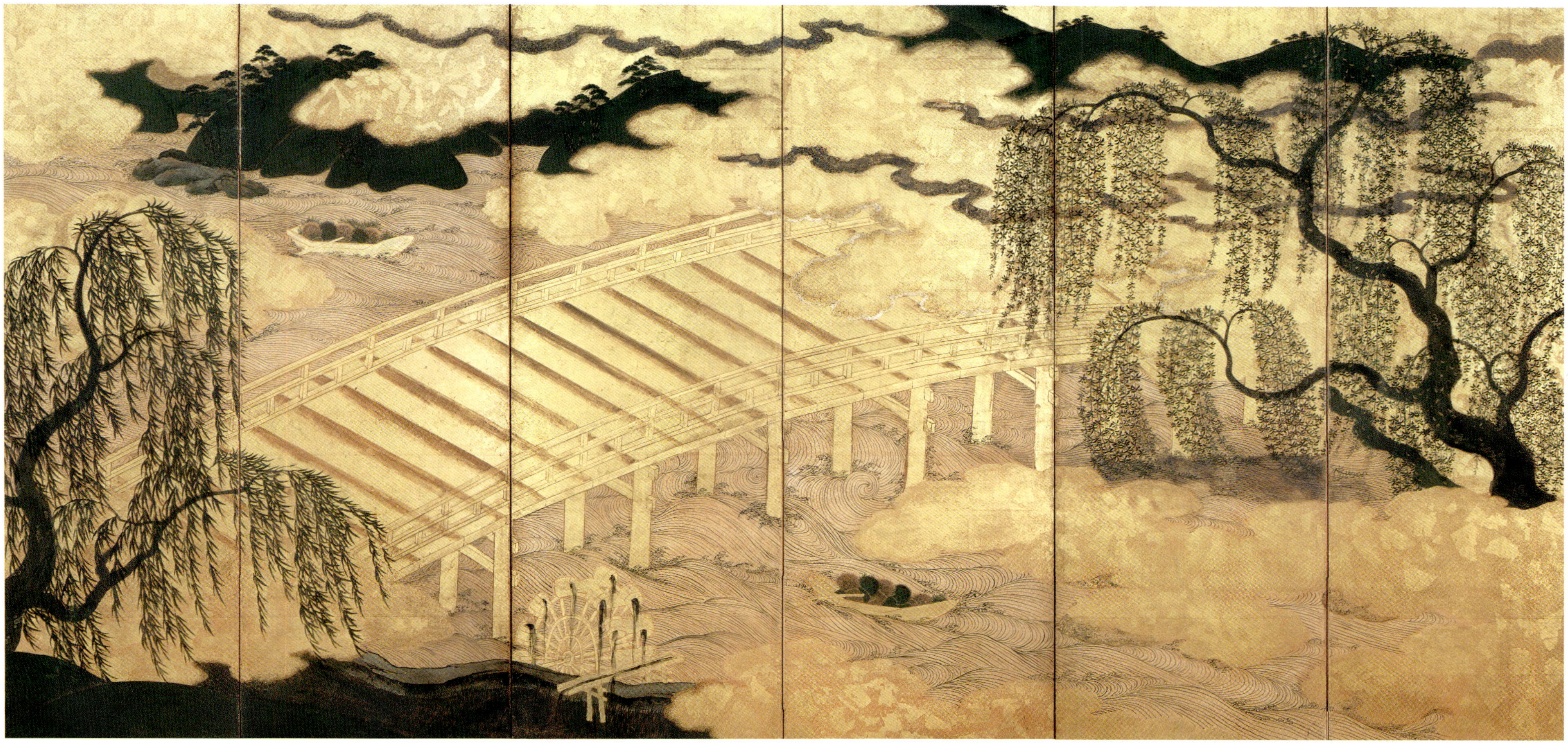

comparison. From the standpoint of composition, motif, and technique, the screens taken at face value would seem to be a mid-sixteenth century link between the earlier, mostly narrative, renditions of Uji and the monumental, simplified Willow Bridge and Waterwheel compositions that were produced in great numbers during the Momoyama (1573–1615) and early Edo periods (see fig. 2). This is not to discount the possibilities that they are a replacement of a lost original representing this important link or that they reflect the taste of an adventurous Edo period patron with extreme antiquarian tastes.

We cannot hope to solve this here, but by treating these screens as representative of compositions produced about the middle of the sixteenth century, we can raise questions that will shed light on them and on Muromachi Yamato-e screen painting in general. How do these screens represent Japanese associations with Uji? How do they relate to traditional depictions of that place? What medieval Yamato-e currents do they draw from? What, if anything, is their ultimate meaning? Because there is relatively little in English about Muromachi screens, it seems appropriate to review the state of our knowledge before proceeding to an intensive investigation of the *Uji River* screens.

WHY THE NEGLECT OF MEDIEVAL YAMATO-E SCREENS?

The Gospel of Painting According to Kano

> Then, two painting traditions developed: one called Yamato-e [Japanese painting] and one called Kanga [Chinese painting]. Yamato-e could attain spirit-resonance but it could not depart from the carefully detailed style. . . . Tosa masters create Yamato-e filled with sensitivity and gentle grace. They paint figures, whether large or small, with simple lines. . . . When depicting pines, they generally paint the female

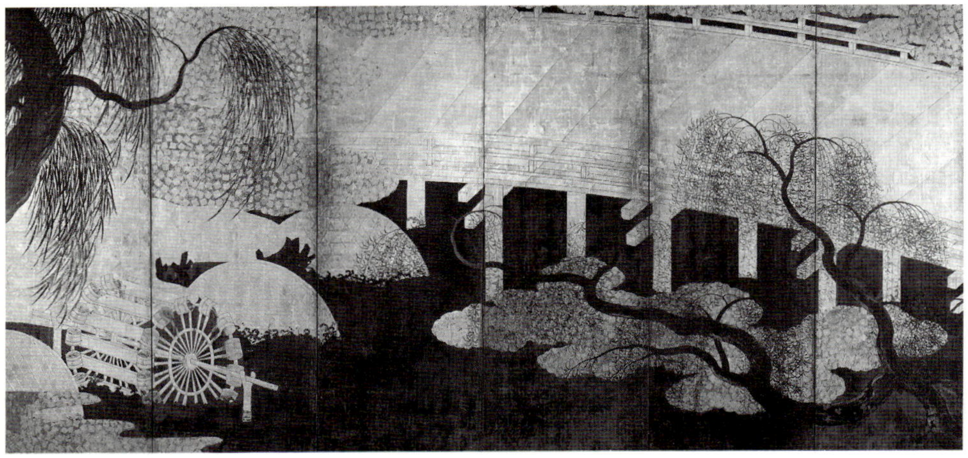
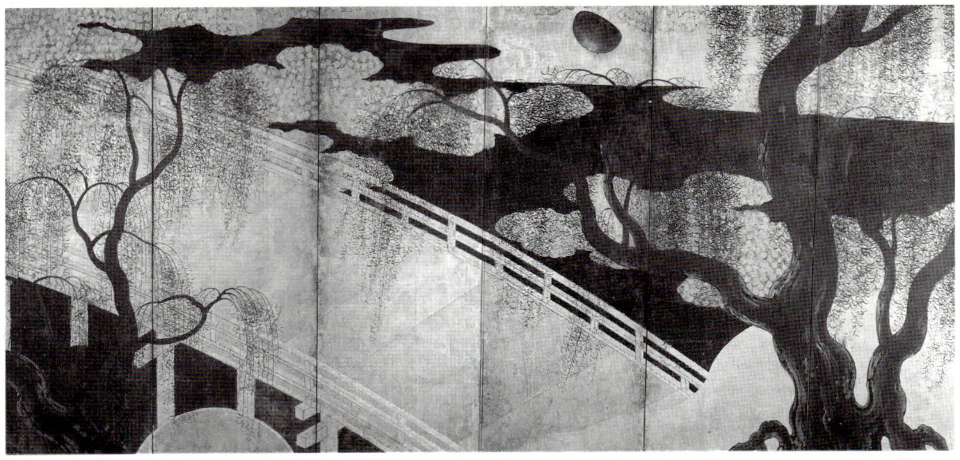

FIGURE 2

Willow Bridge and Waterwheel
Momoyama period, 17th century
Pair of six-panel screens
Ink, color, and gold on paper
Each, 67 x 136 in. (170.1 x 345.3 cm)
The Mary and Jackson Burke Collection

and only rarely paint the male. All the other characteristic features [of Tosa style Yamato-e] can be inferred from these .... The Kano [school] is sovereign of painting schools; its branches extend far and wide. There is no shortage of talent among painters in the family and disciples in the workshop. Kano masters skillfully combine techniques of both the Tosa school and Sesshū, and use them well.[5]

Kano Einō, *Honchō gashi*, 1678

It is a well-known cliché that Japanese culture defines itself by means of opposition to an Other. Until modern times the primary Other was China, and the contrast was drawn under the rubric of *Wakan*, "Japanese-Chinese."[6] From the tenth century when the Japanese of the Heian period (794–1185) gradually transformed the lessons learned from China, they drew a distinction between paintings considered to be in the realm of things Chinese and those that expressed sentiments and themes associated with their own culture. Unfortunately for art historians, this tidy oppositional scheme creates more problems than it solves, for once a foreign style is absorbed into Japanese culture, it quickly undergoes transformations that render the prototype, in most cases, all but unrecognizable—one might say that all painting styles in Japan before the Edo period had their origin in China. When the Japanese turned to the serious writing of art history in the seventeenth century, the Wakan paradigm forced them to shoehorn artists into one category or the other. In reality the stylistic overlap between artists classified as working in the "Chinese mode" and those in the "Japanese mode" was often tremendous.[7]

The Muromachi period felt the renewed effects of Chinese culture in numerous forms after the assimilation that had taken place during the Heian period. Chinese monks fleeing the Mongol invasions rekindled Japanese interest in the culture of the mainland. Newly established Zen monasteries, as well as shoguns and provincial lords, began importing Chinese ceramics, brocades, calligraphy scrolls, flower vases, and tea utensils with a curious insatiability. In the realm of pictorial art, imports from China included traditional Buddhist icons and woodblock books; deities, figures, still-lifes, flowers and birds, and landscapes by Chan (J. Zen) priests like Muqi (active thirteenth century); and the crisply flawless pictures produced by the professional painters of the Chinese Imperial Painting Bureau. The "one-corner," diagonally oriented renditions of landscapes, flowers and birds, flowering grasses and plants, and insects by academy professionals, whether in monochrome or enriched with vegetable or mineral pigment, captivated Japanese collectors and artists. The structured space, clarity of form, and virtuoso brushwork distinguished them immediately from native Yamato-e. Incorporated into the fabric of Japanese painting and collectively known as "ink paintings," or *sumi-e*, during the Muromachi period, these styles served as referents to the authority of China, even as they were being adapted and transformed for Japanese use (see cat. nos. 5, 6, 9, 13). Echoes of the new Chinese painting even found their way into the brushwork of traditional icons and also into Buddhist and secular handscrolls characterized as belonging to the native style.

The critical bias elevating the Chinese lineage above the Japanese lineage congealed during the seventeenth century, as the quotation by Kano Einō opening this section shows. This came about as a result of the aggressive self-promotion that has characterized the activities of the Kano family of painters ever since the lineage began monopolizing the major commissions in the sixteenth century. By the seventeenth century, Kano writers also led the production of painting treatises, a situation that not coincidentally echoed that of the logocentric literati painters of China.[8]

The strategies of both countries' theorists involved the hagiographical presentation of their own lineages' accomplishments set against the backdrop of the disparagement of works produced by rival schools. As a result, over time it became difficult to retrieve information about other kinds of painting by earlier artists less facile with the written word.[9] Kano Einō's essay assumes a tone of objective evaluation: he generously points out the good qualities of his rival Tosa school painters ("Tosa masters create Yamato-e filled with sensitivity and gentle grace") but then undercuts with faint praise ("Yamato-e could attain spirit-resonance but it could not depart from the carefully detailed style"). This serves as a foil for the versatility of his own school ("Kano masters skillfully combine techniques of both the Tosa school and Sesshū [1420–1506, a major talent who worked in the Chinese ink mode] and use them well").

Einō cleverly interjects a reference to the feminine ("When painting pines, they generally paint the female and only rarely paint the male"). The old distinction between the masculine and feminine spheres—another example of the habit of dialectical thinking that produced the rigid division of the Chinese lineage and the Japanese lineage—was articulated, if obscurely, as "masculine painting" (*otoko-e*) and "feminine painting" (*onna-e*) in Heian period Yamato-e. This reverberates with the conventions governing the written language during the Heian period. The official language of statecraft consisted of Chinese characters, which were considered the exclusive domain of men. Women, on the other hand, wrote in a native syllabic script (*kana*), the calligraphic equivalent of Yamato-e (men were free to use either). An early seventeenth century genre screen depicting festivities at the Hōkoku Shrine gives visual evidence of this dichotomy. It shows noblewomen sitting in a room decorated with gilt and polychromed Yamato-e style wall paintings, while warriors next-door occupy a room adorned with Chinese-style monochrome.[10]

Yamato-e, then, became synonymous with the feminine sphere; thus the masculine (in Einō's scheme, meaning the Kano) is represented by Chinese ink painting, with the implicit assumption that the Chinese-painting lineage is the more virile of the two, i.e., stronger, more authoritative, more public. One scholar has suggested that this deep-rooted association of Yamato-e with femininity is responsible for its relative neglect by Japanese art historians, the overwhelming majority of whom are male.[11]

The "Orthodox" Yamato Lineage: Tosa and Other "Elegant" Painters

It is not fair to place all of the blame on Kano treatises for the erasure of the record of Muromachi Yamato-e (although they certainly helped shift attention away from it). The Yamato lineage is not handed to later generations in tidy packages as the Chinese lineage appears—deceptively—to be. The frustrating lack of documentation for Yamato-e results in the temptation to relegate objects not clearly in the Chinese manner to the workshop of Tosa Mitsunobu,[12] as is the case with the *Uji River* screens under discussion. Mitsunobu served as Director of the Imperial Painting Bureau for nearly fifty years, and he also worked for the Ashikaga shogunate. He garnered the highest court rank ever bestowed on a painter, received income from lands awarded by the court and the military, participated in poetry gatherings, and was sufficiently interesting to a number of contemporary courtiers that his activities were recorded in their diaries.

His workshop produced narrative picture scrolls, portraits of warriors and courtiers, traditional Buddhist icons, and large-format screens, including a prototype of the panoramic *Scenes in and around Kyoto* (see cat. no. 15). This versatility, coupled with the fact that Yamato-e painters of this era tended not to sign their works,[13] made it a simple matter to fit all unauthenticated Yamato-e works under the very large umbrella of Mitsunobu.

In truth, Kyoto teemed with competing Yamato-e workshops with which the Tosa family had to wrestle—sometimes unsuccessfully—for the prized post of Director of the Imperial Painting Bureau. Not much is known about these other painters. A set of two picture scrolls entitled *Miraculous Legends of the Circulating Invocation to Amida (Yūzū nenbutsu engi)* gives a good idea of the complexity of the problem.[14] Donated to Seiryōji in 1414, these handscrolls were the joint work of six artists, whose participation is securely recognized only because their names are listed in the accompanying text.[15] In fact, the scenes in the *Miraculous Legends of the Circulating Invocation to Amida* represent the only known works by some of these artists. The widespread destruction and loss of valuable objects throughout the turbulent Muromachi period and the need for replacements kept painters in the Yamato-e tradition busy.[16]

The "Nonorthodox" Yamato Lineage: Fan Shops and Commercial Painting Establishments

At the same time that painters with patrician names like Rokkaku (a branch of the Minamoto family and descendants of an emperor) and Fujiwara were plying their brushes, numerous anonymous plebeian shops catered to a broader clientele. Artistic training, if it could be so described, was probably passed down in-house through the generations. Unrecorded in history, the careers of such painters can be discovered only by chance.

It is important, nonetheless, to take note of their existence. Seemingly typical of this kind of production were the many fan shops, or *ōgiya*, that decorated the Kyoto fans that had been famous throughout the country since the Heian period. These workers might be viewed as part of the larger group of artists—or perhaps we should call them artisans although the distinction is hard to draw, especially because the concept of "art" as we know it did not exist during the period under discussion. There is certainly no question that the concept of "culture" and its necessary accoutrements was fully in place. Later these urban entrepreneurs became known collectively as "town painters" (*machi eshi*). The following excerpt, bearing the early date of 1275, from the *Diary of Lady Nijō* records a transaction with such a fan shop:

> In the seventh month of the year before last when I was preparing to return to the palace after a brief visit to my home, I sent some unmounted fan paper along with a frame of camphor wood to a fanmaker's house, where they were to be pasted together. The paper was decorated with flecks of gold dust on the top and bottom, and the phrase "smoldering ashes" [a reference from the *Tale of Genji* to a secret love affair] was written in white on the blue wave-like design in the center. Seeing this quite ordinary fan paper, the daughter of the house, who painted beautifully, was inspired to design a new fan with an autumn landscape and the line "Though you view the moon from a distant shore" [from the imperial poetry anthology *Kokinshū*]. She pasted her fan paper on the frame in place of the paper I had sent.

The arresting uniqueness of the design produces an unanticipated result:

> Upon my return to the palace at that time GoFukakusa [a retired emperor and Lady Nijō's lover] observed that the style of painting on the fan differed from anything else I had and asked who had given it to me, questioning me with such persistence that I finally told him quite plainly what had happened. It came as no surprise that the beauty of the fan led him to become enamored of the artist, and on several

occasions after that I conveyed messages for them. Finally it was somehow arranged for the girl to come to the palace on the tenth day of the tenth month.[17]

Although the style of the fan was in the Japanese manner, taking its theme from the *Kokinshū*, it "differed from anything else I had." This suggests that these small family-run fan shops were free—perhaps even took it as their stock in trade—to produce a distinctive house style. We might also infer that, because the style was sufficiently unique to arouse the retired emperor's interest, not many of this establishment's fans had previously found their way into court circles. Who then were the clientele of this shop? Although the courtiers were the most literate members of society and produced all the documentary evidence of fan shop activities, it should not be assumed that they monopolized their production. Possibly commoners living on the fringes of court culture were also clients. Such shops may well have had extensive, and wholly unrecorded, business activities in various spheres of society.

Also active in the production of anonymous medieval Yamato-e were painters working in *eya*, "painting shops," a term first seen in the literature of the late Muromachi period.[18] We know about eya because it was the practice for artisans to take as surnames the word for their trade. Along with names like Nuriya ("Lacquer Shop") Sōshi and Ōgiya ("Fan Shop") Yōzōbei, we also find mention for the first time of an Eya So-and-so (sobriquet, Sōyō) in a tea diary from the city of Sakai.[19] The rise of eya is connected, undoubtedly, to the power of the newly affluent urban commoner class (*machishū*) of Kyoto, Sakai, and Osaka, as evidenced by the appearance of the term in diaries from all three cities. An enterprise of this nature, specializing in children's portraits, appears in the screen *Scenes in and around Kyoto* by Kano Eitoku (1543–1590) (Uesugi collection, Tokyo National Museum).

Yūzō Yamane has scoured documents pertaining to the proliferation of these entrepreneurial painting shops. He suggests that the various establishments must have been staffed by ex-fan painters, ex-sutra craftsmen, ex-Buddhist painters, and apprentices who drifted away from Kano and Tosa workshops during the turbulent mid-sixteenth century. This would certainly account for the remarkable diversity of late medieval Yamato-e. Yamane has also reconstructed from diary references of the time the remarkable versatility of eya activities: they produced underpainting for poem-cards, painted fans, decorated lanterns and dolls, drew designs for textiles, decorated shells (for a contemporary pastime, the shell-matching game), and even applied coloring to architecture. In addition, they painted folding screens and sold ink drawings to be pasted on screens (called in the sixteenth century *sumi-e oshi-e*). Many eya seem to have been freelances, working in conjunction with other craftsmen—an important issue in the production of screens during the Muromachi period. Some received training in techniques related to Chinese ink painting (Yūsetsu, the son of the talented Kaihō Yūshō, was one such painter). Others, like the mysterious Tosa Gagakusuke, a man for whom we have a name but no known works, might have emerged from a Tosa workshop.[20]

MUROMACHI YAMATO-E SCREENS

Let us now turn from medieval Yamato-e in general to some specific questions concerning screen painting of the Muromachi period. This area in particular has benefitted from a welcome spate of recent Japanese scholarship, inspired by the discovery of several unique and marvelous objects. This section will touch upon the various functions of Muromachi folding screens, their different types, and some ramifications of their subject matter.[21]

These large-scale paintings present their own special challenges. They were utilitarian, consumable pieces for daily life. Their unwieldy size made them both easy to damage and hard to rescue in case of fire or earthquake. The vast majority became victims of the general devastation of this unstable period. Unlike the easily portable picture scrolls, which often have accompanying texts detailing the circumstances of their production, medieval screens generally employ pictorial imagery only.[22] Given the proposition that most paintings of this period (except portraits) have their inspiration in literary sources, the absence of recognizable referents makes interpretation difficult. When the artist is unknown, the theme obscure, the style not immediately recognizable, and the object difficult to date, it is small wonder that relatively little has been written about individual works.

Status, Use, and Categories of Muromachi Yamato-e Screens

Although the military class was preoccupied with cultural paraphernalia from China, we must not forget that the Ashikaga shoguns forged their cultural identity in part by assimilating aspects of Japanese courtly practice. Warriors incorporated Yamato-e into the architectural decor of their mansions, and they used Yamato-e screens and folding fans for tribute and trade with China and Korea. Thus they continued a tradition dating back to the Heian period. Japanese screens with "thick colors and much gold, green, and blue" are recorded in China in the catalogue of the collection of the Huizong emperor (1082–1135).[23] Golden Yamato-e screens depicting flowers were sent by the shogun Ashikaga Yoshimasa as part of a diplomatic mission to Choson-dynasty Korea in 1443. In 1541 the lord of Suō Province ordered three pairs of golden screens and one hundred fans from Kano Motonobu (1476–1559) as gifts for the emperor of China.[24]

In a country like Japan where the minutest action becomes a sort of ritual, the importance of setting and display for formal occasions brought folding screens to the fore as indispensable objects. Muromachi period diaries refer to them as part of the "equipment" (*gusoku*) necessary for reception room arrangements (*zashiki shitsurai*) along with Chinese objects such as flower vases, incense burners, and trays and other valuable objects calculated to create an impeccable aesthetic atmosphere. Assemblage (*kazari*) became a fine art in itself with various styles and appellations.[25] The desired effect of early Muromachi assemblage was *basara*, or flamboyance. This gave way in the fifteenth century to the aesthetic of *sōgon*, the sublime. It is difficult, however, to distinguish the two, based on actual descriptions of the objects involved. The assemblage was so crucial that what was displayed on a certain occasion was often recorded for posterity. Yamato-e screens play an important role in both schemes.

A prince's diary, the *Record of Things Seen and Heard (Kanmon gyoki)*, from the era in which the aesthetic of the sublime, or sōgon, prevailed, recorded a revealing description of decorations for a reception room (*kaisho*) for the Tanabata festival of the seventh day of the seventh month of 1432. On the preceding day,

> Fine weather. Ornamental setting for Tanabata. A pair of folding screens (*kimigakitsuke* [a special technique of burnished gold] with paintings of pine trees in the four seasons) and three hanging scrolls. Central image a Kannon, borrowed from the chief priest of Hōren'in. These make the reception room arrangement.

Then, on the seventh day,

> Early in the morning people bring flowers and decorate the reception room. Two pairs of folding screens are put up, and seven hanging scrolls are suspended from them.[26]

From this account and others like it, it seems that colorful gilt Yamato-e screens were the prescribed supports from which hanging scrolls in Chinese ink were suspended to achieve the desired aesthetic effect. (Echoes of this medieval notion of display are seen in the gilt and polychromed tokonoma alcoves of the seventeenth century in the audience halls at Nijō Castle, which are often photographed decorated with ink-painting hanging scrolls.[27]) The practice of suspending scrolls from screens originated in China and predated the development of the tokonoma.[28] Chinese-style paintings were even hung from Yamato-e screens during the early phases of the tea ceremony.[29] And Yamato-e golden screens were de rigueur for funeral assemblages, as was the case with the rites for Ashikaga Yoshiharu in 1550.

The relative status of the different kinds of paintings varied according to whether the assessment emanated from the sacred or the secular domain. One sixteenth-century document, a record of practices titled *Collection for the Use of Priests (Sōyōshū)*, places Chinese ink painting and screens with fans (called *kumiōgi nagashi*) "above." "Color painting" (*shikiga*) and "color paintings with burnished gold and silver foil" (*shikiga migakitsuke*) were located "below."[30] Chinese painting receives the honor of being listed first, but it appears to share pride of place with fan screens, which could have been decorated in either the Japanese or Chinese style—or sometimes a mixture of the two in the same screen, as was the case with the Nanzenji fan screens.[31]

Another work, *Mon'ami on Flower Arrangement (Mon'ami kadensho)*, a secular document probably dating from the sixteenth century, gives a different view. The *-ami* in the treatise's title suggests that the author may have been one of the aesthetic advisors to the military class. Not only does *Mon'ami on Flower Arrangement* rank gold screens above all other kinds of painting, it gives a list of eight classifications of folding screens in descending order of importance:[32]

1. *Kimigakitsuke byōbu. Ki[n]* means "gold"; *migaki*, "to polish" or "burnish"; and *tsuke*, "to stick on." It is difficult to know whether the term was sometimes interchanged with what Muromachi diarists called *kinbyōbu*, screens using large sheets of gold foil (roughly five inches [12 cm] square).[33] Yamane describes the laborious technique of *kimigakitsuke* as the application (tsuke) of small flakes and even smaller particles of gold (kin) over mica on paper and then burnishing (migaki).[34] More time-consuming than attaching large, square, uniform sheets of gold, this was an expensive process that had its origins in the decorated papers of the Heian period. *Flowers and Birds of the Four Seasons with the Sun and the Moon* (cat. no. 1) is an example of this technique.

2. *Ōginagashi*, "flowing fans." Fans either attached to folding screens or, later, painted directly on them.

3. *Shikishi*, sheets of paper, usually square, inscribed with poems and then pasted on folding screens.

4. *Deibiki*, thick gold or silver paint. Often used for texture accents on rocks or as underdrawing for calligraphy papers. Difficult to envisage a screen of this.

5. *Yamato-e*. Baffling in this context, because the preceding four categories comprise what we think of today as Yamato-e.

6. *Usudame*, "thin color." Probably denoted painting that used vegetable rather than mineral pigments. Some kinds of Yamato-e, as well as some kinds of Chinese-style painting, used thin pigments, but this probably referred to the Chinese style (see cat. no. 6).

7. *Sumi-e*, ink painting (the Chinese lineage; see cat. no. 13). It will be noticed that this is next to the bottom rank of painting.

8. *Shirohari*, "white sewing." This apparently referred to screens used when someone was giving birth.[35]

This classification confirms that the Japanese of the Muromachi period had a far more elaborate conception of the uses and categories of their six-panel screens than the subsequent, oversimplified Japanese-Chinese, Wakan, distinction would suggest. Also, their conceptualization of the varieties of Yamato-e was very complex. There is the strong implication that Yamato-e in the sixteenth century, despite Kano protests, was considered in various cultural circles to be in no way inferior to Chinese-style painting.

With this brief background in mind, we will be better able to relish the varied problems encountered in studying individual examples of Muromachi period Yamato-e screens.

THE UJI RIVER SCREENS: CONTEXT
Images of the Uji River in History and Literature

From very early times the spectacular scenery around Uji has been celebrated in Japanese poetry and painting. The reasons seem as much logistical as aesthetic: whoever controlled the Uji River commanded most of the crucial strategic link between Ōmi, Kyoto, and the Yamato area, including Nara. The Uji River, known as the Setagawa when it leaves Ishiyama, passes through Kyoto's southern port of Fushimi to merge with the Yodo River shortly before the Yodo disgorges into Osaka Bay. As well as being conveniently close to Kyoto, the hamlet of Uji in traditional times lay also within easy reach of the ancient capital of Nara.

A reference in the eighth-century *Chronicles of Japan (Nihon shoki)* underscored the early strategic importance of Uji as the place where the troops of the (legendary) empress Jingū (r. 201–269) massed to fight a battle.[36] Poems from the earliest poetry anthology, the *Man'yōshū*, reveal that the Uji River was important for the transportation of timber and confirm that the village of Uji saw strife, bloodshed, and death.[37] At the end of the Heian period, great warriors like Minamoto no Yorimasa and Kiso Yoshinaka met their fate on its banks during the battles between the Taira and the Minamoto. A scene from one of these battles, expressing the link between Uji and death in warfare, appears as an image on a fan (fig. 3), which probably dates from the late fifteenth century.

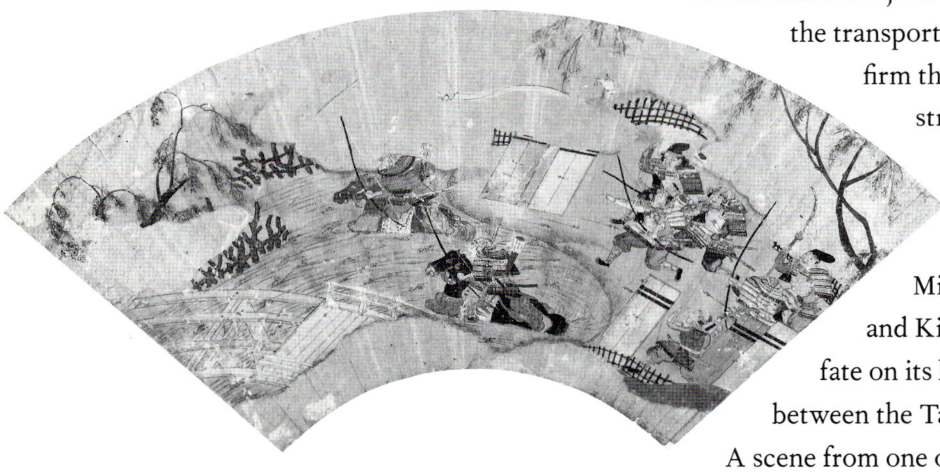

FIGURE 3

Battle on the Uji Bridge
Muromachi period, 15th century
Fan painting
Color and gold on paper
7½ x 18⅞ in. (19 x 48 cm)
Preserved by the Agency for Cultural Affairs (Bunkachō) of Japan

According to a woodblock-printed guidebook for the Uji River produced in 1860, Emperor Kōtoku (r. 645–654) bid Dōshō, the abbot of Gangōji in Nara, to oversee the building of a bridge across this strategic waterway in 646; the guidebook seems to have taken its text from an extant commemorative stone actually dating from 646.[38] It is often said that the Uji Bridge was Japan's earliest bridge.[39] A female divinity, Hashihime, the "Bridge Maiden," became the resident goddess of the bridge (and the literary conceit for innumerable poems about lovers); she was later joined by an unnamed male tutelary deity. The actual maintenance of the bridge was the cooperative task of the powerful Buddhist temples at Nara. Such cooperation was especially important when the bridge was swept away from time to time, owing to the fast-flowing current.[40]

It is hardly surprising then, that when the capital was moved to Heian (Kyoto) in 794, the court aristocracy continued to constitute an obvious presence in the Uji region. The journey from Kyoto to Uji was noted in traditional parlance as being four *ri*, or leagues (a total distance of a little less than ten miles), arduous but not insurmountable. The regent Fujiwara Michinaga (966–1028) maintained a villa there, the Uji'in, later converted to a temple—the Byōdōin—by his son Yorimichi. Michinaga was by no means the only aristocrat with a proprietary interest in Uji. The region provided first-class charcoal for the aristocracy's braziers, good grazing for their horses, and the delicacy known as ice fish (*hiuo*) for their fastidious palettes.[41] That master of the grand gesture Toyotomi Hideyoshi (1537–1598) undoubtedly had these aristocratic associations in mind when he stood on the Uji Bridge several hundred years later and ceremoniously drew water for his tea.[42]

In the eleventh century two sumptuous temples of the Pure Land (Jōdō) Buddhist sect—Jōmyōji and the previously mentioned Byōdōin—were built at Uji. These confirmed in the gestalt of Uji the association with the spiritual life and, particularly, with rebirth in paradise. The hills around Uji came to be considered an especially auspicious site for hermits (most of them aging courtiers) to devote themselves to cutting their ties with the world and concentrate on securing an optimal place in the next world.

Court poetry extolls the natural and fabricated features of Uji. A compendium of traditional associations for place names, *utamakura*, presents one hundred poems by exemplary poets under the listing for Uji.[43] Most of the images in the Idemitsu Museum's *Uji River* screens have their source in classical poetry. These include natural features such as an abundance of various kinds of seasonal mists and clouds (*kasumi, kiri, kawagiri, kumo*),

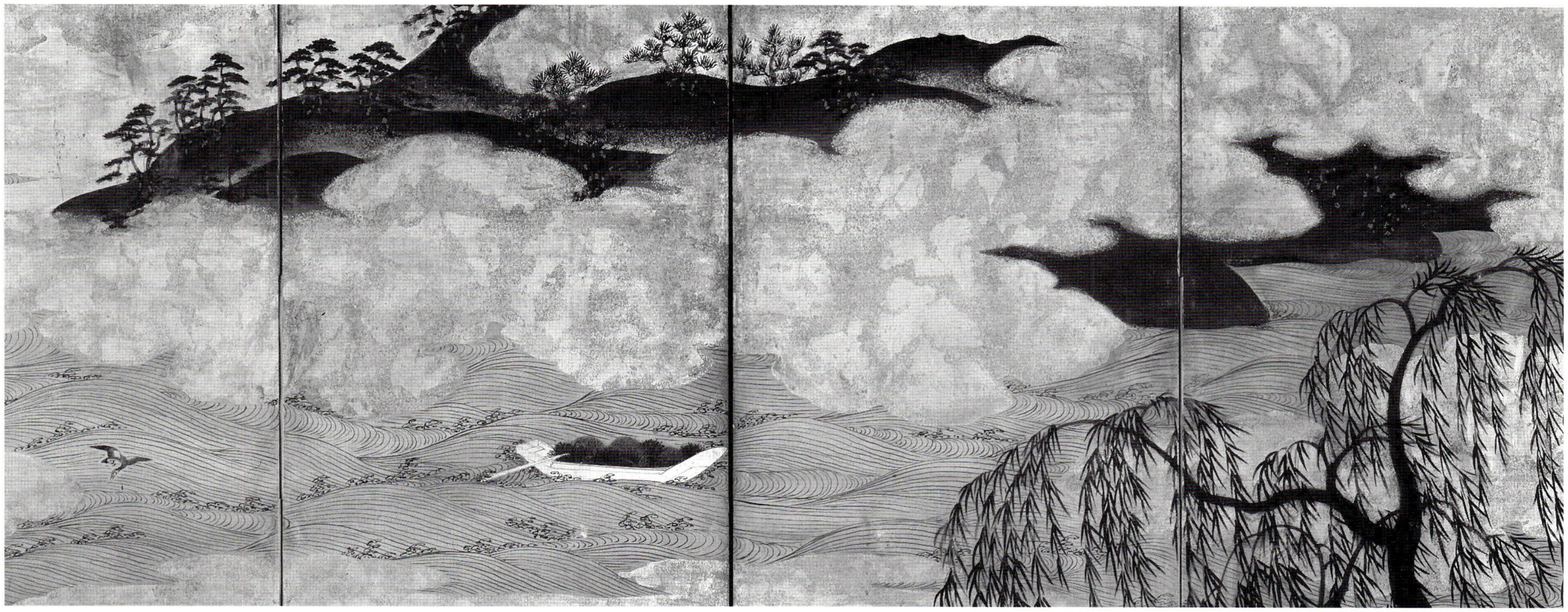

FIGURE 4

Uji Bridge, detail from left screen
CATALOGUE NO. 8

rushing waters, waves, surrounding mountains, and snow and ice (fig. 4). Human presence is indicated by the waterwheel, the fish weirs, the boats carrying brushwood, the fields of ripe rice, and of course the bridge.[44] All these images, used in various combinations, became signals, or markers, for Uji. The Japanese call them *keibutsu*, a word whose nuances are difficult to translate into English.[45] Literally, it means "scenic things," and inevitably the scenic things were tied to seasons or places. One might think of keibutsu as the prefabricated building blocks from which poems and pictures are made.

Other literary associations with Uji have nothing to do with its visual features; rather, they reflect the long-standing practice of associative wordplay in classical poetry. The word *Uji*, for example, has the same pronunciation as another *uji* (written with a different character) meaning "clan." This explains the numerous punning references to clans in the poetry about Uji.

In Uji River
(Uji of the eighty warrior clans)
Along the weir-stakes
Pile the hesitating waves
Not knowing where they go.[46]

Kakinomoto Hitomaro

The word *Uji* also suggests a pun on the word *ushi*, "gloom," and for this reason, Uji came to be associated with sadness. Thus it was the perfect setting to intensify the unhappy mood of the last ten chapters of Murasaki Shikibu's *Tale of Genji*. Being based on poetic conventions, these chapters incorporate nearly all the imagery associated with Uji (which Murasaki may never have visited). The suffusing gloom would be impossible to comprehend without understanding that this is an assigned, not empirical, feature of this lovely place. The suffocating sadness persists throughout the cycle of the seasons over a period of more than a year. A few quotes will suffice to convey the novel's dismal mood in these closing chapters.

> There were mountain villages that had their own quiet charm; but here the tumult of the waters and the wailing of the wind must make it impossible to have a moment free of sad thoughts. He could see why a man on the way to enlightenment might seek out such a place as a means of cutting his ties with the world.[47]

> Sleep was out of the question. The roar of the waters and the whipping of leaves and branches in the violent river winds, which in lesser degree might have moved one to a pleasant awareness of the season, invited gloom and even despair.[48]
>
> Strange, battered little boats, piled high with brush and wattles, made their way up and down the river, each boatman pursuing his own, sad, small livelihood at the uncertain mercy of the waves. "It is the same with all of us," thought Kaoru to himself. "Am I to boast that I am safe from the flood, calm and secure in a jeweled mansion?"[49]
>
> At Uji, the roar of the waters stirred the governor's wife to thoughts of suicide. There could be no rest from her grief. Sadly, she returned to the city.[50]

These depressive ruminations persist throughout the ten chapters. They culminate in Ukifune's attempted suicide.[51] In keeping with Japanese habits of enfolding fictional events into the "reality" of a place, commemorative plaques all over Uji mark the spots at which various events in the narrative "occurred."

The conceptual structure of the *Uji River* screens links them to one of the most fundamental concerns of classical literature: the passage of time as marked by the revolving cycle of the four seasons. Just as the anthologies of classical poetry took the successive seasons as their point of departure, traditional Yamato-e used the visual motifs of the four seasons to amplify the emotions that had found voice in literature. Famous places were usually associated with one particular season (Uji is exceptional in that it rates mention in all four seasons) in addition to being assigned, as we saw in the case of Uji and gloom, a mood or sentiment to impart emotional resonance.

Related Paintings

Even granting that poems and prose are more durable than paintings, one cannot help but be surprised how few pictorializations of Uji survive prior to its appearance on the magnificent golden screens of the Momoyama and early Edo periods (see fig. 2).[52] Uji was sufficiently compelling as a subject to be chosen for representation on a screen in the Seiryōden of the Imperial Palace during the ninth century: the imagery consisted of the red maple leaves of autumn becoming trapped in the river's famous fish weirs—a reminder simultaneously of the place's aesthetic and economic attractions.[53] This may well be one of the first recorded Japanese paintings to break away from subject matter imported from China, but the actual object, which was replaced many times, disappeared long ago in Kyoto's numerous conflagrations.

A case has been made that the famous eleventh century wall paintings of the Phoenix Hall of the Byōdōin represent scenery around Uji, ingeniously interwoven with literary motifs from classical poetry and integrated into a grand symphonic scheme portraying the descent of the Amida Buddha and the various levels of rebirth.[54] It is distressing that these are so ruinous that we are unable to study them as a coherent whole. Discrete motifs associated with Uji include the boats laden with brushwood and the fish weirs.[55]

We are able, however, to get some idea of how Uji was depicted in medieval times. Examining surviving renditions of Uji between the fourteenth and sixteenth centuries will help us to understand which elements of the Idemitsu Museum's *Uji River* screens derive from conventional renderings and which do not. We will thus be in a position to speculate on the ways the designer may have manipulated traditional elements in order to impart particular nuances to the work.

The fifth of the seven handscrolls of the *Picture Scroll of the Miraculous Legends of Ishiyama Temple (Ishiyamadera engi emaki)* seems to be the earliest surviving object to show the Uji River and the Uji Bridge (fig. 5).[56] The set of scrolls pictorializes the thirty-three miracles wrought by the Kannon of Ishiyamadera, whose magical

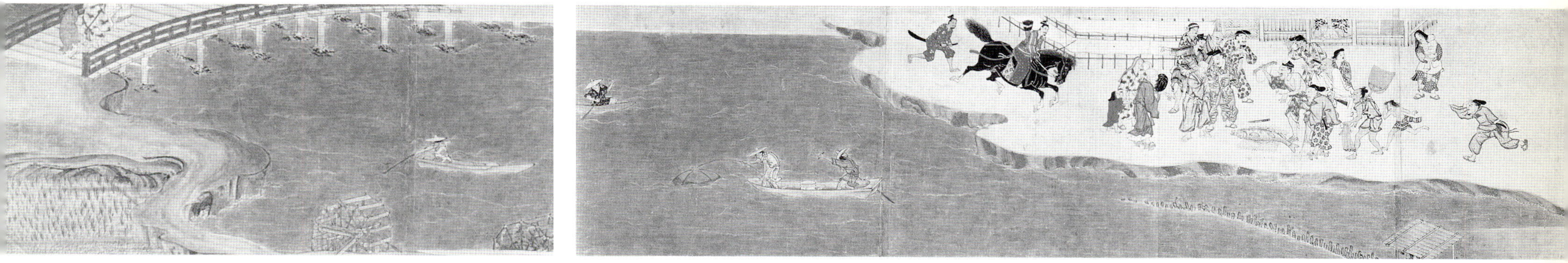

FIGURE 5

Attributed to Awataguchi Takamitsu
(active 1413–1438)
Picture Scroll of the Miraculous Legends of Ishiyama Temple, detail of scroll five
Muromachi period
Handscroll
Ink and color on paper
H: 13¾ in. (33.7 cm)
Ishiyama Temple, Otsu, Shiga Prefecture

powers were not limited to the Ishiyama region but extended far and wide, through time and space. Section three of the fifth scroll tells the story of a man who made the long journey from his hometown in the east to the capital at Kyoto to have a lawsuit settled. He won the case, only to lose his affidavit on the way home. It fell into the Uji River from the Seta Bridge. The distressed man prayed to the Kannon of Ishiyamadera, who appeared in a dream and showed him how to recover his prize. Downstream at the hamlet of Uji, he bought a large fish, cut it open, and retrieved his precious document from the fish's belly. Thus, Uji is portrayed as a place where miracles occur.

The scroll illustrates the Uji section of the tale in a straightforward manner. The artist was a master narrator. An amazed crowd of locals gathers on the main road in Uji Village (known in classical poetry as Uji no sato) to gawk at the spectacle of the overjoyed plaintiff brandishing his document above the gutted body of a large fish. The crowd includes monks (one accompanied by a handsome young acolyte), a mother with a naked unweaned baby, a bird catcher, old people, children of various ages, a mounted samurai, and a fisherman, indifferent to the miracle, tending fish weirs from a river platform in the foreground.

Picture-scroll scenes of Uji such as this helped establish the visual repertoire for depicting and recognizing this famous place. The artist was careful to include the tell-tale scenic elements—the particular constellation of keibutsu—appropriate to Uji. The first marker that the viewer encounters is the row of sticks suggesting the weirs. Because these are not unique to Uji, however, other signals of the place must follow. The waterwheel to the right of the bridge diverts water from the river across a path into the paddies. The wheel is drawn with such precision that one could use it to construct an actual model of the device, and the artist even showed water pouring out of the little scoops on the wheel into a split-bamboo spout. The rushing river eddies around the pillars of the bridge, which are reinforced against the current by protective stones. The context of the setting makes clear that the fishermen in the boats must be catching the region's famous ice fish. A group of pilgrims (perhaps to the Byōdōin) has just begun to cross the bridge, which arches towards the upper right of the composition and disappears into the mist.

Another set of medieval handscrolls, the *Ashibiki-e* (fig. 6), gives a totally different treatment of Uji.[57] These five scrolls, depicting the love affair between a monk of Mount Hiei and a beautiful boy acolyte, include extensive travel scenes, which enable the artist to incorporate a number of beloved scenic spots (*meisho*). The scrolls appear to be a copy of a five-scroll set, the original dating from 1436 and executed by the same Awataguchi Takamitsu with whom scroll five of the *Miraculous Legends of Ishiyama Temple* is associated. But the scene of Uji provides an instructive contrast, for not only does the *Ashibiki-e* seem to be a copy of a copy of Takamitsu's original (essential features having been lost in the repeated transcriptions) but the composition and the selection of motifs that represent Uji are almost wholly different.

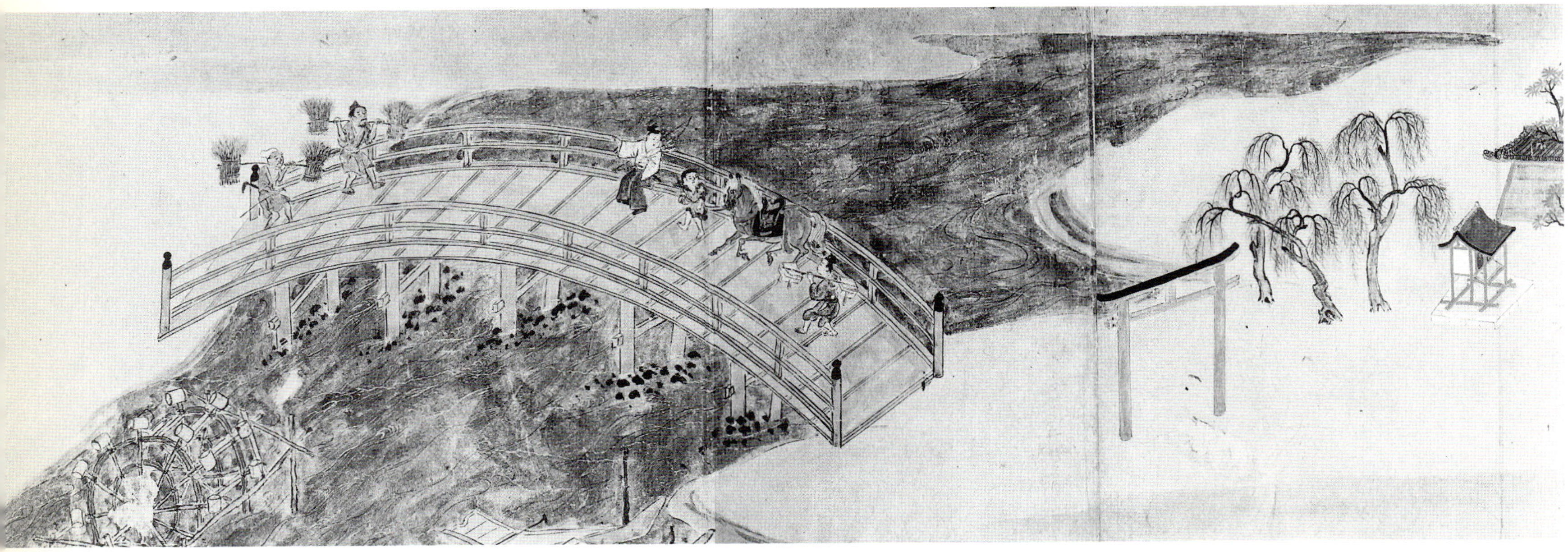

FIGURE 6

Ashibiki-e, detail of scroll two
Muromachi period, copy of an original dated 1436
Handscroll
Ink and color on paper
H: 11⅞ in. (29.0 cm)
Itsuo Museum, Osaka

The acolyte, out of view in the detail reproduced, has just spent the night at Uji and resumed his journey. He has enjoyed the full complement of Uji's charms, to judge from the artist's combining of famous poetical references and everyday features of the actual place. From right to left, these are the rustic row of buildings indicating the shops and residences of Uji, the Byōdōin, autumn maples, a small Myōjin shrine and its torii gate, three willows, the Uji Bridge (with the stones around the pillars), the rapids, moored boats (suggesting ice fish or brushwood), a waterwheel, people bringing in brushwood, and the ubiquitous mists.

Unlike the vision of the empty bridge portrayed in the Idemitsu Museum's screens or the subdued presence of the pilgrims in the *Miraculous Legends of Ishiyama Temple*, the bridge in the *Ashibiki-e* bustles with humanity depicted for its own sake: a samurai, followed by a retainer, has dismounted from his horse, which is being led across the bridge by a page. The rapid current and the churning waterwheel seem to have agitated the horse (a wonderful touch intended to convey the unsettling sound of the rushing water). The samurai points ahead (a stock gesture in handscrolls), perhaps to warn the page of the approaching brushwood-carriers, who are likely to upset the excited animal further. Unlike the crowd of gawkers in figure 5, whose presence is central to the story, this lovingly detailed vignette has nothing to do with the main plot of the affair between the priest and the acolyte. It represents instead the increasing impulse towards genre painting during the sixteenth century. The true offshoots of paintings such as this were the lively genre paintings of the Momoyama period such as that in a two-panel *Uji Bridge* screen of the late sixteenth to early seventeenth century now in the Nezu Museum, Tokyo, in which Uji becomes the backdrop for people at work, on pilgrimage, and at play.

In exchange for the heightened interest in human activity and the increase in Uji's keibutsu in the *Ashibiki-e* (the original artist clearly knew a lot about the traditional scenic indicators for Uji), the specificity that characterizes the *Miraculous Legends of Ishiyama Temple* has been lost. There is a sketchy quality in the handling of the forms that suggests (at least the copyist's) unfamiliarity with the physical aspects of Uji. The waterwheel, for example, stands on its own, incomplete, out of context, with no neighboring rice fields to service. The precisely delineated path by the rice fields in the *Miraculous Legends of Ishiyama Temple* has become a vague wash that could be either path or riverbank. The drawing of the railing of the bridge has been changed into a uniform—

and incorrect—pattern of vertical struts for both the upper and lower tiers (the other depictions show them to have contrasting patterns). Despite his use of a veritable cornucopia of famous scenic markers for Uji, the artist of the *Ashibiki-e* seems to have combined literary sources and previous paintings without much regard for the actual appearance of these phenomena. This rendition shows how motifs go astray after repeated copying of a set image. The artist of the Idemitsu Museum's *Uji River* screens did not fall into that trap; the contrast of these two objects reveals that the artist of the Idemitsu's screens must have had models of excellent quality or he knew Uji firsthand.

A fan depicting the *Scenery of Uji* (fig. 7) brings us closer to the kind of painting that must have served as one of the prototypes for the Idemitsu Museum's *Uji River* screens. Like the latter, the *Scenery of Uji* fan belongs to the category of pure classical Yamato-e "famous-place painting" (*meisho-e*) in which pictures of scenic spots with a long literary or religious history are given a prominent seasonal reference and accompanied by a poem.[58] The *Scenery of Uji* fan adds a twist to the special merger of poem and picture characteristic of traditional Yamato-e in that the poem was inscribed by Ranpa Keishi (1419–1501), a Zen monk prominent in the Chinese literary movement during the Japanese medieval period. Hence the poem is a typical Chinese seven-character quatrain instead of a thirty-one syllable Japanese *waka*. This may account for the somewhat Chinese character of the painting, which includes two Chinese-robed figures in front of a Chinese-style viewing pavilion.

This *Scenery of Uji* fan verifies the existence of a traditional compositional formula from which the designer of the *Uji River* screens must have drawn. In contrast to the famous later renditions represented by the screens in figure 2, which position the viewer on the west (Byōdōin) side so that the current of the river runs from right to left, both the *Scenery of Uji* fan and the *Uji River* screens situate the viewer on the shore opposite the Byōdōin, with the river flowing from left to right. Both show the bridge ascending towards the right and disappearing into mist, the boats with brushwood (in the fan they are securely moored), and the rapids. A significant difference lies in the greater complexity of the Idemitsu Museum's screens. Whereas the fan shows only one season, the screens depict all four. The fan has a limited number of keibutsu; the screens show almost every motif associated with Uji (except, remarkably, the Byōdōin), as well as some, like the waterbirds, that are not in the usual depictions. Comparison with the fan is essential to help us understand how the designer of the Idemitsu's *Uji River* screens modified existing prototypes in order to convey a particular nuance. We will return to this later.

As the sixteenth century progressed, independent, nonaffiliated painters like the previously described eya enterprises entered the scene. Not bound to past traditions, these creative individuals were free to experiment with new ways to treat old subjects. Some of their most innovative designs are found in paintings of monumental scale, as a large group of anonymous late medieval screens attests.[59] The unfathomable diversity of techniques and styles points to what must have been a huge number of workshops, which operated not only in Kyoto but also in Sakai, in Osaka, and most likely in provincial capitals as well. This variety greatly exceeds

FIGURE 7

Scenery of Uji
Inscription by Ranpa Keishi (1419–1501)
Muromachi period, about late 15th century
Fan painting
Color and gold on paper
7 1/8 x 18 3/16 in. (18.1 x 46.2 cm)
Preserved by the Agency for Cultural Affairs (Bunkachō) of Japan

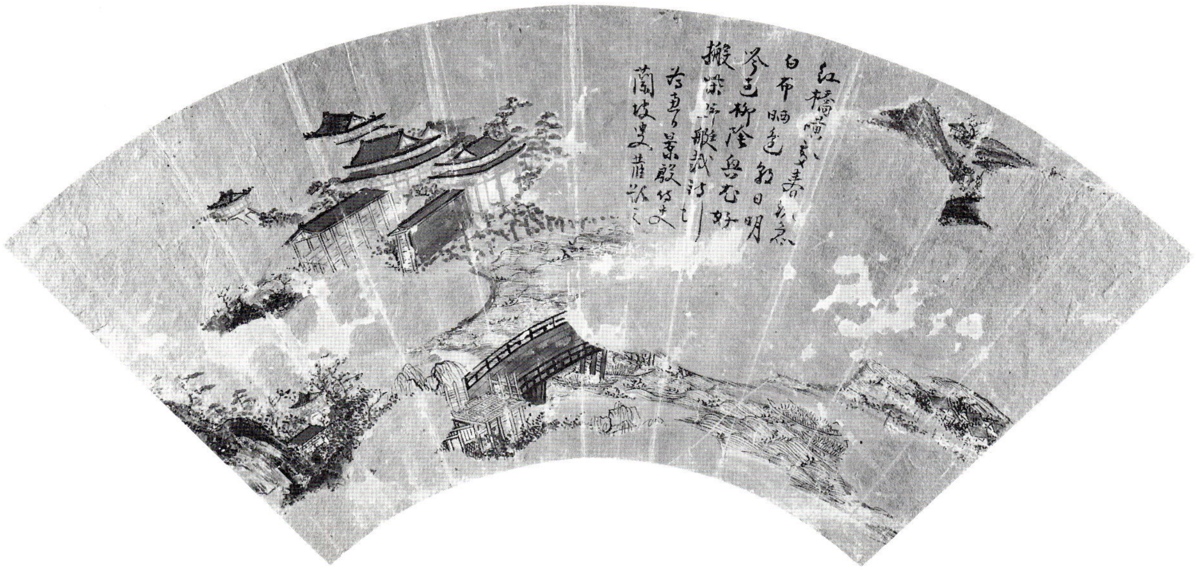

that found in screen paintings belonging to the Chinese lineage. The appearance of these Yamato-e screens is related to the rise of the affluent, educated townspeople called machishū. Keenly interested in the classical past and unfettered by the centuries of developed protocol that often stultified upper-class culture, they were the driving force behind many of the new directions in the arts.

Bridge and Willows (fig. 8) is one example of this uniquely individualistic production. Thought to date from the late Muromachi period, this screen could thus be contemporary with the Idemitsu Museum's *Uji River*. Leaving aside, for the moment, the question of whether the bridge is supposed to represent the Uji Bridge (its shape is straight instead of arched), it has obvious similarities to the Idemitsu's version. In both, a golden bridge ascends to the right over a river that flows from left to right. The willows begin on the right with spring buds and end on the left with the snow-encrusted branches of winter (thus moving the eye in the opposite direction from the river), although *Bridge and Willows* compresses the seasonal cycle by omitting summer and autumn. Furthermore, each of these objects is unique; we cannot discover any others that can be grouped into the same shop style. They clearly demonstrate the complexity of sixteenth century Yamato-e production.

If the *Uji River* screens show a development toward elaboration of detail (they have more scenic markers for Uji than any other extant depiction of the place), *Bridge and Willows* represents the mainstream of evolution leading to the monumentalization and simplification of the theme as represented in high Momoyama art (see fig. 2). The designer of *Bridge and Willows* added only one major motif not seen in earlier depictions: the rock-filled baskets, called gabions, used to prevent erosion of the riverbanks. Otherwise, the traditional keibutsu of Uji have been so ruthlessly abbreviated that the question arises whether this image of an atypical flat bridge, rapids, gabions, willows, an embankment, little low-lying bamboos, and clouds was really intended to represent Uji.

Varied combinations of the motifs associated with Uji continued to be depicted in different media throughout the Edo period. An eighteenth century lacquer medicine case in the Freer Gallery of Art, for example, simply shows the stakes of the fish weirs, the gabions, a river, and willows. Whether implicit or explicit, by the concept known as *mitate* (the cognitive process whereby one set of motifs gives rise to related but absent images), the nuance of Uji rises instantly to mind.

FIGURE 8

Bridge and Willows
Muromachi period, mid-16th century
Six-panel screen
Color and gold leaf on paper
63½ x 142½ in. (161.2 x 361.6 cm)
Private collection, Japan

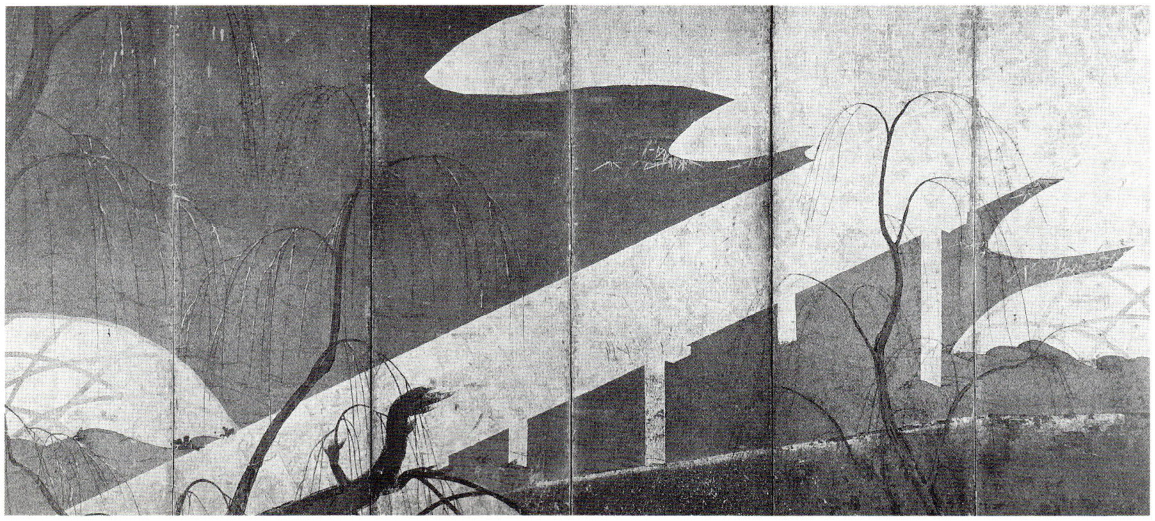

The Style of the Uji River *Screens*

Up to this point we have considered the Idemitsu Museum's *Uji River* screens in comparison to related renditions of the theme. Other aspects can be clarified from objects with different subjects but related styles, such as the two screens called *Landscapes with the Sun and the Moon* (fig. 9). These products of different workshops were assembled as a pair no earlier than the seventeenth century. Nothing is known about the artists. The screens exemplify diverse currents of medieval Yamato-e screen painting, seen by scholars as typifying a polarity. This dichotomy has been variously characterized as the "dynamic" (*dōtaiteki*) versus the "static" (*seitaiteki*) mode; "craftslike" (*kōgeiteki*) versus "orthodox" (*seitōteki*); and, amazingly, "feminine painting" (*onna-e*) versus "masculine painting" (*otoko-e*).[60] Keiko Adachi, recognizing that these appellations are

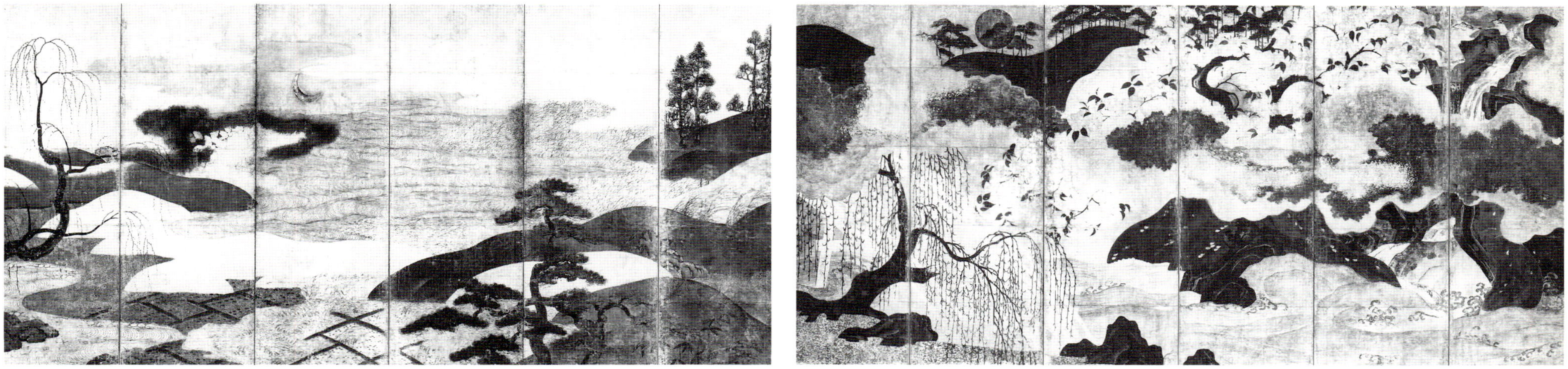

FIGURE 9

Landscapes with the Sun and the Moon
Muromachi period, 16th century
Pair of six-panel screens
Ink, color, and gold on paper with applied cut silver and gold
Right screen: 58¼ x 122 in. (148 x 310 cm)
Left screen: 58½ x 122¾ in. (148.5 x 312 cm)
Tokyo National Museum

too broad to be useful, created the category "other" to accommodate works outside these two groups and ones that exhibit mixed styles (based on their eclectic quality, the Idemitsu Museum's *Uji River* screens seem to be excellent candidates for "other").[61] The static (orthodox) style is associated with Tosa workshops, but when scholars are confronted with such pieces, the best they can usually say is "probably produced about the time of Tosa so-and-so." No names can be attached reliably to any works in the craftslike style. The record seems to have been wholly lost.

The "sun landscape" in the right screen, thought to date from the early sixteenth century, is a spring scene filled with a wild profusion of blossoming cherries and animated by a crashing waterfall. Its rough boldness puts it into the "dynamic" or "craftslike" stream. The abundance of precious metals hints at the participation of artisans skilled in working with lacquer and decorated paper. The appliquéd metal motifs and the sprinkling of gold bits seen in the Momoyama period lacquer box reproduced in figure 10 seem to find kindred expression in this screen, while the contrasting pieces of torn gold and silver foil and minute metallic particles speak of techniques preserved in the papermaker's craft from the Heian period through the middle ages (fig. 11). The irregular gold leaf and small particles of contrasting precious metals as well as the gently arching swells of the water, the dynamic arabesques of the waves, the use of silver particles for the scalloped borders of the golden clouds, the trunk and branches of the leaning spring willow, and particularly the gold-foil bridge (although its direction is reversed) all propose themselves as relatives of elements in the Idemitsu Museum's screens (the left three panels are said to "suggest" the Uji Bridge).[62] Similar kinds of spatial anomalies, such as the bridge disappearing into an ambiguous area in the clouds, appear in both.

The left screen of *Landscapes with the Sun and the Moon*, believed to be of slightly later date—that is, mid-sixteenth century—presents a calmer view and a more rational, measured space. It exhibits a delicate miniaturism and refinement that place it in the "static" or "orthodox" category. Routinely ascribed to an unspecified

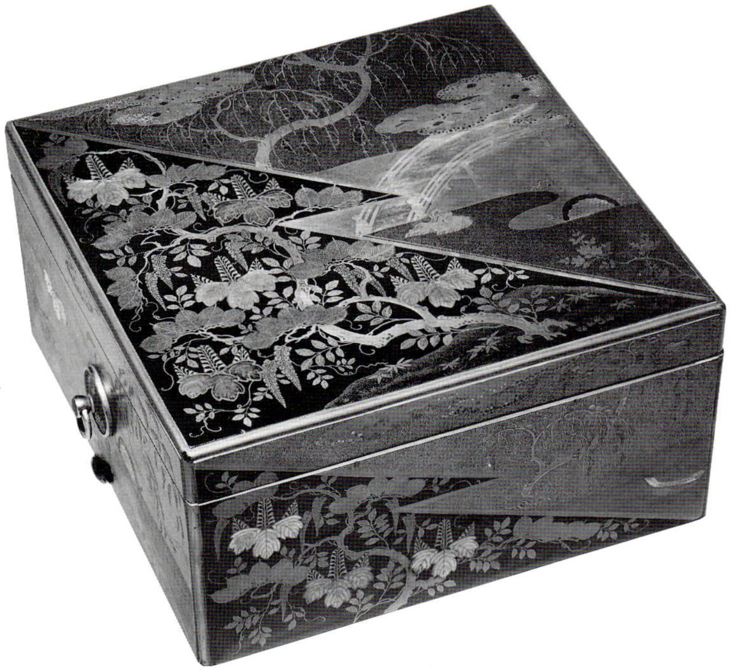

FIGURE 10

Document Box with Design of Willow by the Bridge
Momoyama period, 16th century
Black lacquer sprinkled with gold and silver foil on wood
8¼ x 17[15]/16 x 18 in. (21 x 45.5 x 45.7 cm)
The Metropolitan Museum of Art,
Purchase, Lila Acheson Wallace Fund Gift, 1987,
1987.82 ab

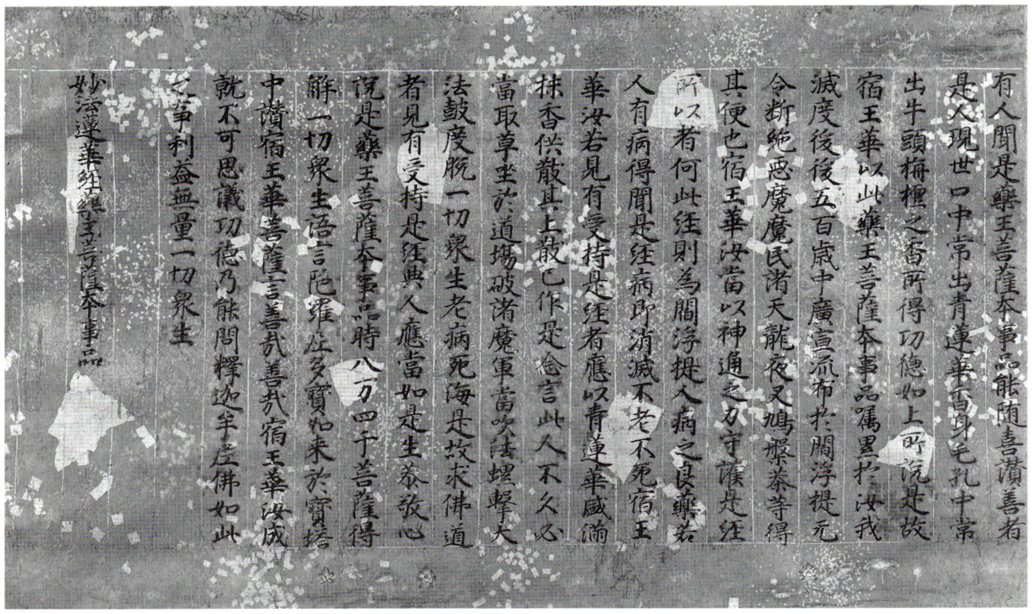

FIGURE 11

Lotus Sutra
Heian period, mid-12th century
Section from a handscroll
Ink on paper decorated with gold and silver foil, threads, and powder, and with pigment
$9\frac{7}{8}$ x $17\frac{1}{4}$ in. (25.0 x 44.0 cm)
Courtesy of The Arthur M. Sackler Museum, Harvard University Art Museums, Gift of Mrs. Donald F. Hyde, 1977.202

Tosa painter, it too has similarities to the Idemitsu Museum's screens that suggest common prototypes. Features that the two share include the passage of water treated as tight coils, the waving autumn grasses, the ripe rice fields at the river's edge giving way to the barren paddies of winter, and the gentle snowfall on willow and paddy at the extreme left of both compositions.

The Idemitsu Museum's *Uji River* screens have features in common with all of the paintings thus far illustrated; yet they are unique. It has been suggested that they represent a collaboration between a Tosa painter and an anonymous town painter,[63] and indeed one can detect a number of anomalies that point to the presence of more than one sense of design working simultaneously. The treatment of the clouds, for example, is different on each screen. On the right screen (fig. 1) some of the golden clouds are edged in silver particles like the treatment in the right-hand screen of *Landscapes of the Sun and the Moon* (fig. 9). The patterning of the water combines the large, gentle U-shaped swells and decorative arabesques of the *Landscapes of the Sun and the Moon* right screen, the "craftslike" Yamato-e style, with the tightly coiled swirls of the "traditional" waves seen on the *Landscapes of the Sun and the Moon* left screen, attributed to the Tosa master. In the *Uji River* screens, the meticulous, delicate, naturalistic drawing evident in the waterbirds and the lovely Chinese bellflowers contrasts inexplicably with the somewhat crude, wavering lines of the water.[64] On the left screen, the space is intelligible and relatively consistent; whereas on the right screen, the disproportionate size of the two boats, the location of the right-hand willow, and the ambiguous terminus of the bridge create confusion about the relative sizes and positions of objects.

There is precedent throughout the sixteenth century for the collaboration of workshops (the subcontracting of Tosa painters to Kano projects and the employment of Hasegawa Tōhaku by Kano Eitoku come to mind). This means that the task of ascribing the *Uji River* screens to a given atelier is daunting. Perhaps it is sufficient to suggest the following:

1. The hard and detailed vision that they exhibit, although it turned out to be unpopular, is not inconsistent with a certain manner of presentation in large-scale painting about the middle of the sixteenth century as seen, for example, in the Chinese-stream works of Kano Shōei (1519–1592).

2. No single prototype would have provided all the motifs contained in this pair of screens. Therefore, the designer must have had access to several old models (like those in figs. 5 and 6) for correctly depicting the numerous features of the Uji region. Such sources could not have been available to, say, the draftsman of the *Ashibiki-e* scroll (fig. 6).

3. Based on evidence for the availability of such traditional models and literary sources, which were often closely kept "secret teachings," we might guess that a Tosa painter participated either as a subcontractor to an eya or as the supervisor of a number of painters with miscellaneous backgrounds. The painting's use of the approved imagery for Uji, along with an adventurous recombination of elements of existing designs, exemplifies the way "new" art is born in Japan. The design seems too innovative but the execution is in places too clumsy to be purely Tosa. During the mid-sixteenth century, the Tosa school was apparently in disarray. In 1569, the

head of the school, Mitsumoto (active 1530–1569), was killed in battle. This may have caused some family members and apprentices to drift away from its gate, taking Tosa secrets with them (as did the later Gagakusuke).

4. The screens were obviously created for a wealthy patron (the gold alone cost a small fortune), possibly a member of the machishū class who had an interest in classical culture but also liked novelty—for the design is traditional, yet also unique.

5. We must not discount the possibility that the Idemitsu Museum's *Uji River* screens could be a copy of an earlier work, perhaps executed in a revivalist spirit during the early Edo period.

Interpretation of the Uji River *Screens*

Are these screens merely beautiful pieces of decorative art? Their solemn dignity—the arresting marriage of cryptic symbol and graceful abstraction found in many of the designs of late medieval Yamato-e screens—invites speculation about their meaning. Part of their allure is, perhaps, that the late medieval Yamato-e tradition is so laconic, largely devoid of textual explication to help tease from it its secrets. Muneshige Narazaki[65] suggests that the Idemitsu Museum's *Uji River* screens, like the *Scenery of Uji* (fig. 7), illustrate a poem by Jakuren (active late twelfth century) from the anthology *Shinkokinshū*, which uses the metaphor of Uji's drifting boats of brushwood to convey yearning and the loneliness of unrequited love:

Although I do not know
The harbor of departing spring
[I do know] the brushwood boats
Of Uji
Floating in the mist

Boats filled with brushwood, Narazaki points out, appear in both classical poetry and Noh drama with the meaning of anguished love. His interpretation is abetted by a label on the screens themselves, which describes them as "Screens of Brushwood Boats" (*shibabune byōbu*). Narazaki believes that the choice of viewpoint from the shore opposite the Byōdōin, which results in the necessity to depict the river flowing in the direction opposite to the natural East Asian flow of composition, is a device calculated to enhance the sense of the speed with which time flees and the present becomes the past. Narazaki's suggestions deserve serious consideration.

Broadening the discussion to encompass the many extant depictions of Willow Bridges and Waterwheels, Keiko Adachi draws a parallel between Uji's existence at the periphery of politico-geographical power, on one hand, and the liminal character of bridges and rivers in general, in an exhaustive survey of literature on the subject.[66] She reminds us that the golden bridge is linked with images of transition, for example, the Pure Land Buddhist theme of the White Path Crossing the Two Rivers (*nika byakudō*).[67] And she evokes the Buddhist conception of "this shore" (*shigan*, the phenomenal world we live in) as opposed to the "other shore" (higan, the transfigured world after death).

It was Shōkin Furuta who introduced the hypothesis that the Idemitsu Museum's *Uji River* screens illustrate Pure Land Buddhist thought.[68] He considers the design of the two shores linked by the golden bridge of transformation to be a pictorialization of religious ideas presented in the *Sutra of Unbounded Life (Kanmuryōjukyō)*. The Uji River is equated with the "river between life and death" (*shōji chūryū*); the waterwheel, a metaphor for the wheel of continual rebirth; and the drifting brushwood boats, the unenlightened human beings who have failed to make the crossing successfully.

Although Furuta's argument is presented subjectively with almost no concrete evidence, I find it appealing. From earliest times the Japanese believed that certain sites possessed noumenal qualities—one might call them "jumping-off places" for passage between worlds. Clearly Uji was considered to be such a place, as was suggested by the inscription in the stone commemorating the erection of the bridge.[69] Even before the creation of the Byōdōin, that ultimate symbol of transformational passage to life after death, Uji was home to religious hermits whose eyes were fixed fervently on the next world. The linkage of Uji with various battles and deaths reinforces the association of crossing to the other world. Not all seekers were destined to die well at Uji: Ukifune's failed suicide in the *Tale of Genji*, like the drifting boats that are synonymous with her name, underscores Uji as a metaphor for the mysterious workings that set human beings adrift in a world in which the wheel of karma grinds ceaselessly. Furuta's connection of the boats in the Idemitsu Museum's screens with rudderless, drifting human souls is reinforced when compared with other extant images of Uji in which all the boats have navigators to guide them through Uji's treacherous rapids or else are safely moored.

Some aspects of the Idemitsu Museum's screens, as yet unremarked by others, reinforce Furuta's interpretation. The migrating geese and ducks in the autumn section can symbolize the transmigration of the soul through its different lifetimes in East Asian Buddhist thought. And while the foreground scenery conspicuously passes through the four seasons—representing the physical world in which change is rapid and relentless—on the distant hills seasonal changes are not to be seen. The designer has purposely contrasted the time-bound with the timeless. Further, even though copious amounts of gold typify the period style of the middle of the sixteenth century, the shimmering golden vision here presents an aura not unlike the golden paradise scenes adorning traditional sutra frontispieces executed in gold paint on indigo paper. Gold has a long history of being equated with paradise in Asian traditions.[70] It seems very likely indeed that the screens offer a view across the Uji River towards the Western Paradise, linked to the mundane world on the eastern side of the river by the golden bridge of transformation. Later versions of Willow Bridge and Waterwheel (see fig. 2) retain something of this nuance, but because they reverse the viewpoint and locate the viewer on the "paradise" side of the river, the idea of crossing to the other shore remains only a faint memory.

Despite our not being able to identify their artist (nor even the school) or their precise period of production, the Idemitsu Museum's *Uji River* screens fascinate scholars precisely because they offer an open-ended reading. Just as the designer's intent comprises one layer of interpretation of a series of texts that includes local histories, Buddhist sutras, and classical poetry anthologies, viewers through the centuries have become participants in an expanding discourse excavating other levels of possible meaning. In a tradition as allusive and self-referential as Japan's, the potential for the accumulation of meanings becomes enormous. If we could locate the historical circumstances under which the screens were produced—say, we learned that they were revivalist works based on medieval models and created in angry reaction to Hideyoshi's tearing down the Uji Bridge in a perverse demonstration of political potency or even to celebrate Ieyasu's rebuilding it in an equally symbolic demonstration of absolutism—even more layers would be added.

It is clear in any case that there is a systematic meticulousness in the arrangement of the images in these screens that indicates the intent to communicate meaning. By probing beneath the arresting surface design of works like these and by digging through the accumulated messages imposed by the designer, the viewer, and the culture at large, we can, after all, begin to decipher the codes communicating cultural meanings in medieval Japanese design.

NOTES

I would like first of all to express deepest gratitude to my student Miki Nishimura, whose meticulous attention to the micro and macro details of this manuscript went immeasurably beyond the call of duty. Thanks are due also to Julia Meech, Karen Brock, and Helen Nagata for providing logistical and conceptual help. My association with Joseph N. Newland, publications manager of The Asia Society Galleries, has been one of the high points of the project; his knowledge, sophistication, patience, and wit kept things moving, even when sometimes they seemed to be moving backwards. In a more unorthodox vein, I would like to include a tribute to Doctors Hinda Sack and Anna Hempstead without whom not a word would have been written. Finally, Don Paulhus and the Somers Field group played important, if intangible, roles in sustaining occasional flagging spirits. Research assistance was provided by the Center for East Asian Studies, Stanford University.

1. In 1960, for example, Matsushita Takaaki was able to write that, based on a combination of extant works and literary references, the names of five hundred ink painters from the Kamakura and Muromachi periods are known. See his *Muromachi suibokuga*, unpaged English foreword. This is not to suggest total neglect on the part of Japanese scholars. Isolated studies began appearing after World War II. An early example is Akazawa Eiji's "Jūgo seiki ni okeru kinbyōbu ni tsuite." For the most extensive recent exhibition, see *Muromachi jidai no byōbue*. See also Michael Cunningham et al., *The Triumph of Japanese Style: 16th-Century Art in Japan*. The 1990s have also seen the burgeoning of studies on individual works.

2. "The term 'Muromachi *Yamato-e*' is a little unfamiliar to us compared with 'Muromachi ink painting.' This is because the words 'Muromachi art' are taken to refer to ink painting, while '*Yamato-e*' conjures up the narrow-eyed, hooked nose illustrations of the illustrated narrative handscrolls of the court" (adapted from the unpaged English section of *Ōta Dōkan kinen bijutsu ten: Muromachi bijutsu to sengoku gadan*). Not a word about Yamato-e is mentioned in the Muromachi volume (vol. 3) of the authoritative *Cambridge History of Japan* (Cambridge: Cambridge University Press, 1990), although the usual paeans are produced for ink painting.

3. See, for example, the inscription on *Trees and Plants of the Four Seasons* (cat. no. 2), written by Kano Tan'yū (1602–1674). Catalogue number 3 also has a traditional ascription, with little reason, to Mitsunobu.

4. Mizuo Hiroshi and Takeda Tsuneo place them at the end of the Muromachi period. Mizuo, "Ujigawazu byōbu," p. 30, suggests a date of the Eiroku era, 1558–1570. See also *Chūsei shōheiga*, cat. no. 54, entry written by Takeda, pp. 46–47. Kuroda Taizō in his entry in *Muromachi jidai no byōbue*, cat. no. 38, p. 238, labels them broadly sixteenth century and indicates that other opinions put them in the Edo period. Those suggesting a seventeenth-century date include two catalogues by the Idemitsu Museum of Arts: *Kaikan jūgonen kinenten zuroku*, caption for cat. no. 81, p. 286; and *Nihon no kaiga hyakusen*, caption for cat. no. 41, p. 145, which labels them Kan'ei era (1624–1644). Adachi Keiko in her descriptive essay for a cluster of related screens in *Keibutsuga—shiki keibutsu*, p. 109, also calls them early Edo, as does Narazaki Muneshige, "Ujigawazu byōbu," p. 98. Jackie Manzies and Edmund Capon, *Japan: Masterpieces from the Idemitsu Collection*, p. 52, picturesquely describe them as a "seventeenth-century anachronism."

5. Kano Einō (1631–1697), *Honchō gashi* (History of Japanese art), preface dated 1678, transcribed in Sakazaki Tan, ed., *Nihon kaigaron taikei*, vol. 2, pp. 369–370. Translation by Carolyn Wheelwright in Bettina Klein, *Japanese Kinbyōbu*, pp. 112–113. See also Quitman E. Phillips's "Honchō gashi and the Kano Myth," p. 47, where he translates the same text. On pp. 55–56, nn. 10, 12, 15–19, Phillips takes Klein and Wheelwright to task for aspects of their translation.

6. This term was coined during the Edo period, but the distinction arose centuries earlier. The Japanese language has many words for both Japan and China. The character for *Yamato* is also read *wa*. For China, the words *Kan* (the Han dynasty and, by extension, Chinese culture) and *Kara* (the Tang dynasty) were frequently combined with the syllables *ga* or *e*, which mean "painting."

7. For an example of the overlap between Kano and Tosa styles, see John M. Rosenfield, "Japanese Painting Workshops and the Gardner Museum Collections," pp. 13–16.

8. This is not to imply that the Kano family was the exclusive producer of treatises in the seventeenth century, although it certainly generated the lion's share. A counterattack by the leading Yamato-e painter of the time, Tosa Mitsuoki (1617–1691) tried to argue for the superiority of Tosa school painting, but his voice was drowned out by the din of Chinese-lineage painters. Mitsuoki's treatise is discussed and partly translated in Makoto Ueda, *Literary and Art Theories in Japan*, pp. 128–144. It should be noted that the dominance of Kano treatises in the seventeenth century gave way to a proliferation of works by painters of miscellaneous schools in the eighteenth and nineteenth centuries.

9. See Phillips, "*Honchō gashi* and the Kano Myth," pp. 46–57.

10. The screen, by Kano Naizen, is reproduced in *Fūzokuga—sairei, kabuki* (Genre painting: festivals and kabuki), vol. 13 of Nihon byōbue shūsei (Tokyo: Kōdansha, 1978), pl. 18.

11. Chino Kaori, in a presentation at the College Art Association annual meeting, San Francisco, February 1989.

12. For a concise discussion in English of Mitsunobu's career, see Karen L. Brock, "Tosa Mitsunobu," in *The Dictionary of Art* (London: MacMillan Publishers), forthcoming 1996.

13. Kano artists began using seals early, but neither Kano nor Tosa painters signed their works until the seventeenth century.

14. Reproduced and discussed in Komatsu Shigemi, ed., *Yūzū nenbutsu engi*.

15. The artists were Rokkaku Jakusai (1348?–1424), a retired Director of the Imperial Painting Bureau and member of a family of painters; Kasuga Yukihide (active 1413–1430), then Director of the Imperial Painting Bureau; Tosa no Kami Yukihiro (active 1406–1443); Fujiwara Mitsukuni (active early fifteenth century), listed like Jakusai as "Former Director of the Imperial Painting Bureau," which is curious because Mitsukuni apparently assumed the title of Director in 1428; Awataguchi Takamitsu (active early fifteenth century), also the head of a workshop, although no works by him survive other than the scenes in this set; and the mysterious "Tayū Hōgen Nagaharu" about whom no information exists. See Klein, *Japanese Kinbyōbu*, pp. 40–42.

16. A case in point is the *Boki ekotoba* (a biography of the priest Kakunyo), a set of ten scrolls originally painted in 1351. After the first two scrolls were destroyed while on loan to the shogun, the painter Kamonnosuke Fujiwara Hisanobu (active fifteenth century) was commissioned to replace them in 1482. Hisanobu is one of the many obscure but capable medieval Yamato-e painters with noble connections whose names have been recorded but whose known works are scarce.

17. *The Confessions of Lady Nijō*, trans. Karen Brazell (New York: Anchor Press/Doubleday, 1973), pp. 83–84. GoFukakusa forces this unsophisticated woman into his bed, but the affair ends badly because "the rustling of her gowns was unusually loud and coarse. . . . But she was without question a beautiful woman . . . despite the fact that she was obviously not of aristocratic birth."

18. The following information on *eya* was taken from Yamane Yūzō, "Eya ni tsuite," pp. 107–117.

19. The diary, the *Suda Sōkyū chaya nikki* (Tea diary of Suda Sōkyū), was written by three generations of tea masters of the Suda family: Sōtatsu, Sōkyū, and Sōhan. See Yamane, "Eya ni tsuite," p. 107.

20. Gagakusuke is mentioned in a diary reference for 1592 as having brought ten underdrawing-prepared poem-cards to one Achamaru. Gagakusuke appears in another diary in conjunction with string puppets in an entry for 1595. See Yamane, "Eya ni tsuite," p. 111. Yoshida Yūji, *Tosa Mitsunobu*, p. 122, mentions Gagakusuke in passing in a reference to the later, largely unknown Tosa painters.

21. For a basic discussion of Japanese screens, see Miyeko Murase, *Masterworks of Japanese Screen Painting: The American Collections*, and the article by Yamane, "Kinpeki shōhekiga no tenkai—kaku ryūha no iwazuru kinchi kōsei o chūshin ni," pp. 114–121.

22. This is an ironic reversal of the situation in the Heian period, when it was customary to append a literary text (poems and prefatory explanations), written on square sheets and pasted on the screens. Conversely, the few surviving Heian picture scrolls have no accompanying explanatory text.

23. Tsuji Nobuo, "Yamatoe byōbu no tenkai," p. 16.

24. This is reported in Klein, *Japanese Kinbyōbu*, p. 166, n. 1, among other places.

25. See Nobuo Tsuji, "Ornament (Kazari)—An Approach to Japanese Culture," pp. 35–45.

26. Adapted from the unpaged English section and p. 119 of the Japanese section of Adachi Keiko, "Muromachi jidai byōbue kō." The *Record of Things Seen and Heard* is the diary of the imperial prince Sadafusa (1372–1456).

27. For an example, see *The Shogun Age Exhibition* (Tokyo: The Shogun Age Exhibition Executive Committee, 1983), p. 97. Thanks to Joseph Newland for this reference.

28. Gail Capitol Weigl, "The Reception of Chinese Painting Models in Muromachi Japan," *Monumenta Nipponica* 25, no. 3 (Autumn 1980), p. 265, n. 34.

29. Ibid., p. 266.

30. Yamane Yūzō, "'Muromachi jidai no byōbue' gaikan—Wakan haigō no sekai," p. 11. Since the writing of this article, Professor Yamane's text has been translated for this volume.

31. For information on the Nanzenji fan paintings, see Takeda Tsuneo, *Nanzenji senmen byōbu* (The Nanzenji fan screens), ed. Nihon no Bun'yō Kenkyūkai (Kyoto: Fujiaato, 1973).

32. Yamane, "'Muromachi jidai no byōbue' gaikan," pp. 11–12. His sources are *Gunsho ruiju* and the manuscript containing the *Mon'ami kadensho*, the *Okazari ki*.

33. See Klein, *Japanese Kinbyōbu*, passim. Yamane, "'Muromachi jidai no byōbue' gaikan," p. 11, posits that *kimigakitsuke* and *kinbyōbu* were interchangeable but admits that there is disagreement among scholars.

34. Yamane, "Eya ni tsuite," p. 12.

35. Yamane, ibid., cites a document called *Sanjō no ki* (Record of the lying-in room) that contains a phrase with this compound in it.

36. *Nihongi: Chronicles of Japan from the Earliest Times to A.D. 697*, trans. W. G. Aston (Rutland and Tokyo: Charles E. Tuttle, 1972), pp. 238–240.

37. See Edwin A. Cranston, *A Waka Anthology*, vol. 1, pp. 33, 77, 78, and 642.

38. This text, as well as a reproduction of the guidebook *Ujigawa ryōgan ichiran* (Continuous view of both banks of the Uji River) is printed in *Kyōto no kan I*, vol. 7 of Fūzoku zue (Japanese famous-place genre painting guidebooks) (Tokyo: Kadokawa, 1979), pp. 418–439. The order to build the bridge appears on p. 426. Mention of the stone, the *Ujibashi dan pi*, is found in Shigehisa Yamasaki, *Chronological Table of Japanese Art* (Tokyo: Geishinsha, 1981), pp. 37, 515, and 603. It is kept at Hashidera Hōjōin in Uji.

39. This is disputed by Kuranishi Shigeru, author of the entry "Bridges" in the *Kōdansha Encyclopedia of Japan* (Tokyo: Kōdansha, 1983), vol. 1, p. 170. He gives that distinction to a bridge in Ikai no Tsu (Osaka Prefecture), built in the fourth century.

40. Shirahata Yoshi, "Yanagi suishazu (Ujibashi)—Meishoe #12," pp. 64–65. See also *Konsaisu Nihon chimei jiten* (Concise dictionary of Japanese place names), ed. Tanioka Takeo and Yamaguchi Keiichiro (Tokyo: Sanseidō, 1987), pp. 146–147.

41. Akiyama Terukazu, "The Door Paintings in the Phoenix Hall of the Byōdōin as *Yamato-e*," pp. 149f and 163. I am grateful to Karen Brock for calling this article to my attention.

42. See Tamamushi Keiko, "Ryūkyō suishazu' to 'Uji no kawase no suisha'—kayō to fūryō to byōbue no kōkyō," p. 873.

43. This is the *Utamakura nayose* (Compendium of poetic place names), thought to have been published in the seventh month of 1659. See Yoshida Kōichi, Jinsaku Kōichi, and Tachibana Ritsu, eds., *Utamakura nayose*, vol. 8 (Tokyo: Koten Bunko, 1974), pp. 61–74. Some meticulous studies of the origins and appearances of various motifs, such as the waterwheel (a technological boon introduced from China in the ninth century), appear in Adachi Keiko, "Nishu no Ryūkyōzu byōbu," pp. 7–22 (see especially her convenient charts, p. 22); Miyajima Shin'ichi, "Shōheiga ni miru kaiga no hen," pp. 119–126; Namiki Seishi, "Kōzu Kobunka Kaikan zō 'Ōgimen shōji' ni tsuite," pp. 25–36; Takeuchi Misako, "The Meaning of Pattern in Rimpa School Painting: *Mitate* and Visual Imagery," pp. 3–10; Takeuchi Misako, "Ryūkyō suishazu byōbu—Shinshutsubon o shōkai o kanete," pp. 7–18; and Tamamushi Keiko, "'Ryūkyō suishazu' to Uji no kawasa no suisha-kayō to furyō to byōbue no bokyo," pp. 859–880. A good, compressed discussion of such motifs appears in Karen Brock's entry for cat. no. 27, *Uji Bridge under the Willows*, in *Autumn Grasses and Water Motifs in Japanese Art from the Suntory Museum of Art* (New York: Japan Society, 1983), pp. 82–83.

44. Images not shown in these screens (but occurring in other depictions of Uji) include red maple leaves, cherry blossoms, the Bridge Maiden, the Guardian God, rain, eulalia (*obana*, a pampas-grasslike plant), *kinohana* plants, dew, deer, rustic huts, ferrymen, the "eighty clans," cloth-pounding, the Amida Buddha, Uji no sato (the hamlet of Uji), Uji no miyako (the capital of Uji), the Isle of Oranges, and Asahiyama.

45. The Japanese writings on keibutsu and keibutsu painting (*keibutsuga*) do not all agree. The fundamental interpretation of the word *keibutsu* can be found in *Nihon kokugo daijiten* (Tokyo: Shogakukan, 1975), vol. 4, p. 138: "1. Things that have a sense of the passing seasons; views of nature; scenery; in [poetry] . . . especially snow, moon, cherries, cuckoo, and often also autumn maples. . . . 2. Remarkable seasonal things: clothing, fruit, special dishes to eat." For art historians' writing on the theme, see the essays in *Keibutsuga—shiki keibutsu*.

46. Cranston, *A Waka Anthology*, vol. 1, p. 193. The poem has also been translated

The waves lingering about the fish-weir stakes
In the Uji, the river of eighty clans of warriors—
Whither they are drifting away
Who knows?

(From Donald Keene, ed., *The Man'yōshū* [New York and London: Columbia University Press, 1965], p. 50.)

47. Murasaki Shikibu, *Tale of Genji*, trans. Edward Seidensticker (New York: Alfred A. Knopf, 1977), vol. 2, p. 782.

48. Ibid., p. 794.

49. Ibid., p. 790.

50. Ibid., pp. 1021–1022.

51. Tamamushi's recent article "'Ryūkyō suishazu' to Uji no kawasa no suisha-kayō to furyō to byōbue no bokyo", pp. 865–866, investigates sources removed from the standard-bearers of high culture, namely, ballads by prostitutes who are thought to have plied their trade (quite literally, in boats) in Uji Harbor in order to service the aristocratic mansions in the environs. She suggests that the phrase (and hence the motif of) "the waterwheel at Uji Rapids" (Uji no kawase no suisha) might have originated in the lyrics of such songs, sung at drinking parties, and filtered upwards into high culture. More to the point, she feels that these songs, having to do with the Uji River's west bank (the Byōdōin side), were upbeat and cheerful, rather similar in tone to the kind of playful paintings known as *giga*, and thus offered a corrective to the association of Uji and gloom. The sources she cites are the twelfth-century *Meikō ōrai* (a title that defies translation) and *Ryōjin hisho* (translatable as "secret writings in the dust on the rafters").

52. Literary evidence points to the popularity of Uji as a theme in long-vanished items of decorative and applied arts. For example, Miyajima Shin'ichi, "Shōheija ni miru kaija no hen," p. 120, traces the connection of various motifs on items of daily use with the notion of *furyū*, a uniquely Japanese term that has the nuance of contemporary chic with a clever spin on it. He cites the case of the retired minister Konoe Michitsugu's pilgrimage to Uji for which a special, gaily colored travel costume was designed: on the right sleeve was the (Uji) Bridge, on the left, a waterwheel, in addition to the motif of pine with wisteria growing from it. Miyajima got this information from an entry in the document *Gukanki*, dated 1369. Surviving painted examples of furyū include a fan thought to date from the second half of the sixteenth century, showing the Uji Bridge and willows in the snow, discussed and illustrated in Namiki, "Kōzu Kobunka Kaikan zō 'Ōgimen shōji' ni tsuite," p. 34, as a possible precursor of the mature Willow Bridge and Waterwheel depictions. The reproduction, however, is indecipherable; a marginally better image appears in Tamamushi, "'Ryūkyō suishazu' to Uji no kawasa no suisha-kayō to furyō to byōbue no bokyo," fig. 2. Objects with motifs suggesting Uji include the underdrawings to an epilogue appended to a fourteenth-century manuscript of the *Tale of Genji*, with waterwheel, brushwood boats, reeds, and geese, cited in Takeuchi, "*Ryūkyō suishazu byōbu—shinshutsubou o shikai o kanete*," p. 30, and underdrawings on a page of linked verse dated 1571 with bridge, willows, and stone-filled baskets, reproduced (dimly) in Adachi, "Nishu no Ryūkyōzu byōbu," fig. 5.

53. Miyeko Murase, *Japanese Art: Selections from the Mary and Jackson Burke Collection*, pp. 160–161, cat. no. 46, the *Uji Bridge* screens in the Burke Collection, quoting Ienaga Saburō, *Jōdai Yamatoe zenshi* (A complete history of classical Yamato-e), rev. ed. (Tokyo: Bokusui Shobō, 1966), p. 29. See also *Keibutsuga—shiki keibutsu*, p. 109.

54. See Akiyama, "The Door Paintings in the Phoenix Hall of the Byōdōin as *Yamato-e*," pp. 144–167.

55. Ibid., figs. 10 and 21.

56. The dating of scroll five to the early fifteenth century is generally accepted, but some scholars dispute it. Sumiyoshi Hiroyuki, a Yamato-e artist working for the shogunate in Edo, visited Ishiyamadera in 1792 and attributed the scrolls to various artists. Scroll five he gave to Awataguchi Takamitsu (active 1413–1438), whose name, we recall, appeared as one of the six artists of the *Yūzū nenbutsu engi* of 1414. Modern scholars have generally followed Hiroyuki's attributions, although some see scroll five as earlier, belonging to the latter half of the fourteenth century. See Yoshida Yūji, *Ishiyamadera engi-e*, vol. 18 of Nihon emaki taisei (Tokyo: Chūōkōron, 1978), p. 115.

57. The obscure title of this scroll—if translated literally, "*picture scroll of foot dragging*"—is a literary convention for mountains and probably refers to Mount Hiei, where the monk who was in love with the acolyte lived. For reproduction, translation of text, and discussion of these scrolls, see *Ashibikie*, vol. 20 of Zoku Nihon emaki taisei (Tokyo: Chūōkōron, 1983).

58. This fan, like its companion piece, figure 4, was detached from a set of sixty fans pasted on a pair of screens, probably of the ōginagashi-type described above, and is now mounted in album format. Both figures 4 and 8, which are painted with thick pigments against a gold background, bear an attribution by Kano Yasunobu (1613–1685) to an unspecified Tosa painter. See Narazaki, "Sasama kezō ōgimen gacho," p. 341, and Yoshida, *Tosa Mitsunobu*, pp. 132–133.

59. The best source bringing these together is *Muromachi jidai no byōbue*.

60. "Dynamic" versus "static" was articulated by Takeda Tsuneo in "Shūtō kachōzu," *Kokka* 1048 (February 1982), p. 31. The "craftslike" versus "orthodox" and "feminine" versus "masculine" appear in Yamane, "Chūsei Yamatoe byōbu ni tsuite—Jitsugetsu shiki kachōzu o chūshin ni," p. 17, cited by Adachi, "Muromachi jidai ebyōbue kō," p. 123. Traditional epistemologies die hard!

61. Adachi, "Muromachi jidai Yamatoe byōbu jitsugetsu kachōzu ni tsuite," p. 16.

62. See *Yamatoe—Miyabi no keifu* (Tokyo: Tokyo National Museum, 1993), cat. no. 98, p. 274, and *Muromachi jidai no byōbue*, cat. no. 14, p. 233.

63. Mizuo, "Ujigawazu byōbu," p. 30, says that these screens' miniaturistic, crafts-like quality suggests to him the influence of craftspeople, as well as the "declining" Tosa school, with machi eshi influence perceptible to boot. Later on the same page, he talks about their having been created by a Tosa painter who subcontracted to the Kano, with machi eshi influence being felt in addition.

64. For example, Mizuo, ibid., p. 24, finds that the treatment of the harvested rice field, the foreground, the distant landforms, distant trees, and the winter willow on the right shows a tendency towards patternization that suggests the hand(s) of machi eshi; the other willows, the water, bridge, boats, and waterfowl speak of Tosa "naturalism."

65. Narazaki, "Ujigawazu byōbu," p. 97.

66. See her entry *Ryūkyōzu* (Bridge and Willows) in *Muromachi jidai no byōbue*, cat. no. 39, p. 238, and her embellishment of the theme in "Nishu no Ryūkyōzu byōbu," pp. 13–14. Especially comprehensive are notes 47–53, which review many facets of religious and literary imagery, including Noh drama.

67. For a reproduction and discussion of the theme of the White Path Crossing the Two Rivers, see John Rosenfield and Elizabeth ten Grotenhuis, *Journey of the Three Jewels* (New York: The Asia Society, 1979), no. 37.

68. Furuta Shōkin, "Yanagibashizu—sono Ujibashizu o megutte sono igi o tou," pp. 8–23. I am grateful to Julia Meech for sending me a copy of this article.

69. See note 38 above. Adachi, "Nishu no Ryūkyōzu byōbu," pp. 13 and 20, n. 54, also touches on this interpretation of the text on the Ujibashi dan pi.

70. See, for example, Klein, *Japanese Kinbyōbu*, passim. Furuta, "Yanagibashizu—sono Ujibashizu o megutte sono igi o tou," p. 19, discusses it in the context of the "seven treasures" of the Pure Land (along with silver, lapis lazuli, and other precious materials). See also the text of the *Sutra of Unbounded Life*, translated in F. Max Müller, ed., *Buddhist Mahayana Texts* (New York: Dover Publications, 1969), pp. 161–201.

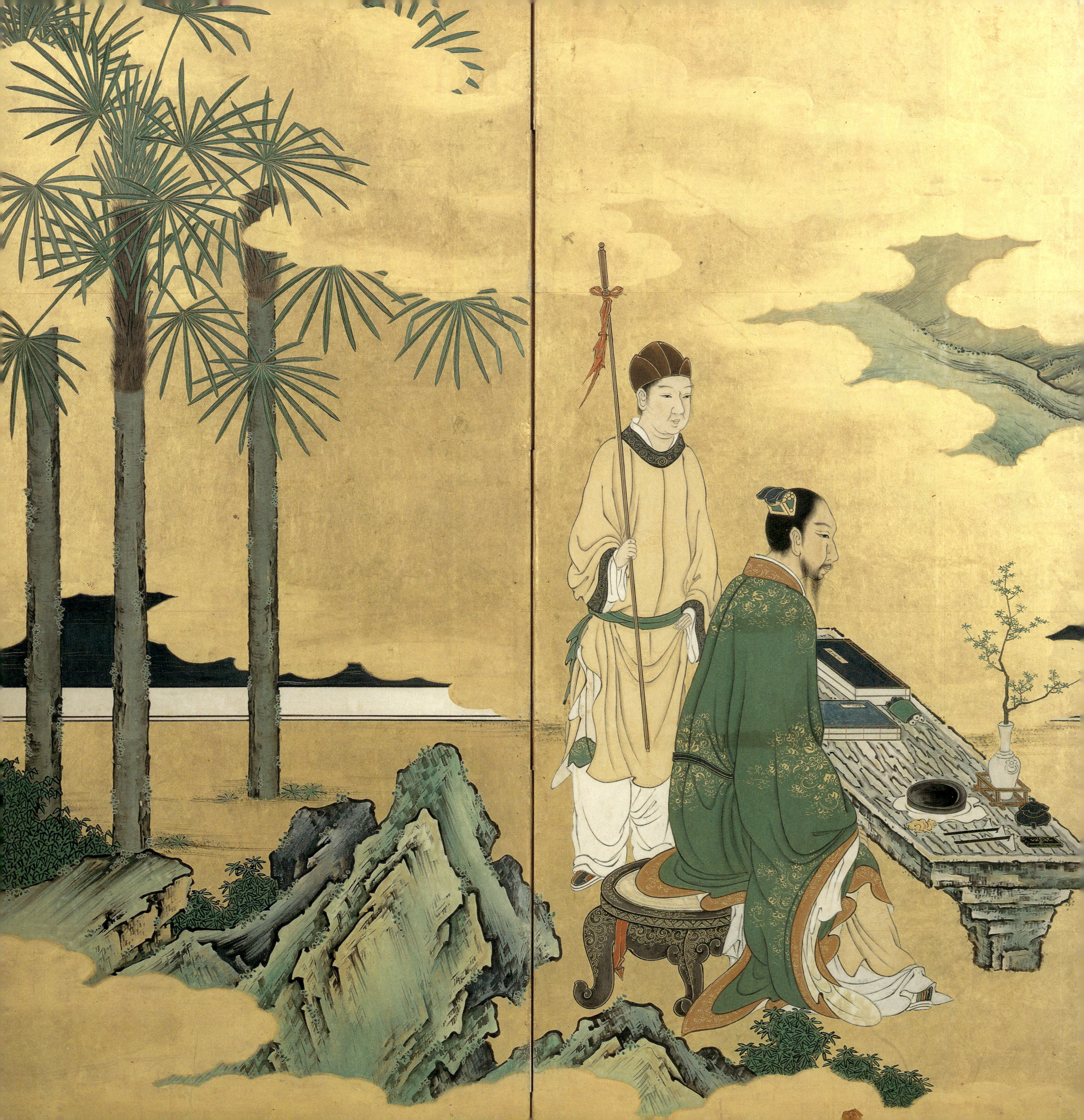

Figurative Screen Painting in the Late Momoyama and Early Edo Periods—Introducing a Recently Discovered Work of the Kano School

THE CURRENT EXHIBITION HAS GIVEN US THE opportunity to introduce to American audiences a recently discovered folding screen of superb quality and considerable historical importance, lately acquired by The Idemitsu Museum of Arts. *The Queen Mother of the West and Dong Fangshuo* (fig. 1; cat. no. 11) raises fascinating questions of connoisseurship and provides valuable insight into the role of the Kano school in the development of screen painting with large-scale figures during the late Momoyama and early Edo periods (1573–1615 and 1615–1868, respectively).

The subject of this painting is a Chinese legend on the auspicious theme of longevity and everlasting youth that has been a favorite of Japanese as well as Chinese artists over the centuries. The Queen Mother of the West (Xi Wang Mu) is a Daoist deity who, the story goes, appeared at the court of Emperor Wu of the Later Han dynasty (202 B.C.E.–C.E. 9) to offer him fruit from the peach tree of immortality, which bloomed and bore fruit only once every three thousand years. Dong Fangshuo was a scholar of that period, a man known for his erudition and eccentricity. According to the tale, Dong Fangshuo pilfered and ate three of the Queen Mother's peaches and thus joined the ranks of Daoist immortals. The seeming incompleteness of the composition suggests that the screen may originally have been paired with another on a Chinese theme; one possibility is that of the Zhou dynasty recluse Tai Gongwang and the Song dynasty poet Lin Hojing, who appear in combination with the Queen Mother of the West and Dong Fangshuo in the sliding-panel paintings from the Guest Hall of Daisen'in at Daitokuji in Kyoto (now in the Tokyo National Museum).

The Queen Mother of the West and Dong Fangshuo screen is in excellent condition and preserves much of the brilliance it must have had on completion close to four hundred years ago. It is almost as if the painting itself possessed the Queen Mother's secret of eternal youth. Works such as this astound with their physical durability as well as their lasting power to move us.

Enveloped in an atmosphere of stillness and tranquillity, the Queen Mother of the West sits at the right

Opposite:
Attributed to Kano Mitsunobu
The Queen Mother of the West and Dong Fangshuo, detail
Momoyama period,
late 16th–early 17th century
Six-panel screen
CATALOGUE NO. 11

side of the composition. She is portrayed not as a living, breathing woman but as a goddess of a faraway land—unapproachable, untouchable—the embodiment of feminine beauty and eternal youth. It is largely through her that the painter, with complete mastery of his art, evokes the mystery and allure of his theme. This technical mastery is apparent especially in the classical features of the figures: their full cheeks and largish noses point to a painter of the Kano school active during the Keichō era (1596–1615) of the Momoyama period, and further, a painter thoroughly versed in the mainstream techniques of that school. *The Queen Mother of the West and Dong Fangshuo* can thus be considered a valuable addition to the known body of figurative *Kanga*, or Chinese-style, screen painting of the Kano school during the late Momoyama period.

Close examination of the figure style yields significant points of comparison with the work of Kano Mitsunobu (1562/1565–1608), the sixth-generation head of the Kano school and son of the great Kano Eitoku (1543–1590). I would like to begin with a close examination of the screen and an exploration of its technical and stylistic similarities to some Kano school portraits of poets, which my studies indicate can be assigned with confidence to Mitsunobu. Next, by comparing the *Queen Mother* screen with other Kanga figure painting attributed to Mitsunobu, I hope to establish the significance of the screen relative to this oeuvre, which has been under re-examination of late by Japanese scholars. Finally, I would like to consider the relationship of this type of Kanga screen painting to the large-figure genre painting that developed slightly later, in the Genna (1615–1624) and Kan'ei (1624–1644) eras of the early Edo period. I would suggest that painters adapted the formal framework provided by paintings such as the *Queen Mother* screen to genre painting to endow their figures with greater impact and immediacy.

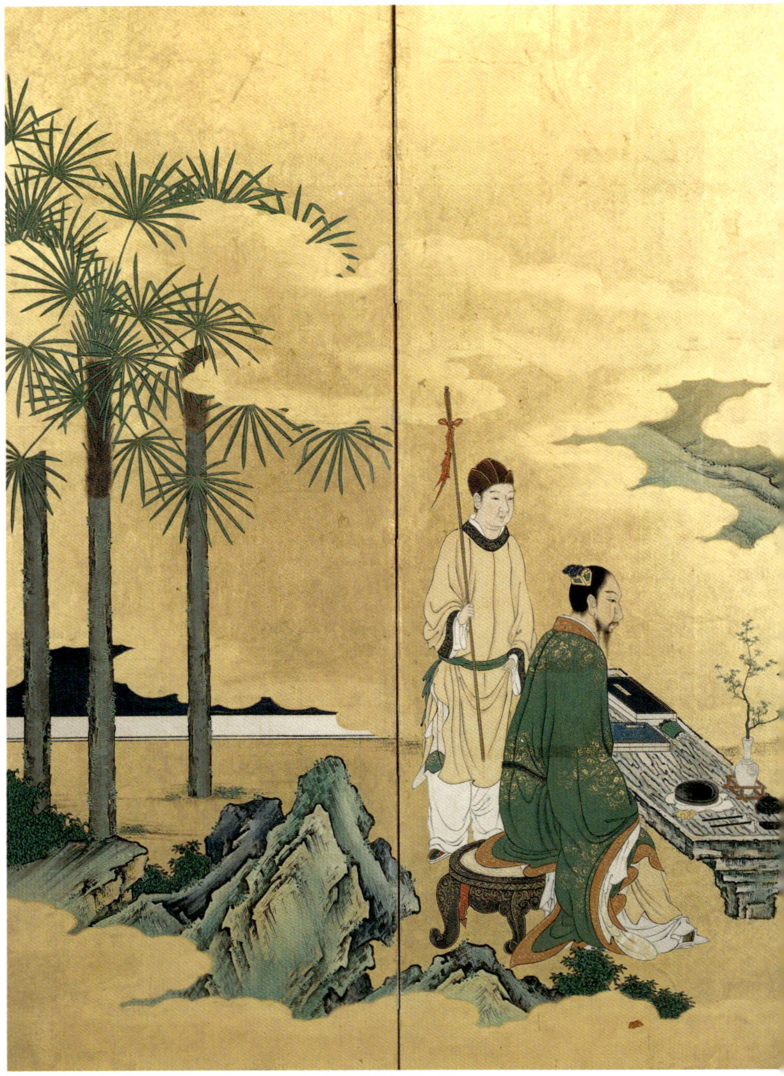

The Queen Mother of the West and Dong Fangshuo

The legend's two main characters are positioned at opposite sides of the composition. On the right, in front of the palace, surrounded by four female attendants is the Queen Mother of the West (see detail, p. 97). She is seated in a chair; at her right an attendant presents the peaches of immortality. The Queen Mother gazes kindly at the attendant to her left, to whom she appears to be murmuring something. On the far left is Dong Fangshuo. The scholar sits at his desk, writing paraphernalia laid out before him, and quietly regards the group of women. Both the goddess and the scholar, while not openly acknowledging each other, are clearly conscious of the other's presence, and this consciousness creates a certain tension. Although the primary theme is an elevated one, the viewer senses that on a different level the painting also implies the romantic attraction between the sexes.

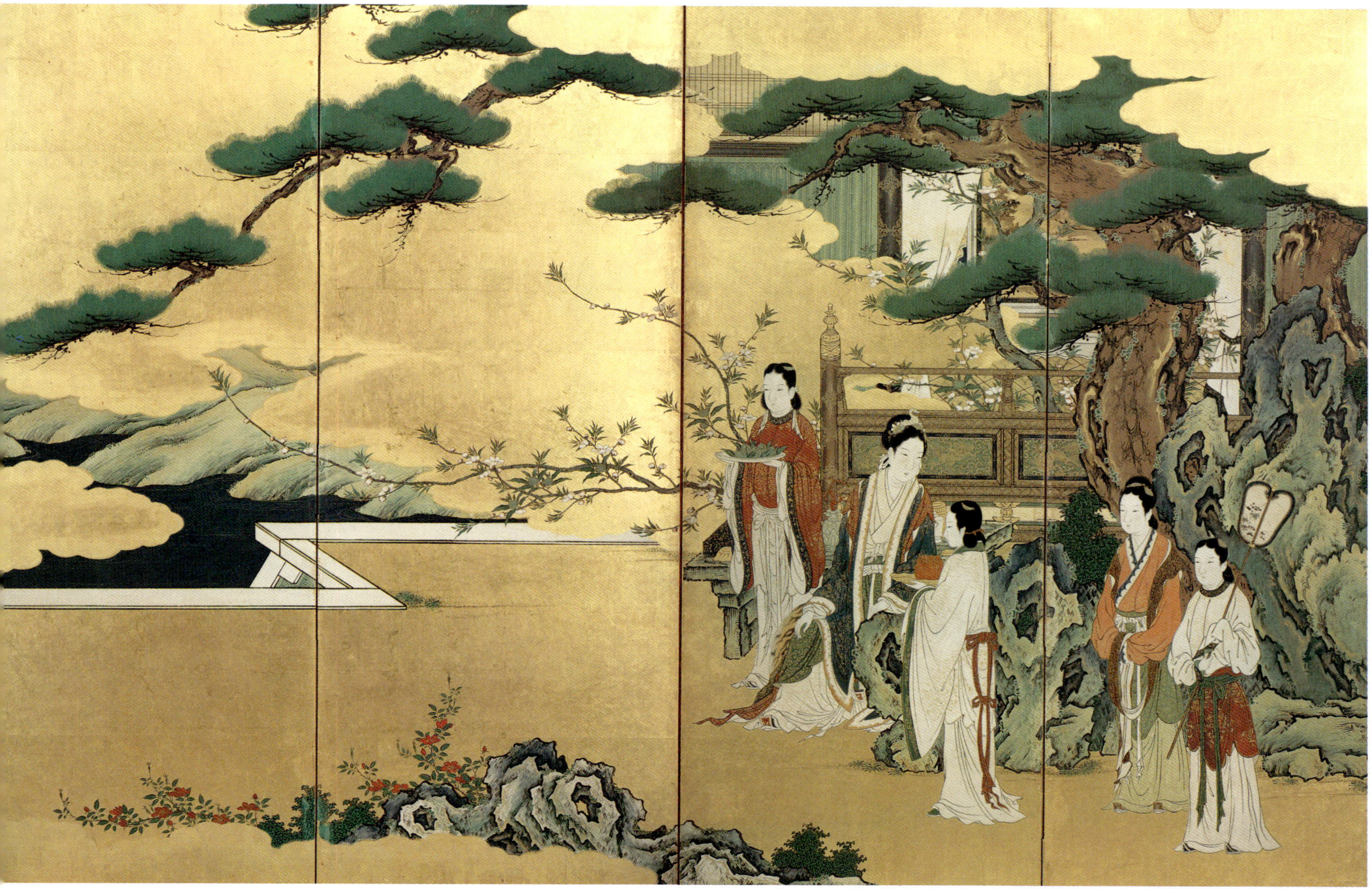

FIGURE 1

Attributed to Kano Mitsunobu
The Queen Mother of the West and Dong Fangshuo
Momoyama period, late 16th–early 17th century
Six-panel screen
CATALOGUE NO. 11

In fact, compositional groupings of men and women similar to this are quite common in genre screens, particularly the category of the receipt of a love letter. The arrangement of figures is also suggestive of the relationship between a woman of the pleasure quarters and a client, as seen in the famous Hikone screen (discussed below). Accentuating this impression is the decorative style of the *Queen Mother* screen: its gold leaf and rich colors evoke a melancholy mood of decadence. In particular, the gold clouds suffusing the space around the figures lend the picture an atmosphere of voluptuousness. A peach tree growing in the palace garden, behind the attendant with the peaches, extends a delicate limb into the center of the composition; it recalls tree and plant forms seen in Kano Mitsunobu's wall paintings of flowering shrubs at Kangakuin, Onjōji, near Lake Biwa—his most famous works—and at Hōnen'in, Kyoto. Elegant and sinuous, the branch echoes the Queen Mother's feminine grace. In front of the palace, a huge pine with gnarled trunk meanders up and out of the composition and then re-enters with a few needle-laden branches near the center of the screen. The trees help establish depth around the figure of the Queen Mother. Three slender palms (*shurochiku*) behind and to the left of Dong Fangshuo serve a similar purpose. This overlapping of palms, also seen in Mitsunobu's wall paintings at Kangakuin and Hōnen'in, seems characteristic of his disposition of trees. The gold clouds weaving in and out among the palms suggest atmosphere occupying that space. Near the bottom of the central panels of the screen a few red flowers that resemble roses lend a charming accent. A mood of springtime quietly suffuses the picture.

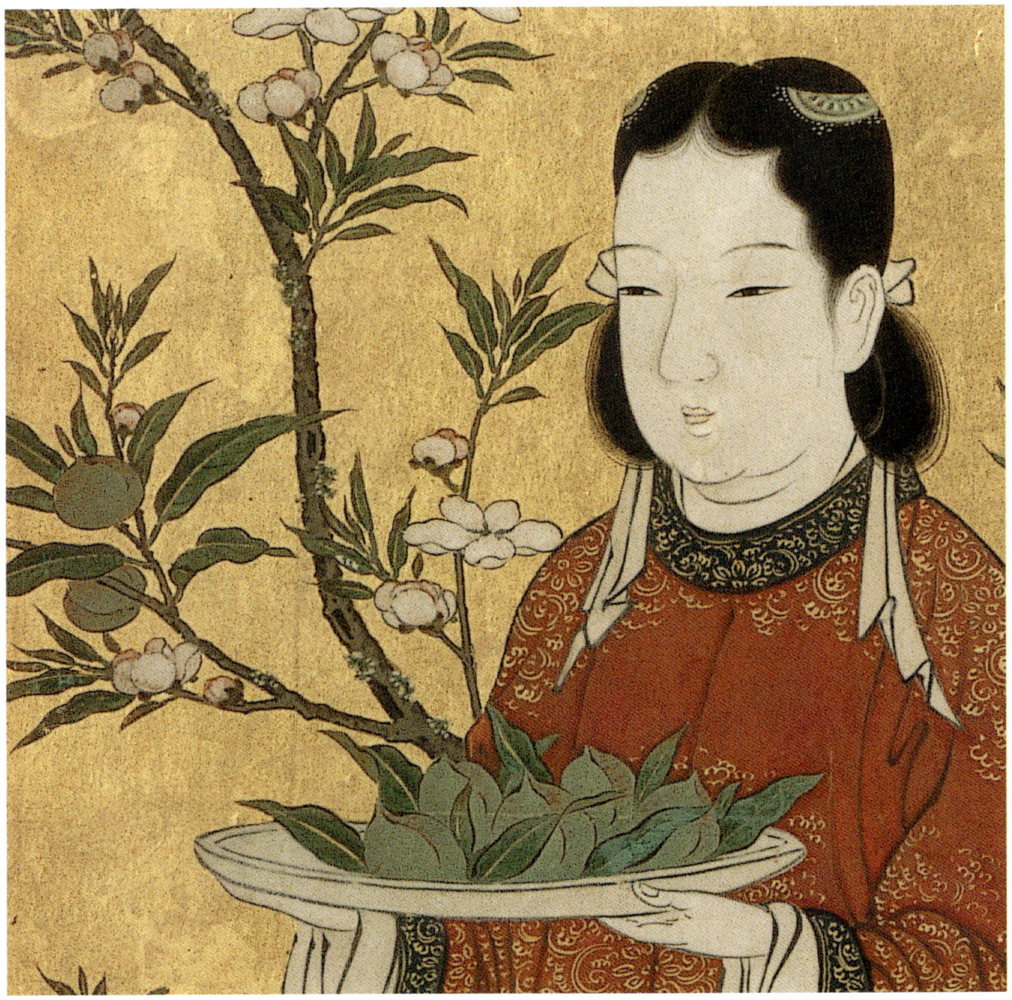

FIGURE 2

The Queen Mother of the West and Dong Fangshuo, detail
CATALOGUE NO. 11

Let us focus on the artist's technique, beginning with the treatment of the figures. Their tallish bodies display idealized proportions, yet the overall effect is natural, not stylized or mannered. The figures' classical features, ideal proportions, and natural, relaxed poses lend the composition an air of calm and tranquillity appropriate to the theme. The technique used in rendering the faces is painstaking in the extreme. After sketching them in ink on a gessolike ground of white earth, the artist applied a coat of white pigment over which he delineated the features in fine brushstrokes: pale ink was used first; then dark ink for the hair, eyebrows, eyes, nose, mouth, and ears; and finally accents to the mouth and lower eyelids were added in dark ink with a very fine brush (fig. 2). Because no red pigment was applied to the lips, the total effect is not so much one of realism as of an idealized, transcendent naturalism that matches the subject.

Turning to other pictorial elements, one notes first that considerable care has been taken in the rendering of the large, fantastically shaped ornamental rock at the right, a motif that plays an important role in conveying the "Chinese" flavor of Kanga paintings such as this. The underpainting was done in gold and pale malachite green; next came texture strokes in dark ink, followed by a wash of ultramarine. This technique resulted in a heavy buildup of pigment, which contributes to the feeling of weight and volume. Finally, one cannot help but be impressed by the artist's meticulous attention to detail in the rendering of textile patterns, the monochrome ink landscape adorning the one-panel screen (*tsuitate*) just visible within the palace, and the tiger skin on which the Queen Mother sits.

The delicate, pliantly graceful peach branch with its appearance of inner vitality, the solid and substantial rocks, and the suggestion of space and atmosphere through the disposition of trees and clouds point to the hand of a painter of the Keichō era, and all these features are consistent with the style of Kano Mitsunobu.

Mitsunobu's Poet Portraits

Let us now turn to Mitsunobu's figure style, beginning with two sets of the Thirty-Six Immortal Poets painted on wooden votive plaques (*kasen-e*). These ideal portraits of long-dead classical poets—a theme particularly popular during the Kamakura period (1185–1333)—follow established conventions and a standard iconography yet reveal technical and stylistic nuances that I believe bear comparison with the treatment of the figures in the Idemitsu Museum's *The Queen Mother of the West and Dong Fangshuo*.

In keeping with standard Kano school practice, the set of the *Thirty-Six Immortal Poets* of about 1590 at the Munakata Shrine, Fukuoka Prefecture (hereafter called the Munakata Shrine set) follows the iconography of the thirteenth century Narikane scroll and depicts each poet seated on a *tatami* mat.[1] Of the original thirty-six, only one, Minamoto no Shigeyuki, has been lost. Painted against a yellowish white background, these portraits convey a soft and delicate image in contrast to the sumptuous effect of other sets that employ a gold ground.

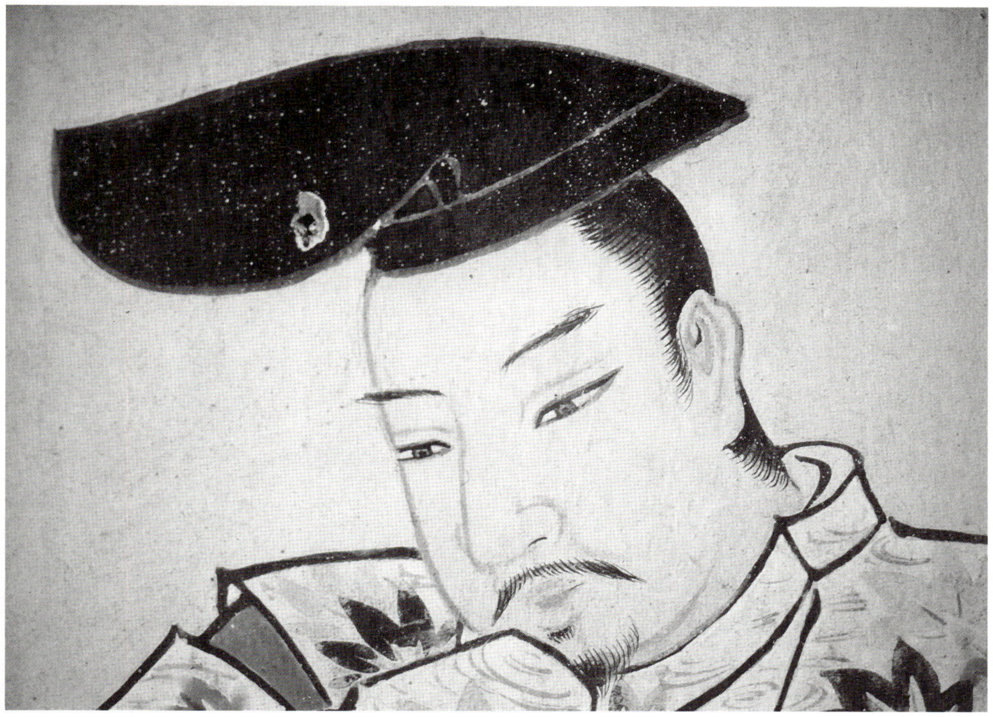

FIGURE 3

Attributed to Kano Mitsunobu
Fujiwara no Okikake, one of
Thirty-Six Immortal Poets, detail
Momoyama period, about 1590
Color and ink on wood
20½ x 14⅛ in. (52.0 x 36.0 cm)
Munakata Shrine, Fukuoka Prefecture

The poets' relaxed poses, classical features, and slightly downturned gazes combine with their brightly colored garments to create an effect at once serene and sparklingly fresh. The painstaking treatment of their faces involved drawing in ink over the ground (probably a mixture of white earth and yellow ochre), painting over the drawing with white pigment, retracing the underdrawing in pale ink, and then applying a coat of yellow ochre (fig. 3). The lines of the face were then redrawn in pale ink or cinnabar. Next the artist carefully delineated the hair, beard and mustache, eyebrows, eyes, nose, mouth, and ears in dark ink. Finally, with fine, dark brushstrokes, he applied accents to the lower eyelids and the mouth. The clothing was painted in the *horinuri* technique in which the artist used deft, modulated brushwork to delineate the drapery folds and then painted up to but not over those brushstrokes. The method imparts a subtle, natural sense of movement to the human form. The garments display a variety of textile patterns, including chrysanthemums and trellislike *tachiwaki*, waves, bellflowers, and phoenixes, executed in vivid pigments such as cinnabar, malachite, ultramarine, and gold. Overall, the paintings exhibit the fresh, bright palette characteristic of *Yamato-e*, traditional Japanese-style painting as practiced since the Heian period (794–1185). Of the Kano school votive poet portraits from the Momoyama period, the Munakata Shrine set are exceptionally vivid.

The "Kuninobu" seal impressed on the Munakata Shrine portraits is that of Kano Eitoku, Mitsunobu's illustrious father. Shrine records suggest, however, that the set was dedicated to commemorate the completion in 1590 of the Hetsumiya subshrine, sponsored by the warlord Kobayakawa Takakage. At that time Eitoku was occupied with the production of wall paintings for the Jurakudai Palace of the ruler Toyotomi Hideyoshi, and Eitoku died the same year; therefore, it seems unlikely that the great master was directly responsible for these poet portraits. It makes more sense to regard them as an early work of Eitoku's direct heir and pupil, the young Mitsunobu. The poems inscribed on the upper portion of the compositions, in squares resembling the decorative papers known as *shikishi*, can be confidently assigned to the hand of Shōgoin Dōchō (1555–1608), a priest with close connections both to Hideyoshi and to the Munakata Shrine.

The recently discovered set of the *Thirty-Six Immortal Poets* of about 1603 at Myōhōin, Kyoto (fig. 4),[2] is complete and in excellent condition. The classical facial features, accomplished brushwork, and refined palette immediately identify the set as a product of the mainstream Kano school during the Momoyama period. The Myōhōin set closely resembles the Munakata Shrine set except for a luxurious effect that derives from the former's gold ground and the generous use of gold in the rendering of the fabric patterns. The fact that they share the same format, medium, technical details (such as the use of the horinuri technique for drapery and the application of fine, dark accents to the lower eyelids and mouth), model, and mood suggests that the painter of the Myōhōin set was either Kano Mitsunobu or an accomplished member of his atelier.

The various wall paintings at Myōhōin attributed to Mitsunobu and his workshop imply that the Kano master had connections with that Kyoto temple. The works include a group of slender pines adorning the entry hall and paintings of Chinese historical figures and Daoist immortals in the Ichinoma of the temple's Daishoin building (specifically, those adorning a set of decorative sliding panels [*chōdaigamae*], the *tokonoma* alcove, and the recess for the staggered shelves).

It should also be noted that some of the structures within the Myōhōin temple complex are known to have been transferred from the old Shōkōin Palace, which had served as the residence of the above-mentioned Shōgoin Dōchō after he was made chief priest in charge of Hideyoshi's massive project, the building of the Great Buddha at Hōkōji, completed in 1595. The Great Buddha Hall and the nearby Shōkōin Palace both burned in 1602 and were rebuilt between 1603 and 1605. Mitsunobu and his atelier, which had close ties to Hideyoshi, are assumed to have undertaken production of the palace wall paintings on that occasion. These historical circumstances, combined with the stylistic clues discussed above, raise the possibility that the Myōhōin set of the *Thirty-Six Immortal Poets* was painted by Mitsunobu or a member of his coterie to commemorate the rebuilding of the Shōkōin and was later moved to Myōhōin. Although no documentation has been found to substantiate the theory that Mitsunobu himself painted the Myōhōin set, the stylistic and technical similarities between it and the Munakata Shrine set are undeniable. The major difference, as already noted, is the prolific use of gold, which gives the Myōhōin set a lavish, sophisticated effect in contrast to the fresh innocence of the Munakata Shrine set. This change in decorative emphasis could be ascribed to the artist's maturation during the thirteen to fifteen years that elapsed between the two works. We should also bear in mind that the Munakata Shrine set was intended for a provincial shrine—a circumstance that would be consistent with the use of Eitoku's "Kuninobu" seal on a work produced by his workshop under the young Mitsunobu's direction—whereas the Myōhōin set was in all likelihood painted in connection with one of Hideyoshi's major construction projects after Mitsunobu had assumed leadership of the Kano school. This would account for differences in the artist's approach to his work and, specifically, in the effort expended on lavish decorative effects.

The calligraphy of the poems inscribed shikishi style on the Myōhōin set relates closely to the work of Shōgoin Dōchō, and in view of the probability that the set was produced to commemorate the rebuilding of the Shōkōin Palace, it seems likely that Dōchō himself brushed these poems as he did those on the Munakata Shrine set. This could indicate that the Myōhōin *Thirty-Six Immortal Poets*, along with the Munakata Shrine poet portraits and the restoration of Onjōji's Kangakuin, was a collaborative effort by Mitsunobu and Dōchō.[3]

I would suggest that the Munakata Shrine and Myōhōin sets of the *Thirty-Six Immortal Poets* are the work of Kano Mitsunobu and that the Idemitsu Museum's *The Queen Mother of the West and Dong Fangshuo* is without question stylistically and technically comparable with them—lending credence to the theory that the Idemitsu screen is the work of Kano Mitsunobu.[4]

FIGURE 4

Attributed to Kano Mitsunobu
Fujiwara no Okikake, one of *Thirty-Six Immortal Poets*, detail
Momoyama period, about 1603
Color and ink on wood
Myōhōin, Kyoto

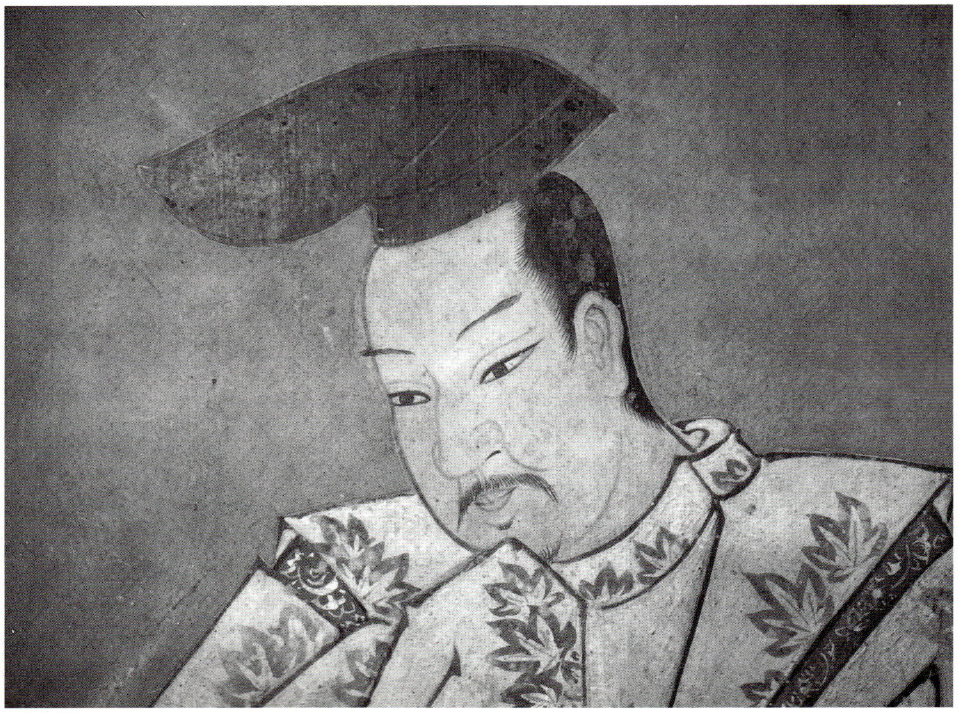

Mitsunobu's Kanga Figure Painting

To test the theory that the Idemitsu Museum's *Queen Mother* screen is the work of Kano Mitsunobu, let us compare it with other Kanga figure painting in the style associated with this artist. Because our focal point is a richly colored gold screen painting, I will examine several Mitsunobu-style paintings in this mode and will concentrate on those that seem most likely to be by Mitsunobu himself.[5]

The previously mentioned wall paintings of Myōhōin—*Chinese Figures* and *Daoist Immortals* in the Ichinoma of the Daishoin—are generally judged to be by Mitsunobu himself because the trees and rocks are similar in style to those in Mitsunobu's flower-and-bird paintings. Because the figures' faces display none of the characteristics that I have noted in the Munakata Shrine and Myōhōin poet portraits, however, I am inclined to view the wall paintings as the work of a lesser artist in Mitsunobu's circle rather than the master himself.[6]

The folding screen *The Minghuang Emperor and Yang Gueifei* in the Freer Gallery of Art, Smithsonian Institution, Washington, D.C. (fig. 5), depicts seven episodes in the tale of Emperor Xuanzong of the Tang dynasty (618–906), known as Minghuang, and his beloved consort Yang Gueifei—a story made famous in the *Song of Everlasting Sorrow* by the Tang poet Bo Juyi. The painting displays the attenuated pines and slender figures associated with Mitsunobu, and the composition is cleverly divided into seven sections by overlapping strata of gold clouds. Yet one senses artifice in the handling of the clouds, as well as a lack of variety in their spatial relationships. Whether in the far right, far left, or central portion of the composition, the clouds are always behind and the pines in front. The interweaving of clouds and branches seen in *The Queen Mother of the West and Dong Fangshuo* is absent. The attenuation of the figures goes beyond idealization to distortion, and the tiny hands and feet—which bring to mind the passage about these characteristics of Mitsunobu's style in Kano Ikkei's book of painters' biographies, *Tansei jakuboku shū*—come across as a mannerism. Compared with the Munakata Shrine and Myōhōin poet portraits, the treatment of the human form is neither natural nor subtle. In my view, the Freer screen should be seen as the work of a follower, not of Mitsunobu himself.

The Idemitsu Museum's screen *Scenes of Tartars Hunting on Horseback* (fig. 6; cat. no. 12),[7] which may have been reduced from a larger screen, has a remarkably unlively composition for a heroic theme of this nature, especially when compared with a painting of the same subject by Kano Sōshō (1551–1601) in the Asian Art Museum of San Francisco or one by Kano Jinnojō (active late sixteenth–early seventeenth century) in the Freer Gallery of Art. In both the San Francisco and the Washington screens, a complex grouping of numerous small figures conveys a strong sense of movement. Several masses of figures, each visually tied to the next, are disposed across the composition to create a unified, organic whole that vibrates with kinetic energy. The Idemitsu screen possesses no such complex unifying device: each of the Tartar horsemen is a discrete entity in a fragmented composition. It has been argued that this type of depiction refers to a more primitive style of hunting.[8] That is, the painter of the Idemitsu's *Tartars Hunting on Horseback* adopted a more archaic model than that followed by either Sōshū or Jinnojō. At the same time, we can discern in the Idemitsu screen a number of features characteristic of Mitsunobu's style. The Tartars' curiously still faces and downcast eyes accord with what we have seen in the poet portraits at the Munakata Shrine and Myōhōin, and the sinuous pine is similar to forms seen in Mitsunobu's wall paintings. On the basis of these observations, I believe there is a strong possibility that the Idemitsu's *Tartars Hunting on Horseback* is by Mitsunobu.

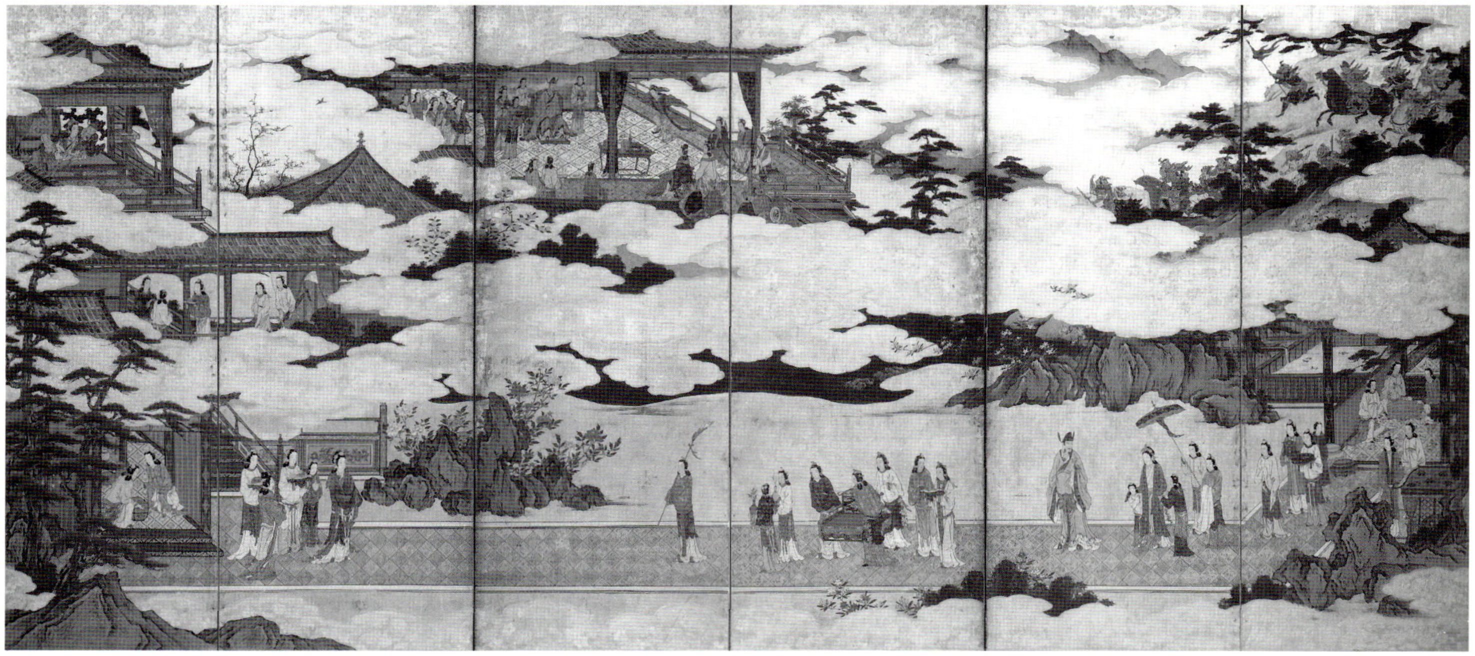

FIGURE 5

The Minghuang Emperor and Yang Gueifei
Momoyama period
Pair of six-panel screens
Color and gold on paper
Each, 62¼ x 145⅝ in. (158 x 365.9 cm)
Courtesy of the Freer Gallery of Art, Smithsonian Institution, Washington, D.C.
01.20/01.21

The two-panel screen *Boats Escorted by Mounted Tartars*, seventeenth century, now in the Museum of Fine Arts, Boston (fig. 7), appears originally to have been part of a set of sliding doors. Because the painting is no longer intact, the precise theme of the work is unclear. Seemingly presenting a portion of a procession, it is quite different from the typical image of swirling groups of stouthearted men on galloping horses. Like the Idemitsu's *Tartars Hunting on Horseback*, the Boston screen lacks the lively movement seen in the compositions by Sōshū and Jinnojō and seems to represent a more archaic style. The branch that snakes out from the left side of the tree trunk at the far right of the right-hand panel is almost identical to a sinuous limb growing from the left side of the Chinese black pine (*maki*) in Mitsunobu's sliding doors *Chinese Black Pine and Aronia* at Hōnen'in. Furthermore, the contemplative faces and downcast eyes correspond to what we have seen in both *Tartars Hunting on Horseback* and the Munakata Shrine and Myōhōin poet portraits. Although no attribution has been made heretofore, stylistic evidence points to the hand of Mitsunobu.

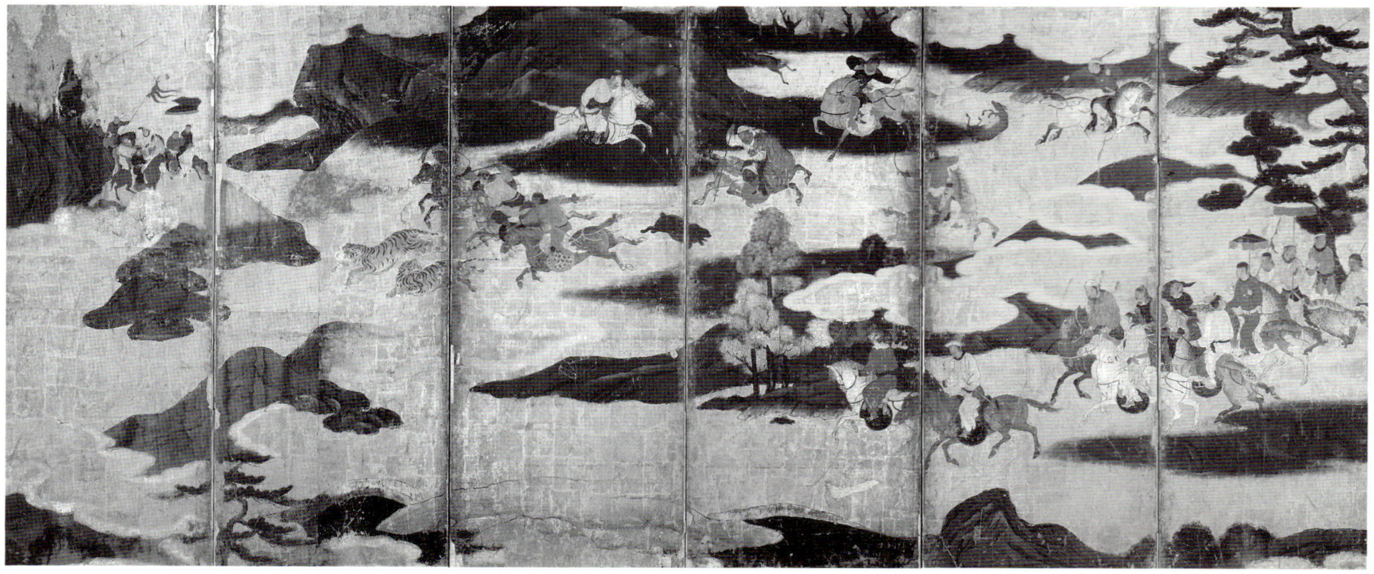

FIGURE 6

Scenes of Tartars Hunting on Horseback
Momoyama period, beginning of 17th century
Six-panel screen
CATALOGUE NO. 12

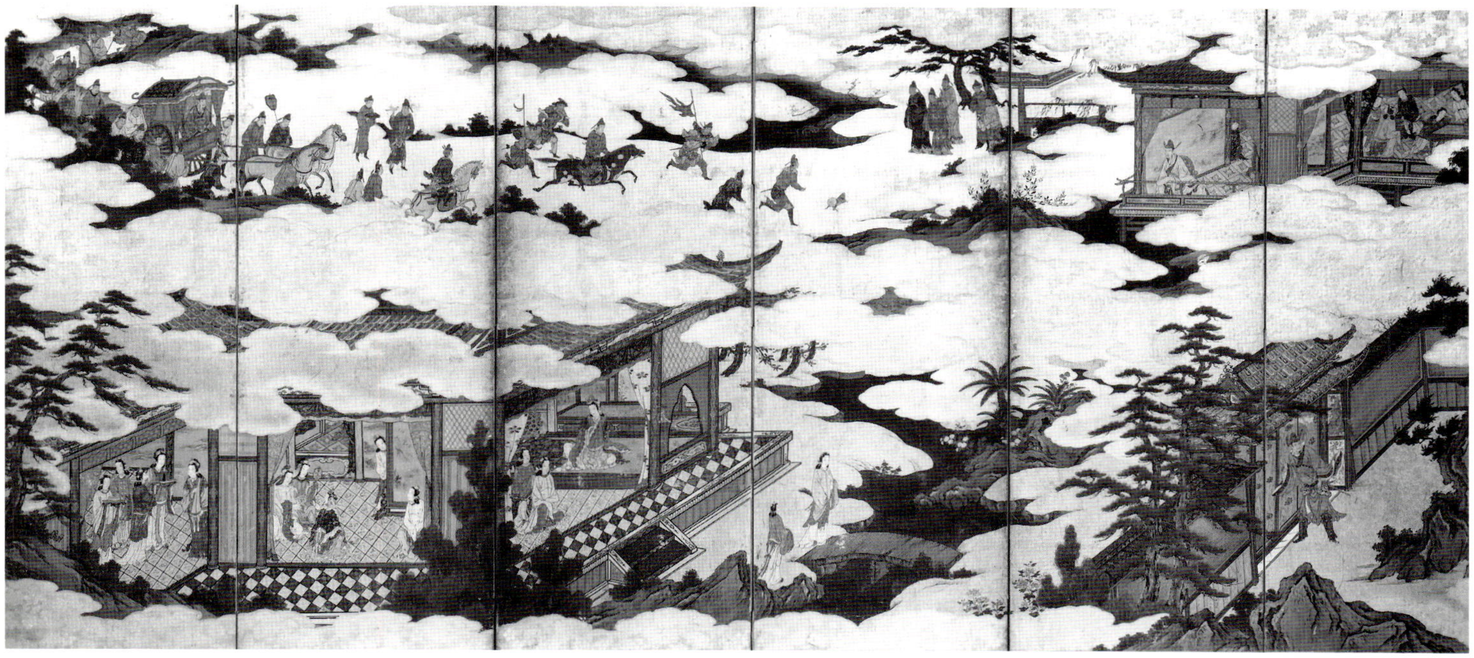

Of the five large-scale figure paintings discussed, then, the Idemitsu *Scenes of Tartars Hunting on Horseback* and the Boston *Boats Escorted by Mounted Tartars* seem most likely to be genuine works of Kano Mitsunobu. Because both paintings have been altered in format, it is difficult to compare them with *The Queen Mother of the West and Doug Fangshuo* in terms of composition. One element we can profitably compare, however, is the use of gold clouds within the painting.

Mitsunobu's wall paintings at Kangakuin and Hōnen'in are distinguished by the use of gold clouds to convey a sense of atmosphere. Instead of drawing attention to themselves as design elements, these clouds quietly occupy the three-dimensional space constructed by the careful arrangement of motifs—floating between trees, for example. The same approach is apparent in *The Queen Mother of the West and Dong Fangshuo* in which clouds fill the space established by the three slender palms at the far left without conveying any sense of drifting. In the Idemitsu *Tartars Hunting on Horseback* and the Boston *Boats Escorted by Mounted Tartars*, the gold clouds play a similar role. By contrast, in the Myōhōin *Chinese Figures* and the Freer *The Minghuang Emperor and Yang Gueifei*, trailing clouds appear to drift across the composition. Whereas the former three paintings have a number of small clouds patched together to form one or two large, enveloping clouds, the latter two paintings

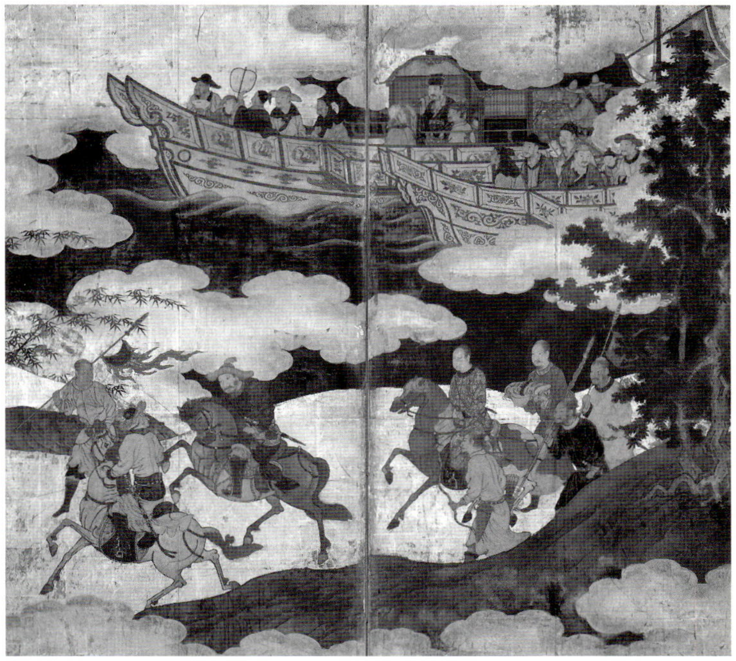

FIGURE 7

Kano School
Boats Escorted by Mounted Tartars
Momoyama period, 17th century
Two-panel screen
Ink, color, and gold on paper
68 x 75 in. (173 x 190 cm)
Fenollosa-Weld Collection,
Courtesy, Museum of Fine Arts, Boston
11.4450

display long, continuous clouds that give the appearance of horizontal movement. We see here a basic difference in compositional function.[9] Combined with our earlier observations regarding the treatment of figures, this comparison lends weight to the idea that the Boston *Boats Escorted by Mounted Tartars* and the Idemitsu *Tartars Hunting on Horseback* and *The Queen Mother of the West and Dong Fangshuo* can be grouped within the oeuvre of Kano Mitsunobu.

Of these three works, it seems to me that *The Queen Mother of the West and Dong Fangshuo* is the most successful. The main reason is probably that the manner of painting is better adapted to the portrayal of dignified, idealized figures, such as the Queen Mother of the West or Yang Gueifei, than to the rough-and-tumble genre subject of hunters galloping over the countryside. That is to say, the painter of these screens was more at home with a static treatment of the human figure than a dynamic one. The most obvious representative of static figure painting is portraiture. In this sense, the qualities of the Boston *Boats Escorted by Mounted Tartars* and the two Idemitsu screens tally with the image of Mitsunobu as an artist with considerable experience in portrait painting.

Even taking into account differences in the state of preservation, *The Queen Mother of the West and Dong Fangshuo* stands out among the three works in terms of its cohesion and its skillful creation of an evocative ambiance appropriate to the subject matter. Of the extant Kanga figure paintings in the manner of Mitsunobu, *The Queen Mother of the West and Dong Fangshuo* displays the greatest skill, substance, and depth. At the same time, the technique that yields such depth can be discerned also in the *Thirty-Six Immortal Poets* of the Munakata Shrine and the Myōhōin, both assignable to Mitsunobu. It seems to me, therefore, that the Idemitsu Museum's highly accomplished *The Queen Mother of the West and Dong Fangshuo* has a better claim to a place in Mitsunobu's oeuvre than the Kanga figure paintings hitherto attributed to him.

As compelling as it is, this work is obviously not a real portrait but rather a generalized, idealized image of the human figure—much like a conventional poet portrait. It is true, as Teisuke Toda has pointed out, that in enlarging the proportions of figures within a composition an artist highlights their individuality and that this technique consequently intensifies the impact and immediacy of the figures.[10] Even so, when idealized and stereotyped figures are incorporated into the highly decorative format of the gold screen, the result is no more than a faint echo of reality. Such are the limits of Japanese Kanga figure painting.

Nevertheless, this large-figure decorative format has the potential to bring to life a world outside our ordinary experience. To artists involved in genre painting, it offered a mode of expression that permitted the conflation of fantasy and reality. The first decades of the Edo period, from 1615 to about mid-century, witnessed the production of a large number of gold screen paintings that depict the transient amusements of the pleasure quarters. In such works, the decorative style dilutes the reality of the figures as flesh and blood yet paradoxically highlights and magnifies the desires that motivate them. The impact of the reality thus conveyed is in fact very intense. It is as if the remote, stylized Chinese figures of the Kanga screens were reincarnated in the following era as voluptuaries of the pleasure quarters, gaining in the process a liveliness they never had before.

Toda has characterized the development of Kanga figurative screen painting in the following terms: "The figures become extremely stereotyped, and . . . the composition is standardized until it becomes a ready-made template into which the artist can insert interchangeable sets of figures."[11] Without question, Japanese Kanga figure painting during the late Momoyama period tends to be highly decorative, color and design are emphasized, and the treatment of figures becomes increasingly stylized. At the same time, the enlargement of the figures for the sake of greater impact and immediacy becomes part of a standard formal vocabulary for animating a world beyond daily life. This vocabulary helps bring a new sense of reality to figure painting with the emergence

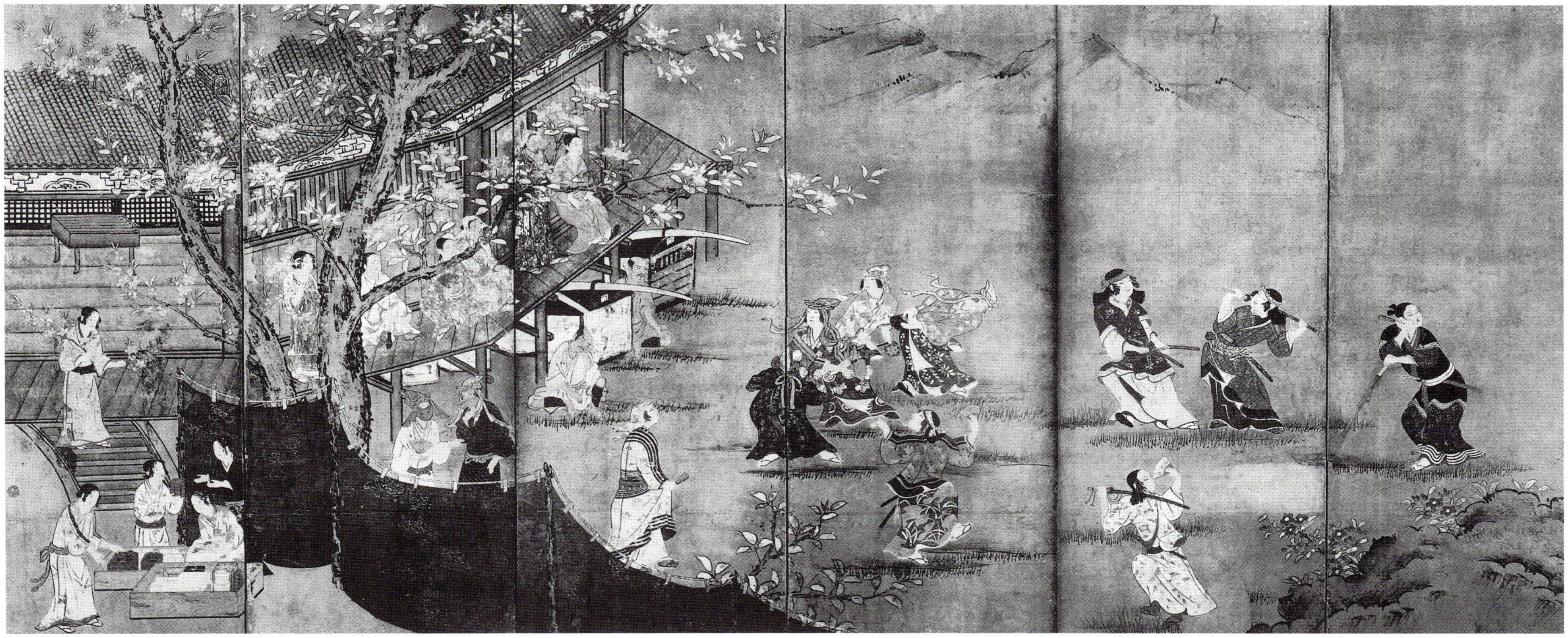

FIGURE 8

Kano Naganobu (1577–1654)
Amusements under the Cherry Blossoms
Edo period, early 17th century
One of a pair of six-panel screens
Color and ink on paper
58⅞ x 140 in. (149.4 x 356.1 cm)
Tokyo National Museum

of Edo period genre scenes, which constitute some of the most appealing art of that time. I believe that the Kano painters recognized this basic mode of expression as an effective means of endowing human figures with the appearance of objective reality and embraced it as a style appropriate to the depiction of those who haunted the pleasure quarters.

Kanga Figure Painting and Genre Painting

The history of Japanese genre painting begins with the tiny figures of the Scenes in and around Kyoto (*rakuchū-rakugaizu*), dating from the late Muromachi period (see cat. no. 15). But by the early Edo period, much larger figures appear in depictions of the amusements of the pleasure quarters. This evolutionary process culminates in the Kanbun era (1661–1673), when we begin to see Pictures of Beauties (*bijinga*) in which a large portion of the composition is filled by a single full-length female figure. The trend toward larger figures has been said to reflect an impulse to penetrate deeper into the subject and an increasingly mature mode of figurative expression. To this interpretation I would propose an additional factor. We should bear in mind first that, in addition to the well-known *Amusements under the Cherry Blossoms* by Kano Naganobu (1577–1654), dating from the early seventeenth century (Tokyo National Museum; fig. 8), there are a number of anonymous proto-ukiyo-e genre paintings that display the accomplished technique and stylistic idiosyncrasies associated with the Kano school. These include the so-called Honda Heihachirō and Sen-hime screen (Tokugawa Art Museum, Nagoya; fig. 9) and the anonymous Hikone screen (Ii Naoyoshi, Hikone, Shiga Prefecture), both of the early seventeenth century. Such works also represent a trend toward the enlargement of the human figure in genre painting. It seems to me that, in terms of their basic mode of expression, the high quality Kano-style genre paintings mentioned above are strongly influenced by Kano school Kanga figure painting of the late Momoyama period. Judging from extant works, all the major early themes—Scenes in and around Kyoto, screens of Westerners (*nanban byōbu*), depictions of the Gion Festival, and scenes inside

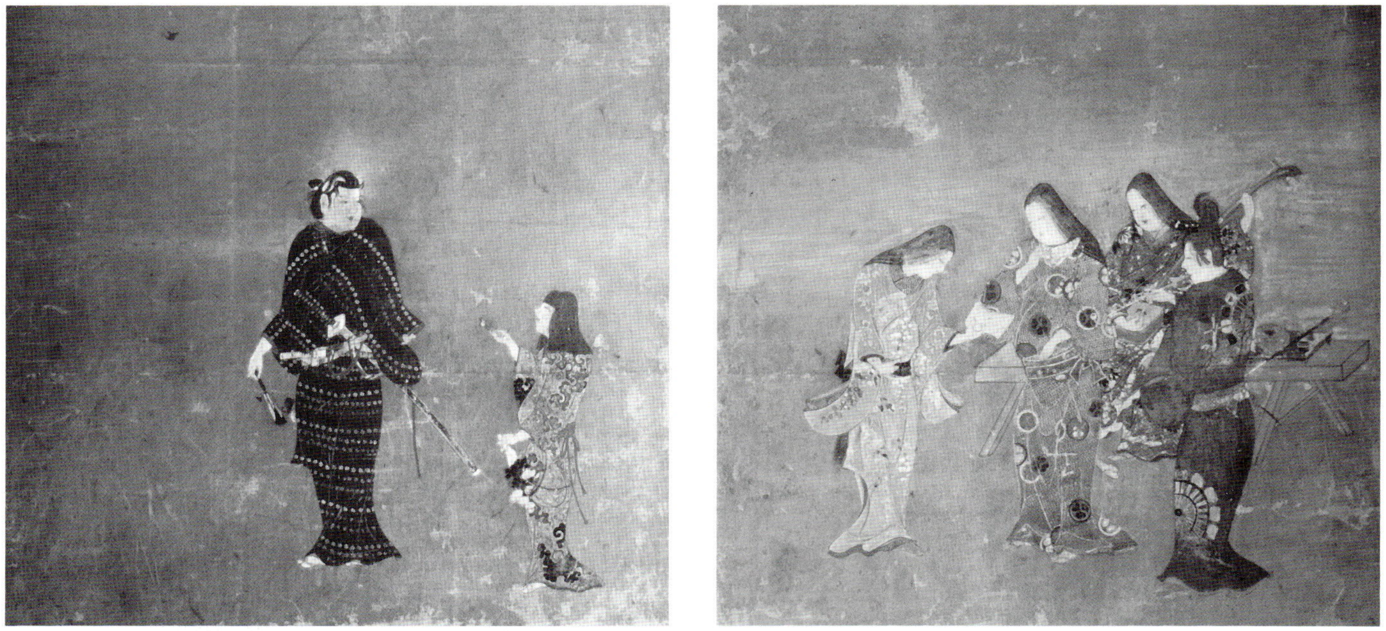

FIGURE 9

Honda Heihachirō and Senhime
Edo period, early 17th century
Two-panel screen
Color and gold paint on paper
28⅝ x 62 in. (72.7 x 157.5 cm)
Tokugawa Art Museum, Nagoya

the pleasure quarters—were first treated by Kano artists. Of course, thematically speaking, *The Queen Mother of the West and Dong Fangshuo* has little in common with pictures of the licensed entertainment districts known as the pleasure quarters and their denizens, but disparities in content do not preclude a formal relationship.[12]

Scholars have long agreed that, during the early Edo period, the Kano school, which claimed the highest prestige and authority among Japanese painters, helped carry out the Tokugawa shogunate's cultural and educational policy by producing rather stuffy, academic, didactic paintings on Confucian themes, under the leadership of Kano Tan'yū (1602–1674). As I have indicated, however, some of the most accomplished and expressive large-figure genre paintings made during the first few decades of the seventeenth century display clear stylistic affinities with the Kano school. It is apparent, in other words, that some of the same artists charged with disseminating Confucian values through art—including such leading figures as Naganobu—were simultaneously using their impeccable technique to paint appealingly warm-blooded images of the pleasure quarters. The works summon a universal response to the subject matter and often have such depth that they invite psychological analysis. Because some of them succeed in part by recalling Chinese tales or events involving noted Japanese personages, I would submit that only painters of the Kano school could have combined such literary, mythical, and historical knowledge with the technical mastery apparent in these genre scenes.

Figure painting in the Amusements category differs from both pure portraiture and painting on mythical, legendary, or allegorical subjects; it conveys neither the tension and immediacy of the former nor the distance of the latter. Here the perception of the viewer moves freely between reality and fiction. Although the figures are imaginary, the extremely familiar and accessible themes invite the viewer to empathize. There is a quality of intimacy that is absent from most Japanese figure painting; this intimacy brings with it an immediate and vivid sense of reality. The figures, although anonymous, are very much like people whom the viewer has met or known. Yet, because they are anonymous, they can be portrayed as the embodiment of a certain image or ideal. Furthermore, in order to elicit another level of recognition and response from the viewer, well-known themes or events can be superimposed on these anonymous, idealized figures. This type of genre screen, in short, represents a highly advanced form of figure painting. It was almost inevitable that the Kano school, which was at the forefront of innovation during this era, would be involved in its development. Let me conclude by examining the relationship between Kanga figure painting and large-scale genre works with reference to several representative examples of the latter.

The group of dancing women depicted in the left screen of the famous pair of six-panel screens *Amusements under the Cherry Blossoms* by Kano Naganobu (fig. 8) can be identified as performers of women's Kabuki, a form of entertainment practiced by courtesans. This subject places the work solidly in the Amusements category. At the same time, the central female figure of the right screen and the central male of the left screen have been said to represent Yang Gueifei and the Minghuang Emperor, respectively—or, alternatively, the shogun Tokugawa Hidetada's wife and their son Kunimatsu.[13] It seems certain that Naganobu intended this allusion to ancient Chinese themes and important contemporary figures. By painting his pleasure seekers so that they could be identified with lofty personages, the artist rescued his painting from commonness and vulgarity, just as Kano Hideyori established an elevated tone in his famous genre painting *Maple Viewing at Takao*, seventeenth century (Tokyo National Museum), by inserting a sacred motif, the roof of Jingoji, near the upper edge of the composition. This can be regarded as a standard device of Kano school genre painting. That Naganobu's work lends itself so readily to association with the Chinese theme of Minghuang and Yang Gueifei strongly suggests that the artist had prior training and experience with Kanga subjects. *Amusements under the Cherry Blossoms* thus provides powerful evidence of the impact of Kanga figure subjects on proto-ukiyo-e painting in the early Edo period.

The well-known work called Honda Heihachirō and Senhime (fig. 9), falls into a category of genre scene popular during the first half of the seventeenth century—the receipt of a love letter. Traditionally, it has been associated with the tragic love story surrounding the shogun Tokugawa Hidetada's daughter Senhime and his retainer Honda Heihachirō. A strong indication that this is more than an anonymous genre scene is the hollyhock crest of the Tokugawa clan in the pattern of the kimono worn by the main female figure (Senhime) and also in the fabric of what appears to be the painting's original mounting.[14] The genteel faces of these large-scale figures, with their full cheeks and refined expressions, point to a master of the Kano school; my own theory is that the screen is the work of Naganobu or a follower.[15] In any case, we can surmise from the skill with which the artist opens the door to various interpretations that his style and technique, much like those seen in Hideyori's *Maple Viewing at Takao*, are founded on rigorous training. We might also speculate that any painter capable of portraying anonymous figures with such presence that the viewer associates them with specific personages must have had the benefit of considerable experience in portraiture.

The uniquely expressive six-panel Hikone screen is arguably the most appealing of all Edo period genre paintings.[16] With its subtle hint of decadence and ennui, it goes beyond the depiction of superficial enjoyment to convey something of the pleasure seeker's inner psyche. Over the years the screen has been the subject of numerous studies and various interpretations. To begin with, it is generally acknowledged that, in addition to depicting amusements of the pleasure quarters, the work represents the traditional Kanga theme of the Four Accomplishments: music, *go* (and similar games), calligraphy, and painting. A number of scholars have gone much further, however, positing that the screen refers to or dramatizes a specific series of events.[17]

Without discussing these theories, I would like to offer my personal interpretation—that the Hikone screen might reflect the twilight of the artist's own career. The painting style, like that in the two previously discussed works, points to the hand of someone who had received rigorous professional training. Specifically, the technical prowess apparent in both the flawless composition and the accomplished monochrome landscape painting adorning the folding screen depicted at the left leave little doubt that the artist was of the Kano school. We can be fairly certain that the screen was produced sometime in the Kan'ei era. This raises the possibility that the setting is the Misujimachi pleasure quarters in Kyoto, which functioned as a kind of cultural salon until the licensed district was relocated to Shimabara in 1641. It was during the Kan'ei era that Kano Tan'yū assumed leadership of the Kano school, and older artists, such as Naganobu, were no longer in demand.

Perhaps it is a trifle farfetched to interpret this composition as that painter's swan song. But the skill with which the artist superimposed the Kanga theme of the Four Accomplishments upon this scene of the pleasure quarters bespeaks a firm grounding in Kanga themes and techniques. Furthermore, it seems likely that a painter who had mastered the compositional and expressive techniques necessary to evoke such a variety of narrative interpretations must have had considerable training and experience in figure painting on themes relating to specific Chinese legends, allegories, and historical anecdotes.

The realist tendency of this period was an attempt not to reproduce the world precisely as it is seen but to endow the human figure, however idealized, with a sense of actuality. This mode of expression surely cannot be divorced from the art of portraiture, be it the idealized portrayal of poets or the depiction of the powerful to emphasize their majesty and dignity. In both Kanga figure painting and genre painting we see the same idealized and decorative treatment of the human figure; the same quiet, dense, evocative quality conveyed through the use of gold and rich colors; and the same classical features. In fact, *The Queen Mother of the West and Dong Fangshuo* contains a presentiment of genre painting for, in addition to the auspicious theme of longevity, there is a hint of the worldly subject of amour.

In short, it is reasonable to suppose that the artists responsible for the genre paintings that we have examined also had experience with Kanga figure subjects and portraits of the ruling class. By increasing the proportions of their figures relative to the format and, at the same time, obliquely alluding to distinguished personages, they imparted a sense of actuality to these figures while maintaining a dignity and refinement that transcended the subject matter. The large-figure Kanga subjects produced during the Keichō era, near the end of the Momoyama period, anticipated this development and, for this reason, they occupy a place of special significance in the history of Japanese painting.

In such Kanga figure paintings as *The Queen Mother of the West and Dong Fangshuo*, a sumptuously decorative and patterned effect, combined with an idealized and stereotyped treatment of the human figure, robs the figures of life, diluting their immediacy and impact. Nonetheless, when the Kano genre painters of the first half of the seventeenth century applied that inherited compositional mode to the anonymous yet familiar figures of the pleasure quarters, they endowed those subjects with a quality of objectivity and breathed life into Japanese figurative screen painting. The Idemitsu Museum's *The Queen Mother of the West and Dong Fangshuo* sheds light on the role of the Kano school in the stylistic evolution that yielded the extraordinarily appealing proto-ukiyo-e painting of the early eighteenth century.

NOTES

1. See the author's "Munakata Taisha no Kuninobu-in sanjūrokkasenzu hengaku," pp. 166–184. The Narikane scroll is one of two Kamakura period handscrolls (later cut into separate sections) that formed the basis for subsequent depictions of the Thirty-Six Immortal Poets.

2. See the author's "Kōdaiji no sanjūrokkasenzu hengaku," pp. 22–32.

3. Although a set of the *Thirty-Six Immortal Poet* plaques at Kōdaiji, Kyoto, has been attributed by some to Mitsunobu, I would suggest for reasons (discussed ibid.) that need not be detailed here that the Kōdaiji set represents a stylized version of Mitsunobu's portrait style as interpreted by a slightly later artist.

4. Assuming that Mitsunobu was indeed a portrait painter, we may hypothesize that the large-scale treatment of figures seen in *The Queen Mother of the West and Dong Fangshuo* relates to the treatment of figures in traditional portrait painting.

5. In addition to the works discussed below, I believe that Mitsunobu painted portions of the wall paintings *Twenty-Four Paragons of Filial Piety* in the Ohirunoma of Nanzenji, Kyoto. Although two painted wooden shell containers at the Ise Shrine have been generally accepted into the oeuvre of Mitsunobu and are suggestive of his manner, there are certain stylistic problems with that attribution; and, inasmuch as they cannot be meaningfully compared to the screen *The Queen Mother of the West and Dong Fangshuo*, they will not be considered here.

6. Problems relating to the architecture of the Daishoin make it impossible to determine authorship of the paintings.

7. See the author's "Dattanjin shuryō byōbu no hissha no tegakari."

8. See Suzuki Hiroyuki, "Kisha to kari (Dattanjin shuryōzu byōbu o megutte," pp. 13–30.

9. See the author's "Sakura, momo, kaidōzu byōbu," pp. 37–39, which discusses a painting of peonies that appears to be an early work of Kano Naganobu. It contrasts the treatment of gold clouds in the Naganobu work with that seen in Mitsunobu's wall paintings at Kangakuin and Hōnen'in, and concludes that Naganobu's treatment represents an older aesthetic.

10. Toda Teisuke, "Kangakei jinbutsuzu byōbu no rinkaku," p. 132.

11. Ibid, p. 135.

12. For example, the funerary portraits of women produced during the Momoyama period, which by their nature tended to idealize their subjects, provided a stylistic framework for the large-scale female figures that appeared later in purely secular genre scenes. The formal affinity is underscored by the fact that many such commemorative portraits, notably the anonymous *Portrait of a Lady*, early seventeenth century, now in the Yamato Bunkakan, have been admired over the years as pictures of beauties.

13. Yamane Yūzō, *Yūraku fūzokuzu gaikan—Yagai fūzokuzu o chūshin ni*, p. 80.

14. Mr. Tokugawa Yoshinobu of the Tokugawa Art Museum informs me that this crest belongs to the Owari branch of the Tokugawa clan.

15. See the author's "Sōōji byōbu no hissha ni tsuite," pp. 9–32.

16. Reproduced in Penelope Mason, *A History of Japanese Art* (New York: Harry N. Abrams, 1993), pp. 238–239, and in color in Richard Lane, *Images from the Floating World: The Japanese Print* (London: Alpine Fine Arts Collection, 1978), pp. 26–27.

17. See Okudaira Shunroku, "Hikone byōbu ni tsuite: Kyōzō kankei to gachūga no mondai o chūshin ni," pp. 12–25.

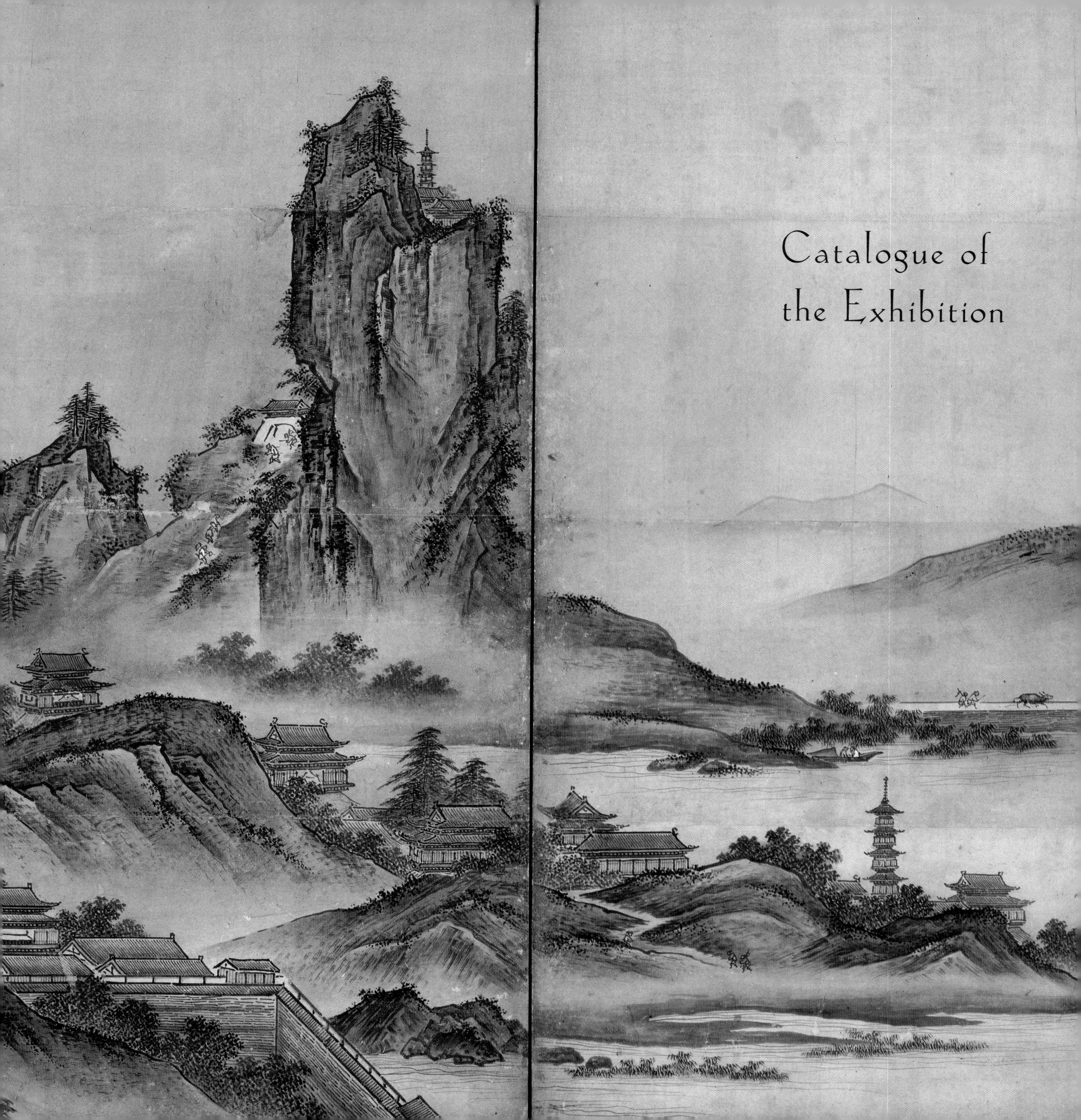

Catalogue of the Exhibition

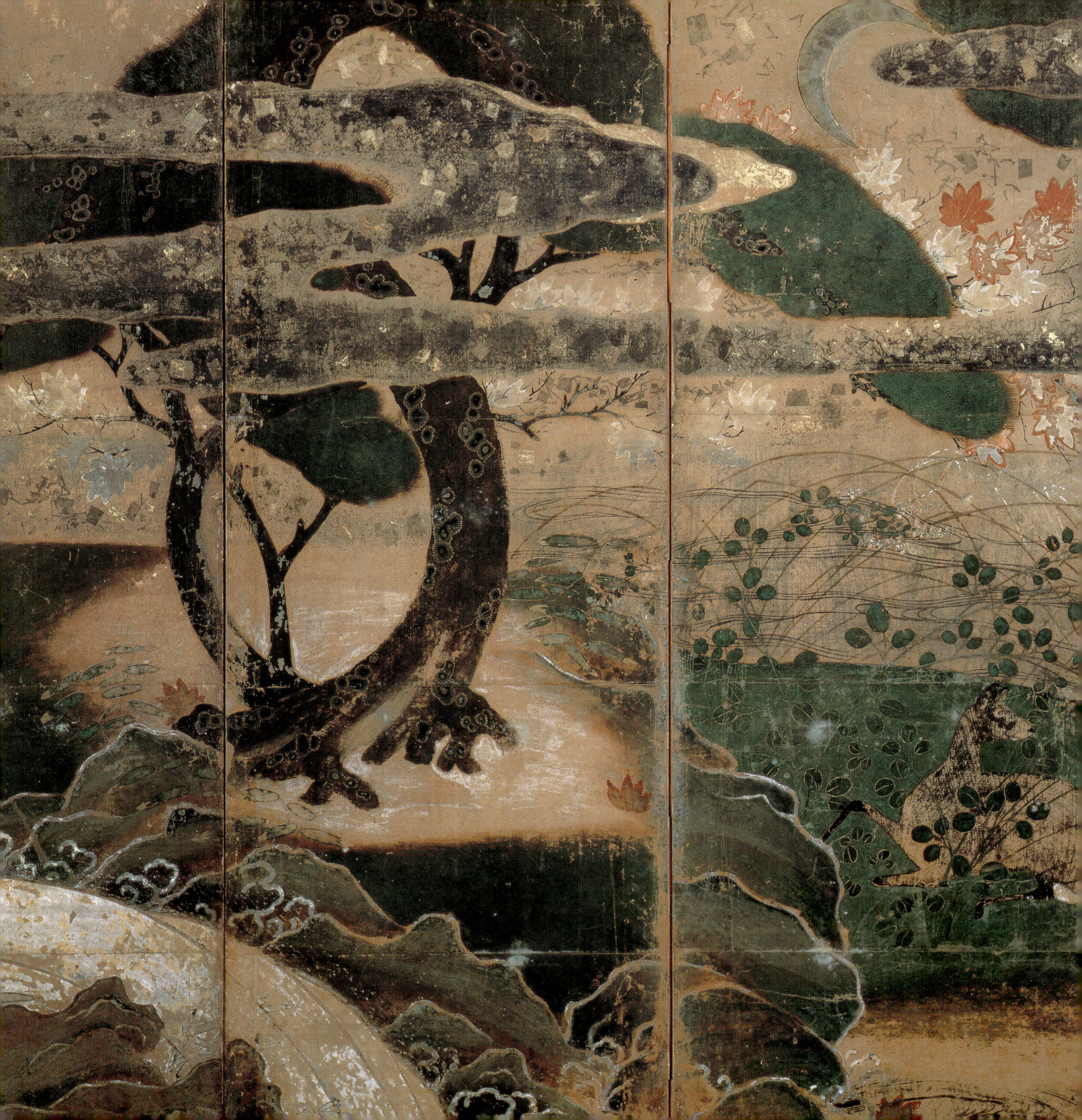

2

Flowers and Birds of the Four Seasons with the Sun and the Moon

Muromachi period, 15th century
Pair of six-panel screens
Color on paper
Each, 61 x 127½ in.
(154.8 x 323.6 cm)
9206

IN THE RIGHT SCREEN a pheasant watches protectively over his hen and chicks under a spreading willow and a blossoming cherry tree. The breeze scatters the white cherry petals, creating delicate patterns on the ground. The setting in the left screen is at water's edge, where an antlered deer calls out as his doe rests in the thicket of bush clover under a pine tree and a scarlet maple. White chrysanthemums in full bloom grow beside a rushing stream. The subject of this pair of screens was especially common in indigenous, Yamato-e painting from the Heian period (794–1185) onwards. The delicate brocadelike willow leaves and pearly cherry blossoms convey the passage of time from spring to early summer; the maple leaves, bush clover, chrysanthemums, and pampas grass are the flora of autumn and early winter.

Screens like these having a metallic disc and metallic crescent set into the paper surface exemplify a type of Yamato-e painting referred to as Sun and Moon Screens. The Idemitsu Museum's screens are extremely rare because few remaining Sun and Moon Screens include the progression of the seasons. The two screens are effectively connected by abstract bands of silver mist (now blackened by oxidation). The appearance of the sun and moon adds a day-to-night progression to the seasonal progression in this dreamlike world.

The use of pieces of metal for the sun and moon, cut and torn strips of gold and silver, and gold and silver dust, as well as the gradation of silver in the mist, are all techniques that appear in decorative papers. The white outlines and contours of the rocks and ground, painted in *gofun* (a white gessolike pigment made from crushed shells), and the fingerlike splashes of water from the stream also appear frequently in lacquerware. The art and technique of the paper or lacquer craftsman, therefore, probably played an important role in the production of these screens.

From the standpoint of subject matter, technique, and style, the screens display qualities unusual among extant Yamato-e screens of the Muromachi period. Assigning a date of production to a painting with so few stylistic counterparts is extremely difficult. Because of the resemblance of the motifs to ones that appear in lacquerware and painting from the late fourteenth century, the present writer concludes that these screens were probably produced in the first half of the fifteenth century.

Opposite: detail from left screen

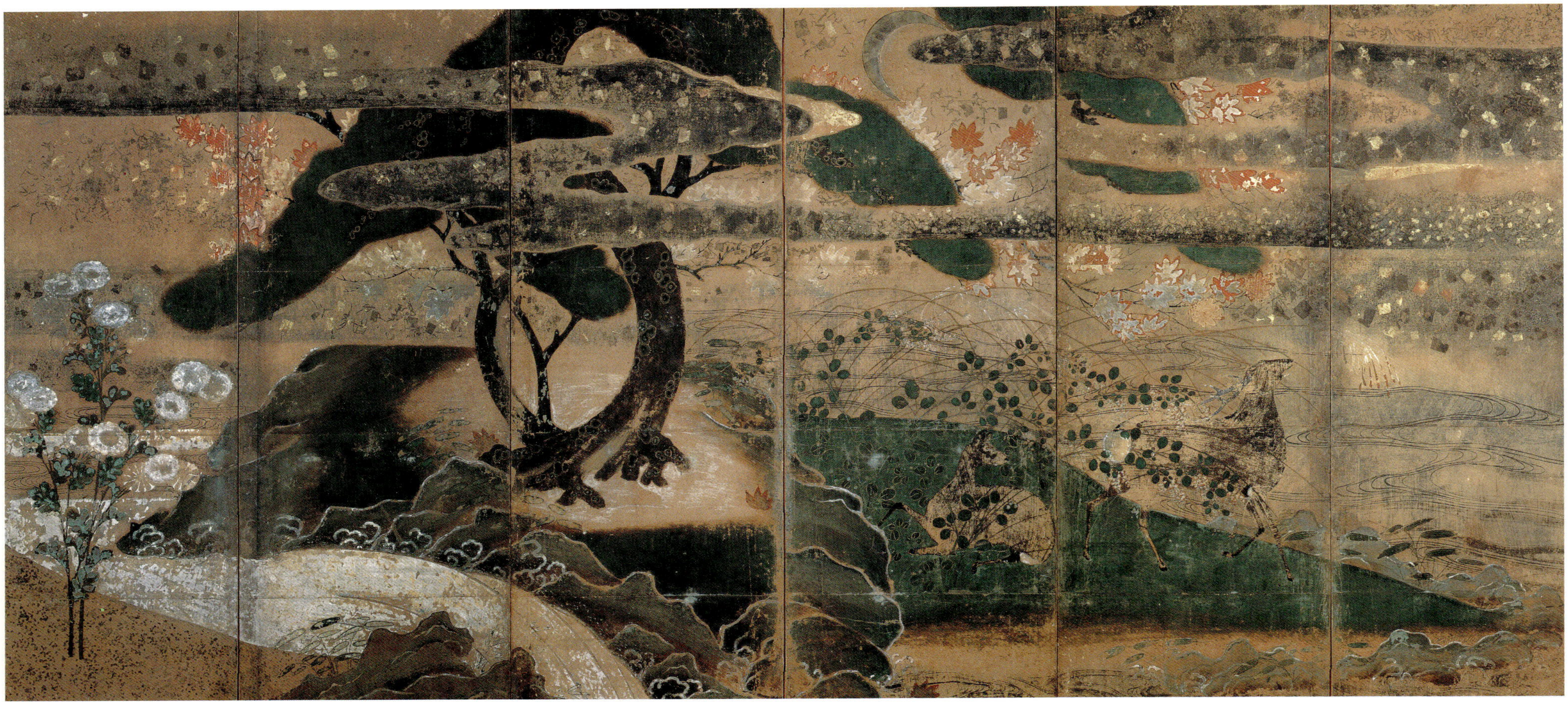

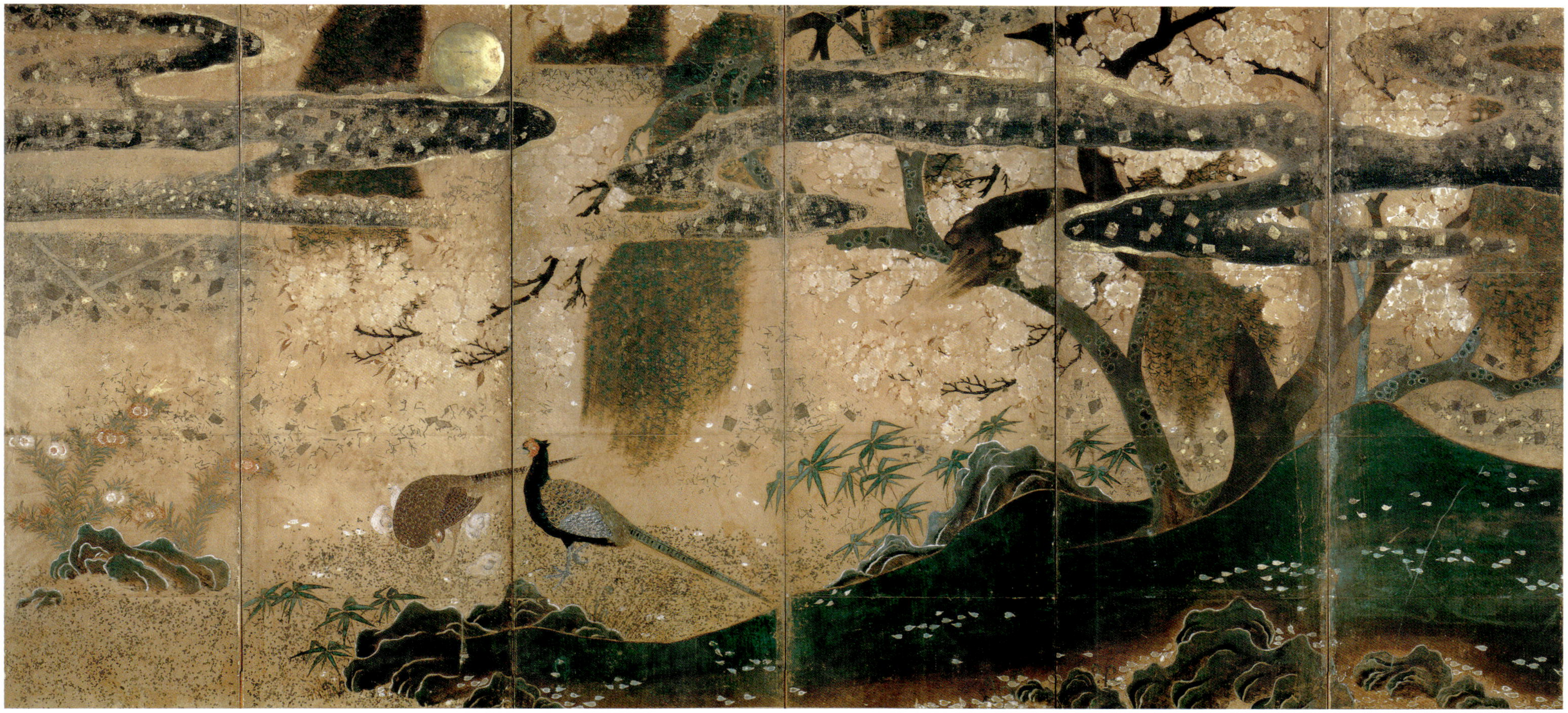

2

Trees and Plants of the Four Seasons

Muromachi period, about 1500
Pair of six-panel screens
Color on paper
Each, 65½ x 128¾ in.
(166.8 x 327.0 cm)
9769
Important Cultural Property

Screens shown in their entirety on pages 14–15.

BLOSSOMING RED PLUM, *kumazasa* bamboo grass, spearflowers, lilies, hydrangeas, bellflowers, patrinia, bush clover, pampas grass, and scarlet maple leaves are presented across the panels of this pair of screens. A small grove of pines graces distant snow-capped mountains in the upper left corner of the left screen. These motifs, arrayed from right to left, correspond to the progression of the seasons from the red plum blossoms of spring to autumn foliage and the snowy mountains of winter.

A shimmering layer of mica covers the surface of the picture. Over it are scattered fine particles of silver, which have blackened from oxidation. The seasonal floral motifs are set within this richly decorative surface. When the work was new, before the silver oxidized, the combined silver and mica must have glittered like mist rising in sunlight.

The unusual split shape of the roots of the pine tree and the technique used in applying the silver-and-mica mist are closely related to the screen painting *Pine Trees on a Shore*, fifteenth century, in the Tokyo National Museum. The appearance of indigo in the mist especially resembles the mist with indigo in the Pine Trees on a Shore scene in the fourteenth century illustrated narrative handscroll *Miraculous Legends of Ishiyama Temple* (Ishiyamadera, Ōtsu, Shiga Prefecture). Similar examples of such use of indigo can be seen in screen paintings depicted in the narrative handscrolls *Miraculous Legends of Matsugasaki Tenjin Shrine*, 1311 (Hōfu Tenmangu Shrine, Yamaguchi), and *Boki ekotoba*, a biography of the priest Kakunyo, 1351 (Nishihonganji, Kyoto).

Inscriptions by the painter Kano Tan'yu (1602–1674) on both of the Idemitsu Museum's screens read "the brush of Tosa Mitsunobu" and were written to authenticate the painting as the work of this late Muromachi period master of Yamato-e painting. Although a thorough analysis of the painting in relation to a specific artist will have to be completed in the future, it is reasonable to identify *Trees and Plants of the Four Seasons* as the work of an artist in the Tosa school of about the year 1500.

Opposite: detail from left screen

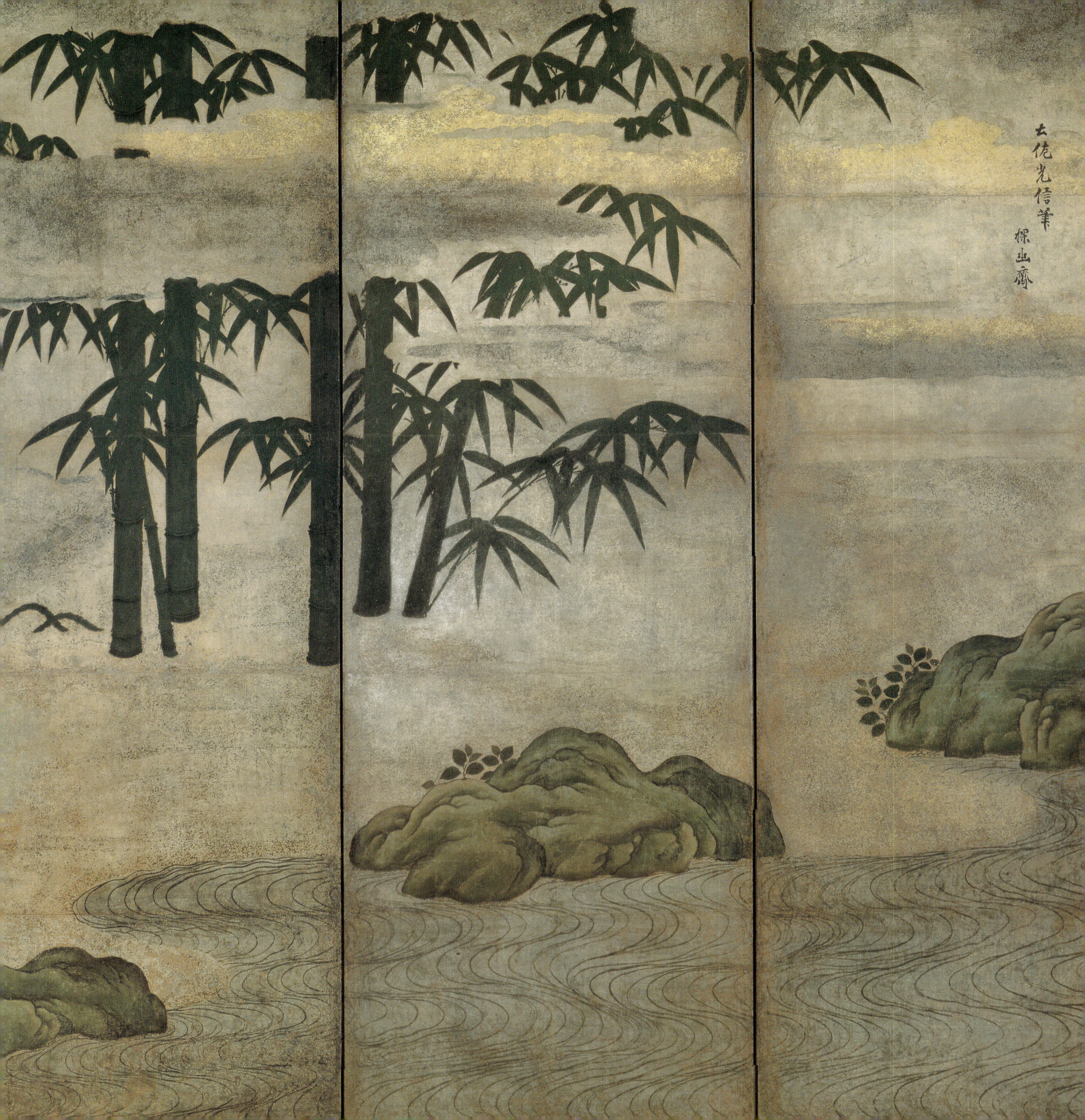
土佐光信筆
探幽齋

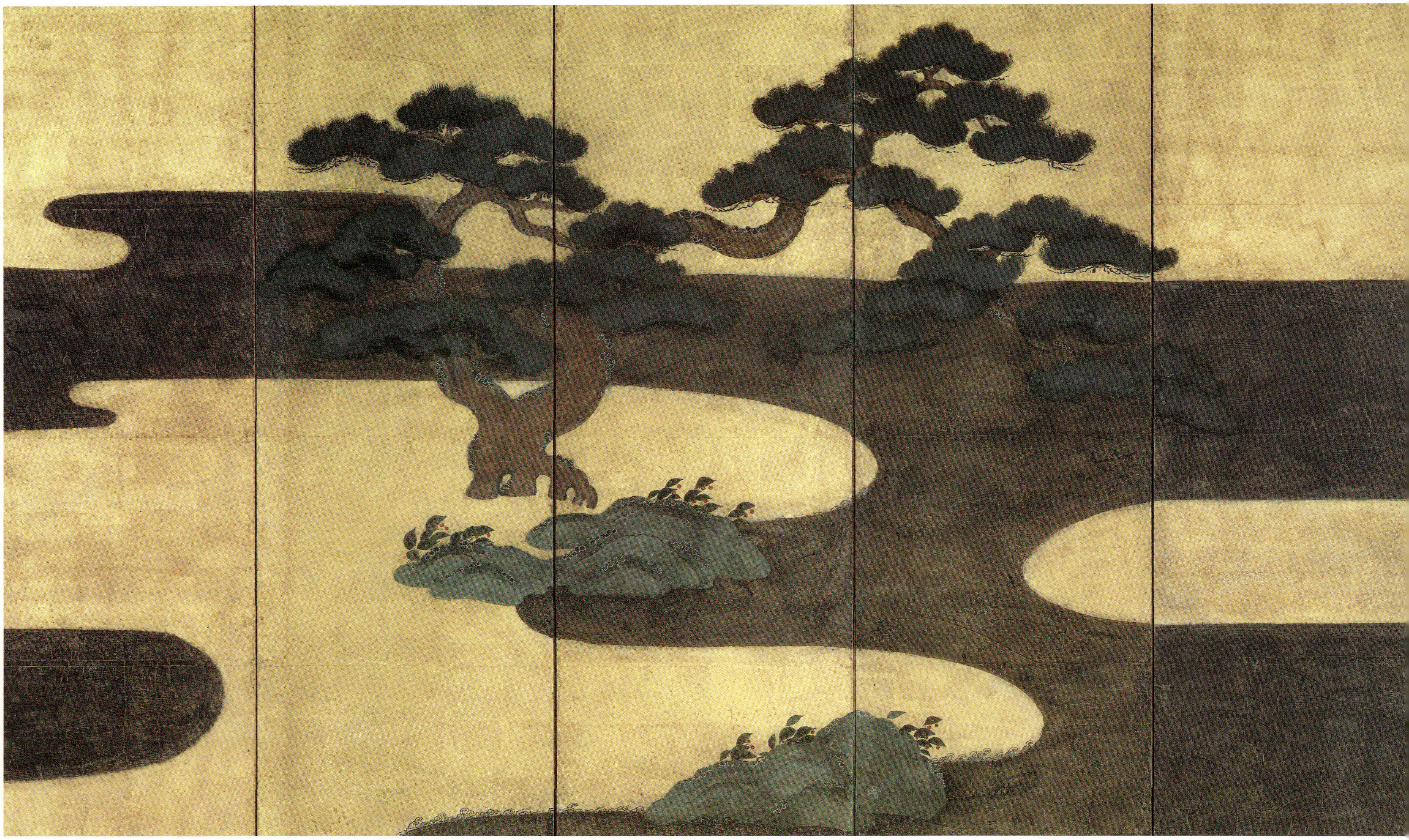

3

Pine Tree

Muromachi period, early 16th century
Six-panel screen
Color and gold leaf on paper
56½ x 109½ in.
(143.8 x 278.4 cm)
10765

A SINGLE GREAT PINE TREE with gracefully spreading limbs stands on an abstract bank of gold. Rounded stones with blooming spearflowers are placed as if to suggest spatial recession. Gentle ripples in fine lines of silver ink lap the rocks and the golden shore. The form of the pine tree and the composition of the banks, rocks, and water are characteristic of traditional Yamato-e style. The stone at the right edge, which is inclined too far to the right, and the weighting of the overall composition to the left give a slightly diffuse impression. Close inspection of the screen reveals that the gold application and the water in the second panel from the right differ from the rest of the painting; also, to the left of the center of the first panel, there is a damaged portion that matches in shape and position the pine needles in the second panel. Furthermore, traces of metal fittings suggest that the painting was originally on a set of sliding panels (*fusuma*), the second panel having been added when it was remounted as a single folding screen. Restored to its original state without the second panel, the painting would have a much more stable composition, balanced around the central pine tree.

This screen is undoubtedly a work of the late Muromachi period. Determination of its exact stylistic relationship to contemporary works, such as the Idemitsu Museum's *Trees and Plants of the Four Seasons* (cat. no. 2), the screen *Pine Trees* in the Tokyo National Museum, and representations of mural paintings in narrative handscrolls such as the *Pictures of Longing for Extinction (Boki-e)*, repaired in 1482 (Nishihonganji, Kyoto), will have to await further research.

The inscription at the upper right corner of the screen reads "certified by Tosa Mitsunari to be a work of the brush of Sakonoe Shōkan Fujiwara Ason Mitsunobu." In other words, the Edo period painter Tosa Mitsunari (1646–1710) gives his guarantee that it is the work of the late Muromachi period painter Tosa Mitsunobu (1434–1525). As in many paintings later assigned to Mitsunobu, however, there is no firm stylistic or documentary evidence to support the attribution. The painting can nevertheless be recognized as the work of a Tosa school artist active in the early sixteenth century.

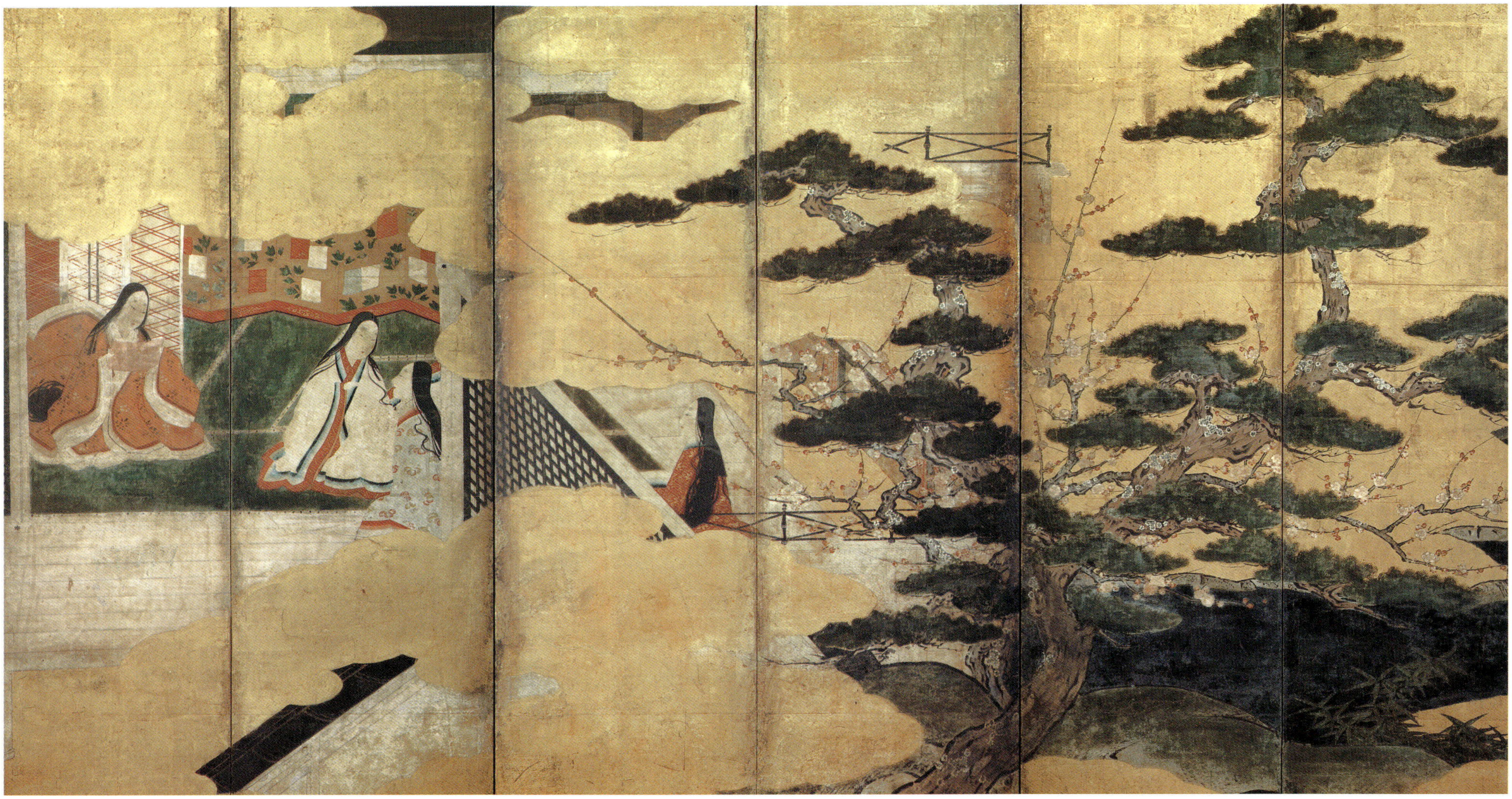

4

Scenes from the Tale of Genji

Muromachi period, first half of 16th century
Pair of six-panel screens
Color and gold leaf on paper
Each, 62¼ x 110¼ in.
(158.2 x 279.8 cm)
9404

JAPAN'S GREATEST LITERARY CLASSIC, the *Tale of Genji*, was written by Murasaki Shikibu, a court lady, during the Heian period, about the year 1000. This long, psychologically probing novel recounts the life and romances of Hikaru Genji and his descendants. The earliest extant handscroll illustrations of the *Tale of Genji* date from the twelfth century, and it subsequently became a staple of Yamato-e; many paintings of the theme were produced in various formats, from handscrolls to folding screens.

Centered on a grove of pine, plum, and bamboo—the Three Friends of Winter—at water's edge, the left and right screens of this pair combine to create one large scene. The right shows an autumn scene from the "At Writing Practice" chapter of the *Tale of Genji*; the left probably shows a spring scene from the "Fern Shoots" chapter. They belong to the "Uji Chapters," the final ten chapters of the *Tale*, which recount events after Genji's death.

In the "At Writing Practice" scene, the young captain (*chūjō*) looks longingly toward Ukifune, who has taken Buddhist vows and retired to a life of contemplation. Although she appears in full view seated at a desk for practicing calligraphy, Ukifune is hidden from the captain's gaze by a lattice-and-bamboo screen. In keeping with the rules for becoming a nun, her hair is cropped to shoulder length, while her attendants' tresses still spill down their backs.

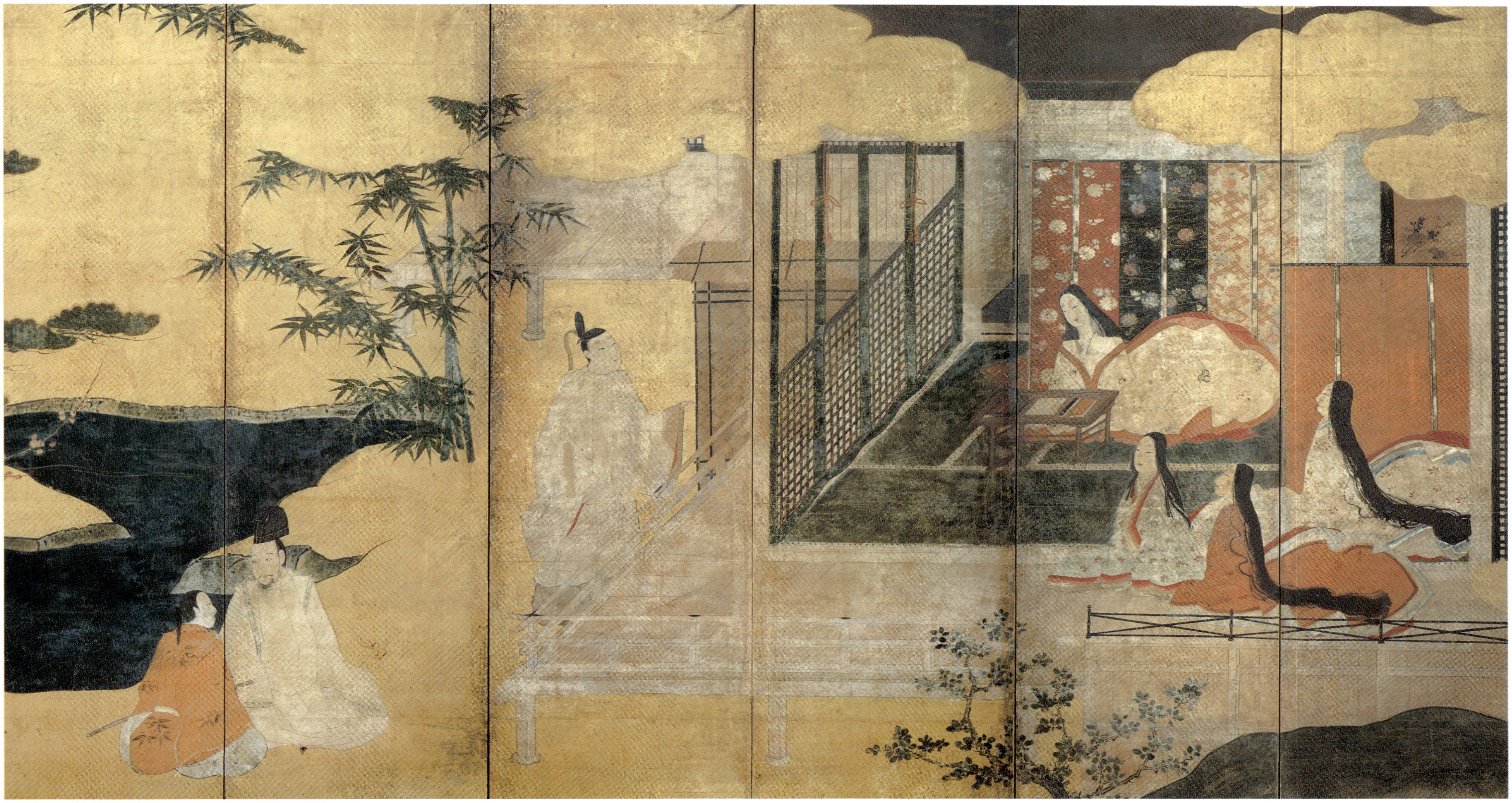

The scene in the left screen is difficult to identify but probably represents a scene from the chapter "Fern Shoots." The principal figure, seated reading at the left, is most likely Nakanokimi, who receives a basket of fern shoots (barely visible on the veranda owing to damage to the painting) from a monk from a nearby monastery. The red plum in the painting figures as an iconographic element of that chapter.

From the style of brushwork in the trees and rocks and the easy, relaxed air of the figures, it is clear that the artist was a master of Chinese-style ink painting, possibly a member of the Kano atelier active in the late Muromachi period. A pair of Muromachi period screens with scenes from the *Tale of Genji* attributed to Kano Eitoku (1543–1590) are in the Imperial Collection, but the Idemitsu Museum's screens probably predate them.

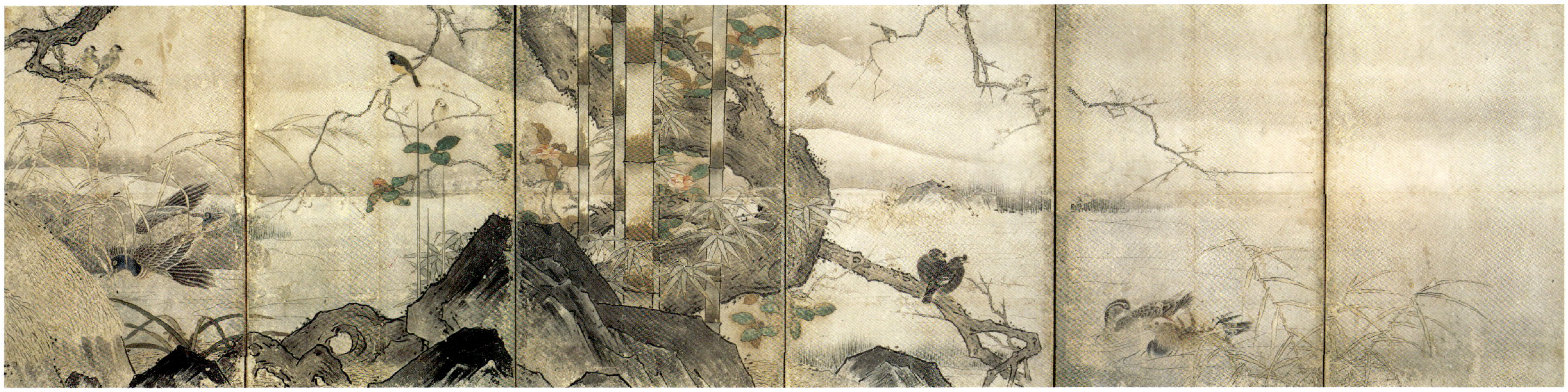

5

ATTRIBUTED TO SESSHŪ TŌYŌ
(1420–1506)

Flowers and Birds of the Four Seasons

Muromachi period, 16th century
Pair of six-panel screens
Ink and color on paper
Each, 42½ x 150 in.
(108.0 x 381.0 cm)
1602

SESSHŪ TŌYŌ, the greatest master of ink painting in Japan, left many works of ink monochrome landscape painting, but also associated with Sesshū's name are a number of paintings of Flowers and Birds of the Four Seasons in ink and polychrome. These works are thought to be the result of his study of flower and bird painting during his sojourn in Ming China from 1467 to 1469. A tradition of flower and bird painting in the polychrome Yamato-e mode had existed in Japan for centuries, but Sesshū was among the first to adopt the Chinese style, which combined strongly modulated ink lines with lively mineral pigments. His models were most likely flower and bird paintings in the hanging scroll format by artists of the Chinese Imperial Painting Academy, such as Lüji (active late fifteenth century).

Motifs of the four seasons are represented in rich colors across the pair of screens. The banks and hills in the middle distance and background appear in light ink, which creates the illusion of recession in space. Within this landscape setting are represented peonies, bamboo, pine, lotus blossoms, plum, camellias, and reeds. A kingfisher in flight eyes the surface of the water, as if looking for food, and pairs of Mandarin ducks, *pa-pa* birds (relatives of the mynah), sparrows, and finches enliven the scene. The minute brushwork that describes the delicately rendered birds and blossoms contrasts with the heavier lines used in the rocks and trees. Sesshū's adaptation of the hanging scroll format to the expansive pictorial space of the folding screen is clearly evident in the exaggerated manner in which the branches of the pine and plum trees stretch across the panels.

Although this work lacks both signature and seals, the style of the brushwork and the coloration closely resemble other screen paintings of flowers and birds associated with Sesshū, such as the pairs in the Kosaka collection, the Maeda Ikutokukai, and the Freer Gallery of Art, Smithsonian Institution, Washington, D.C.

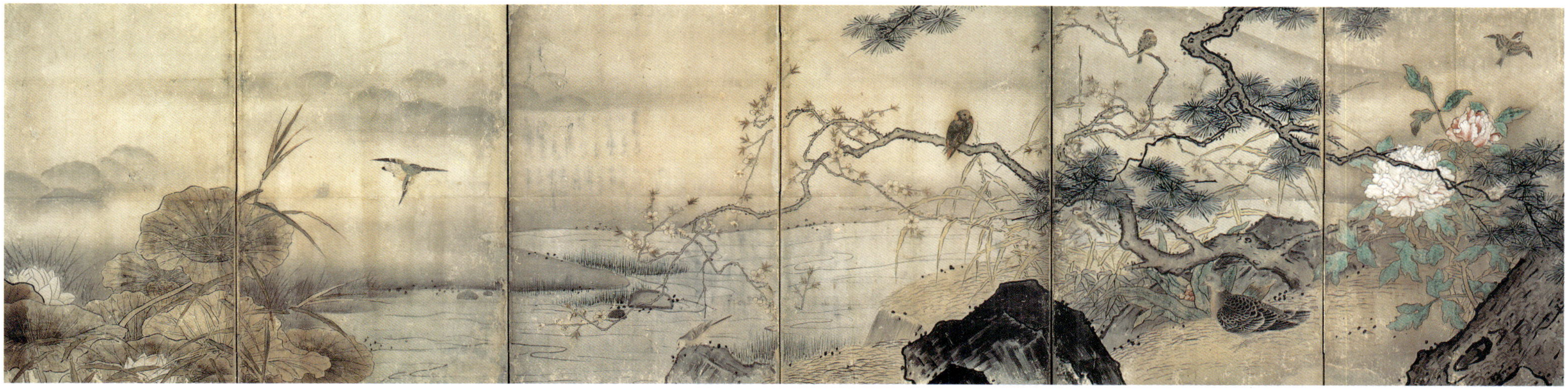

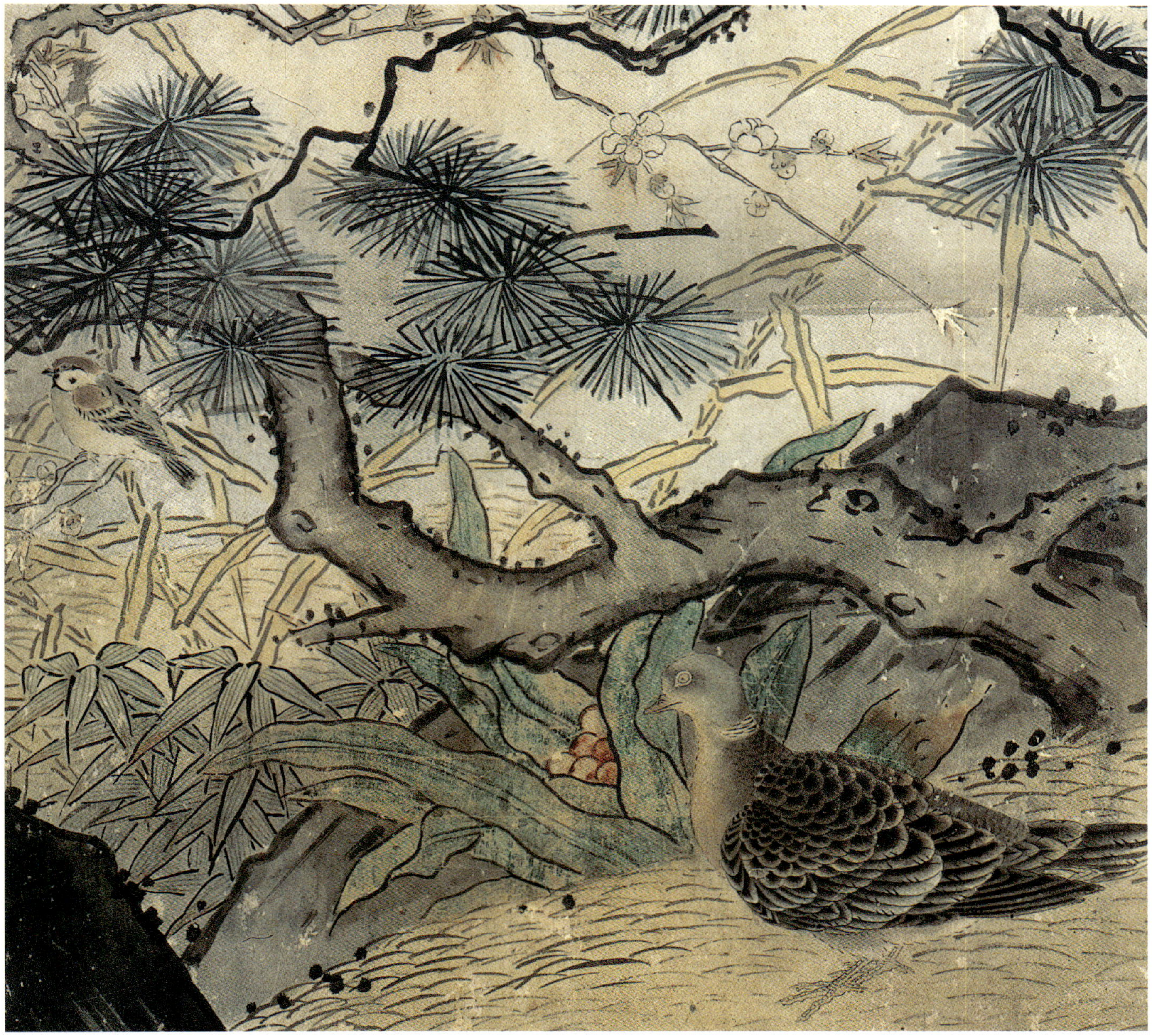

Detail from right screen.

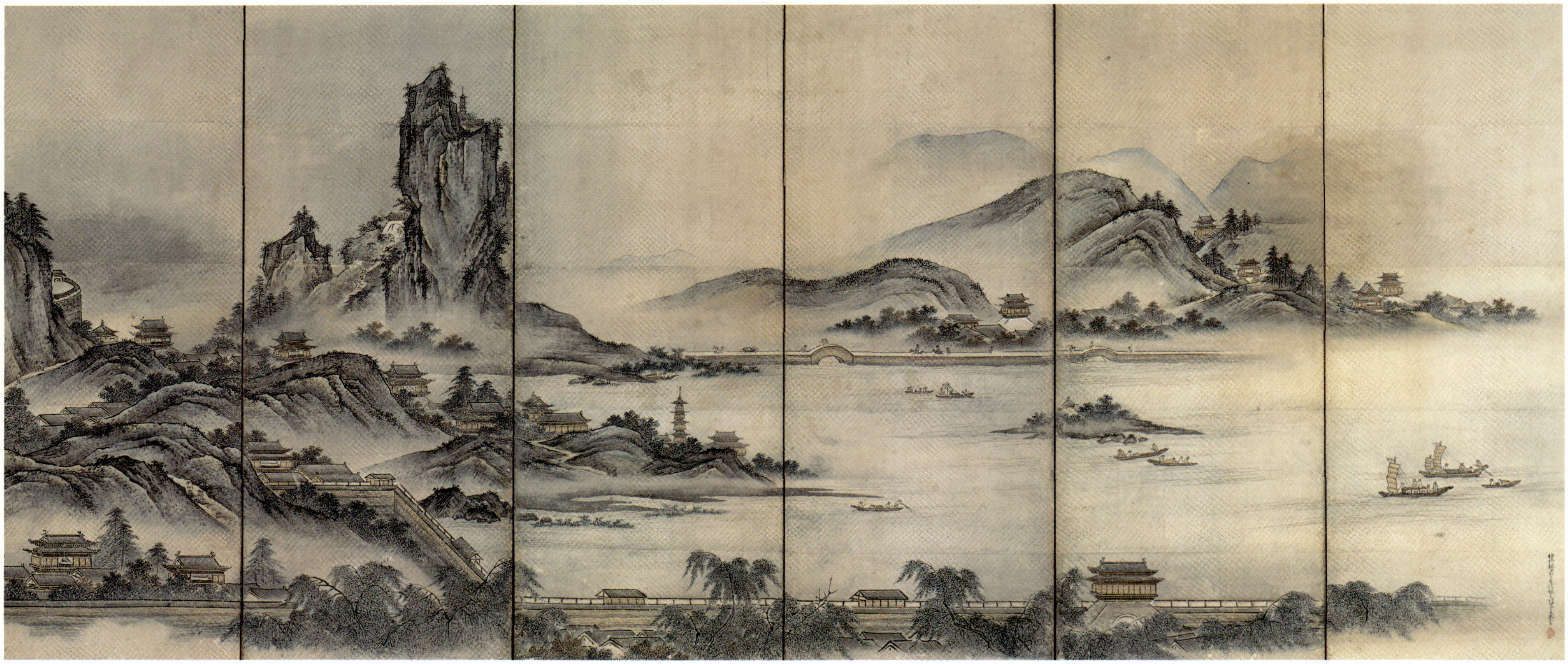

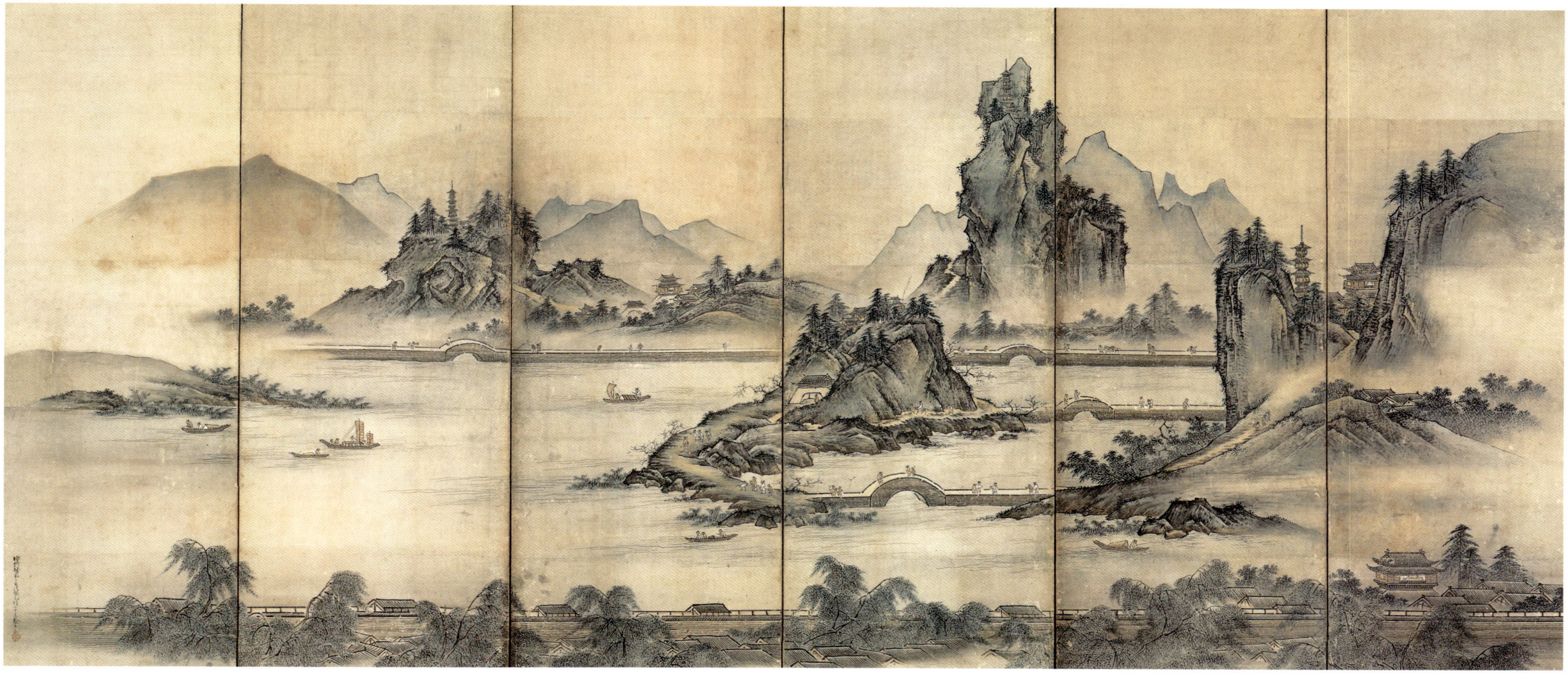

6

KANO MOTONOBU (1476–1559)

West Lake

Muromachi period, dated to 1550
Pair of six-panel screens
Ink and light color on paper
Each, 68 x 152¼ in.
(172.8 x 386.8 cm)
10762

THE ENTIRE VIEW of fabled West Lake in Hangzhou, China, unfolds on this pair of screens, which are unified by the long embankments built by the poets Su Dongpo (1036–1101) and Bo Juyi (772–846). In the right screen we can see Mount Gushan, Beigao Peak, and Lingyin Temple; in the left screen, Nangao Peak, Jinci Temple, and the other sites of the Ten Views of West Lake. The buildings, mountains, and rocks are executed with strong black lines, following the *shin*, or "block script," mode of landscape painting perfected by the Chinese painters of the Southern Song academy Ma Yuan (active about 1190–1225) and Xia Gui (active about 1180–1224).

The inscriptions at the lower left corner of the right screen and the lower right corner of the left screen read "painted by the former servant of Echizen, Kano Hōgen Motonobu, age 75." Under each inscription is a red urn-shaped seal that reads "Motonobu." According to Nobuo Tsuji's research, the rank of *hōgen*, "Eye of the Dharma"—an honorary Buddhist rank conferred upon accomplished painters and other artists and artisans—was awarded to Kano Motonobu when he was about seventy years old by the lord of Echizen Province. The inscription indicates Motonobu's having served the lord of Echizen before attaining the rank of hōgen. The style of the painting and signature and the shape of the seal strongly suggest that the work comes from the hand of Motonobu himself. The self-assured, logical composition of the painting is representative of his late work.

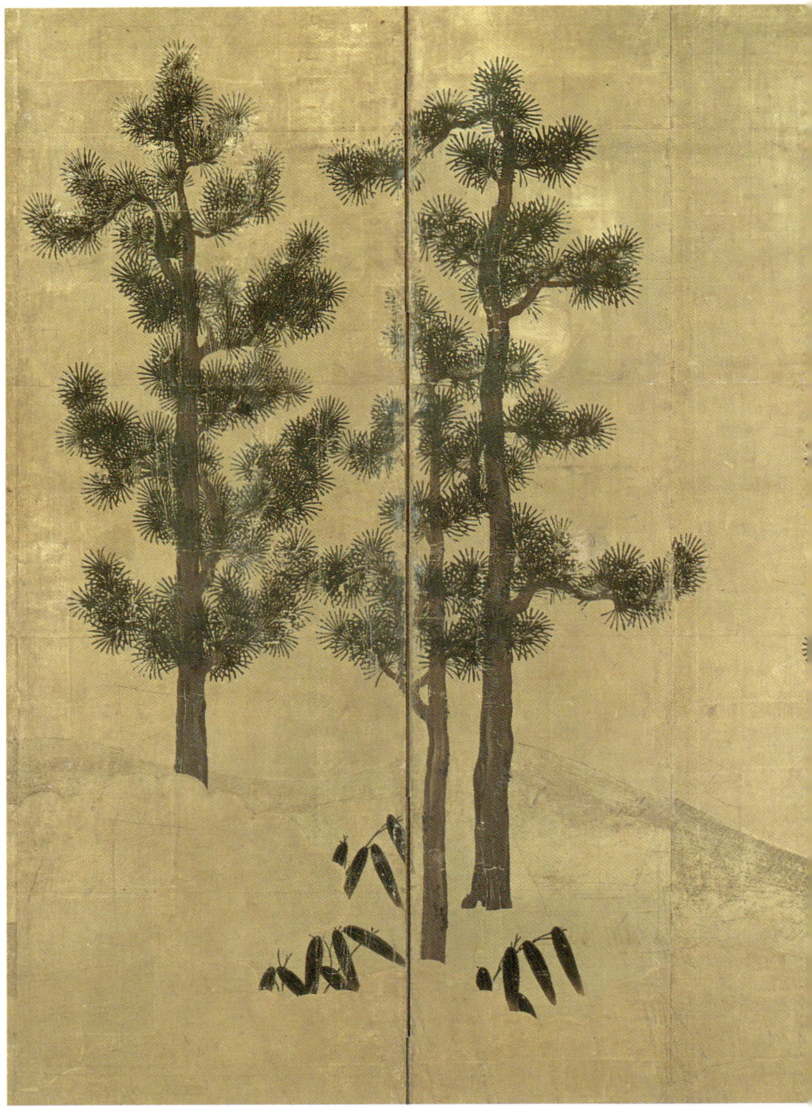

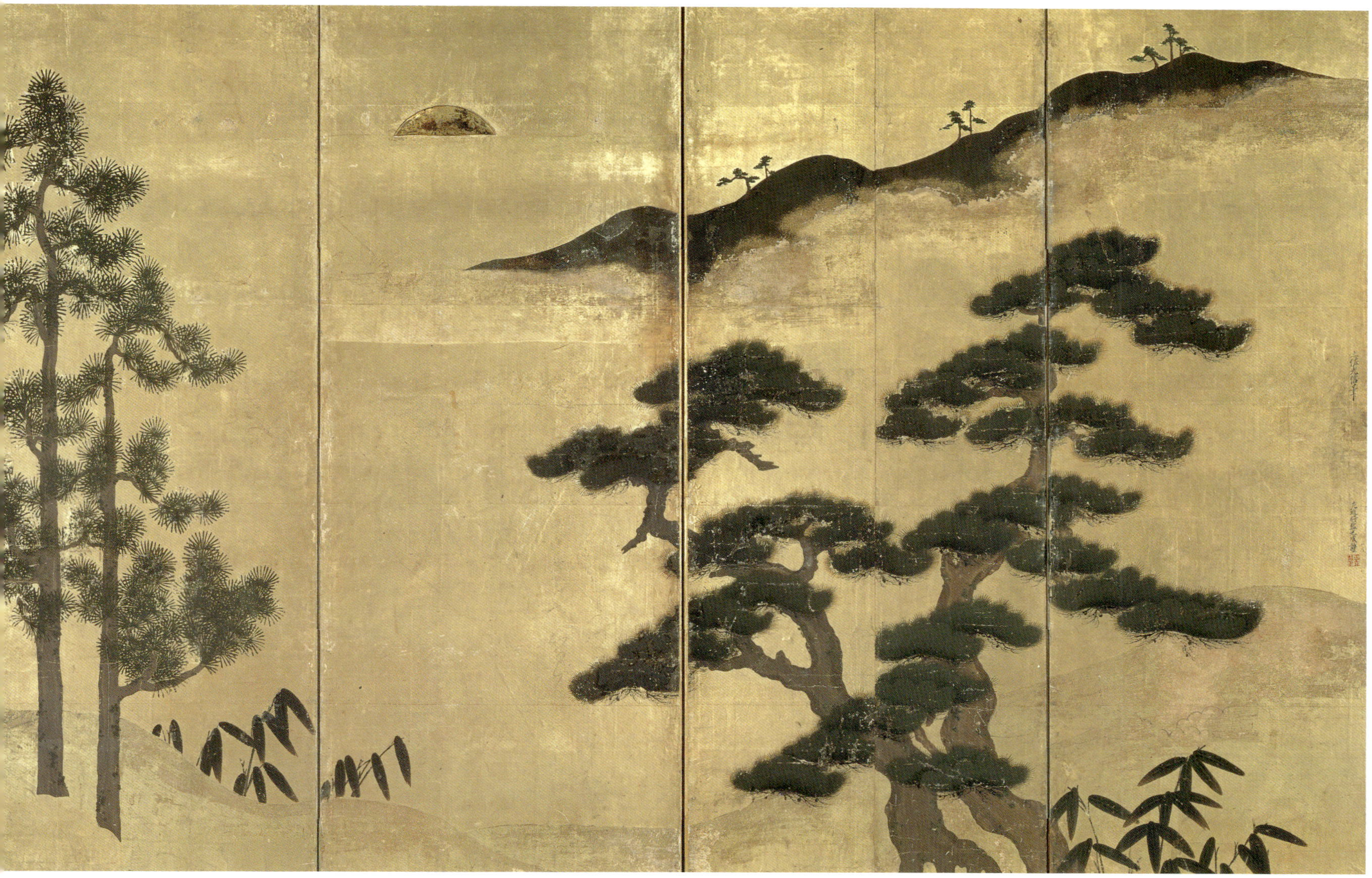

7

Pine Trees and Chinese Black Pines

Muromachi to Momoyama period,
possibly mid-16th century
Six-panel screen
Color and gold leaf on paper
65 x 144¾ in.
(164.9 x 367.6 cm)
10764

TWISTING PINE TREES (J. *matsu*) contrast with straight-trunked Chinese black pines (J. *maki*) in a magical setting of gold-leafed ground and clouds. A semicircular metallic plate has been fitted into the surface of the painting to represent the sun setting beyond the distant mountain ridge. Perhaps this painting was originally paired with another that included the moon, as in *Flowers and Birds of the Four Seasons with the Sun and the Moon* (cat. no. 1). The pine trees with their gently curved trunks, clawlike roots, and delicate twigs and needles resemble in general style the pines in other Muromachi period screen paintings in the present exhibition (particularly cat. nos. 2 and 3). Other features of the work, namely the flat, scallop-edged gold clouds and the grouping of the trees in the front plane of the painting, seem more characteristic of paintings of the late sixteenth and early seventeenth centuries. The condensed delicacy discernible in *Trees and Plants of the Four Seasons* (cat. no. 2) appears to have given way in the present screen to a more expansive, dynamic aesthetic.

The inscription at the right edge by Tosa Mitsunari (1646–1710) attributes the painting to Tosa Mitsunobu (1434–1525), but it was probably painted by an artist of a later generation.

8

Uji River

Muromachi to Momoyama period,
possibly mid-16th century
Pair of six-panel screens
Color and gold leaf on paper
Each, 64½ x 130 in.
(164.0 x 330.0 cm)
2726

Screens shown in their entirety on pages 32–33.

THE GREAT BRIDGE over the Uji River south of Kyoto spans the entire right half of this pair of screens. Below it small boats loaded with brushwood float downstream amid the swirling current. A waterwheel irrigates the field in the foreground of the right screen. In both screens gold clouds part to reveal hills on the opposite bank. Five willow trees are depicted, from right to left, with the delicate young leaves of spring, with full summer foliage, and leafless, covered with winter snow. This seasonal sequence is further articulated in the rice fields flooded in summer, ready for the autumn harvest, and barren in winter.

The decorative nature of this painting results from the flat, patterned willow trees, from the generous coloration of the waterfowl, and especially from the high degree of craftsmanship evident in the painted surface—in the use of gold, for example. Instead of an even layer of gold leaf, irregularly shaped pieces have been arranged within the clouds' scalloped contours, and fine particles of gold *sunago* (literally, "sand") have been added to heighten the glimmering effect. This complex surface treatment and the intricate curves of the swirling rapids are the type of design elements that one would encounter in lacquerware and other decorative arts of the late sixteenth through the early seventeenth century.

There are numerous examples of paintings with similar pictorial motifs, and they are generally recognized as representations of the great bridge at Uji. An early depiction of the bridge appears in the narrative handscroll *Miraculous Legends of Ishiyama Temple* (Ishiyamadera, Shiga Prefecture), and the theme of boats carrying brushwood has its origins in the thirteenth century imperial poetic anthology *Shinkokinshu* and other medieval poetry. Incidentally, in recent years it has been suggested that these screens were produced in the early Edo period (seventeenth century) retaining the style of Muromachi period Yamato-e screen paintings.

Opposite: detail from left screen

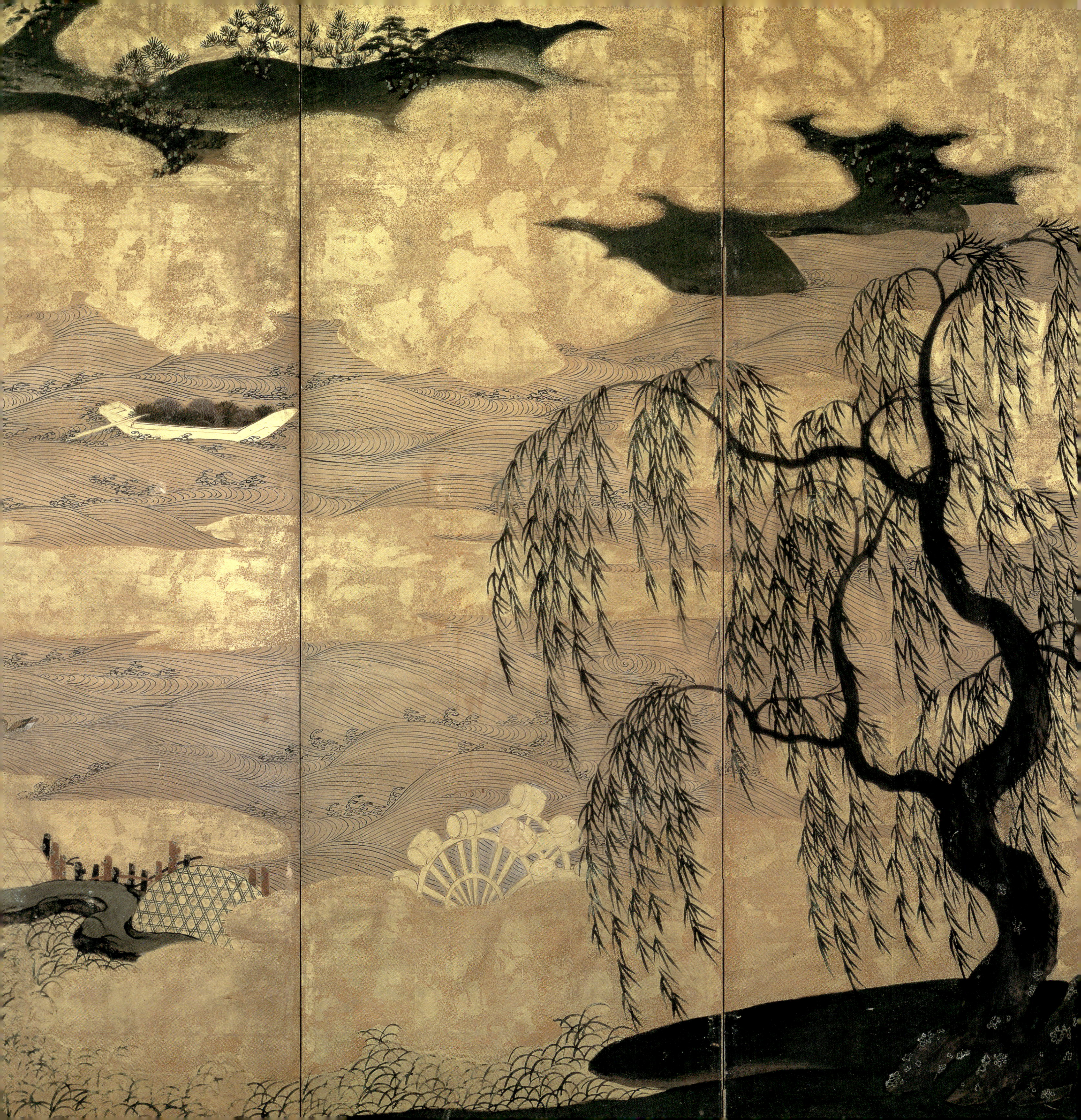

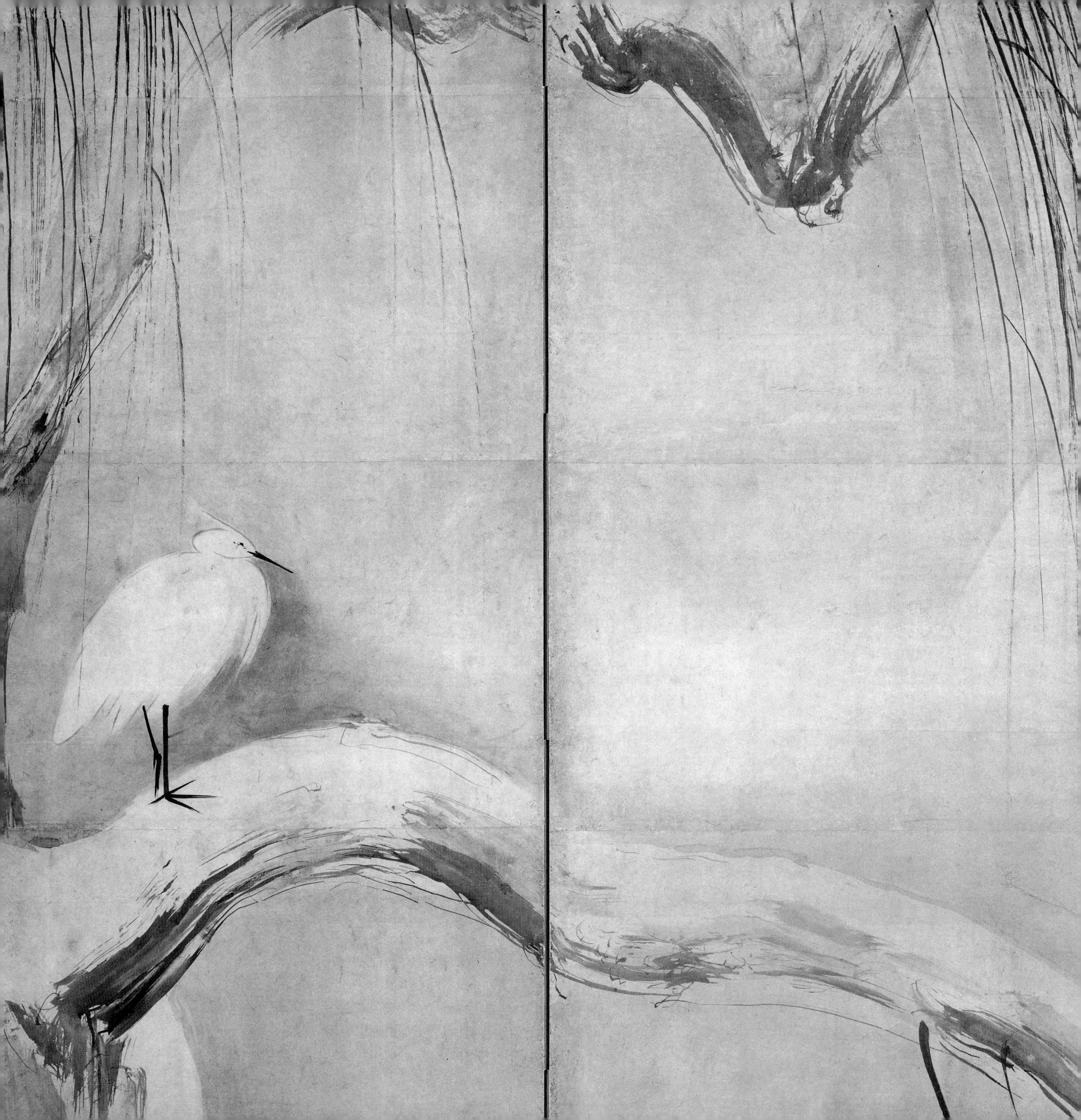

9

HASEGAWA TŌHAKU (1539–1610)

Crows and Pine and Egrets and Willow

Momoyama period, 16th century
Pair of six-panel screens
Ink and light color on paper
Each, 67 x 153 in.
(170.5 x 388.6 cm)
11257

HASEGAWA TŌHAKU was one of the great painters of the Momoyama period (1573–1615). In his formative period he was influenced by the Kano school, which dominated the most important commissions of the day. By about 1590, Tōhaku had established his own distinct style, and he competed with the Kano and other painters, such as Kaihō Yūshō (1553–1615), for the lucrative patronage of the powerful warlords who controlled the capital.

The present work, which was discovered rather recently, is a fine example of the bold, broad-gestured style of such Tōhaku masterpieces as the sliding-panel painting of a giant maple tree in Chishakuin, Kyoto, and the folding screens of pines in mist in the Tokyo National Museum, both from the late sixteenth century. Although the work lacks visible signatures and seals, the stylistic attribution to Tōhaku has been confirmed by infrared photography, which revealed seals reading "Tōhaku" in the lower portion of the outer right and left panels. At one time the screens were attributed to Sesshū, as is evident in scratched-out signatures reading "Sesshū" on the same outer panels.

The brushwork of the Crows and Egrets screens is in the long, flowing manner of the triptych of the bodhisattva Kannon, crane, and monkeys by Muqi (active thirteenth century), a Chinese painter during the Southern Song dynasty. The triptych is kept in the Zen Buddhist monastery Daitokuji in Kyoto, where Tōhaku had opportunities to study it directly. In the present work Tōhaku deftly "performs" the mode of painting associated with Muqi's triptych. The similarity is particularly marked in Tōhaku's execution of the pine tree draped with vines.

Egrets in bare willows in winter often appear in Japanese paintings. However, crows do not seem to have been a popular theme, as these carrion-eating birds were thought to be impure, given their association with death. Chinese paintings frequently show *pa-pa* birds (a type of Chinese bird related to the mynah), which closely resemble crows. In the Idemitsu Museum's screens, Tōhaku has painted crows, which, unlike pa-pa birds, he could observe directly in Japan. He completes his iconoclastic gesture by depicting a family of crows, conveying a message of familial love rather than impurity. The egrets, which mate for life, are appropriately represented as a pair.

A single dandelion under the crows' nest and the bare snow-covered branches of the willow indicate a shift in season from summer to winter. There is the suggestion also of a contrast in sound—from the noisy cawing of the crow family to the silent flight of the egret in a muted snowscape.

Opposite: detail from left screen

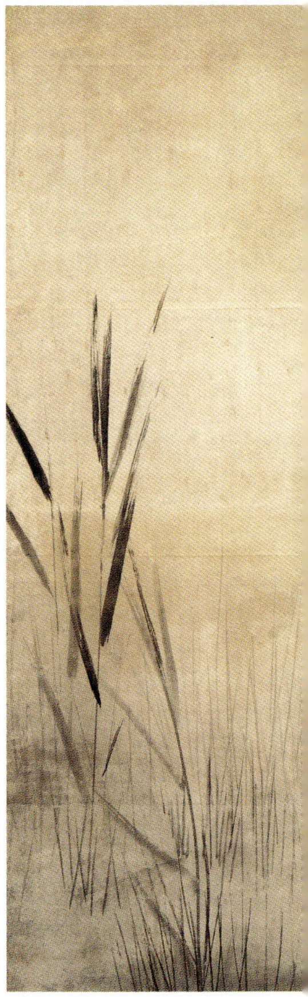

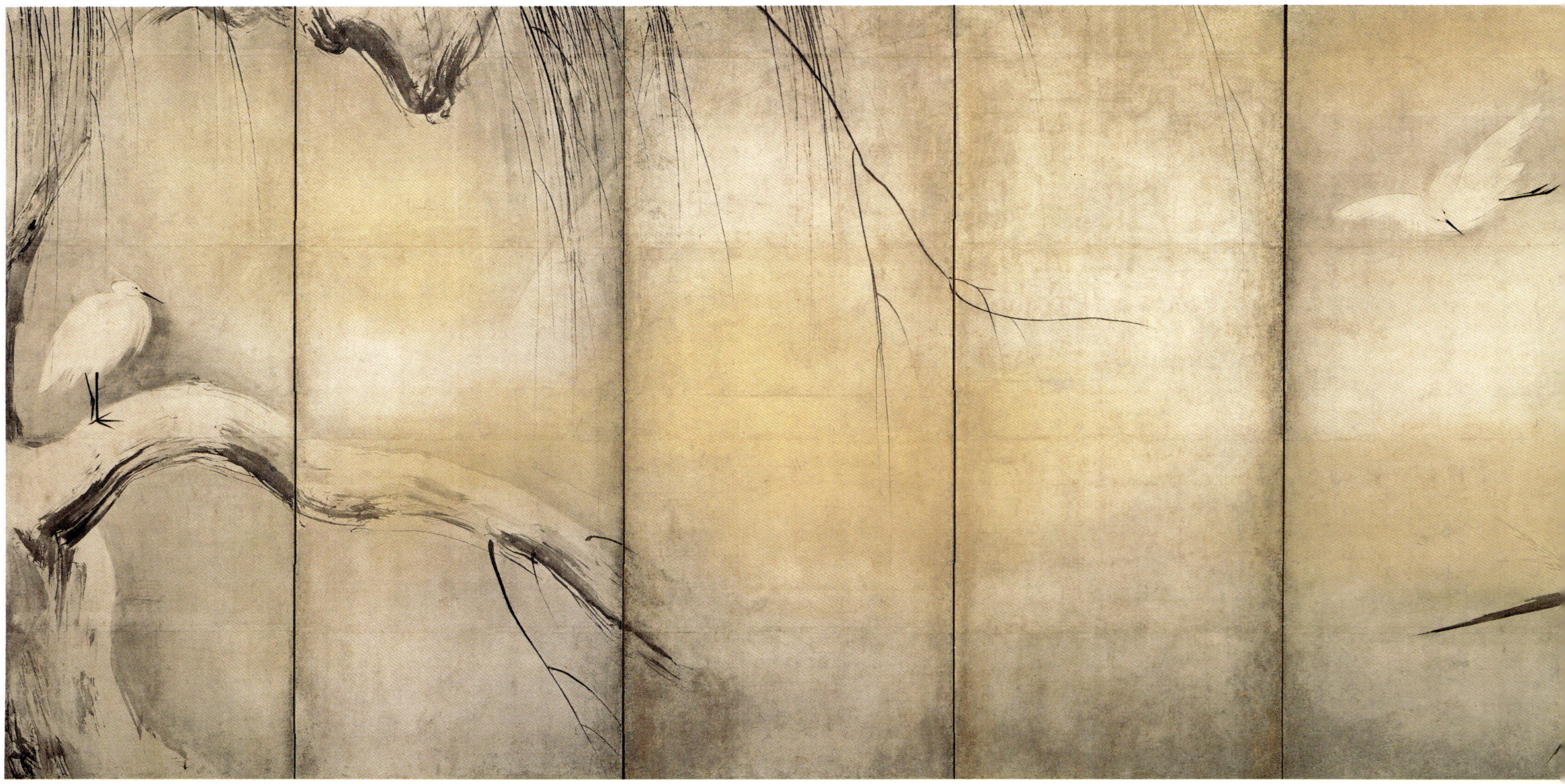

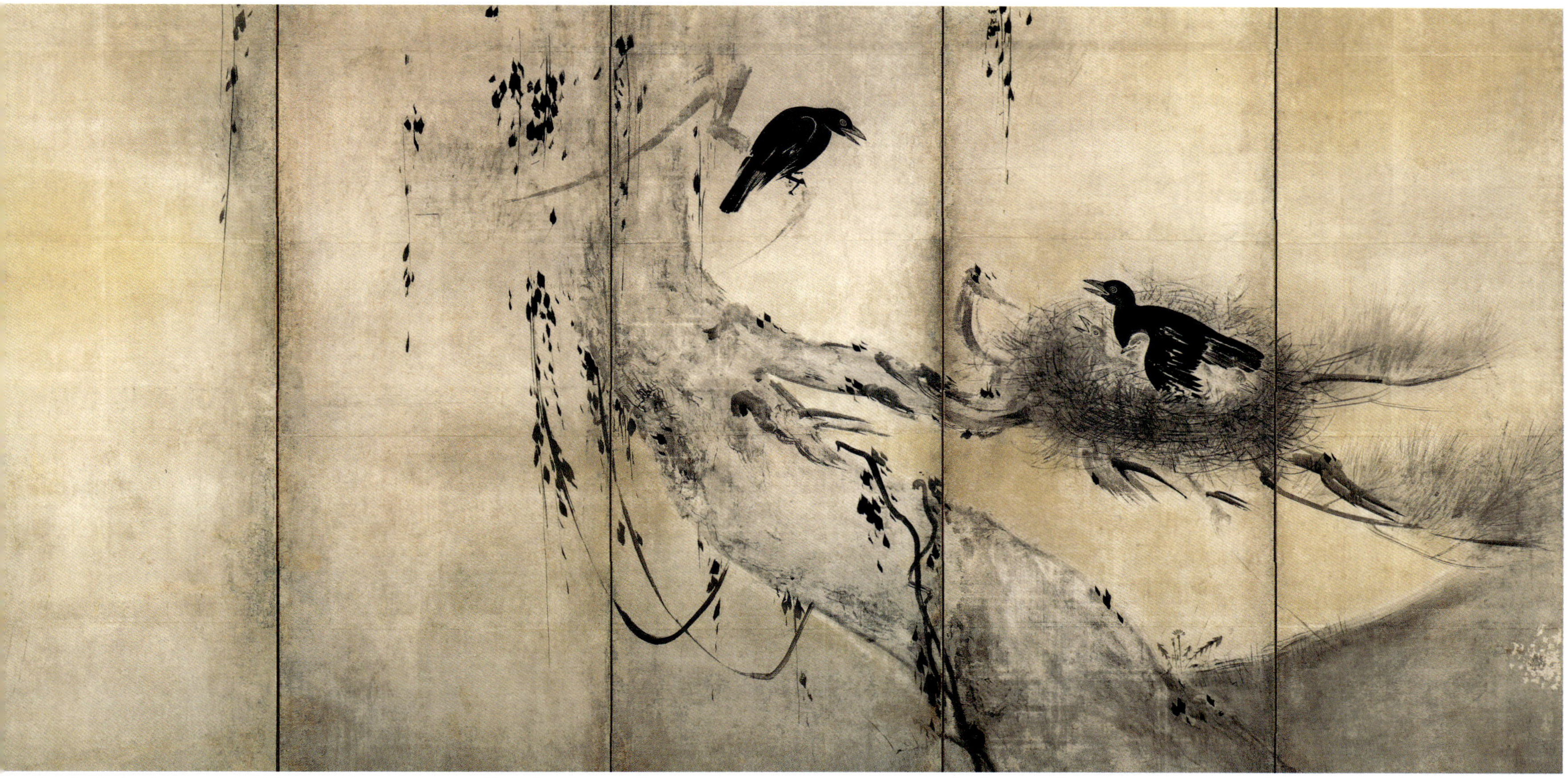

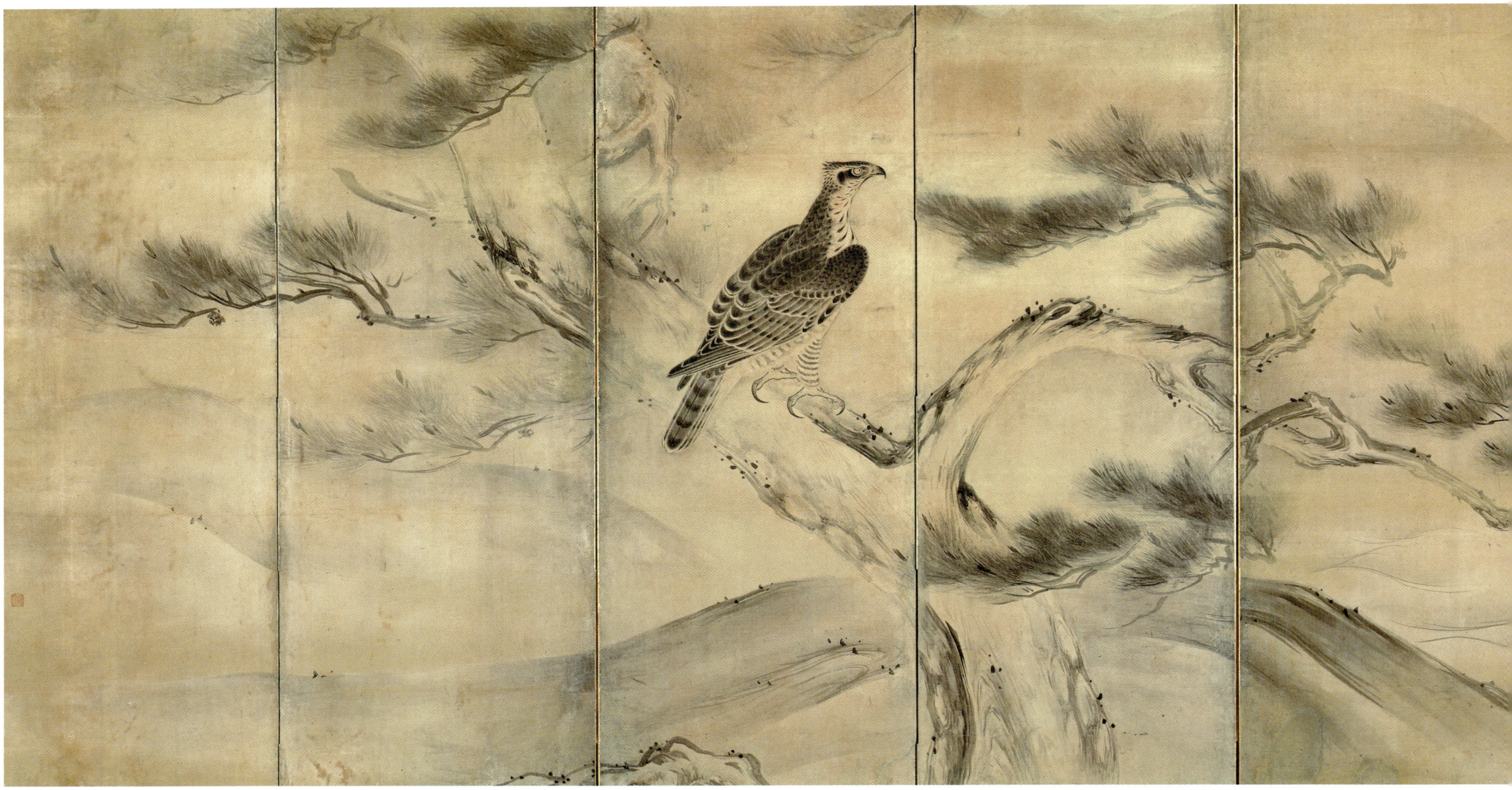

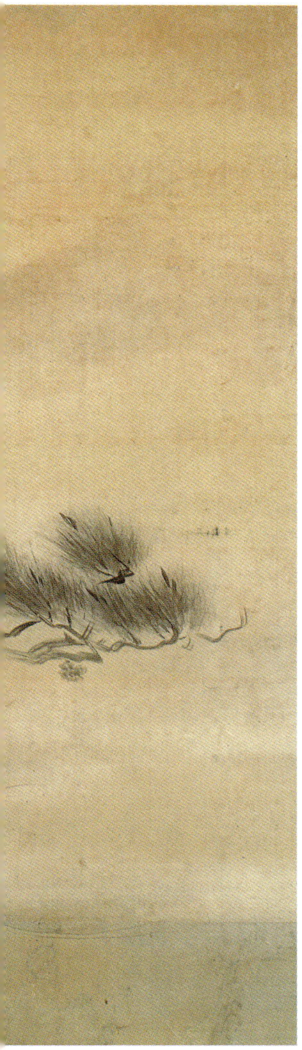

20

SOGA CHOKUAN (ACTIVE 1596–1610)

Hawk and Pine Tree

Momoyama period, late 16th century
Six-panel screen
Ink and gold paint on paper
69¼ x 151¼ in.
(176.1 x 384.4 cm)
10825

THE PAINTER SOGA CHOKUAN was active in the late Momoyama period, at the beginning of the seventeenth century. Although little is known about his life, many of his paintings remain. The majority depict hawks and falcons in monochrome ink. Apparently, Chokuan lived in Sakai, south of modern Osaka, and several works by him and his son Nichokuan (active first half of seventeenth century) have been handed down in temples at Mount Kōya and the region south of Nara. A Soga school lineage constructed by Nichokuan claims that he and his father were descended from Soga painters such as Jasoku (active late fifteenth century) and Sōjō (dates unknown) at Daitokuji in Kyoto, but concrete evidence to confirm this claim awaits discovery.

This single screen was probably originally one of a pair. Chokuan presents a hawk perched in a wind-blown pine tree that, reaching across all six panels, fills up the entire pictorial space. Following the Momoyama preference for bold, dynamic compositions, Chokuan has pulled the pine tree to the foreground, where it gains an immediacy that directly confronts the viewer. The highly accomplished brushwork ranges from the minutely descriptive in the raptor's feathers to broad sweeps in the tree trunk and branches. The austerity of the setting is maintained by keeping landscape detail to a minimum, obscured by gold mist.

Hawks were a favorite subject of the warrior elite of the late medieval and early modern periods. Numerous paintings show mounted samurai using them to hunt pheasants and waterfowl. The hawk was a symbol of bravery, as expressed in Chokuan's lone bird, stolid against a driving wind in a bleak landscape. It is generally assumed that, because most of Chokuan's and Nichokuan's paintings were of hawks, their patrons were primarily members of the samurai class.

22

ATTRIBUTED TO KANO MITSUNOBU
(1562/1565–1608)

The Queen Mother of the West and Dong Fangshuo

Momoyama period,
late 16th–early 17th century
Six-panel screen
Color and gold leaf on paper
65½ x 146 in.
(166.5 x 370.4 cm)
11891

Screen shown in its entirety on pages 56–57.

EXHIBITED FOR the first time, this extremely well preserved screen was discovered and acquired very recently by the Idemitsu Museum of Arts. In the single screen—which probably was originally paired with another—the artist depicts Xi Wang Mu, the Queen Mother of the West, a Chinese mythological figure from at least as far back as the Han Dynasty (206 B.C.E.–C.E. 220). The man seated in the left half of the picture is identifiable as Dong Fangshuo, who, according to legend, stole the queen's peaches of immortality, held in this scene by one of her attendants. This story was part of a diverse repertory of themes from Chinese lore that included paintings of Daoist immortals (such as the sliding-panel paintings from Ryōanji, Kyoto, now in The Metropolitan Museum of Art, New York), Tartar hunters, and episodes from the Chinese classics (such as the screen painting *Song of Everlasting Sorrow* in the Freer Gallery of Art, Smithsonian Institution, Washington, D.C.). Paintings of the Queen Mother of the West and Dong Fangshuo held great appeal for aristocratic patrons versed in the Chinese classics.

This screen, with its exquisite draftsmanship, rich and vivid colors, and carefully designed composition, could only have come from the deft hand of the most assured professional painter. The treatment of the pine tree with its gently curved ranks of needles, the combination of bold outlines and sharp texture-stroke faceting on the rocks, and the smoothly flowing calligraphic contour lines on the figures' drapery make the painting immediately recognizable as the product of a Kano school artist of consummate skill, most likely Kano Mitsunobu, who was active from the latter half of the sixteenth century through the beginning of the seventeenth century. The figures' faces, the banks at the water's edge that gradually recede into the background, the acutely angled rocks, and the gracefully extended branches are all characteristic of Mitsunobu's style.

The statuesque figures in a richly decorative garden setting are similar in scale to figures in seventeenth century genre paintings of groups of people, such as the famed Hikone screen, 1624/1644 (Ii Naoyoshi, Hikone, Shiga Prefecture). The theme of principal characters accompanied by attendants appears in another of the Idemitsu Museum's screens, *Beauties under the Cherry Blossoms* (cat. no. 23). Perhaps paintings of characters from Chinese lore by masters of the Kano school, like *The Queen Mother of the West and Dong Fangshuo*, provided the inspiration for later genre screens of people in the pleasure quarters. In any case, the present work is a valuable point of reference for an analysis of Mitsunobu's style. It also provides an indication of the central style of Kano school painting from the end of the sixteenth through the beginning of the seventeenth century.

Opposite: detail

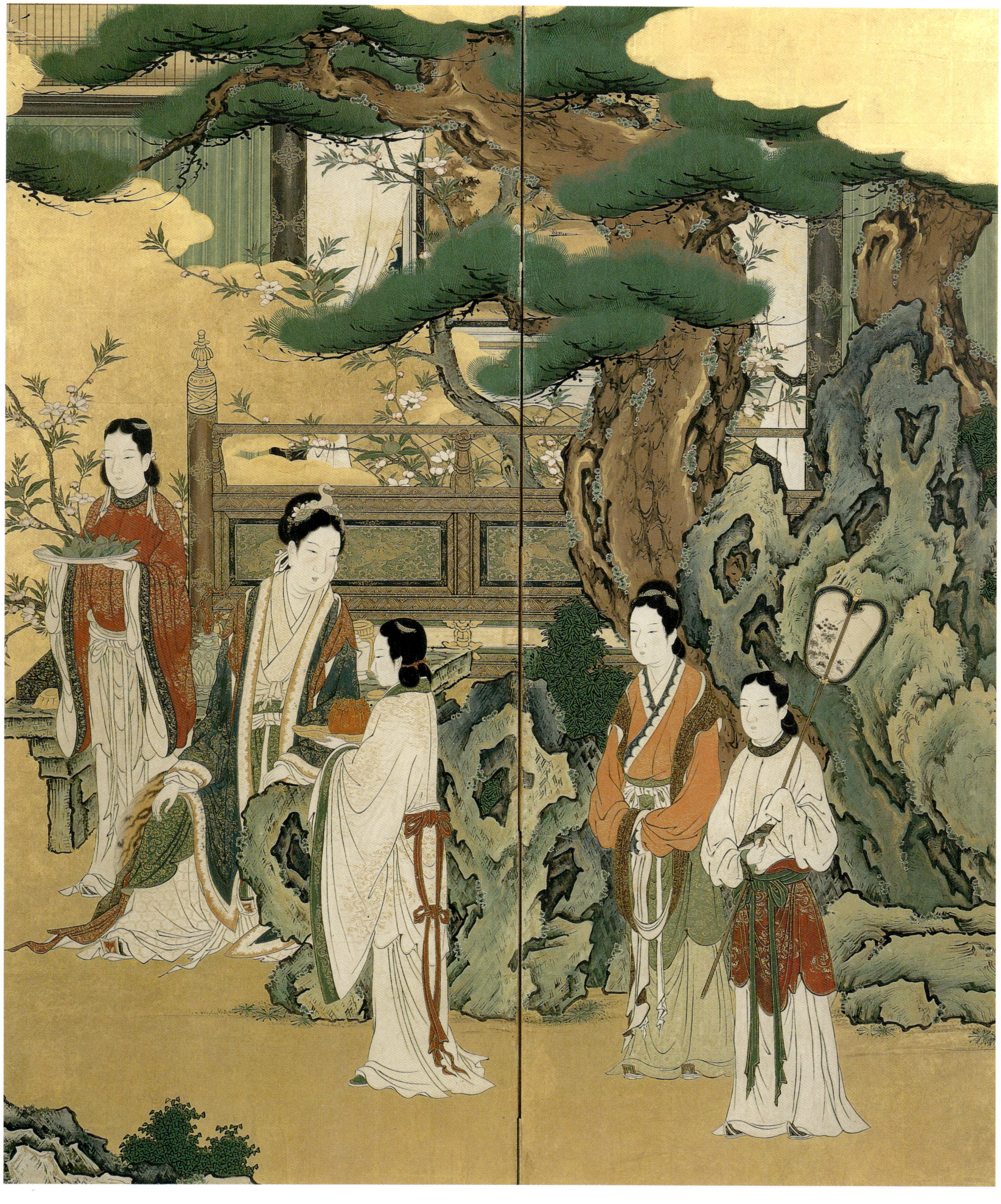

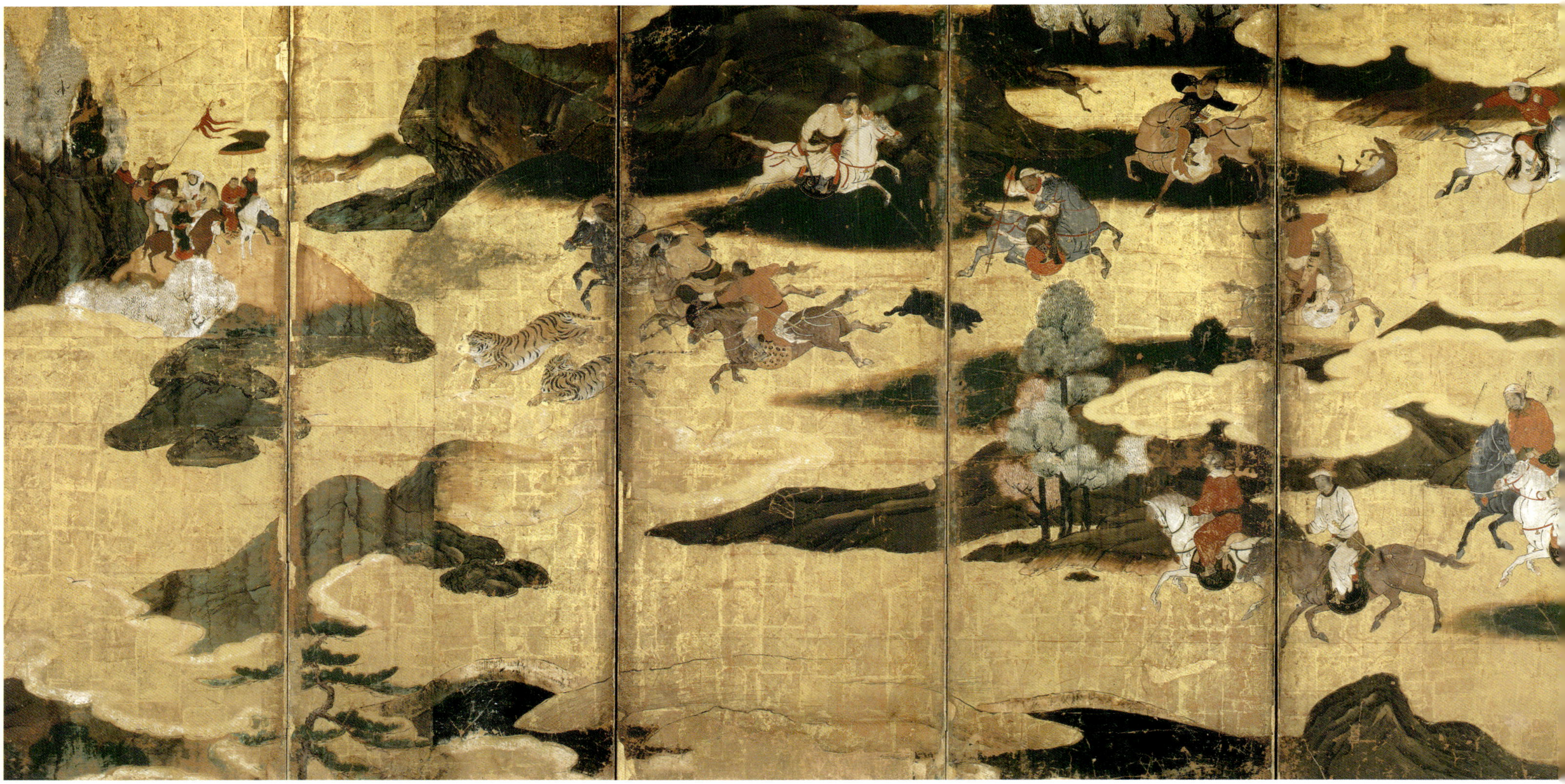

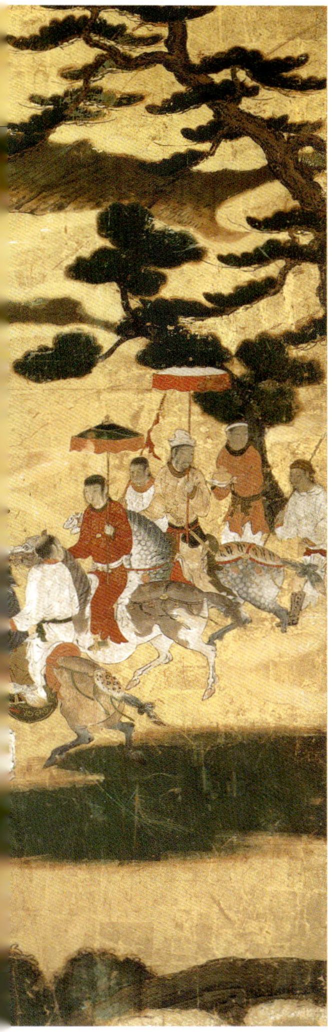

12

Scenes of Tartars Hunting on Horseback

Momoyama period, beginning of 17th century
Six-panel screen
Color and gold leaf on paper
65¾ x 149½ in.
(167.0 x 379.4 cm)
9542

THESE SCENES BELONG to a genre of painting that depicts the Mongol nomadic Tartar peoples of northern China. Sometimes they were paired with scenes of polo players, as in a late sixteenth century pair of screens in the Asian Art Museum of San Francisco. Frequently painted by Kano school artists of the Momoyama through early Edo period, scenes of Tartars Hunting on Horseback were popular among the equestrian samurai warriors.

The Tartars' faces and the markedly accented ink lines in their clothing are characteristic of the Kano school style. The consummate skill displayed in the lineament suggests a superior artist active about the beginning of the seventeenth century. The quiet aspect of the depiction of the Tartars is close in style to the paintings of the *Thirty-Six Immortal Poets* bearing "Kuninobu" seals and dedicated in 1590, located in the Munakata Shrine in Fukuoka Prefecture. Although Kuninobu was a name used by Kano Eitoku (1543–1590), these paintings are recognized as the work of his son Kano Mitsunobu, who was active from the late sixteenth century through the early seventeenth. In addition, the gentle curve in the pine trees in the upper right corner is a hallmark of Mitsunobu's manner. Compared with the *Tartars Playing Polo and Hunting* screens in San Francisco, which are thought to be by Eitoku's younger brother Kano Sōshū (1551–1601), and screens in the Freer Gallery of the Smithsonian Institution in Washington, D.C., which bear "Motohide" seals and are thought to be the work of Sōshū's son Kano Jinnojō (active late sixteenth–early seventeenth century), the present screen exhibits an antique quality within the realm of Kano-style figures. This aspect is in keeping with the older style often noted in Mitsunobu's painting. It drew on a Kano school style that preceded Eitoku's grand manner, which became dominant in the Momoyama period. Therefore, it can be concluded that these screens were produced by Kano Mitsunobu or by a close member of his atelier.

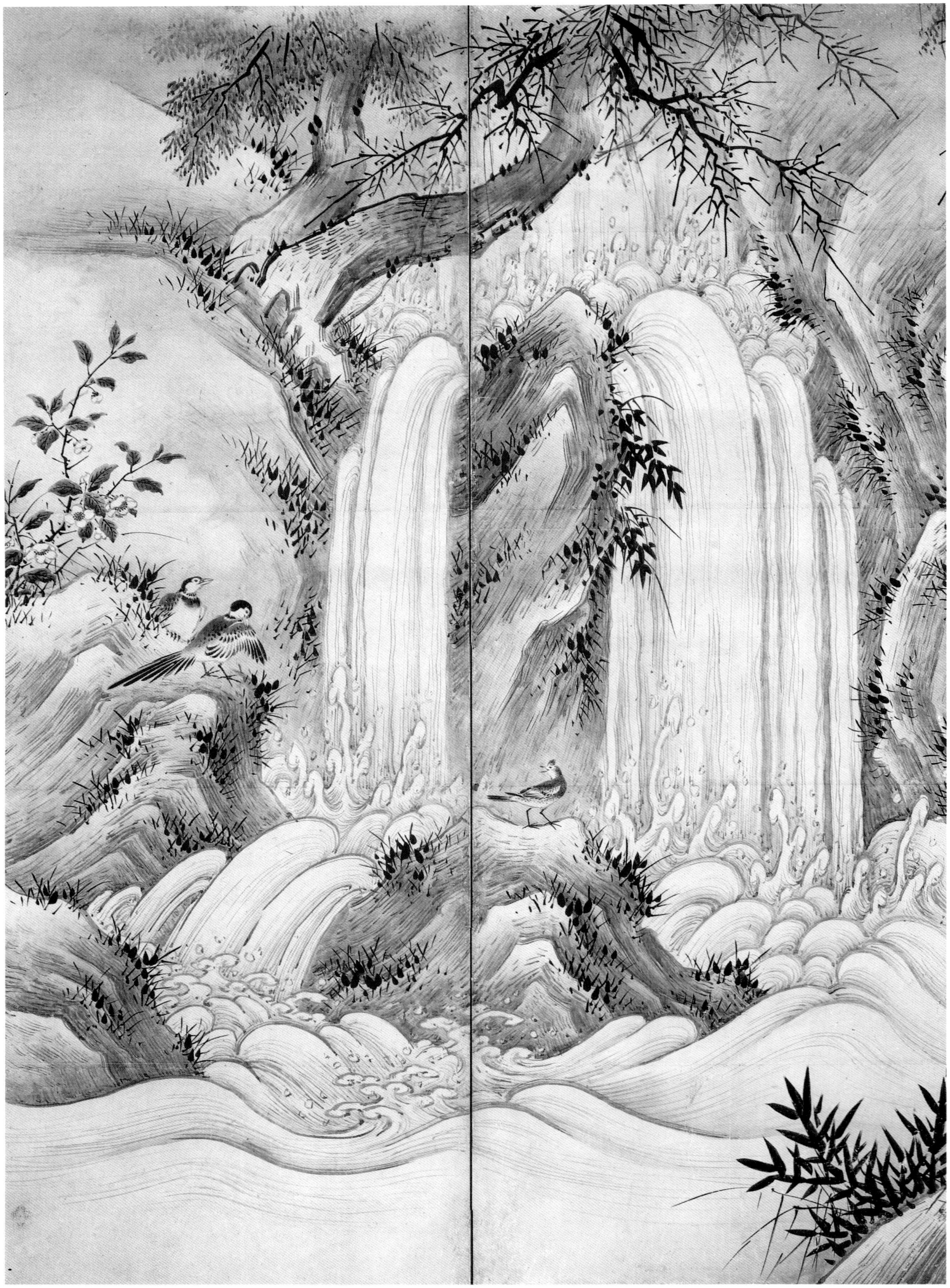

13

KANO SCHOOL (SEAL OF MOTONOBU)

Flowers and Birds of Spring and Autumn

Momoyama period, early 17th century
Pair of six-panel screens
Ink on paper
Each, 66½ x 147 in.
(169.2 x 373.4 cm)
10392

IN THE RIGHT SCREEN, golden pheasants, white egrets, and songbirds are arranged in a springtime setting of streams and grassy banks verdant with bamboo, dandelions, and plum blossoms. In the left screen, distant snowy mountains provide a backdrop for geese, wagtails, and finches among Chinese hibiscus and other flora characteristic of autumn and winter. Joined together by a gently flowing stream fed by a waterfall at the left edge of the left screen, the two screens form a panorama of spring and autumn flowers and birds. The composition across the pair of screens is evenly accented with motifs at the right and left edges and at the center.

Urn-shaped seals reading "Motonobu" are impressed at the lower right corner of the right screen and lower left corner of the left screen, but compared with the sliding-panel paintings at the temple Reiun'in and other works by Kano Motonobu (1476–1559), the lines and expression of the branches in the present work display a cautious, timid quality not apparent in the confident works of that early sixteenth century master of the Kano school. The extended, stretched character of the plum and other branches closely resembles that of the plum trees in the sliding-panel paintings by Kano Mitsunobu (1562/1565–1608) in the Kangakuin subtemple of Onjōji in Shiga Prefecture. The mannered gesture of the plum branch dipping into the stream in the right screen is a motif that also appears in the sliding panels by Kano Eitoku (1543–1590) in the Jukōin subtemple of Daitokuji in Kyoto. Judging from the delicately placed brushstrokes and generally light appearance of the birds, however, the present work is more properly considered to be a copy of a Motonobu painting, by Eitoku's son Mitsunobu or another Kano school painter active in the early seventeenth century.

Both details from left screen.

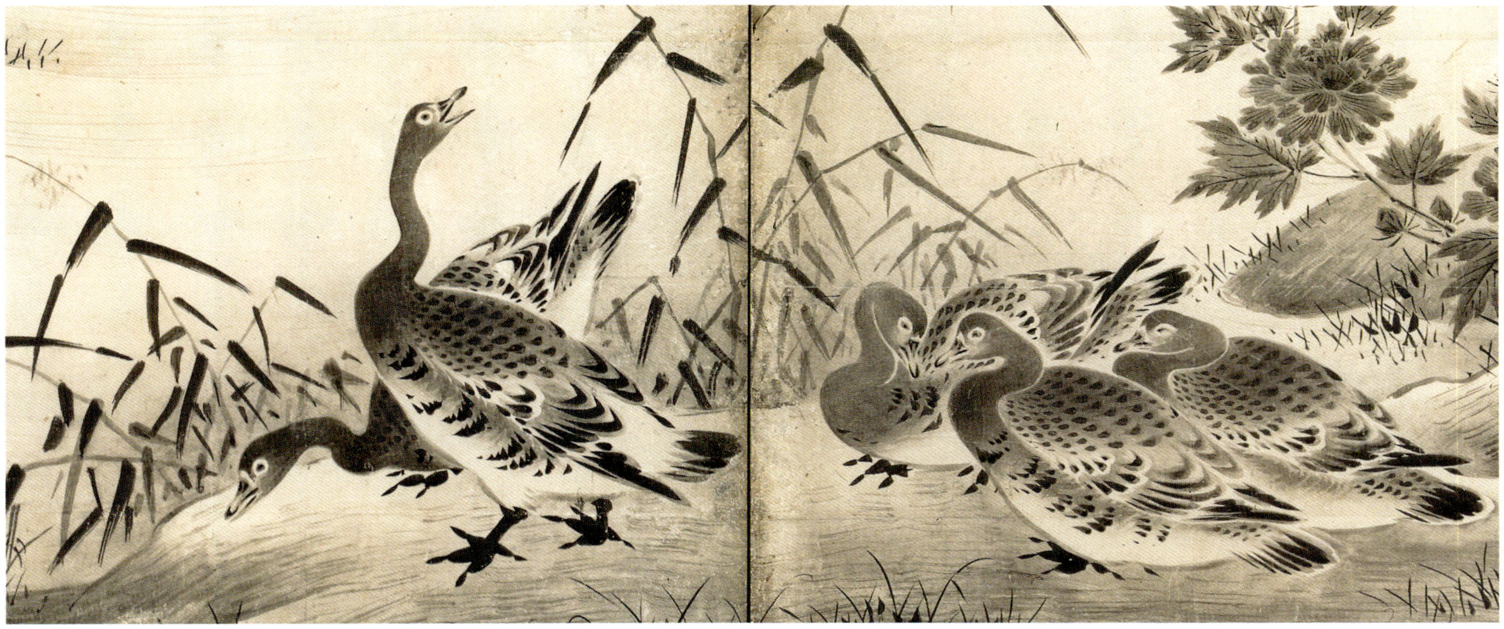

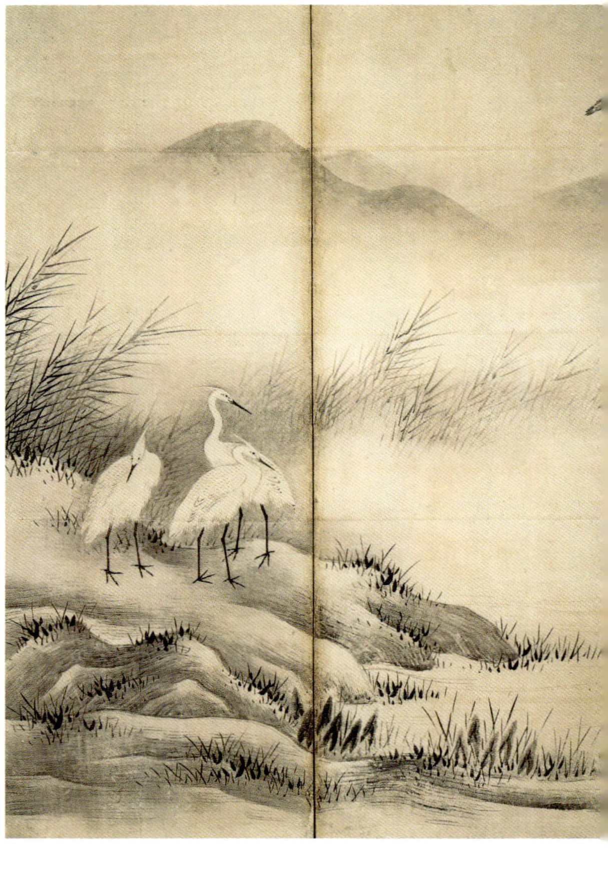

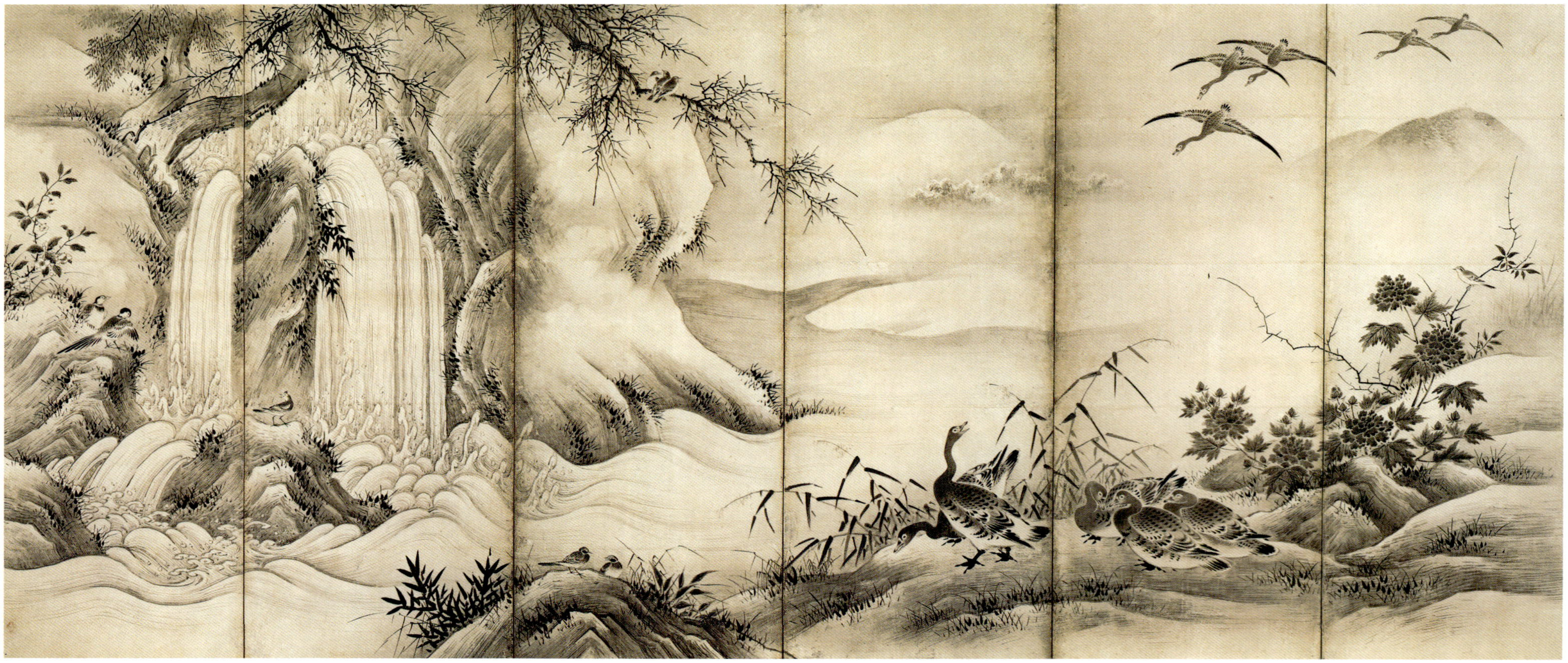

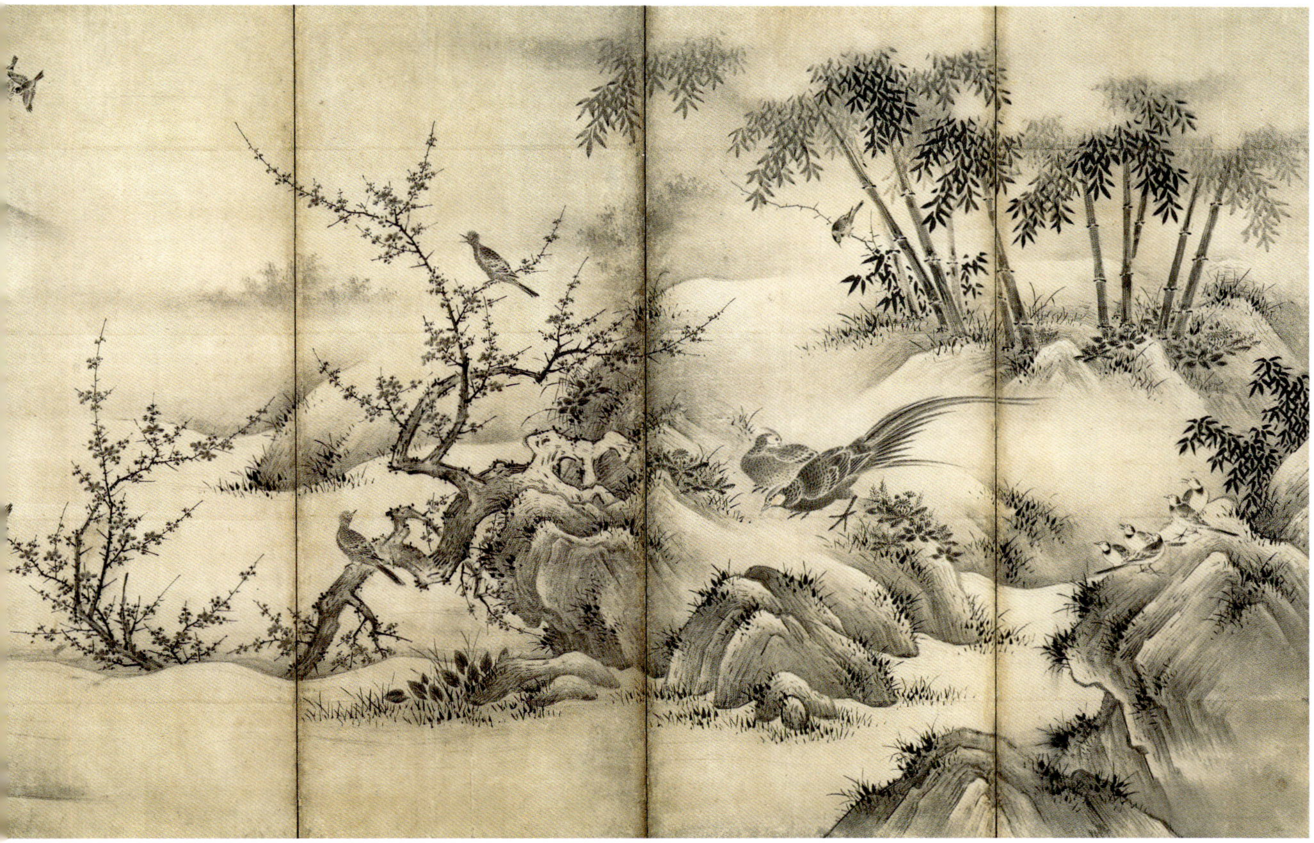

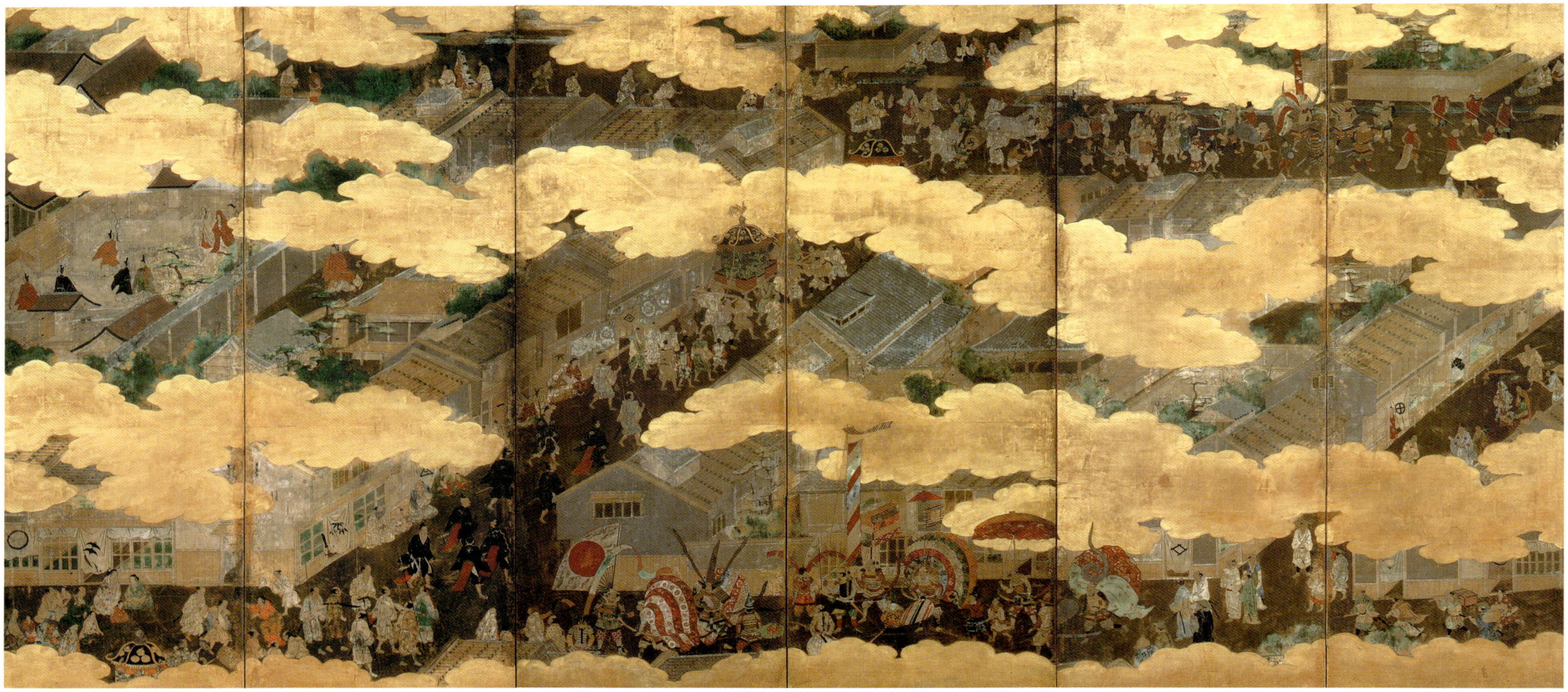

14

Gion Festival, Kyoto

Momoyama period, Keicho era, 1596–1615
Pair of six-panel screens
Color and gold leaf on paper
Each, 67½ x 143½ in.
(171.5 x 364.2 cm)
2684
Important Cultural Property

THE GION FESTIVAL, Japan's most famous, is a summer festival that originated in the ninth century to appease spirits believed to have caused an epidemic in Kyoto, the old imperial capital. The procession of decorated carts—the smaller called *yama* (mountains) and the larger called *hoko* (halberds)—began as a sacred rite thought to ward off angry plague-causing spirits, but over time it took on the festive character of a parade. Canceled during the Ōnin War (1467–1477), the festival was revived in 1500. Then, with the support of Kyoto's newly prosperous merchants, artisans, and money-lenders, it grew to spectacular dimensions during the economic boom of the late sixteenth through early seventeenth century.

The right screen depicts the yama and hoko floats being paraded through the capital in the first part of the festival. The left screen shows the procession of portable shrines accompanied by fantastically costumed warriors in the second part of the festival. The composition is directly derived from screens depicting Scenes in and around Kyoto (*rakuchū-rakugaizu*) in which the city's streets are arranged along horizontal and diagonal lines. The painting itself gives a closeup view of only the district in which the festival was held. Paintings of the Gion Festival, such as the Idemitsu Museum's pair, are one of many types of "genre" paintings that had their origins in themes within screen paintings of Kyoto.

Among the oldest of the Gion Festival screen paintings, this pair was likely painted in the 1590s. The figures' elegant, refined expressions follow the Kano style of the Momoyama period, so it is not unlikely that a late sixteenth century master of the Kano atelier executed this painting.

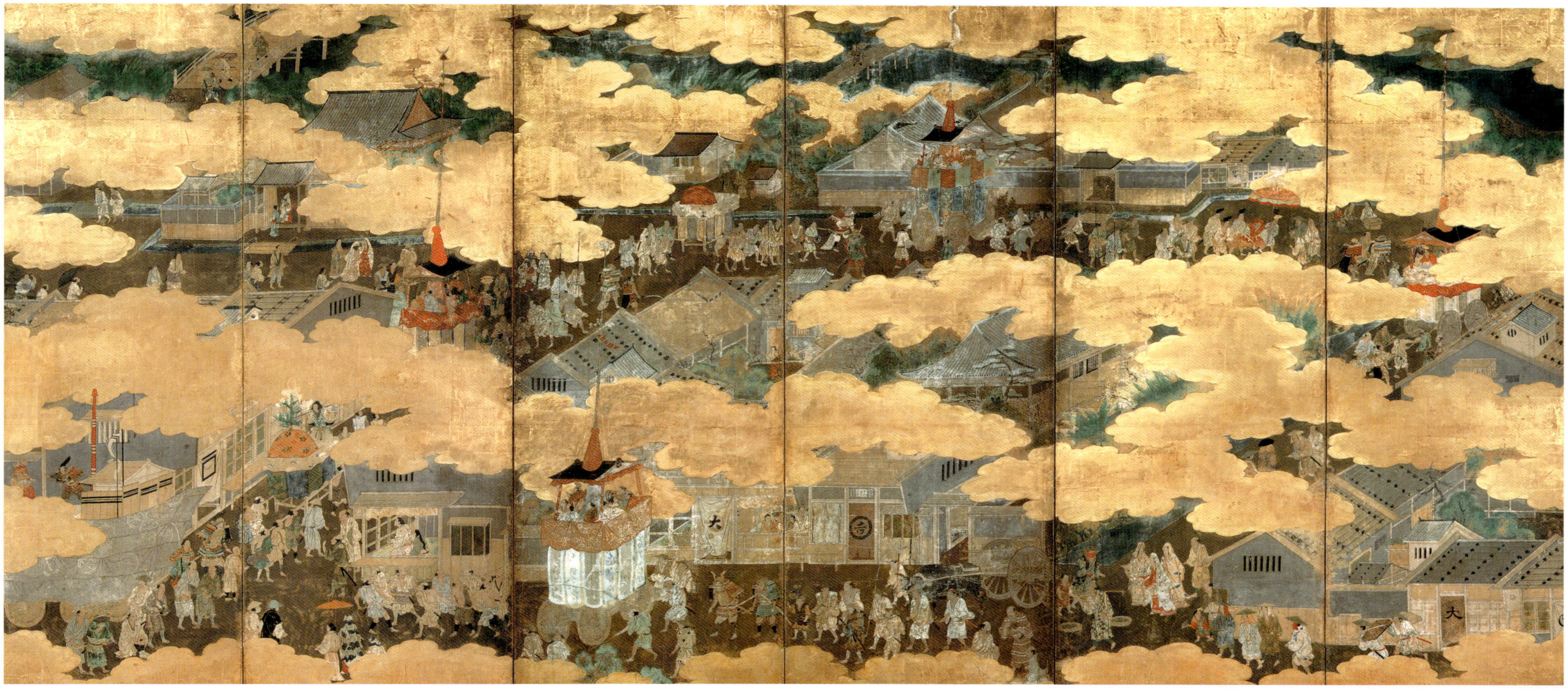

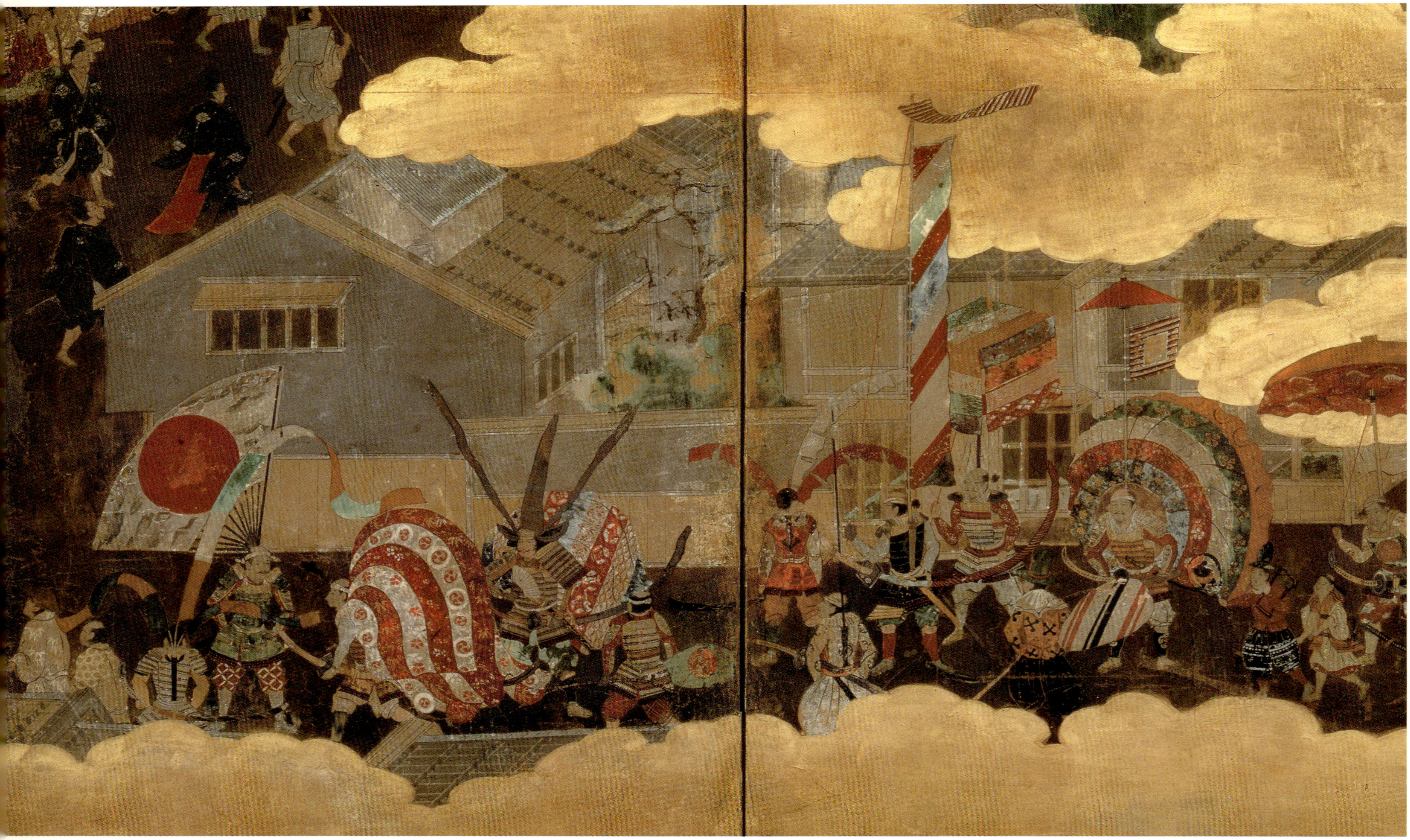

Detail from left screen.

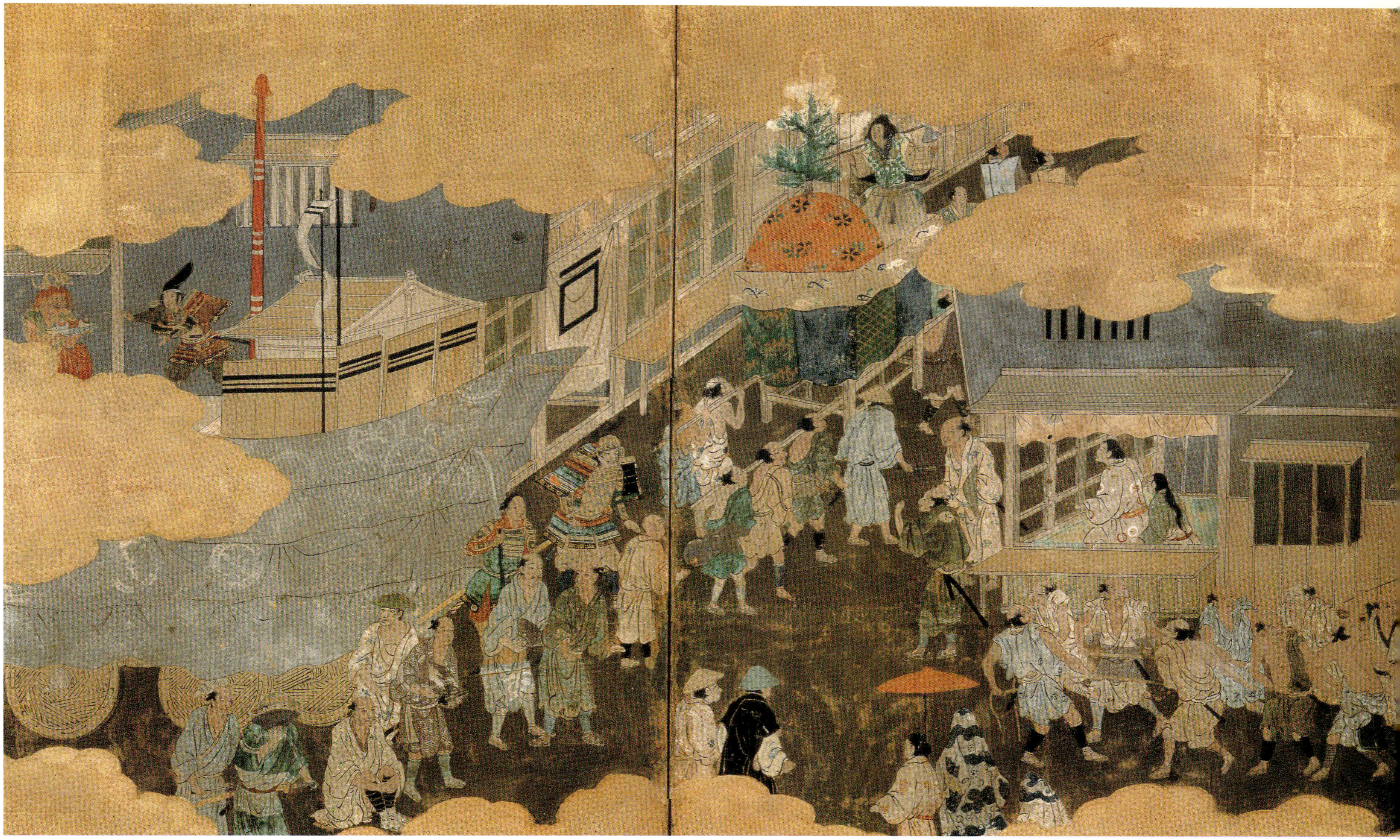

Detail from right screen.

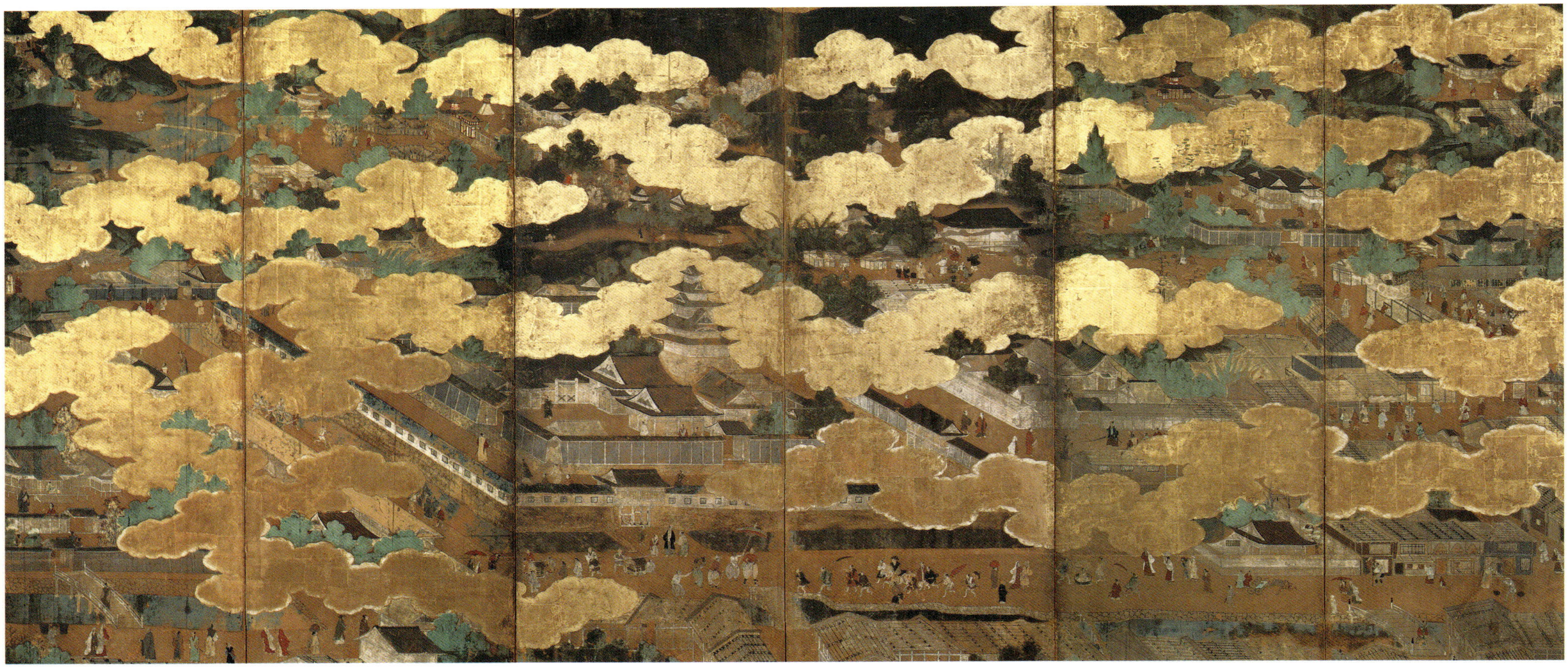

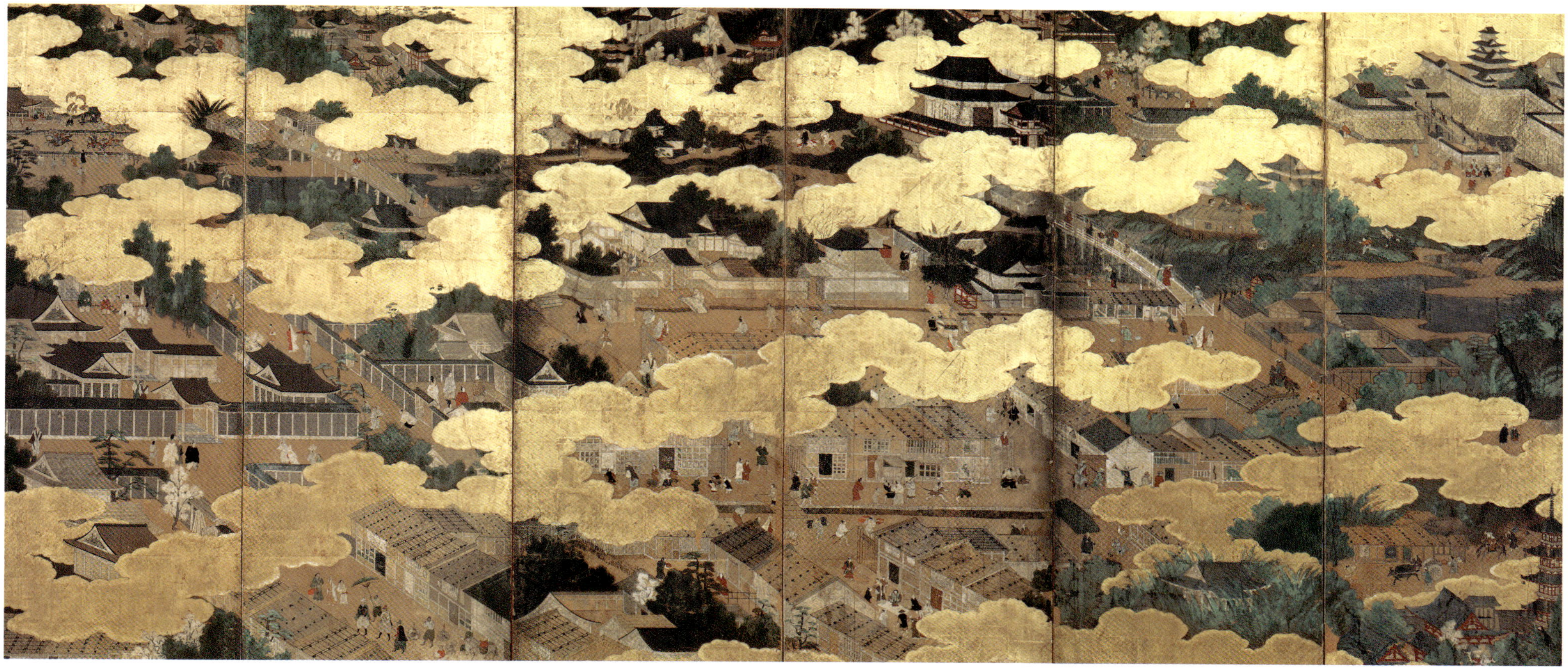

15

Scenes in and around Kyoto

Momoyama period, early 17th century
Pair of six-panel screens
Color and gold leaf on paper
Each, 66¼ x 146 in.
(168.1 x 371.0 cm)
10172

SPREAD ACROSS THE TWELVE panels of this pair of screens and partly hidden by stylized clouds of gold leaf are famous locales in the old imperial capital. The annual cycle of life unfolds in streets lined with the houses of Kyoto's merchants and craftsmen. In the hills that border the city to the north, east, and west, celebrated temples and shrines are set in a landscape of lush bamboo groves, blossoming cherry trees, and forests of evergreens. Some of the more notable sites represented in the present work include two temples, Tōji with its five-story pagoda (right screen, lower edge of first panel from right) and Kiyomizudera (right screen, upper edge of fourth panel from right), the Gion Shrine (right screen, upper edge of fifth panel from right), the Imperial Palace (right screen, sixth panel from right), and the Togetsukyō Bridge in Arashiyama (left screen, upper edge of sixth panel from right).

The earliest known pair of screens of Scenes in and around Kyoto date from the early sixteenth century. The present work seems to show the capital in the first two decades of the seventeenth century and was probably painted about that time. This dating is based on the depiction of Fushimi Castle, which was built in 1597 and dismantled in 1623 (right screen, upper right corner); Nijō Castle (left screen, fourth panel from right), which was remodeled in 1626; and Kitano Shrine, which was rebuilt in 1607 (left screen, first panel from right).

Although the painting is faded and the slightly simplistic rendering of motifs lacks the sophistication of the finest examples of this genre, the pantalooned Westerners with exotic animals such as the so-called Chinese musk cat (right screen, lower edge of fifth panel from right), the horse race at Kamo Shrine (right screen, upper left corner), the Kabuki performance near Kitano Shrine, and similar scenes add human interest to the broad panorama of temples, shrines, and residential streets.

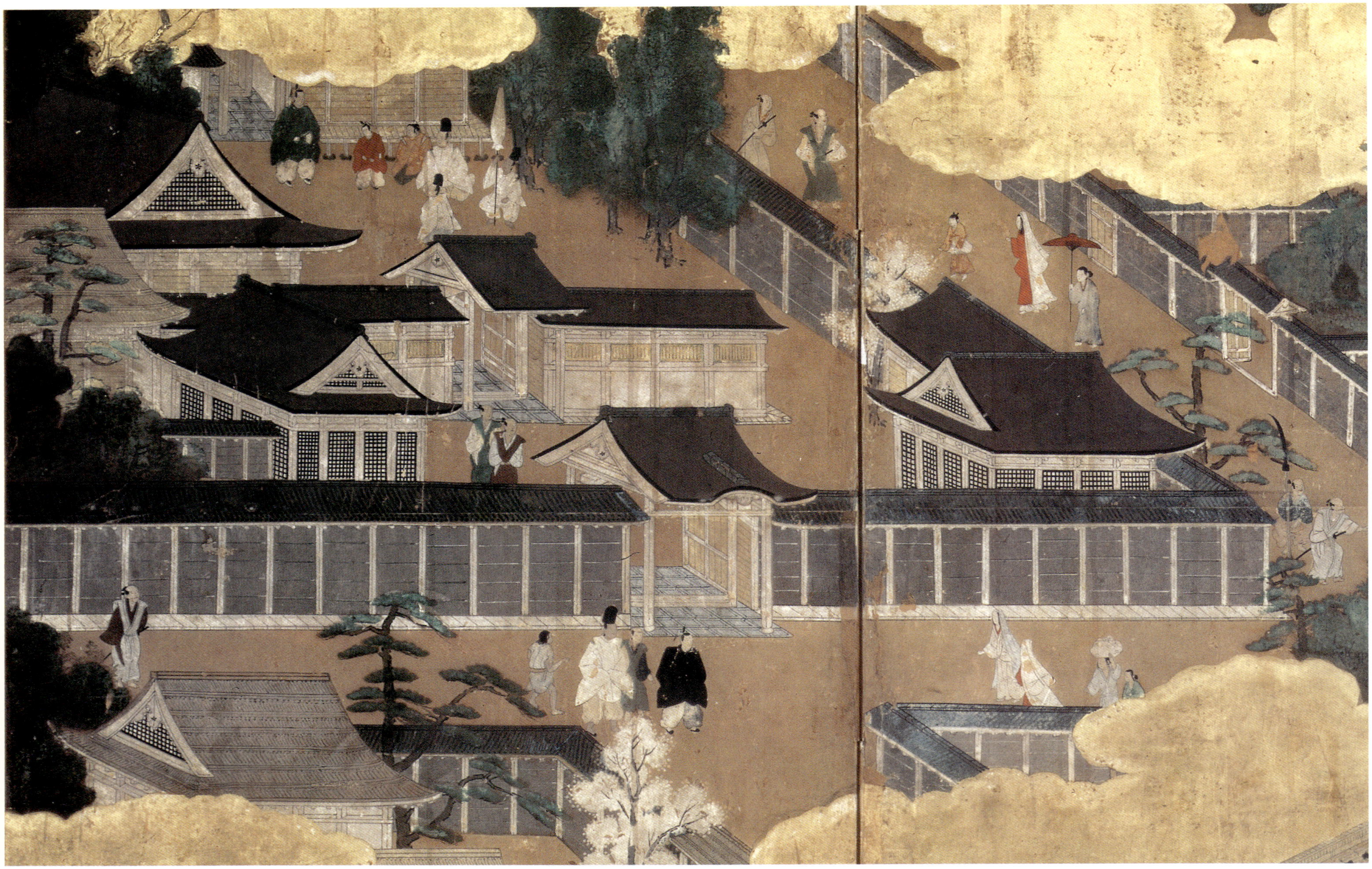

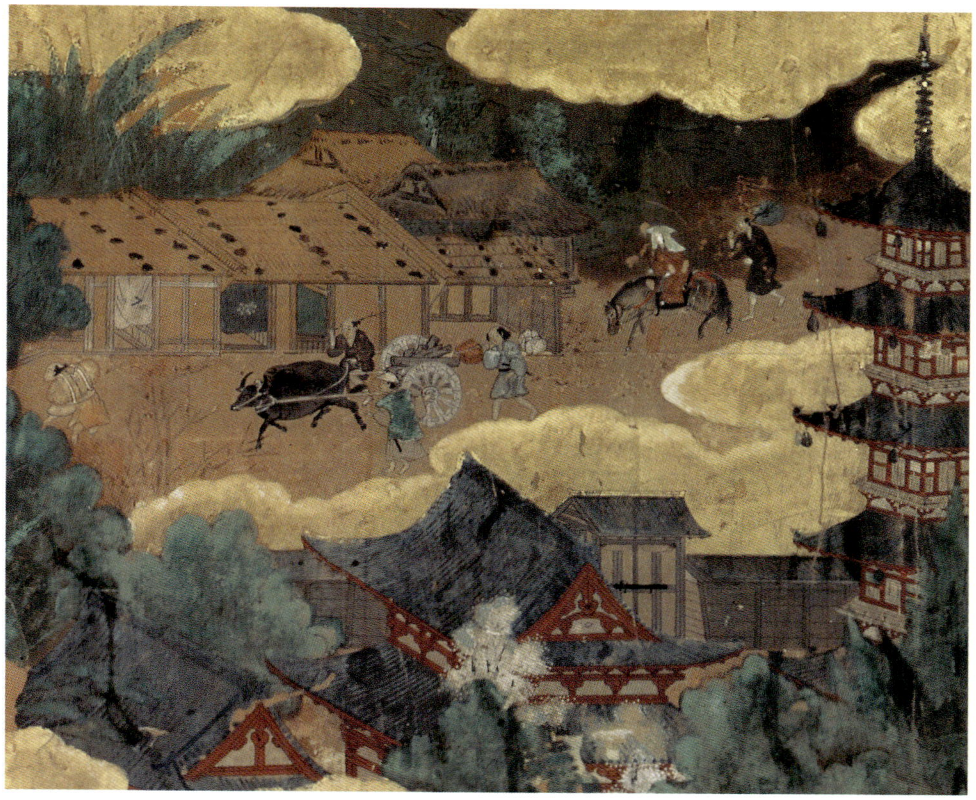

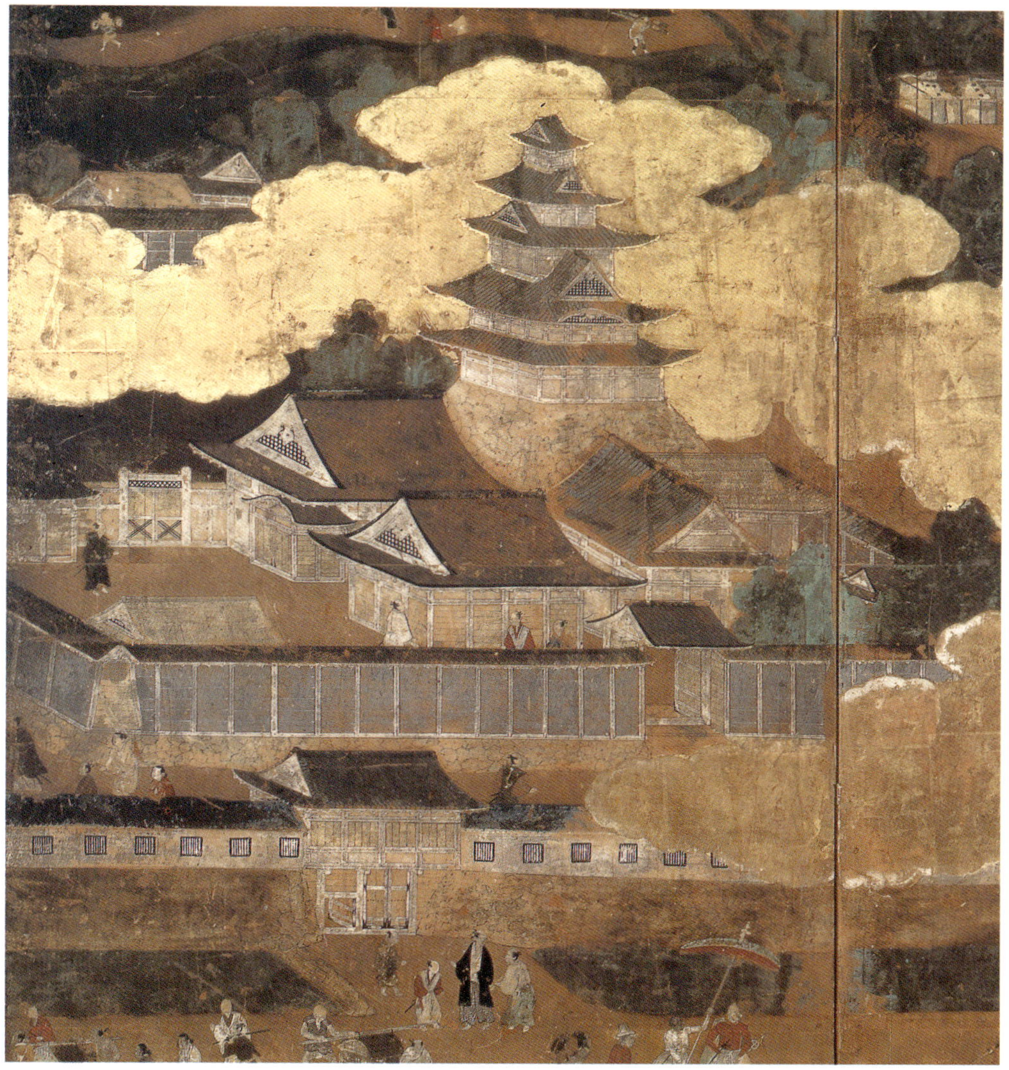

Above right: detail from right screen of Tōji pagoda

Above: detail from left screen of Nijō Castle

Right: detail from right screen of Fushimi Castle

Opposite left: detail from right screen of Imperial Palace

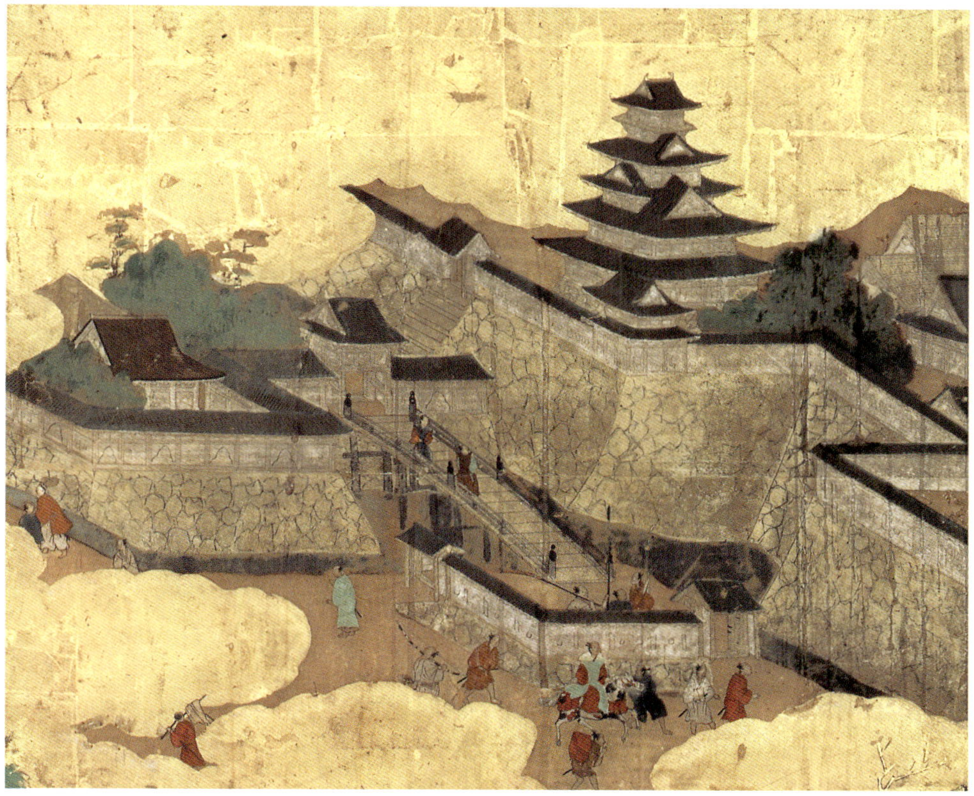

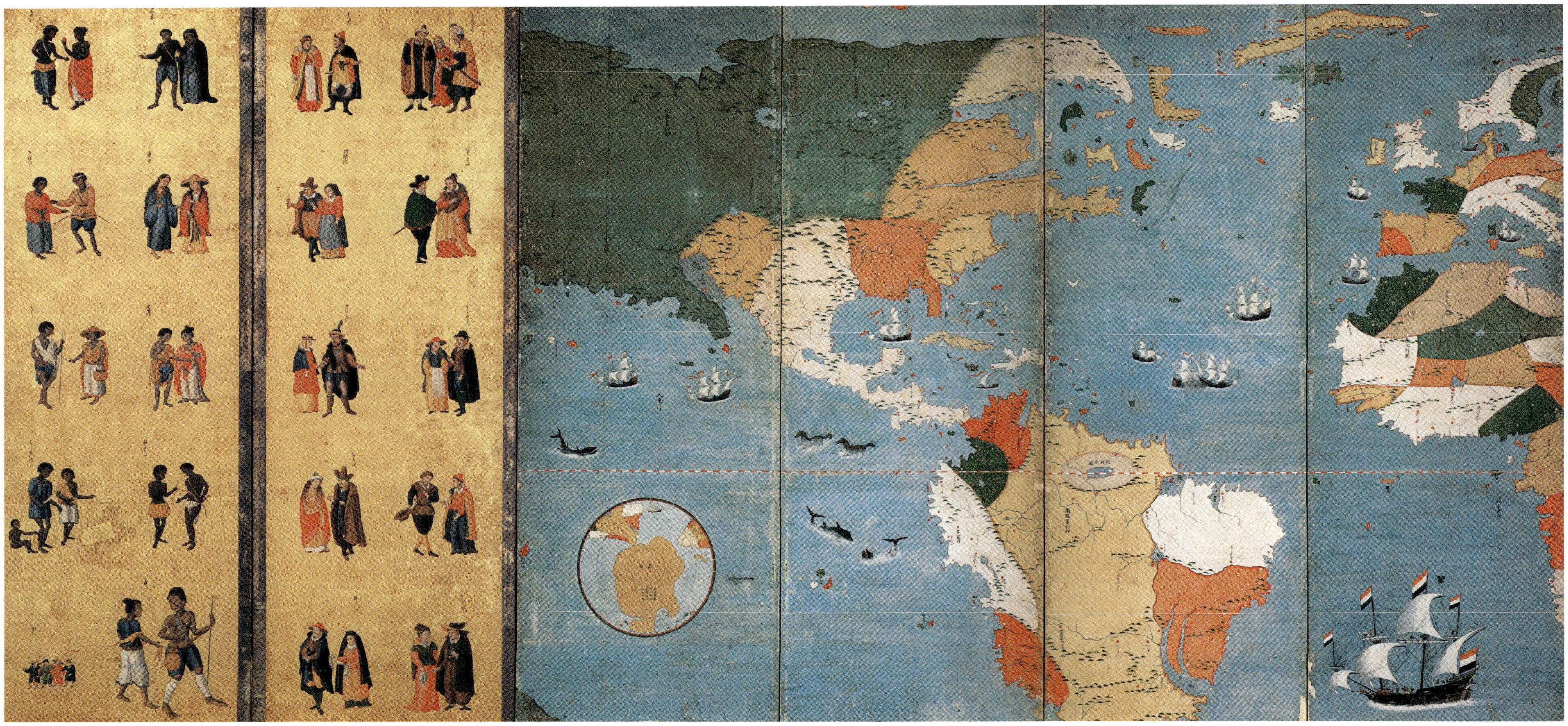

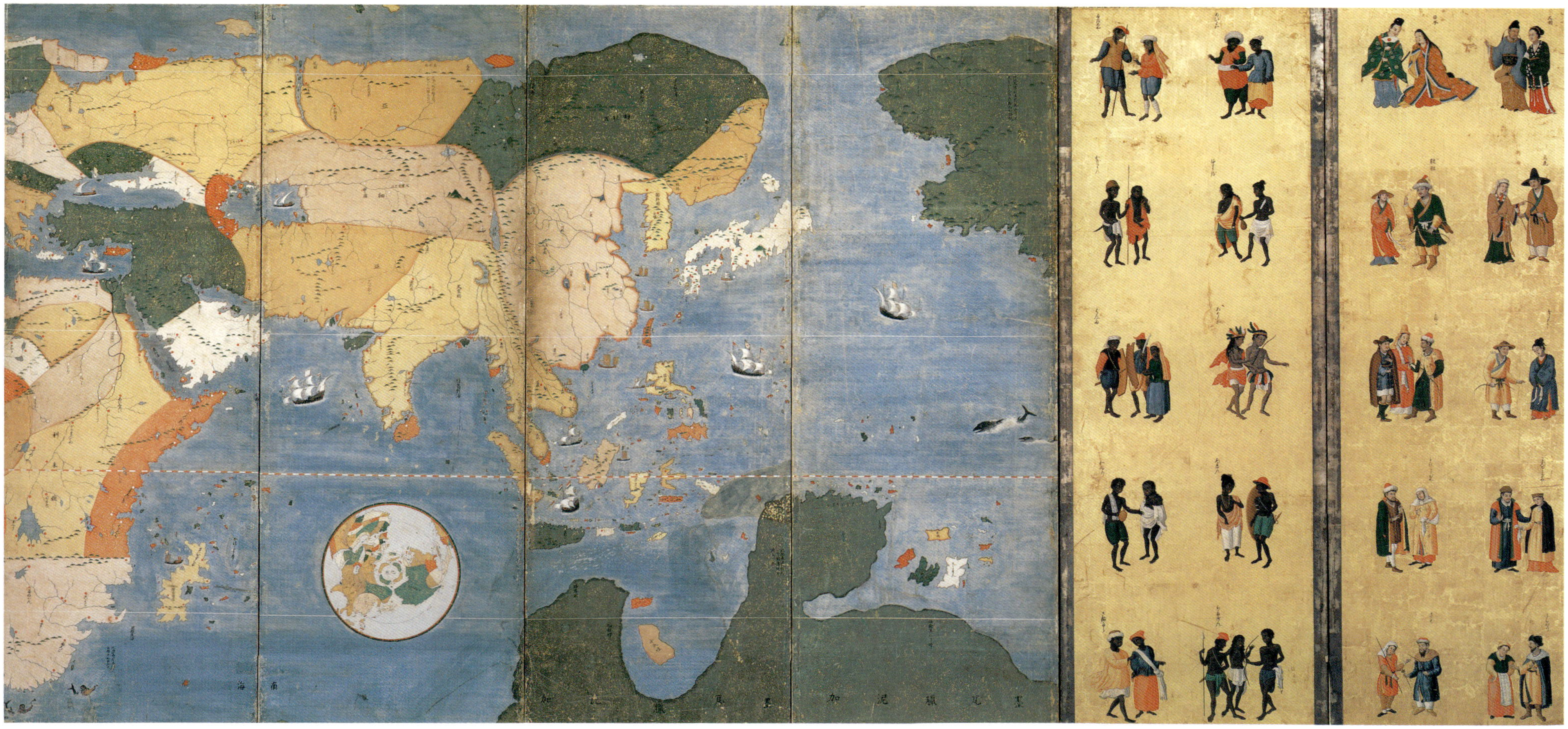

16

Map of the World and People of Various Lands

Edo period, 17th century
Pair of six-panel screens
Color on paper
Each, 67¼ x 143¼ in.
(170.7 x 364.0 cm)
9106

THE FIRST WESTERNERS to appear in Japan were a group of lost Portuguese sailors in 1543. The ensuing century was marked by frequent contact and cultural exchange with Europeans, which resulted in the introduction to Japan of firearms, Christianity, and Western-style painting and mapmaking. The numerous Western-style paintings extant in Japan and abroad indicate that ateliers of Japanese painters were actively producing works based on the visual materials newly available through the prints, paintings, religious icons, and maps that European visitors brought with them.

The *Map of the World* painted across the middle panels of this pair of screens derives from one produced in 1592 by the Dutch cartographer Petrus Plancius (1552–1622). He divided the world into western and eastern hemispheres and included smaller depictions of the northern and southern hemispheres. Willem Janszoon Blaeu (1571–1638) produced a version of Plancius' map in 1607, and it is upon this version that the map in the Idemitsu Museum's screens is based.

From the style of the figures in the four *People of Various Lands* panels, it can be surmised that they postdate the map. The chiaroscuro modeling in the faces and clothes resembles that of other Western-style paintings from the Momoyama period, such as the figures in the screens *Twenty-Eight Cities and Map of the World* in the Imperial Collection. The probable source for these figures was the woodblock-print edition of *Complete Pictures of the Various Lands (Bankoku sōzu)*, published in 1645.

Overleaf: detail of right screen

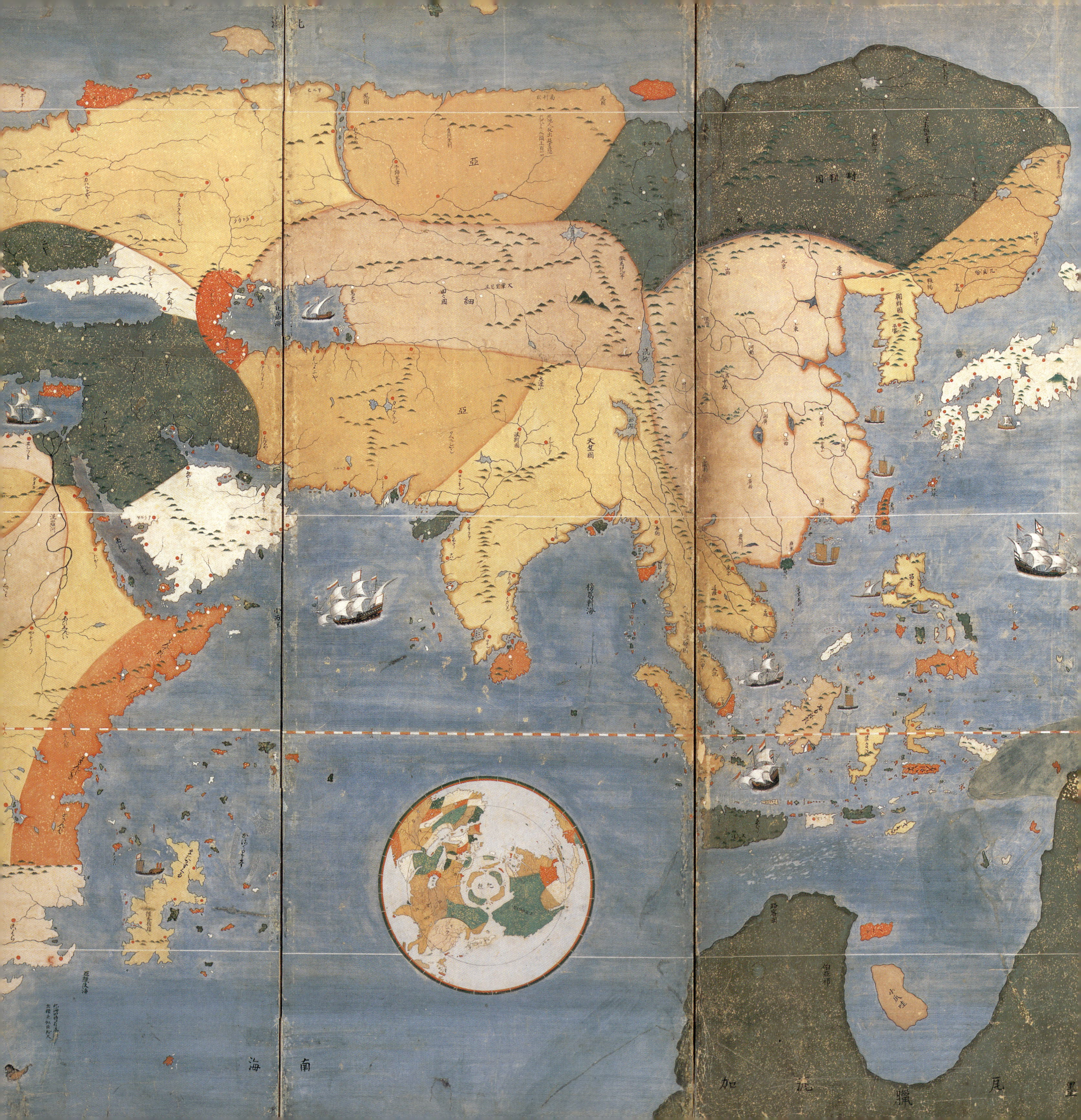
北
南海
墨瓦臘泥加

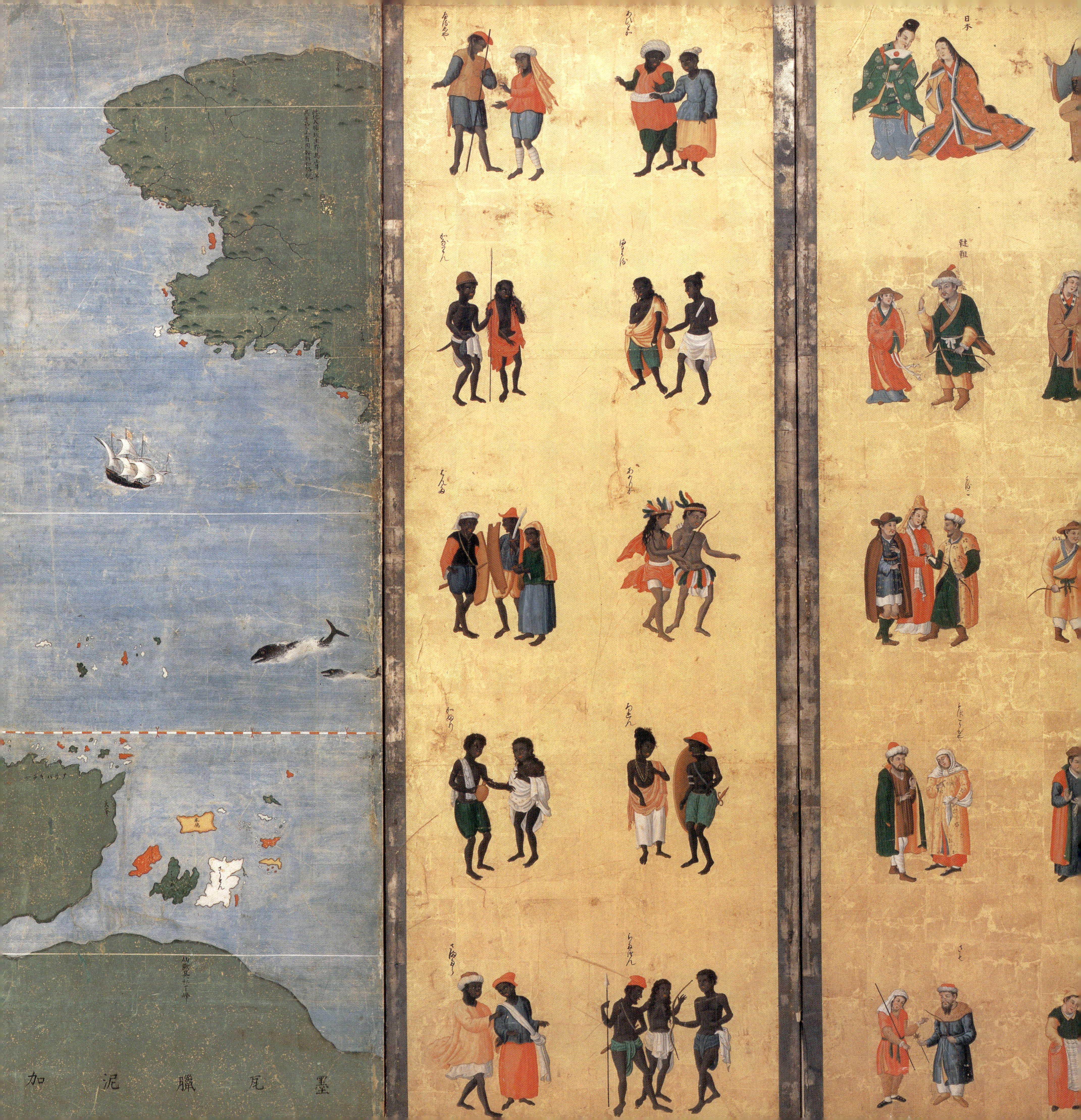
墨瓦臘泥加
日本

17

KANO NAONOBU (1607–1650?)

Minamoto no Nakakuni Hearing Kogō Playing the Koto and Ziyou Visiting Andao

Edo period, 17th century
Pair of six-panel screens
Ink and light color on paper
Each, 67 x 151½ in.
(170.3 x 385.2 cm)
9934

Opposite: detail from right screen

KANO NAONOBU was the younger brother of Kano Tan'yu (1602–1674), the official painter to the Tokugawa shogunate. Naonobu founded the Kobikichō branch of the Kano school of painters in Edo. In this pair of screens he presents two of the most famous episodes from Japanese and Chinese literature—in the right screen, the Kogō episode from the *Tale of Heike*; and in the left, the scene from classical Chinese literature in which the poet Ziyou visits his friend Andao.

Kogō was a lady in the court of the emperor Takakura (r. 1168–1180). Famed for her beauty and musicianship at the *koto*, she had been sent to comfort the emperor after the loss of his favorite, Aoi. Kogō's entrance into the imperial court forced her to leave her lover, Major Counselor Reizei Takafusa, whose love for her only increased with the separation. Emperor Takakura soon grew fond of Kogō, much to the consternation of the empress. Taira no Kiyomori, the father of both the empress and Takafusa's wife, realized that his daughters would never be happy while Kogō remained at court. He decided to exile her, but Kogō learned of his intention and disappeared. The emperor was heartbroken, and when he heard that Kogō was in Sagano (on the western outskirts of Kyoto), he sent a messenger, Minamoto no Nakakuni, to find her. On a moonlit night, after searching and searching, Nakakuni heard the music of the koto coming from a humble shack and thus discovered Kogō. This is the moment portrayed in the screen. It is also the climax of a later Noh play based on the chapter. It therefore would have been recognizable to Kano Naonobu's samurai patrons, who were aficionados of the Noh theater.

The story of Ziyou, a poet of the Jin dynasty (1115–1234), began one wintry evening as he sat at home drinking and reciting poetry. Suddenly he remembered his reclusive friend Andao and, on the spur of the moment, set out on the long boat ride to his friend's hermitage. When at last he reached the mooring near Andao's lodge, Ziyou just as abruptly decided to return home without seeing his friend. Asked why, Ziyou replied simply that he had been excited by the prospect of visiting his friend but that he lost his enthusiasm upon arrival. In other words, Ziyou was more interested in the journey than actually seeing his friend. The episode is generally interpreted as an expression of the freedom from social convention of the Chinese scholar-recluse.

The choice of these two scenes may have had something to do with the strong seasonal element in the texts on which they are based. The setting of the Kogō episode is Sagano, overgrown with autumn grasses under a harvest moon. The Ziyou story, by contrast, takes place on a snowy night in deep winter. Both scenes are filled with a sense of the pathos of lonely lives.

The screens were executed in the spare, light-handed manner established by Kano Tan'yu—the first of the Kano painters to move to Edo at the invitation of the shogun—which became the signature style of the Kano painters in Edo. Naonobu's use of broad areas of gray washes conveys the mysterious atmosphere of a misty autumn evening in the Kogō screen and serves equally well to highlight unpainted areas that represent snow in the Ziyou screen. Leaving large areas blank, he reduced both scenes to their essential motifs, which are accented with red and blue washes.

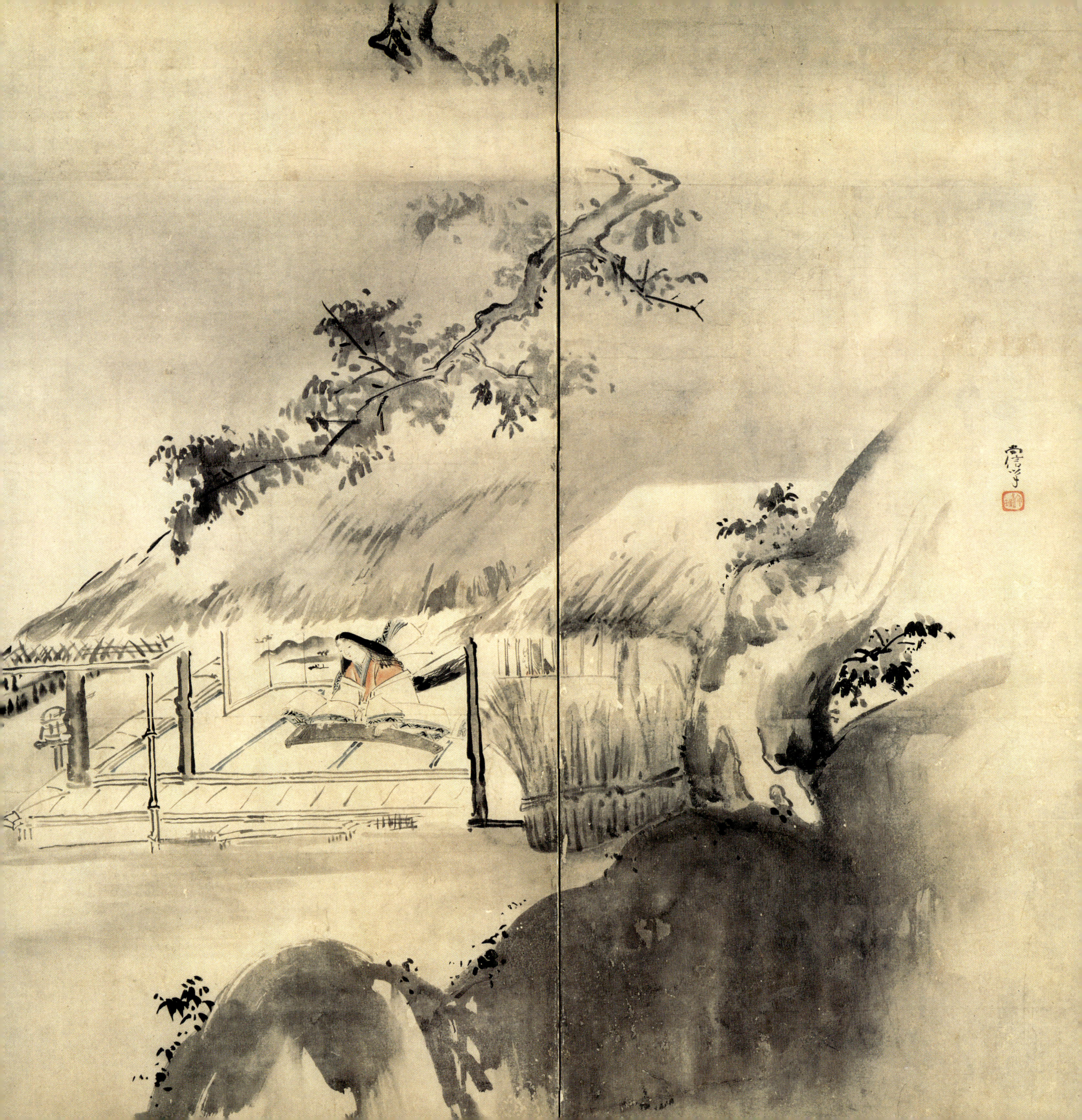

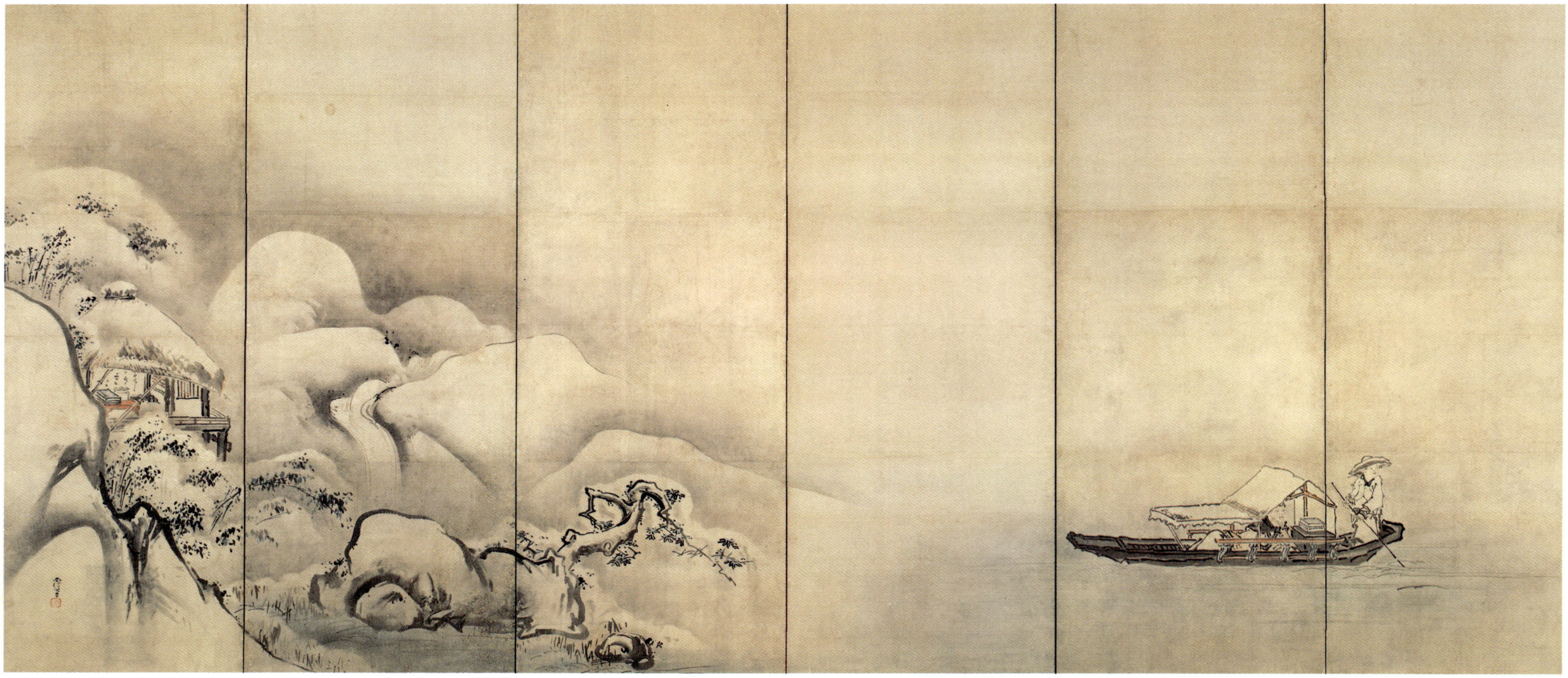

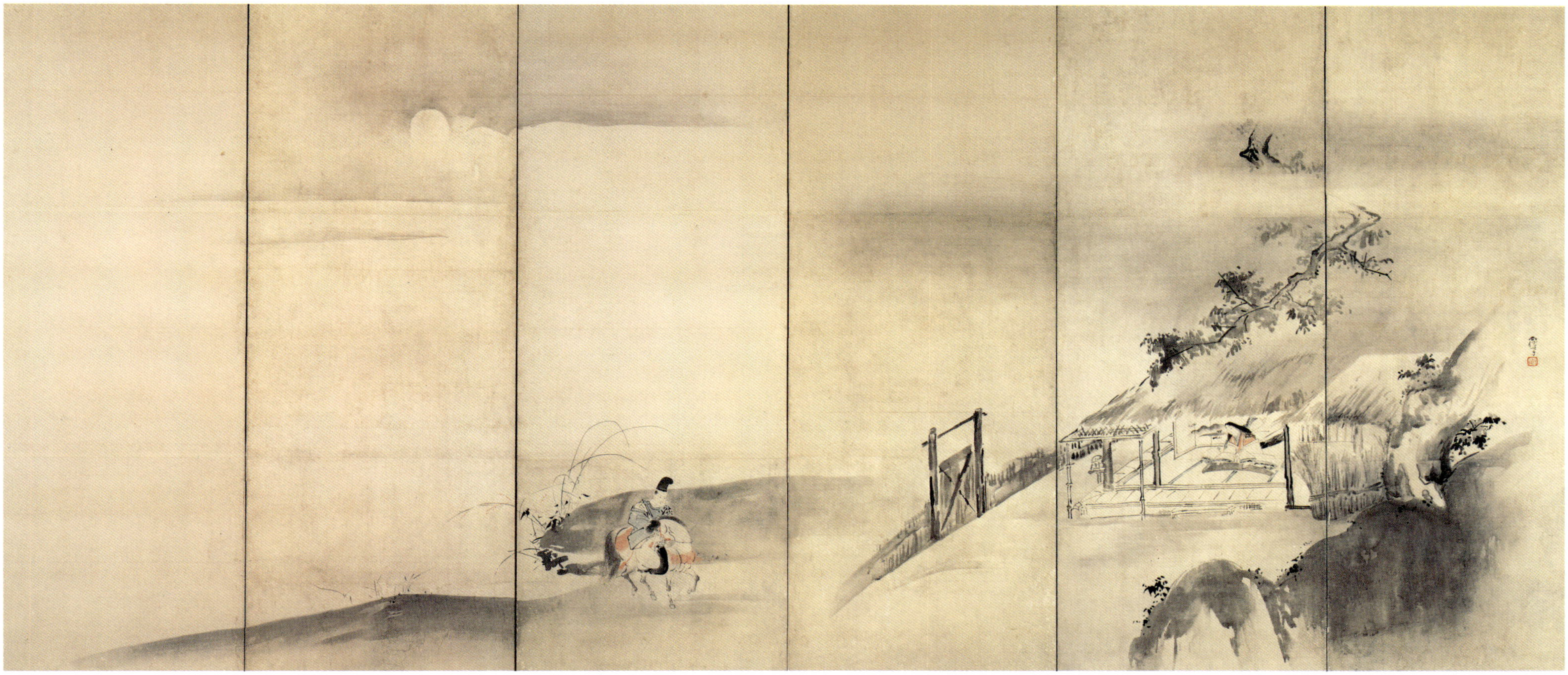

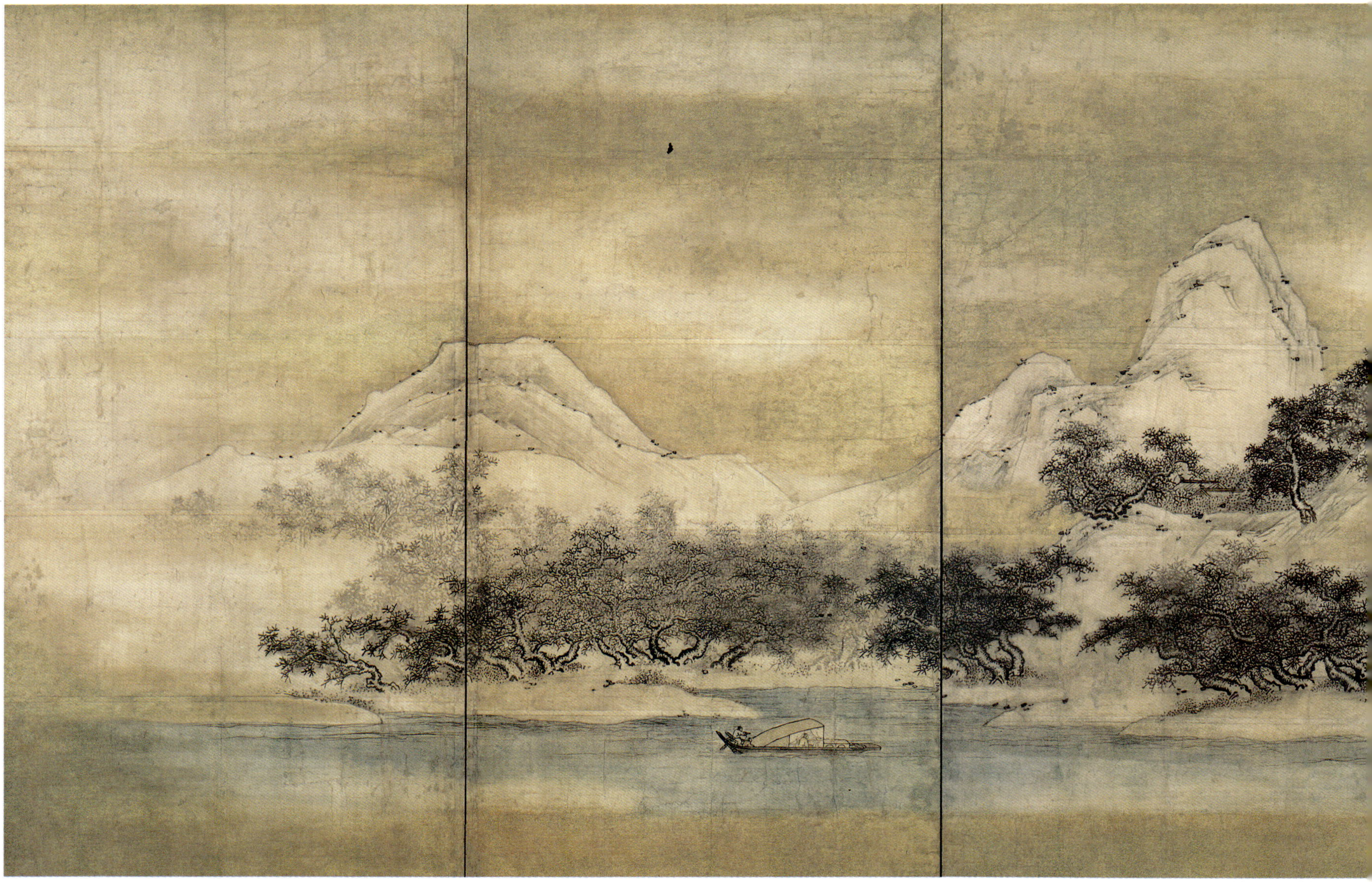

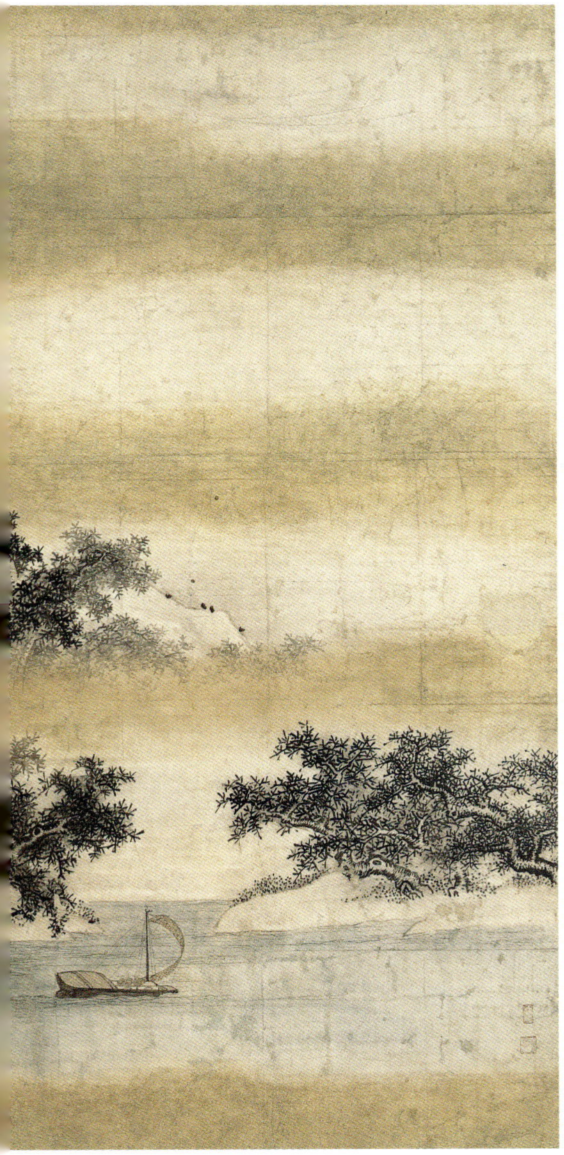

18

Winter Landscape

Edo period, 17th century
Four-panel screen
Ink, light color, and gold on paper
72¼ x 143¾ in.
(183.2 x 365 cm)
10766

TWO SMALL RUSH-ROOFED BOATS glide past a shore lined with groves of bare trees against a background of towering snow-covered peaks. The icy blue water, stark branches, and uniform white of the mountains and ground convey the chill of deep winter.

Tradition maintains that this screen was formerly a set of sliding-door panels at Daitsūji, a temple in Nagahama, Shiga Prefecture, with which the painters Kano Sanraku (1559–1635) and his adopted son Sansetsu (1590–1651) were closely associated. In addition, the painting bears two seals reading "seal of Kano Sanraku." Both seals differ, however, from Sanraku's standard seals. Thus it would be hasty to conclude, based on the seals alone, that the painting is by Sanraku. In terms of style, particularly in such motifs as the heavily outlined, thick, twisting trees, this work more closely resembles the work of Unkoku Tōgan (1547–1618). The contour of the distant mountains and the exaggerated curve of the sailboat's sail match such motifs in Tōgan's paintings. *Winter Landscape* lacks, however, the brusque directness of expression that distinguishes Tōgan's best paintings. Rather, it can be characterized as possessing the refined clarity of paintings by Tōgan's son, Tōeki (d. about 1639). *Winter Landscape* is, therefore, tentatively assumed to be a work not of Kano Sanraku but of Unkoku Tōeki or another artist of Tōgan's atelier.

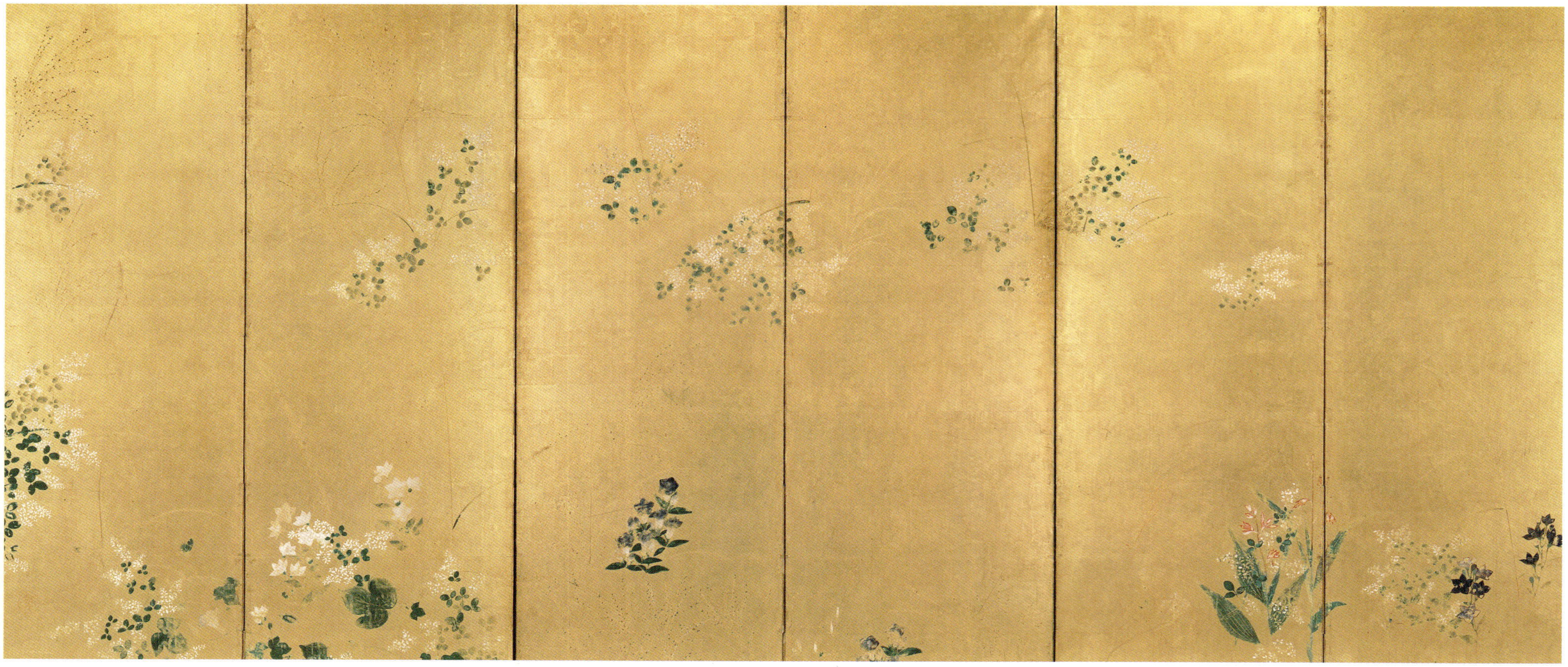

19

ATTRIBUTED TO TAWARAYA SŌTATSU
(ACTIVE FIRST HALF OF 17TH CENTURY)

Autumn Grasses

Edo period, 17th century
Pair of six-panel screens
Color over gold leaf on paper
Each, 67¼ x 148½ in.
(170.8 x 377.2 cm)
1762

PRECIOUS LITTLE is known about the life of Tawaraya Sōtatsu—even the dates of his birth and death remain uncertain—but it is apparent from mentions of him in his contemporaries' diaries that he was active as a painter in Kyoto from about 1600 to about 1644.

One characteristic of Sōtatsu's art is his imaginative use of motifs purely for their decorative nature. This free use of forms harks back to the Yamato-e roots from which he created his own unique style. Indeed, Sōtatsu is best remembered as the painter whose decorative style and frequent use of traditional Japanese imagery formed the basis of the Rinpa style as formulated by Ogata Kōrin (1658–1716).

In this pair of screens, delicate bush clover, bellflowers, and gossamer strands of pampas grass gone to seed seem to dance in the moonlight in autumn's crystal night air. They are scattered across an even ground of gold leaf under a half moon of silver leaf, which has tarnished over the centuries. Round seals that read "Inen" appear in both screens; the "Inen" seal is frequently found on works associated with Sōtatsu.

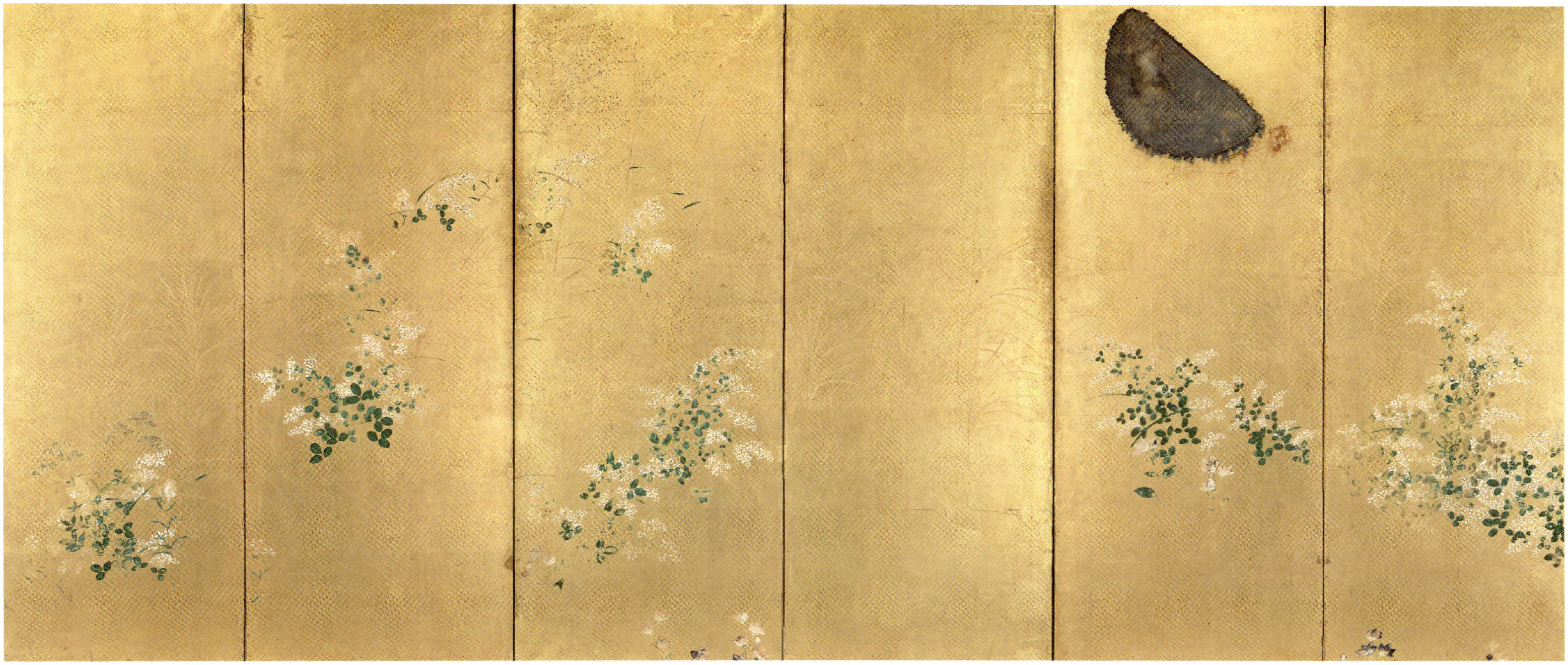

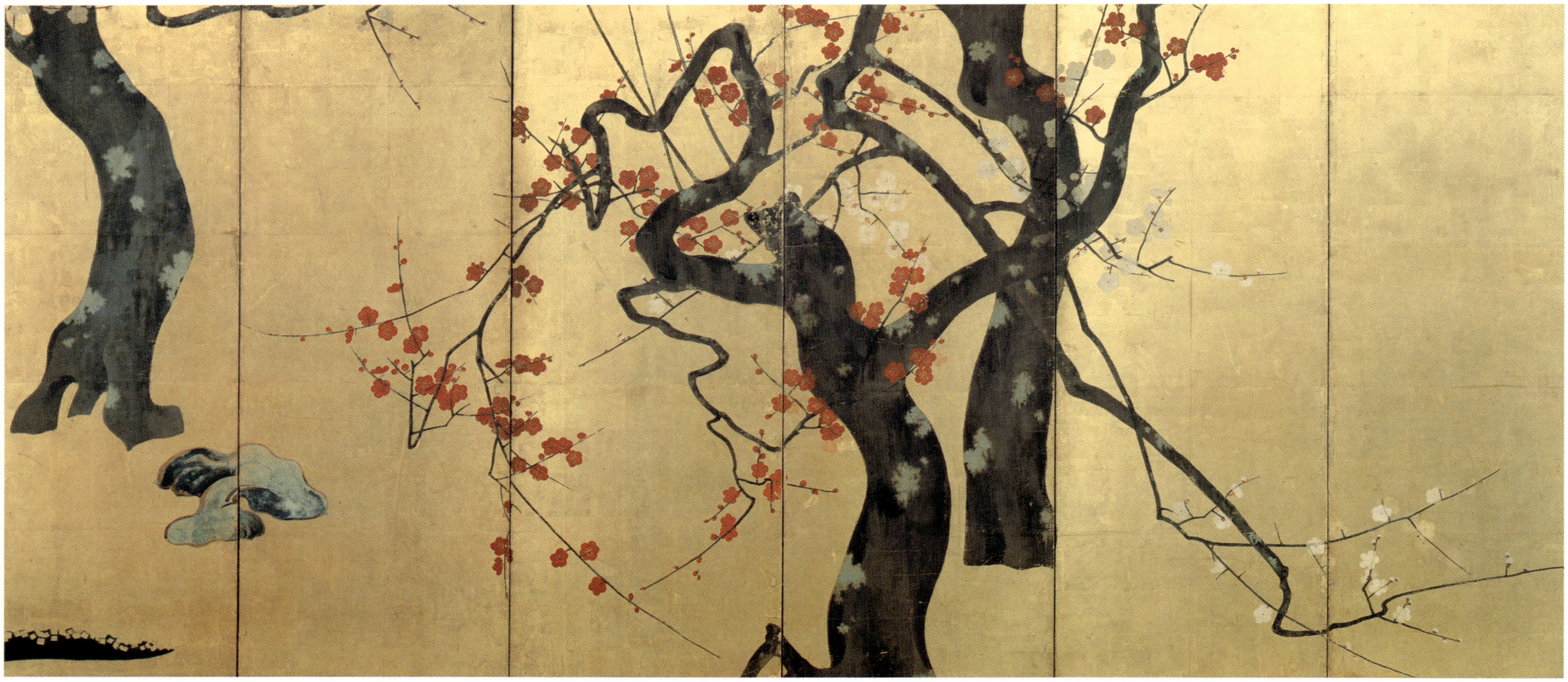

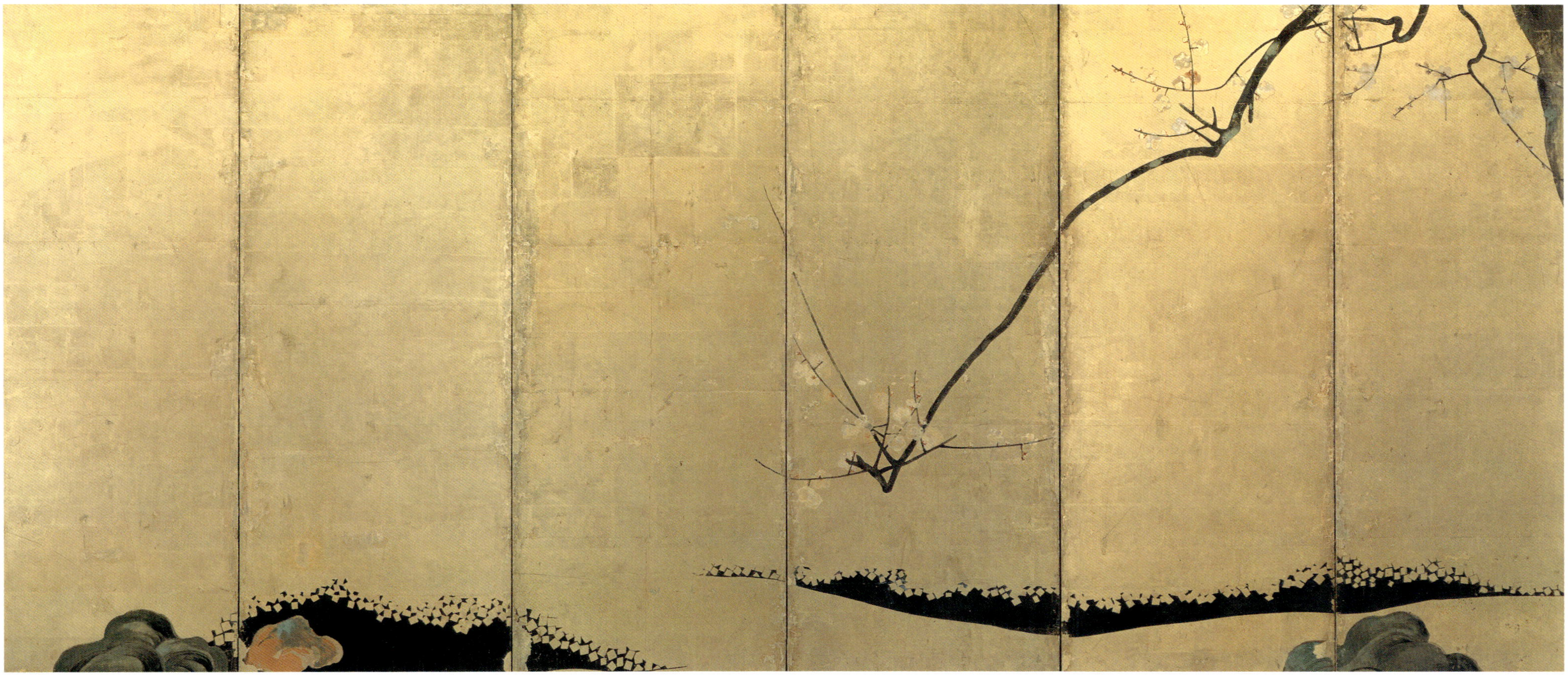

20

ATTRIBUTED TO OGATA KŌRIN
(1658–1716)

Red and White Plum Trees

Edo period, 17th century
Pair of six-panel screens
Color over gold leaf on paper
Each, 65¾ x 143½ in.
(167 x 364.4 cm)
1763

THIS WORK WAS long thought to be a masterpiece by Tawaraya Sōtatsu, although it lacks both signature and seal. The intense emotional expression that comes through the form and color of the blossoming plum trees could only be the work of an artist of Sōtatsu's caliber. The plum trees in the center of the left screen are a masterly harmonization of naturalistic representation and decorative abstraction. In this aspect the work more closely resembles the formal character of *Red and White Plum Trees* in the MOA Museum in Atami than paintings by Sōtatsu.

The plum trees, rocks, and water in other parts of the painting are of yet a different style, however, one closer to the works of artists after Kōrin (such as Watanabe Shikō [1683–1755], for example). It is also possible that these motifs were added in later years, in which case the original work would have consisted of the left screen only.

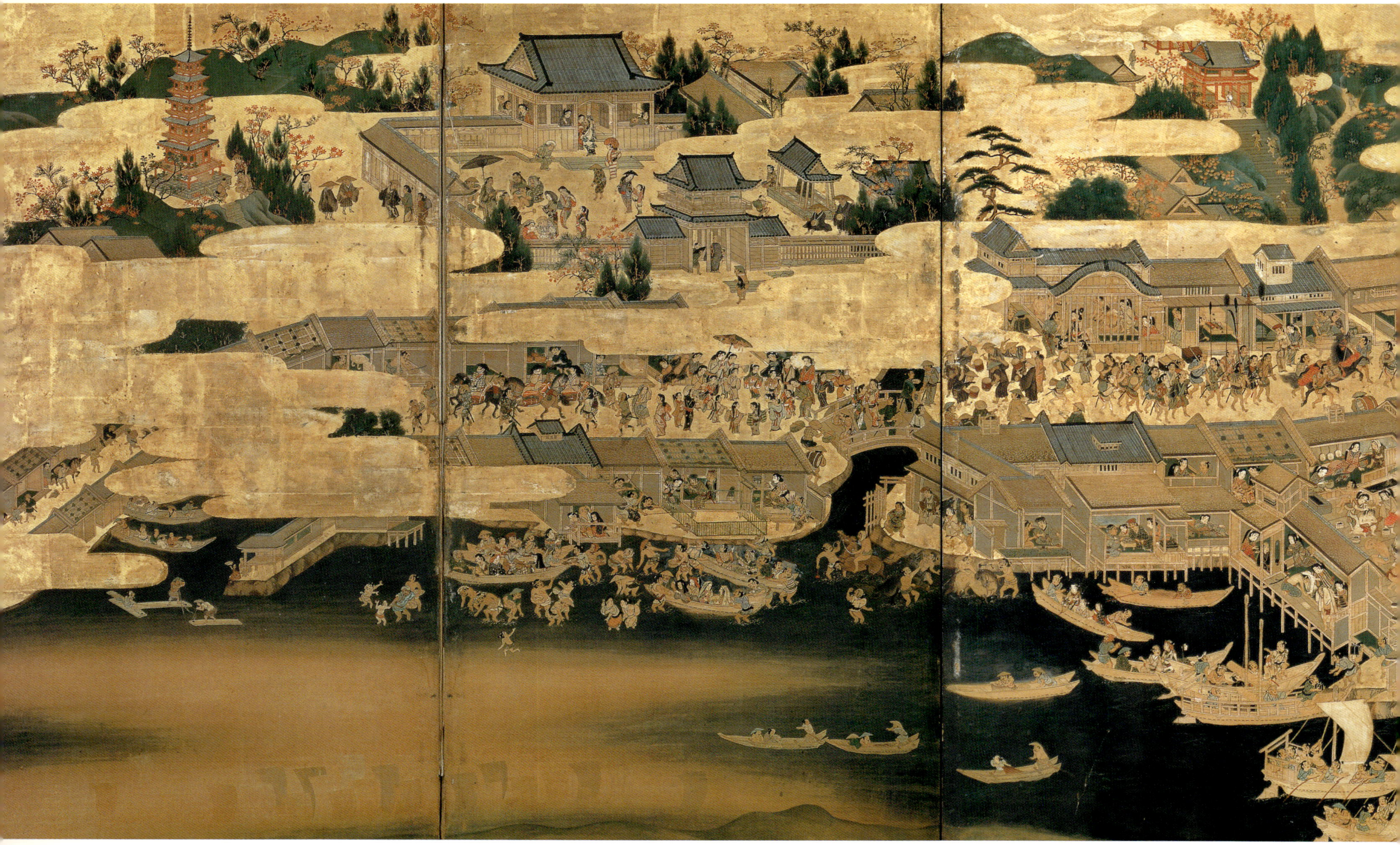

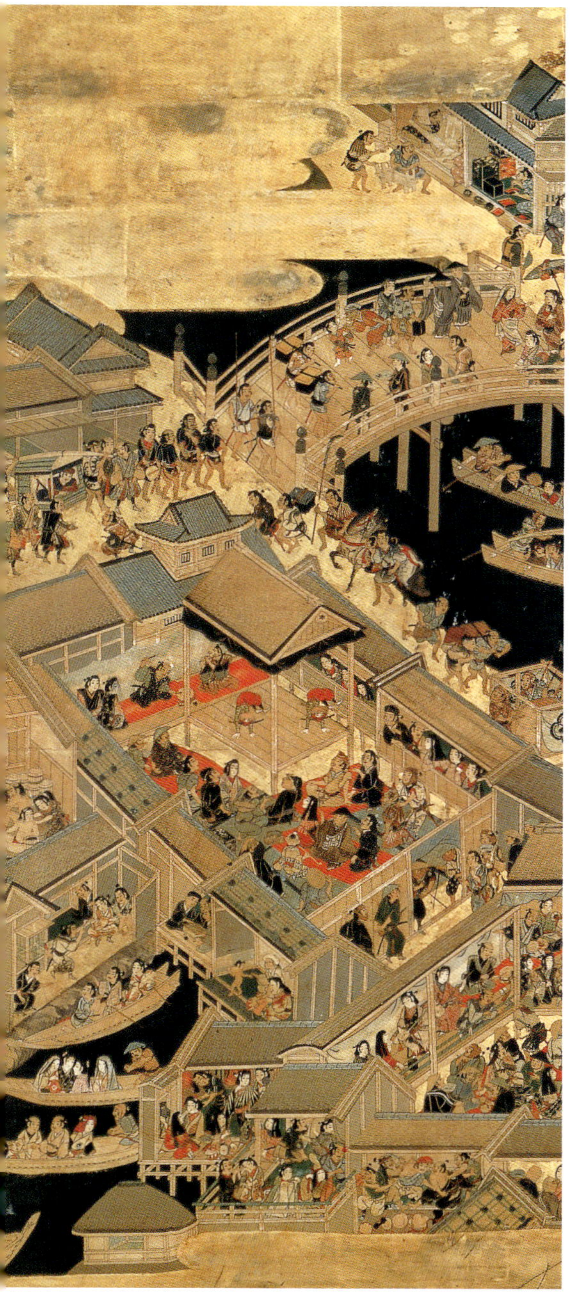

21

Famous Views and Entertainment Centers in Edo

Edo period, Kan'ei era, 1624–1644
Pair of eight-panel screens
Color and gold leaf on paper
Each, 47¾ x 198 in.
(121.5 x 502.6 cm)
2689

CENTERED ON EDO CASTLE, these screens represent the famous sights of the Tokugawa shogunate's administrative seat and the people who lived there. The anonymous painter depicted the old pleasure quarter of Moto-Yoshiwara and the theater district as they likely appeared from the 1620s through 1640s. The screens themselves were possibly produced about the same time.

The artist framed this panorama of Edo (Tokyo) with blossoming cherry trees in the Asakusa vicinity at the right edge of the right screen and scarlet maple leaves at Zōjōji at the left edge of the left screen. This follows the older convention in *Scenes in and around Kyoto* (see cat. no. 15) of incorporating a seasonal sequence into the depiction of famous places in the capital. Some of the notable sites in Edo include, in the right screen, Mount Ueno and Kan'eiji, the official temple of the Tokugawa family, where many shoguns were laid to rest; Sensōji, a popular temple founded centuries before the Tokugawa shogunate; Shinobazu Pond; the Tōshōgū mortuary shrine of the first shogun, Ieyasu; Kanda Myōjin Shrine; and the old licensed pleasure quarter of Moto-Yoshiwara. In the left screen are Edo Castle; the bridge called Nihon-bashi, Edo's commercial hub; the Kabuki theater entertainment district; and the Tokugawa's tutelary temple, Zōjōji.

Although many of the Tokugawa's new monuments and symbols are portrayed in these screens, most striking is the ordinary citizens' excited pace, which permeates the sixteen panels. The screens are a virtual textbook of fashion, fads, and festivals in the years before the city was incinerated in the Great Meireki Fire, of 1657. In the Asakusa section at the Sanja Festival, several figures sport European-style dress with hats and pantaloons, a popular fashion in early seventeenth century urban centers. Another important detail, the fact that the Kabuki performers in the left screen are young men (*wakashū*), dates the scene before the 1652 prohibition against young male performers.

The facial expressions and gestures of the citizens of Edo are full of playful energy, reflective of the spirit of the city as it mushroomed in size during the boom years of the early seventeenth century. The immediacy of the rendering of the lifestyles of the people suggests an artist who lived among his subjects and could observe them carefully. Although the painting does not possess the finesse and polish of the work of an artist of the Kano academy, for example, it does deftly convey the atmosphere of life in Edo's early years. The Idemitsu Museum's *Famous Views and Entertainment Centers in Edo* has particular historical value because it is considered the oldest extant representation of the city on folding screens.

Opposite: detail from left screen

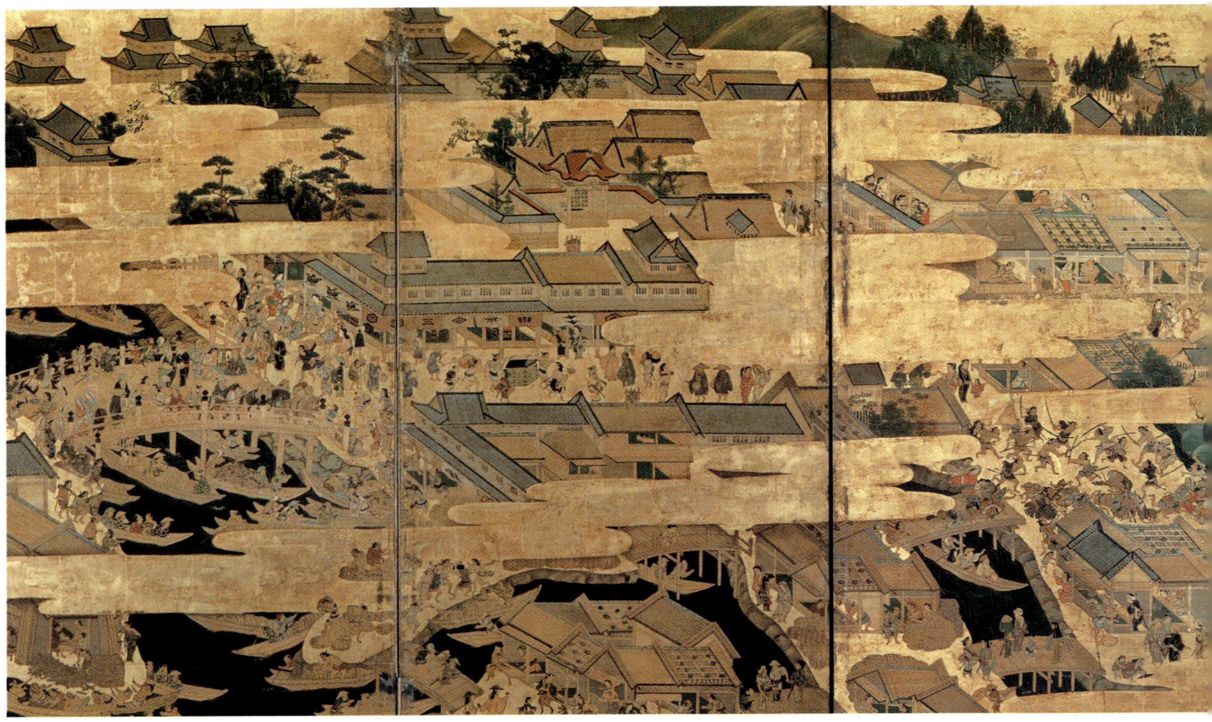

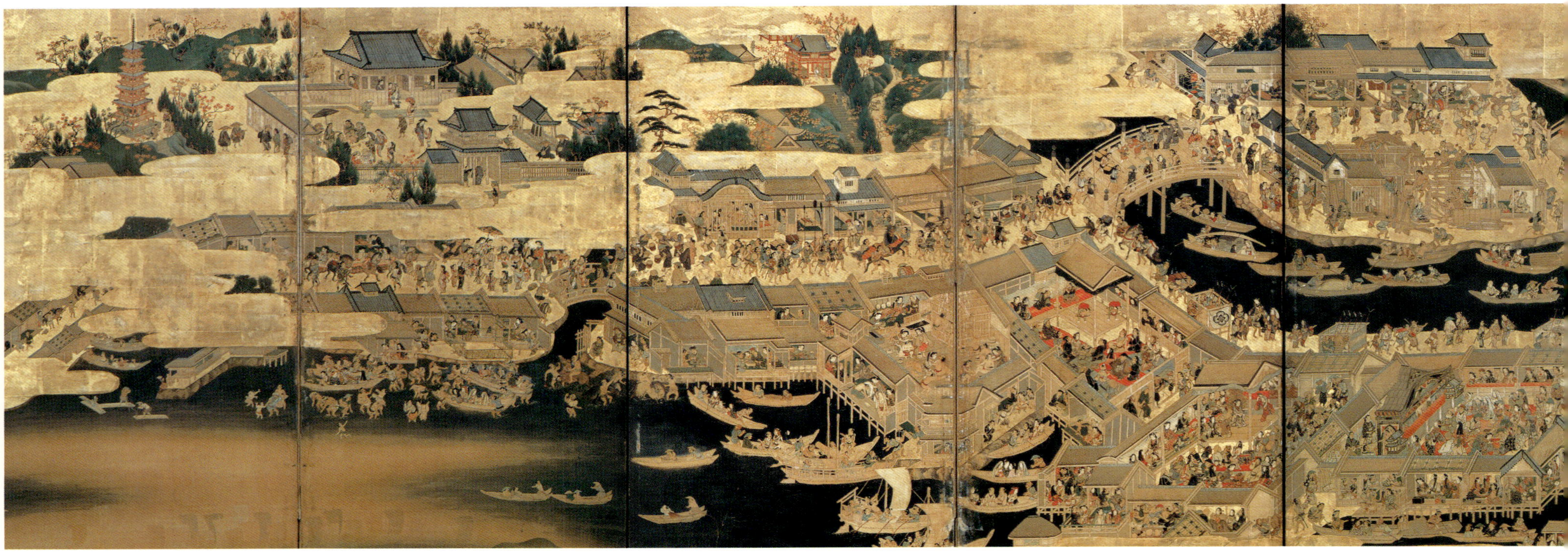

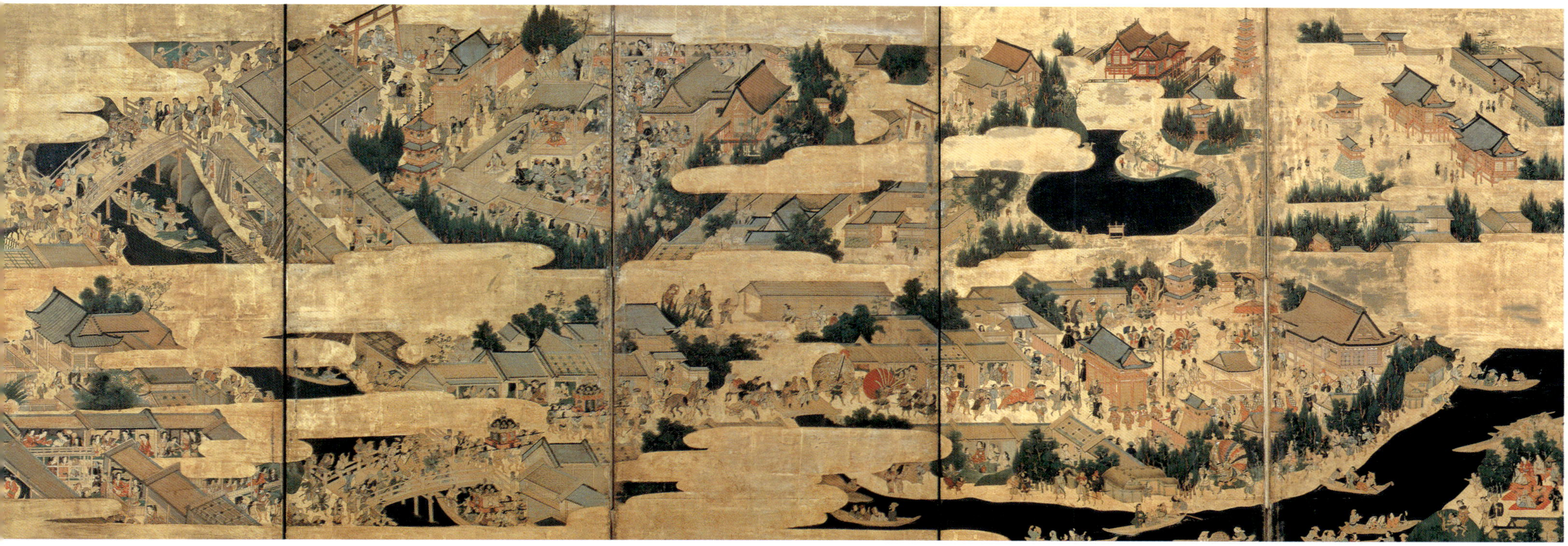

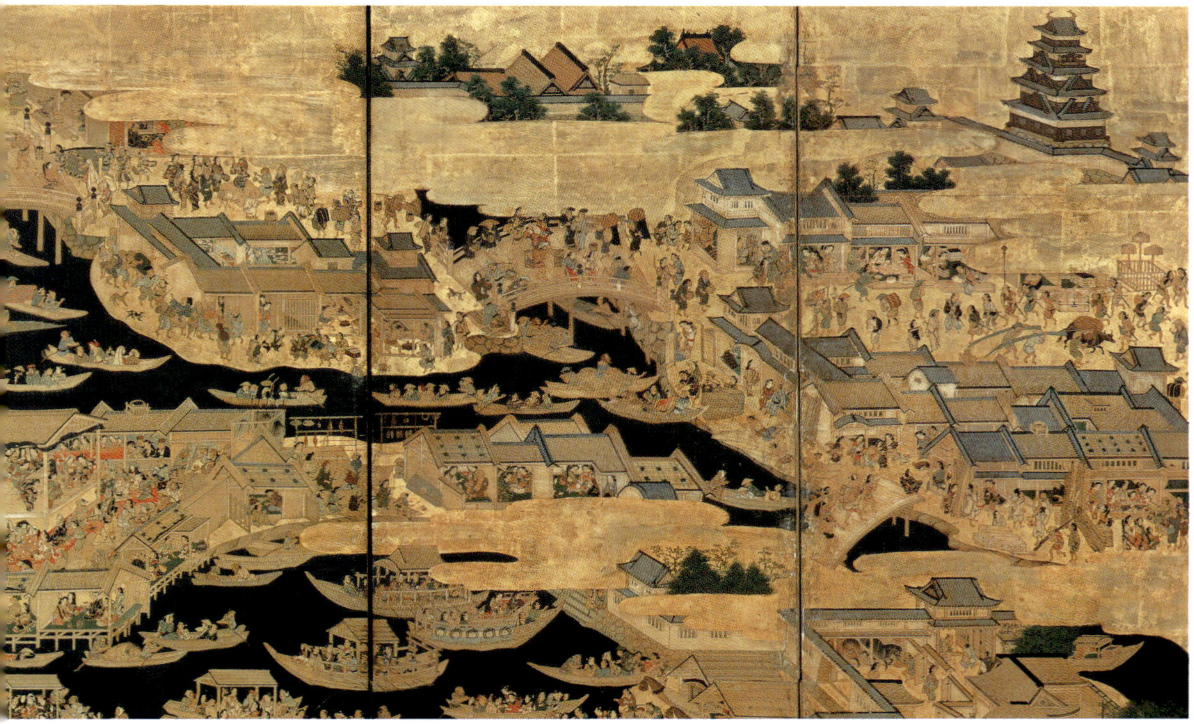

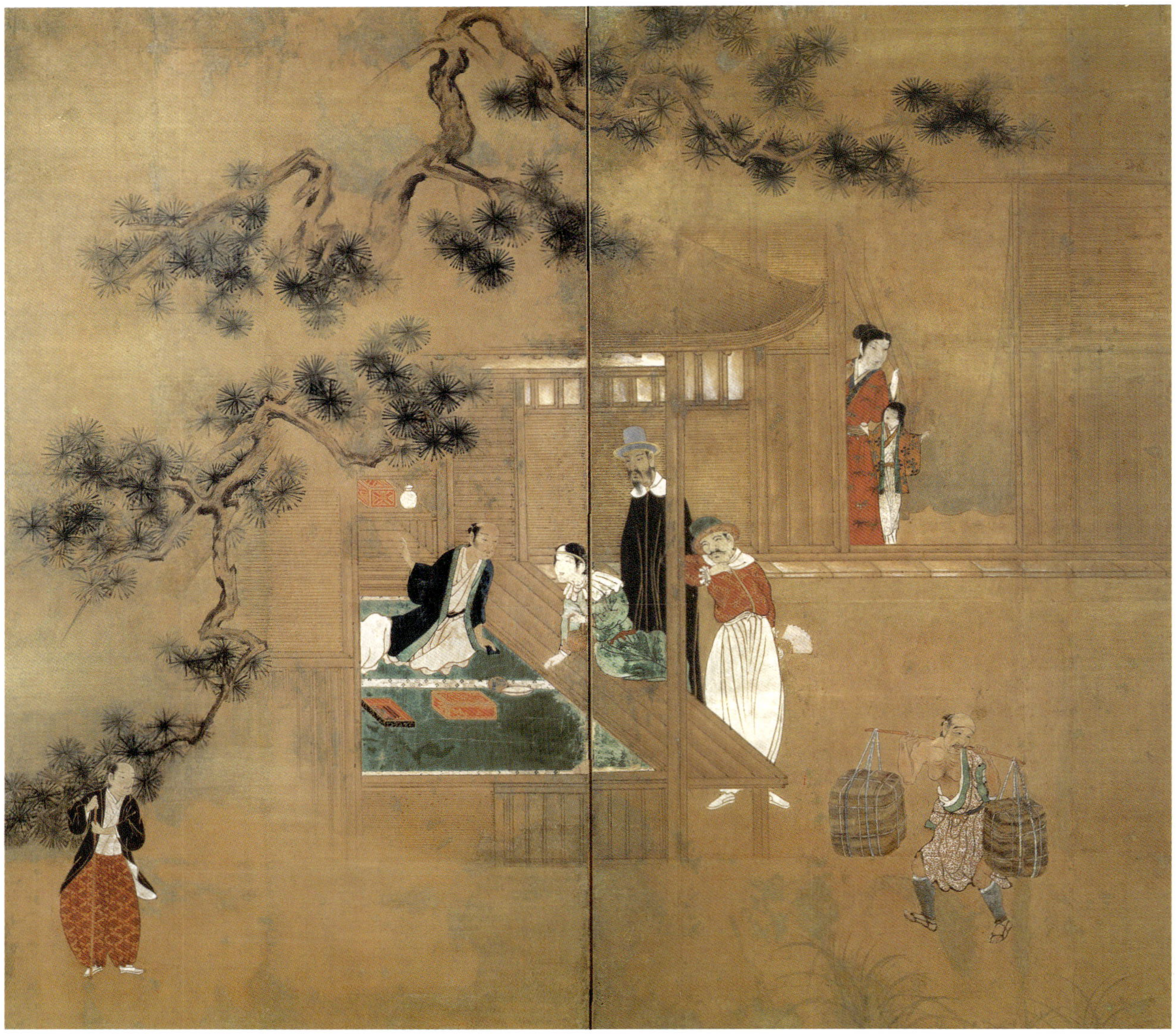

22

Westerners in Japan

Edo period, mid-17th century
Pair of two-panel screens
Color on paper
Each, 67¼ x 74½ in.
(170.8 x 189.2 cm)
2720

A GROUP OF EUROPEAN VISITORS to Japan—possibly Portuguese or Spanish—are represented shopping on a street in an unidentified locale. They have already purchased a great deal, as is evident from the packed bundles that their porters struggle to haul.

The anonymous artist has opposed the right and left screens by subtly shifting his gaze from the Westerners, who are greater in number and central to the right screen, to the Japanese, who eye the visitors curiously but with some caution in the left screen. Within this contrastive composition, both the Europeans and the Japanese are represented with expressive faces that show off the painter's sure-handed draftsmanship. Two distinctly differentiated types of pine trees effectively frame the scenes from above and below. Their gesticulating branches bear some resemblance to pine trees in works by the early Edo period artist Iwasa Matabei (1578–1650), such as the *Yamanaka Tokiwa* handscroll paintings in the MOA Museum in Atami. It would be hasty, however, to assign authorship of the present work to Matabei. More likely, it is the work of someone a generation later, who perhaps started in Matabei's atelier.

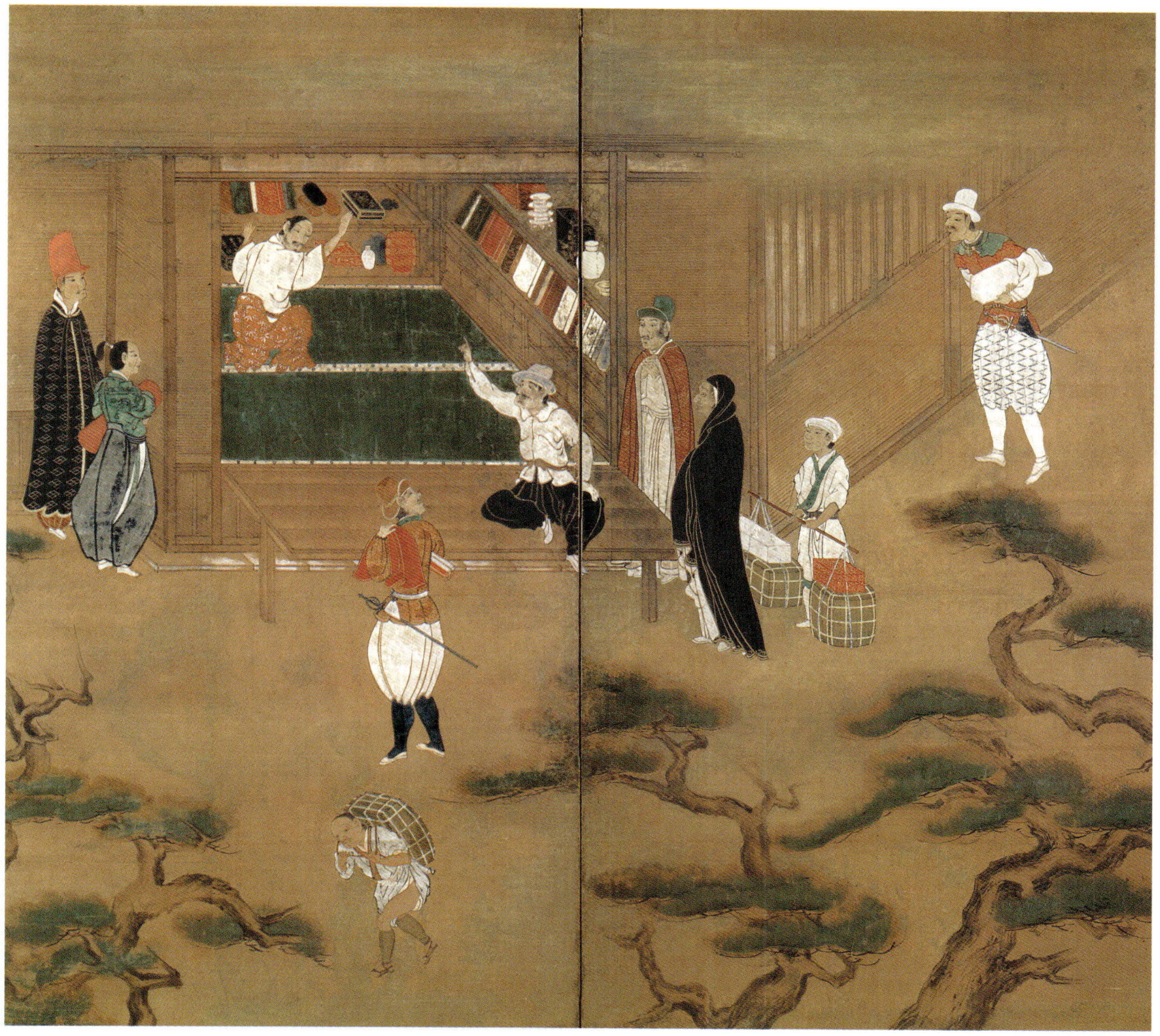

23

Beauties under the Cherry Blossoms

Edo period, mid-17th century
Two-panel screen
Color and gold leaf on paper
71¾ x 74¼ in.
(182.5 x 188.5 cm)
2707

UNDER A WIZENED CHERRY tree in full bloom, beautiful women enjoy elegant pastimes. Seated near the veranda, one lady strums a *shamisen*, and the other reads a letter while a young attendant prepares ink for a response. Their companion outside holds a long *kiseru* pipe, and her young assistant opens a box containing another shamisen. This combination of music and reading could be a parody of the Chinese theme of the Four Gentlemanly Accomplishments of zither (C. *qin*, J. *kin* or *koto*), literature, chess (C. *weiqi*, J. *go*), and painting. Although only music and reading appear in this screen, the other two may have been represented in an accompanying screen, now lost.

The anonymous artist of this screen took special care in the arrangement and gestures of the five figures, but what is perhaps most remarkable is the painstaking detail in the clothing. This almost excruciating precision, along with the figures' hand gestures and faces, could have been influenced by the early Edo period artist Iwasa Matabei (1578–1650); but the work is probably not by his hand.

The women portrayed in this screen are most likely women of the pleasure quarters (*yūjo*)—a popular theme throughout the Edo period. Their mastery of traditional arts, their fine costumes, and the elegant surroundings made them celebrities of their day; and many paintings idealizing their existence remain. The present work, with its richly patterned cherry blossoms and wisteria and gorgeously clothed figures, is a masterpiece most likely dating from the Kan'ei era (1624–1644).

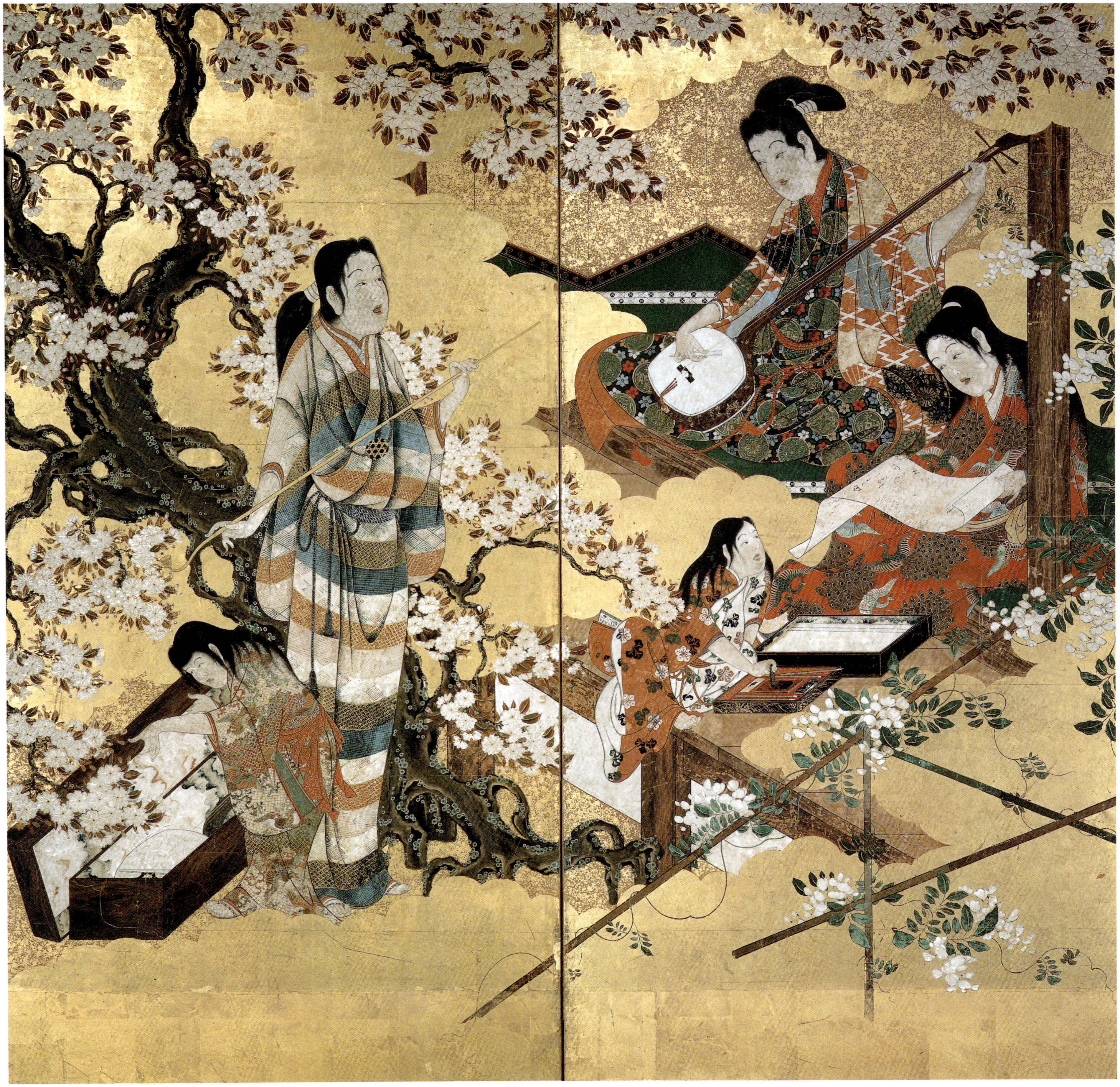

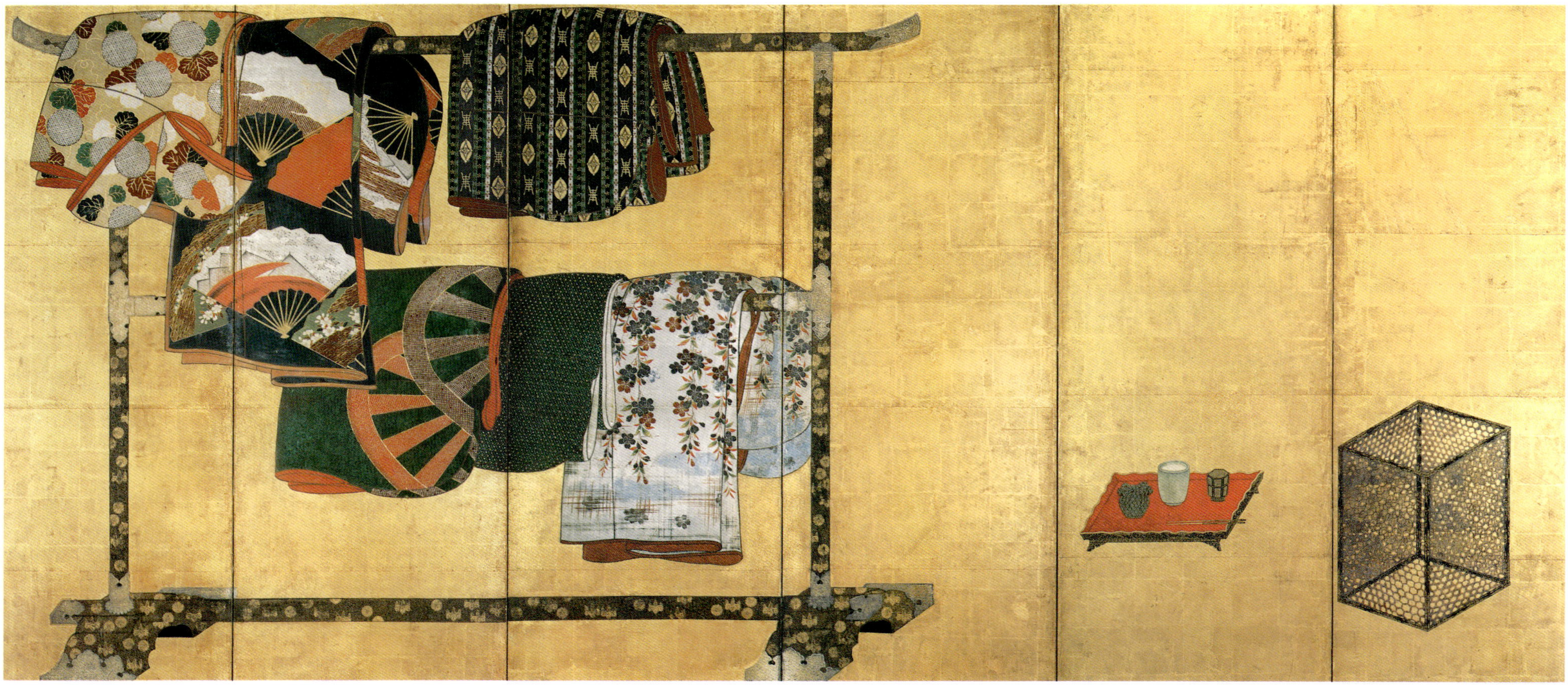

24

Whose Sleeves? (Tagasode)

Edo period, mid-17th century
Pair of six-panel screens
Color and gold leaf on paper
Each, 67 x 144 in.
(170.4 x 366 cm)
2727

IN THE RIGHT SCREEN, a young girl's long-sleeved kimono (*furisode*), protective amulets, and six other kimonos are hung on a bamboo kimono rack. Two sets of quilts are piled in a heap on the floor nearby. In the left screen, six kimonos are draped casually over a lacquered kimono rack (*iko*) decorated with a pattern of chrysanthemums and paulownia in gold *maki-e* (decoration made by sprinkling metallic powders into damp lacquer). Nearby are placed a tray with utensils for incense and a wire drying coop for kimonos. Curved lines bring out the soft quality of the kimonos. Painstakingly rendered patterns and fabrics enliven this still life.

As the title indicates, the owners of the gorgeous robes are nowhere in sight. Although the women—perhaps courtesans—do not appear, their kimonos serve to remind us of them. This use of possessions to suggest their absent owners is also characteristic of seventeenth century Dutch still life painting.

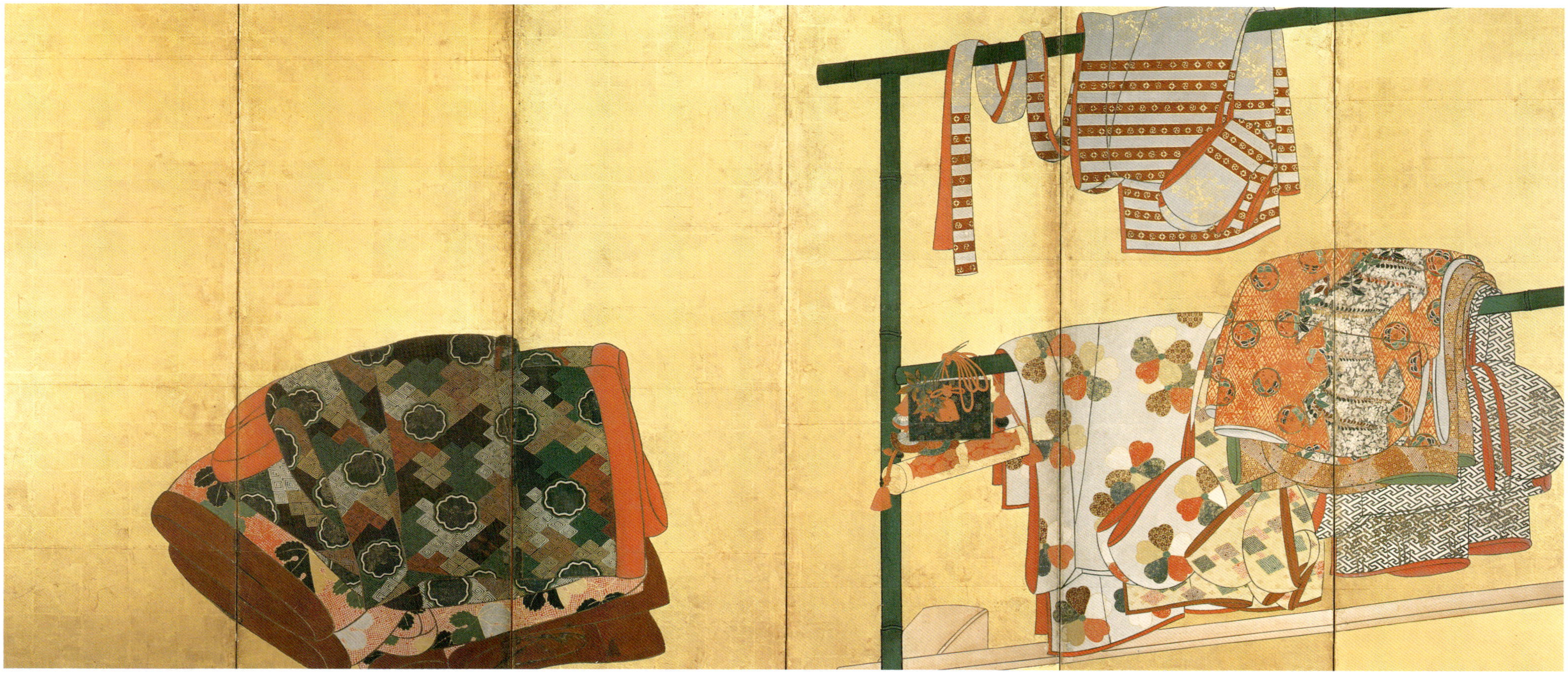

25

Scenes from the Tale of Heike

Edo period, mid-17th century
Pair of eight-panel screens
Color and gold leaf on paper
Each, 67 x 208½ in.
(170.3 x 530.0 cm)
2722

THIS PAIR OF SCREENS illustrates scenes from the Genpei Wars between the Minamoto (or Genji) and the Taira (or Heike) clans during the late Heian period. This clash is immortalized in the epic *Tale of Heike*, which recounts how the Taira clan fell from its glorious position in the imperial court to near extinction at the hands of the Minamoto, a fierce and daring clan from eastern Japan.

The first four panels of the right screen show the battle of Ichinotani, which occurred in 1184. Minamoto no Yoshitsune, the brother of Yoritomo (who would later become Japan's first shogun), executes a surprise attack on the Taira at their stronghold in Ichinotani, near the modern city of Kobe. As the *Tale of Heike* describes the event, Yoshitsune and his men attack from steep mountains and almost catch the Taira off guard. Their presence is revealed, however, when three deer, startled by the massive cavalry movement of the Minamoto forces, dash toward the Taira's stronghold (deer would ordinarily run into the mountains for cover). The second panel shows the deer and the beginning of the cascade of Yoshitsune's soldiers down the cliff face immediately above the Taira's fortified palatial buildings.

Having lost the day at Ichinotani, the Taira flee across the Inland Sea to Yashima, only to be pursued by Yoshitsune's forces. The battle of Yashima appears in the left four panels of the right screen. In one of the most memorable moments of this battle, a Taira woman in the bow of a ship holds up a fan. According to an oracle, if a Minamoto archer managed to hit the fan, the Minamoto would win the battle; but, if not, the Taira would prevail. As the artist carefully shows in the sixth panel, the fan is carried into the air by the arrow, and again the Minamoto emerge victorious.

The left screen shows the famous naval battle of Dannoura (near modern Shimonoseki) in which Minamoto no Yoshitsune defeats the fleet of the Taira. In this final, decisive confrontation, the Minamoto with three thousand ships overwhelm the Taira, who have only a thousand. As in the right screen, the two sides are identifiable by their flags: white for the Minamoto, red for the Taira. One of the most poignant moments in the entire *Tale of Heike* is depicted in the upper left corner of this screen. Rather than be captured by the despised enemy, the Nun of the Second Rank, the widow of Taira no Kiyomori and grandmother of the emperor, takes the eight-year-old emperor Antoku in her arms and tells him to pray to the Ise Shrine to the east and to the Paradise of Amida in the West. A moment later, still holding the emperor, she plunges into the waves and drowns them both.

Among the many extant paintings illustrating episodes of the *Tale of Heike*, battle scenes of Ichinotani and Dannoura are the most common. The Idemitsu Museum's screens are unusual in that they expand in eight panels rather than six and they include the battle of Yashima. The question of who painted the screens remains open, but it is safe to assume that the artist was influenced by the Tosa school.

Opposite: detail of seventh and eighth panels of left screen showing the widow of Taira no Kiyomori with Emperor Antoku, plunging into the waves

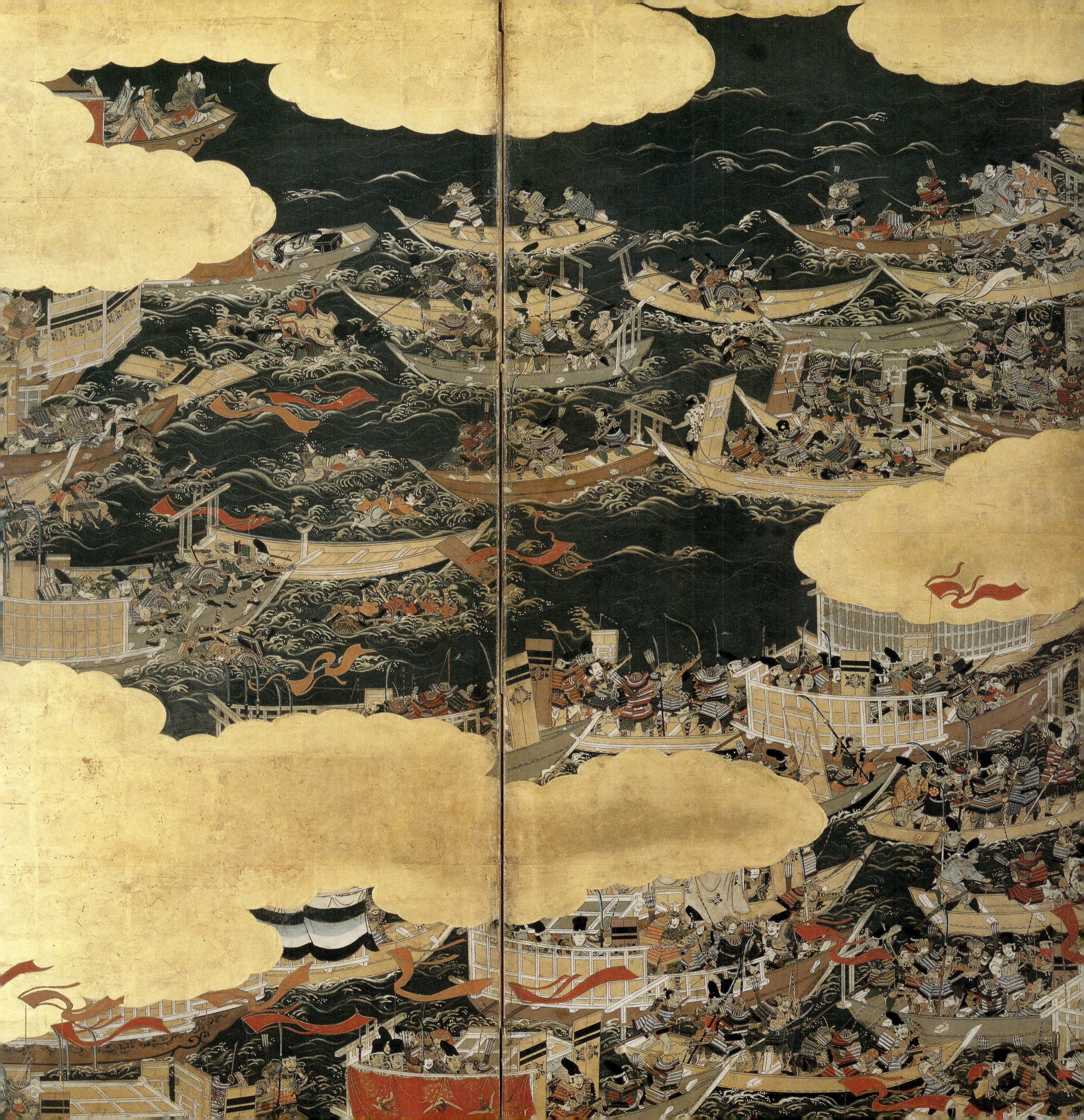

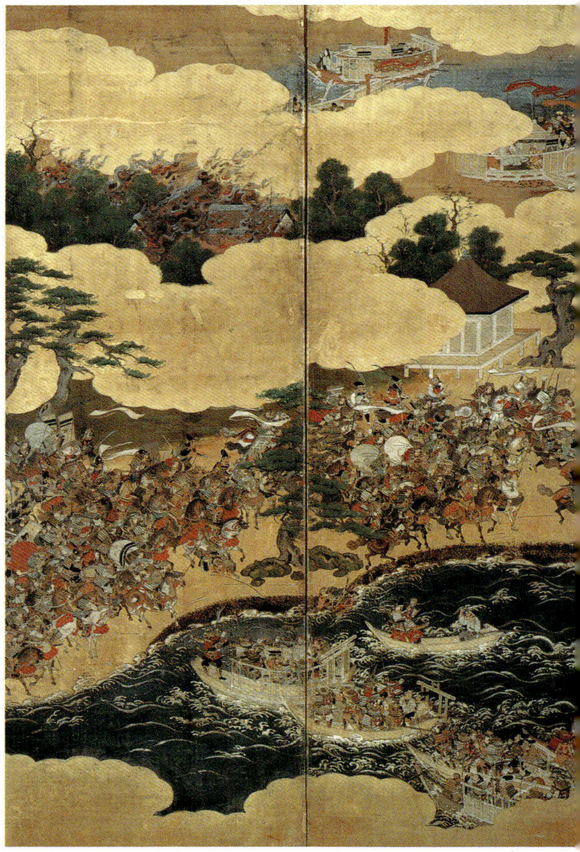

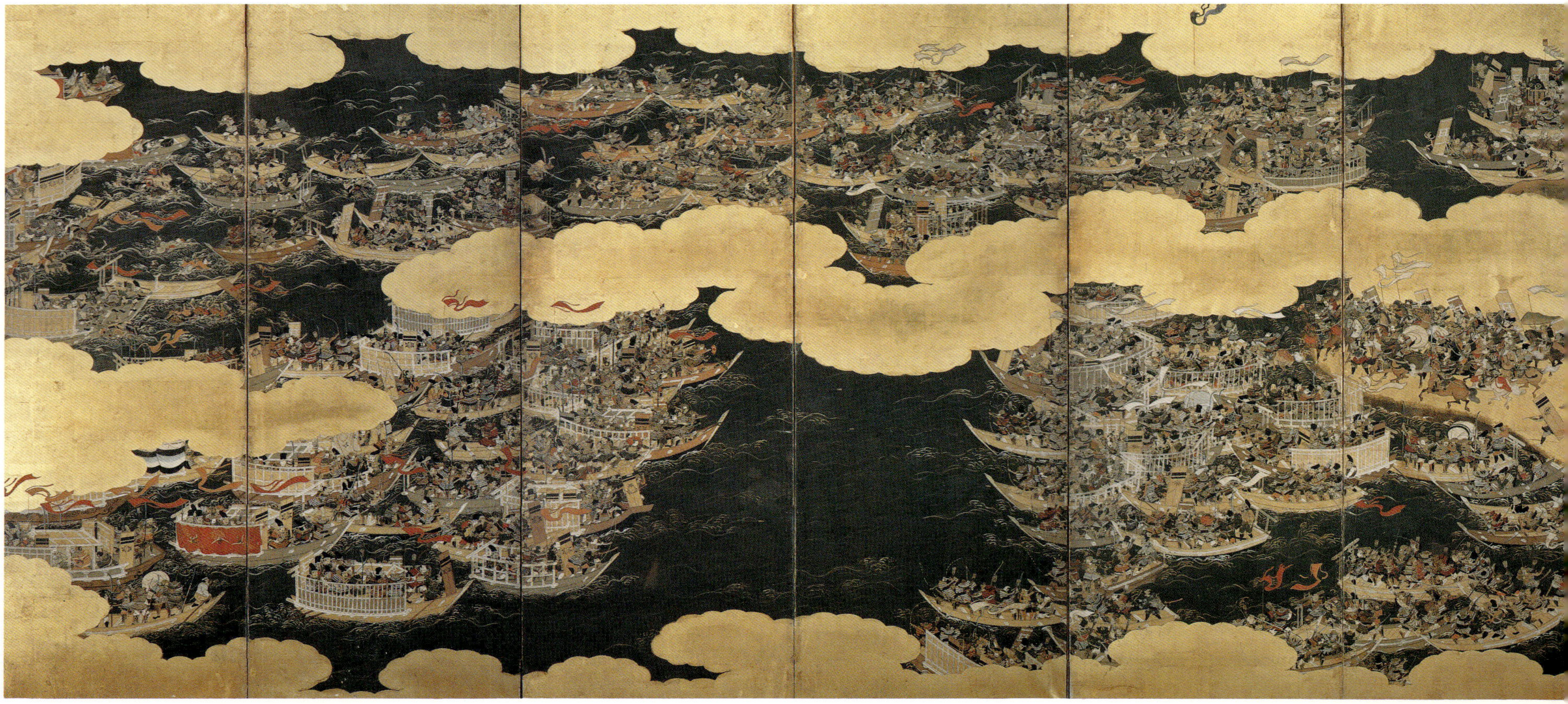

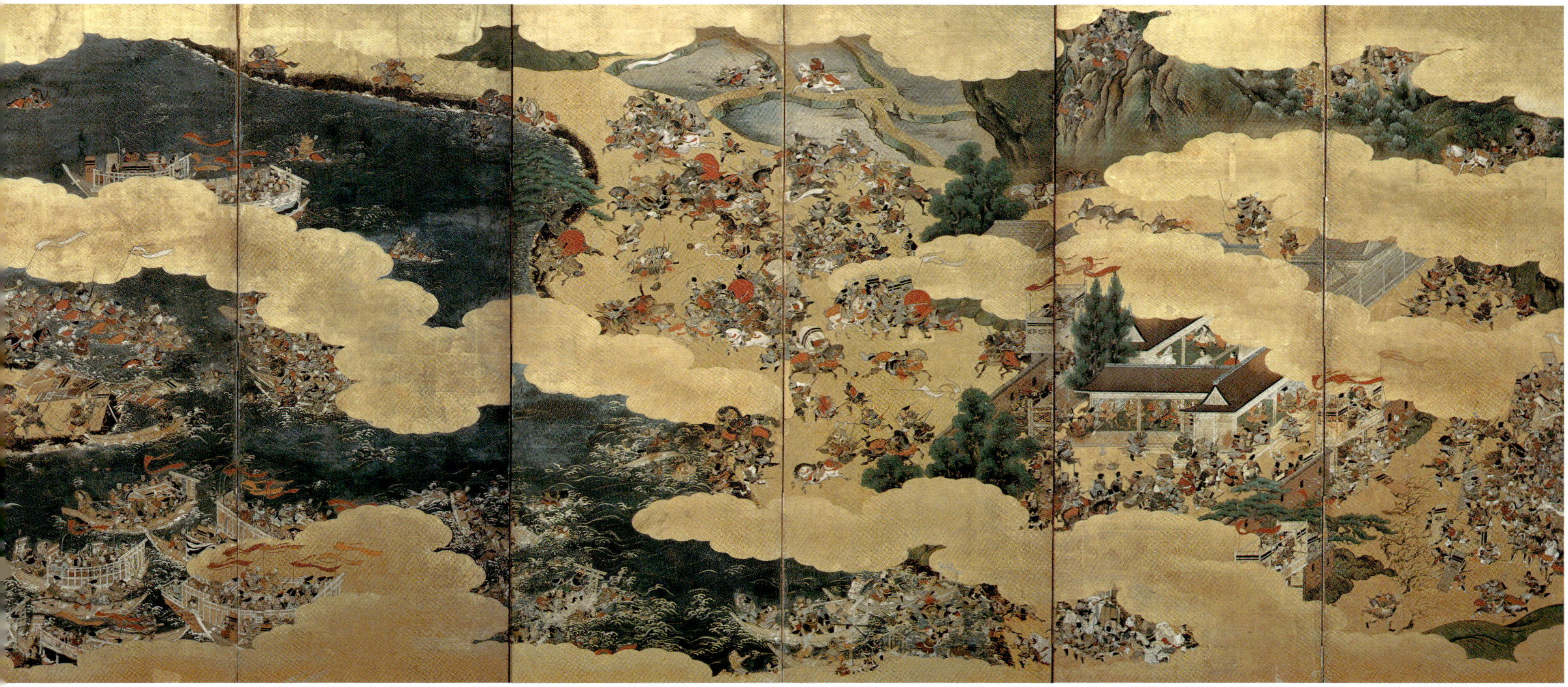

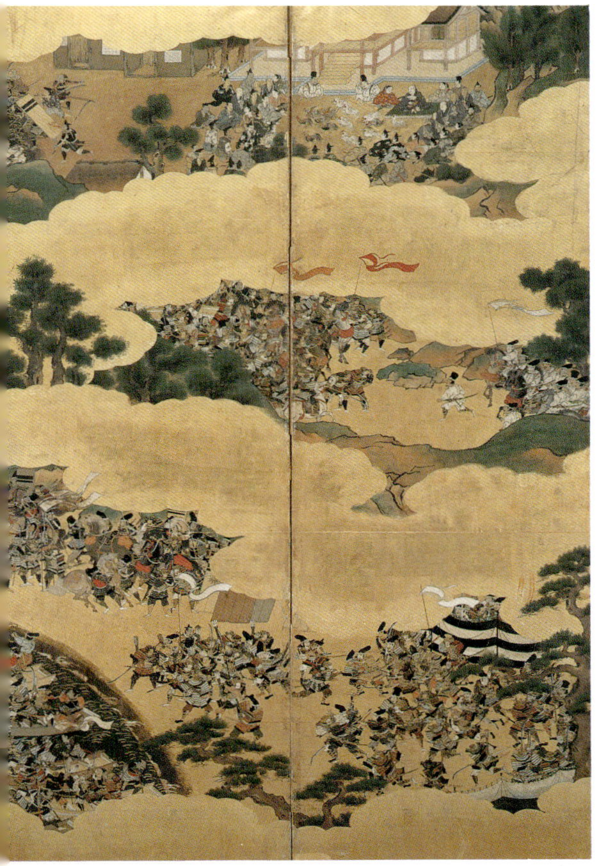

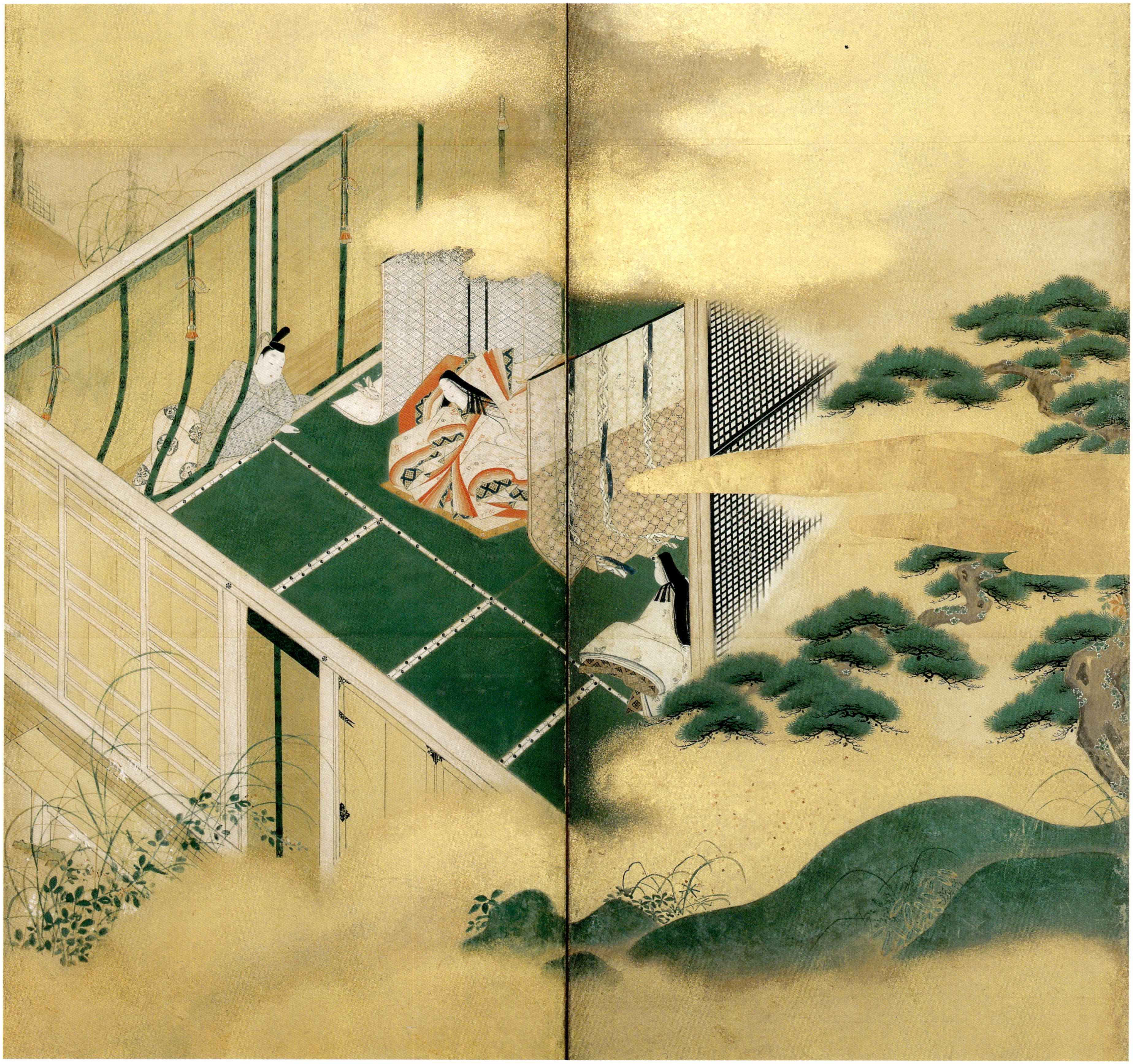

26

KANO TAN'YU (1602–1674)

Scenes from the Tale of Genji

Edo period, dated to 1669
Pair of six-panel screens
Color and gold leaf on paper
Each, 64¾ x 147¾ in.
(164.4 x 375.2 cm)
9933

KANO TAN'YU was the official painter to the Tokugawa shogunate and founder of the Kajibashi branch of the Kano school. Taught by his father, Takanobu (1571–1618), Tan'yu displayed genius at an early age and eventually developed a distinctive style characterized by a light, refined touch that created meaning in the blank areas of his compositions. Tan'yu's reserved style represented a major departure from the dominant style of the Kano school that preceded him. He is therefore known as the founder of the Edo Kano school and was, moreover, the artist most responsible for establishing the foundation for the styles of various schools of artists throughout the Edo period. Adept at Chinese-inspired ink painting, Tan'yu also devoted much of his energies to the indigenous Yamato-e mode in which native themes were painted in mineral pigments.

The "Sacred Tree" and "Channel Buoys" chapters of the *Tale of Genji* supply the subjects for this pair of screens. Among the most stirring of the many chapters of this great Heian period classic, these episodes describe the meeting of Genji with two of his former lovers. In the "Sacred Tree" chapter, Genji visits Lady Rokujō, who, having been forsaken by him, has decided to accompany her daughter, a Shinto priestess, to the Ise Shrine. At a temporary shrine in Sagano, the lonely wilds of western Kyoto, Rokujō and her daughter prepare for their departure. Genji arrives and is so moved when he and Rokujō exchange poems that he begs her to stay in the capital. Although the lady does entertain second thoughts, her mind is made up and she soon departs with her daughter. The right screen shows the moment on a fall evening when Genji and Rokujō meet for the last time.

The "Channel Buoys" chapter describes, among other events, Genji's pilgrimage to the Sumiyoshi Shrine and his chance encounter with a former lover, the lady of Akashi. In Tan'yu's painting, Genji arrives at the shrine by oxcart with his entourage just as the boat of the lady of Akashi appears offshore. Neither expected to see the other. The lady, ashamed of her lower social status, shyly covers her face with the sleeve of her many-layered kimono. As the story goes, Genji, speechless with surprise, sends the lady of Akashi a poem and a message inviting her to the capital, but she declines the invitation. Like the "Sacred Tree" episode, "Channel Buoys" involves Genji's seeing a former lover and asking her to join him again but ultimately being refused.

This work is particularly valuable as one of the very few paintings by Tan'yu of the *Tale of Genji*. In addition, the sumptuously decorative gold clouds and mist display the artist's mastery of the style of earlier Muromachi period paintings in the Yamato-e mode. While paintings of the *Tale of Genji* tend to follow established patterns of motifs and composition, Tan'yu's painting is completely original in every aspect. Bearing signatures and seals reading "from the brush of Hōin [seal of the Dharma (Buddhist Law)] Tan'yu, age 68," this pair of screens is a masterpiece from the end of the artist's life.

Opposite: detail from right screen

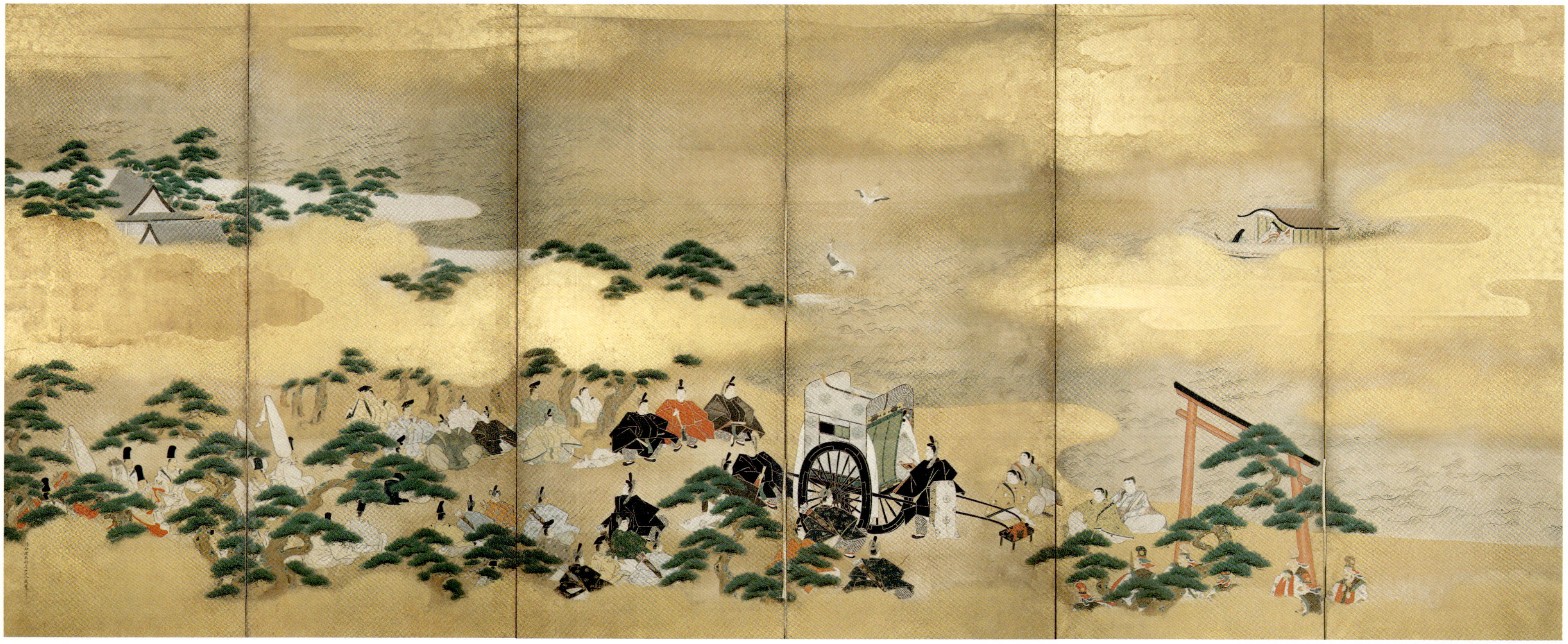

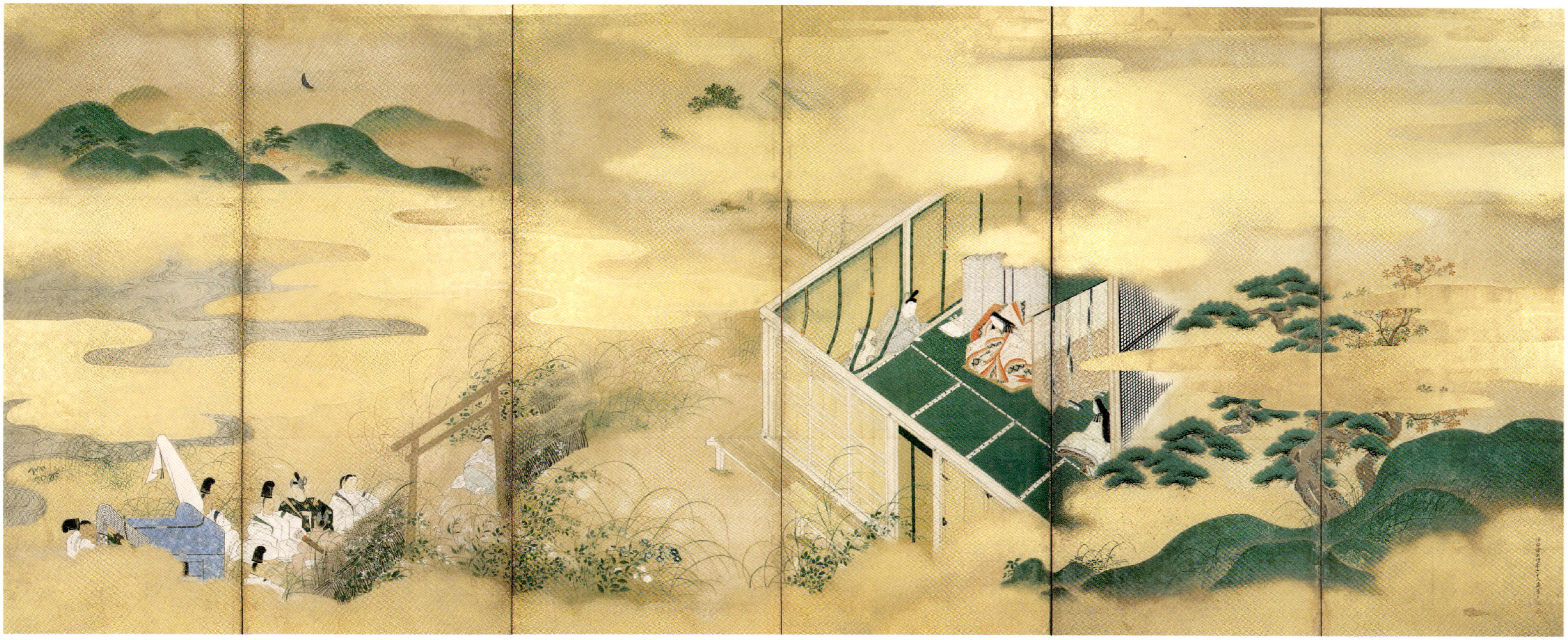

27

KANO TSUNENOBU (1636–1713)

Rolling Waves

Edo period, late 17th century
Pair of six-panel screens
Color and gold leaf on paper
Each, 71½ x 151½ in.
(181.5 x 385.2 cm)
10393

KANO TSUNENOBU WAS the eldest son of Kano Naonobu (1607–1650?) and the nephew of Kano Tan'yu (1602–1674), who founded the Kano school at Edo. Tsunenobu succeeded his father as head of the Kobikichō branch of the Edo Kano school and, after the deaths of his father and his uncles Tan'yu and Yasunobu (1613–1685), directed the whole Kano school organization. Like Tan'yu, Tsunenobu was assiduous in his efforts to record paintings that he inspected and made voluminous collections of reduced-scale sketches called *shukuzu*. After Tsunenobu's death, his descendants in the Kobikichō branch wielded tremendous authority and prospered as "painters of the inner chamber [of the shogun's residence]" (*oku-eshi*) to the Tokugawa shogunate.

Seagulls dance above the spray blown from a sea of violently churning waves. Tsunenobu captured the atmosphere of the stormy Japanese seacoast in the rhythmic undulations of waves breaking over sharp rocks. An element of abstraction pervades the painting—for example, in the mannered fingerlike wave-tips and strong ink accents on the rocks, which combine to create an animated surface.

The artist signed his name ceremoniously on both screens as "Fujiwara Tsunenobu," recalling the spurious lineage to a noble family that the Kano created for themselves. The dimensions of the screens are greater than standard folding-screen size (*hongen*, approximately 59 inches high by 129 or 133 inches [150 x 330/340 cm]), so it is possible that they were conceived for a special ceremony or other exceptional occasion.

Opposite: detail from left screen

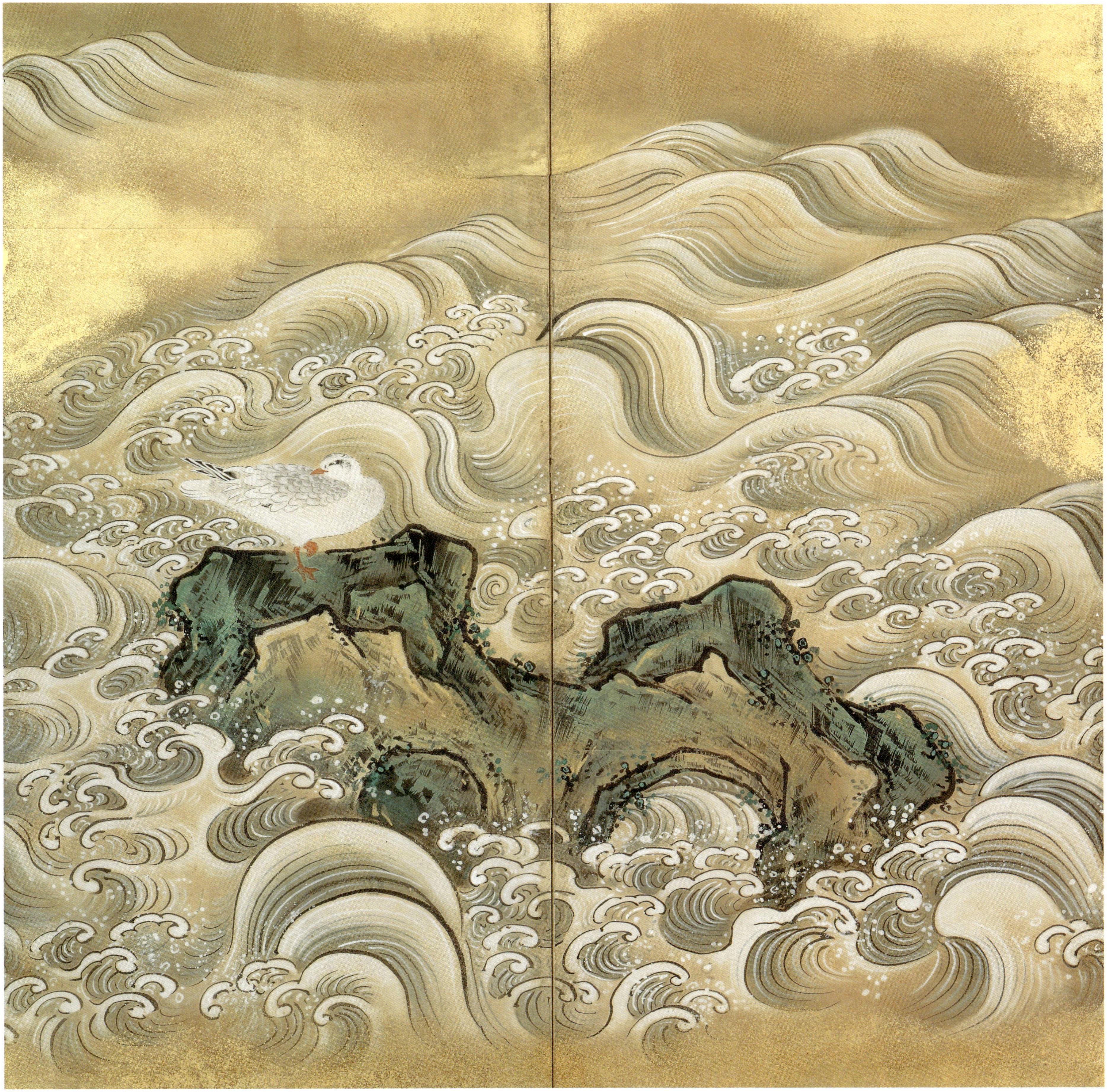

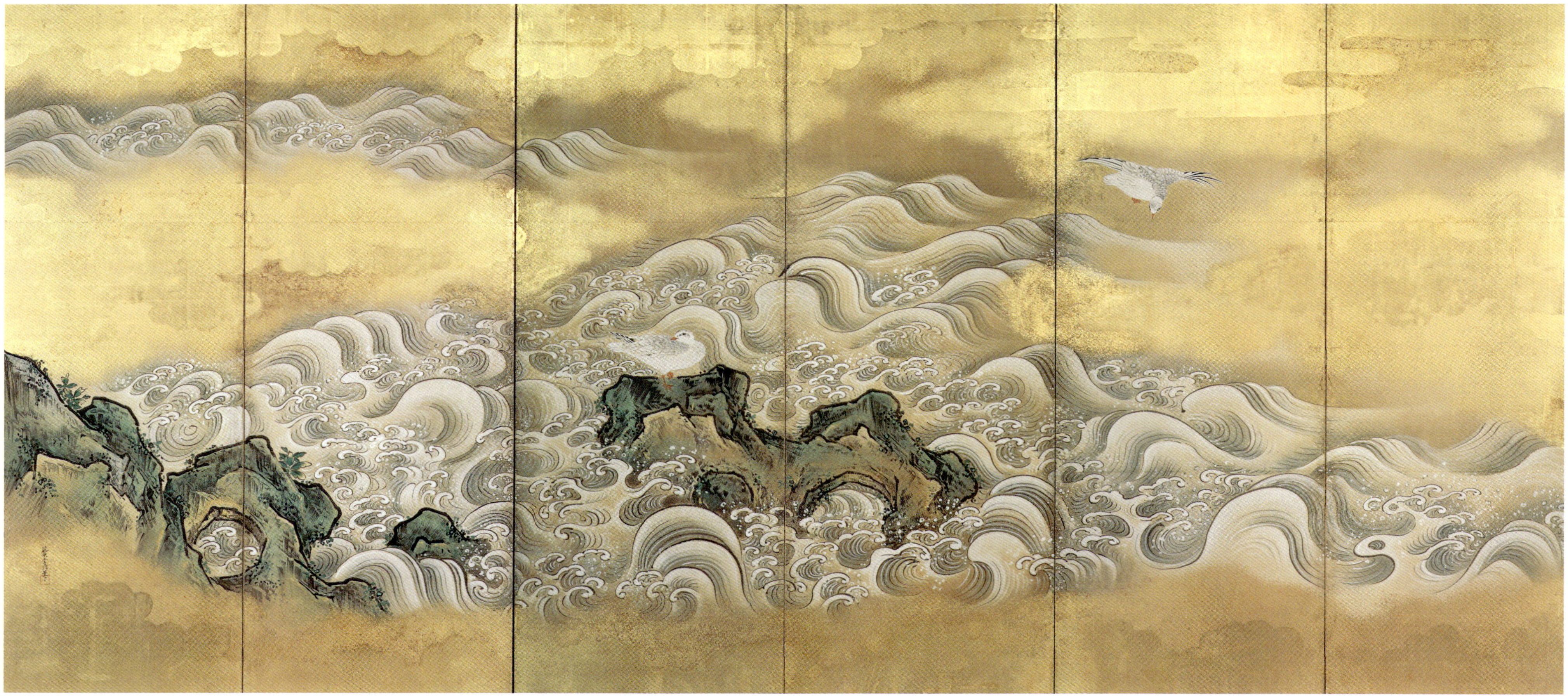

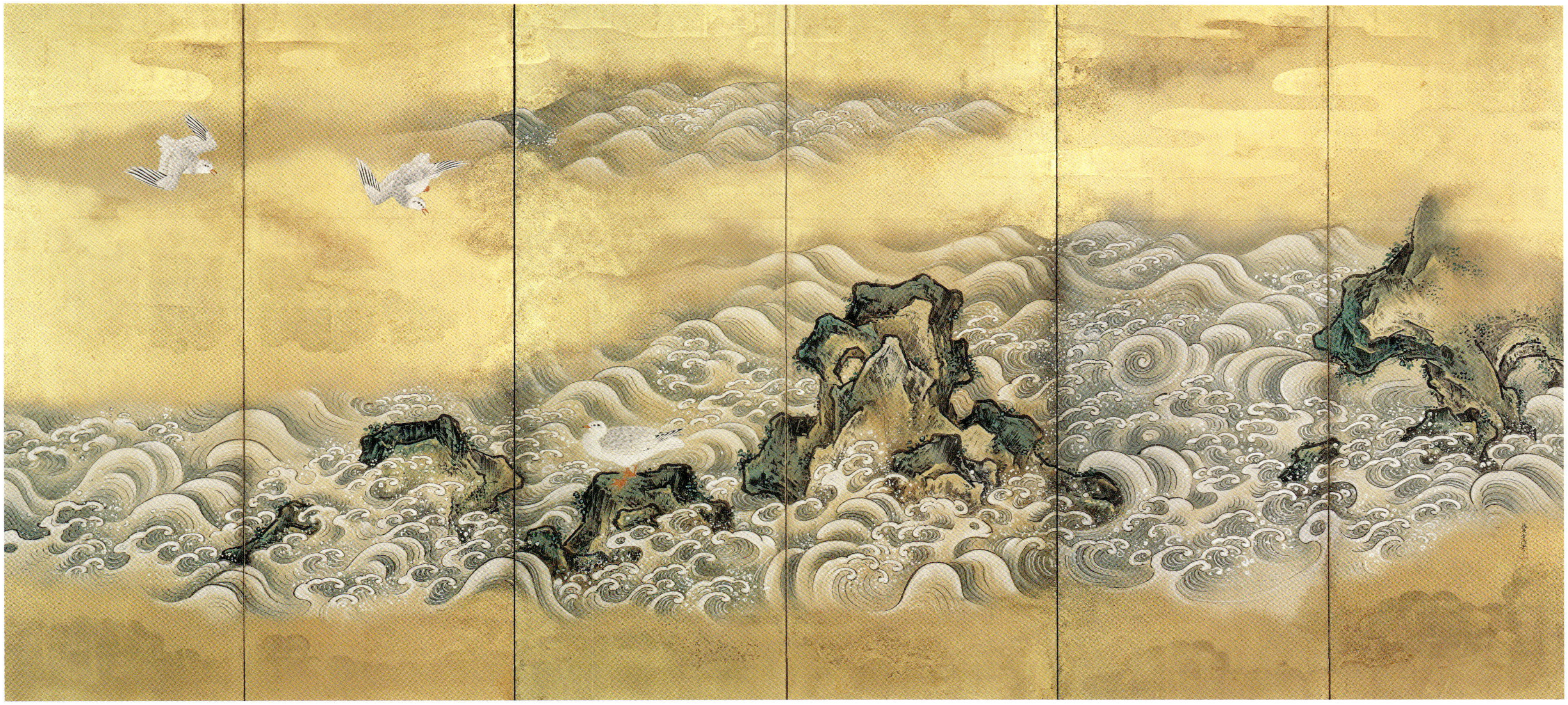

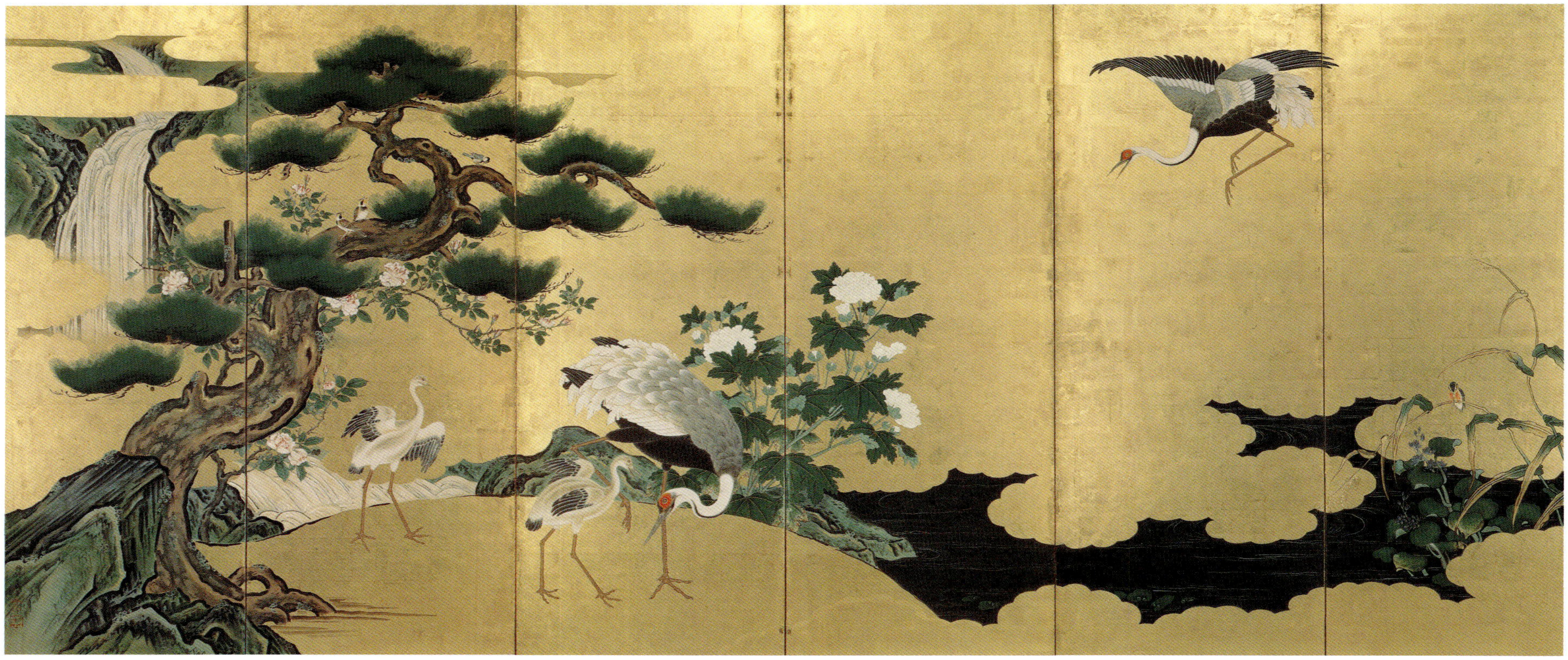

28

KANO EINŌ (1631–1697)

Cranes

Edo period, late 17th century
Pair of six-panel screens
Color and gold leaf on paper
Each, 67 x 149¼ in.
(170.3 x 379.2 cm)
9360

JAPANESE CRANES, birds of paradise, peonies, irises, pines, and azaleas in the right screen are paired with Asian white-naped cranes, Chinese hibiscus, roses, and a pine in the left screen. All of these motifs are set in a glimmering world of gold clouds and gold ground accented with green moss-covered rocks and an indigo pool fed by a cascading waterfall. The assembled flowers and birds are the essence of auspicious imagery: paired birds of paradise and cranes symbolize marital fidelity and longevity; the family of four white-naped cranes, the mother bending attentively toward one of her chicks, represents the fulfillment of parental duty and sacrifice. Einō's grouping of classically Japanese flowers and birds in one screen, counterposed with their "exotic" continental relatives (white-naped cranes, roses, and hibiscus are not native to Japan) in the other, further heightens the splendor of the painting.

The artist of these newly discovered screens, Kano Einō, was the third-generation head of the Kyoto branch of the Kano school. He succeeded the Momoyama and early Edo period giants, Kano Sanraku and Sansetsu. The author of the *History of Painting in this Realm* (*Honchō gashi*), the first history of Japanese painting, Einō is better remembered as a historian and theorist than as a painter, but his many extant works (many of which are in American collections, such as the Museum of Fine Arts, Boston) attest to his ability as a painter. The large motifs that fill the picture and are textured with bold brushstrokes in the Idemitsu Museum's screens display Einō's mastery of the grand style perfected by Eitoku and Sanraku. The composition, in which pine trees anchor the right and left edges and in which the background is negated by bringing the principal motifs to the foreground, follows the standard formula established in the paintings of Kano Motonobu over a century earlier. The snaking curves of the pine trees with their stylized groups of needles are more decorative than their more naturalistically rendered antecedents, as in *Flowers and Birds of Spring and Autumn* (cat. no. 13), for example.

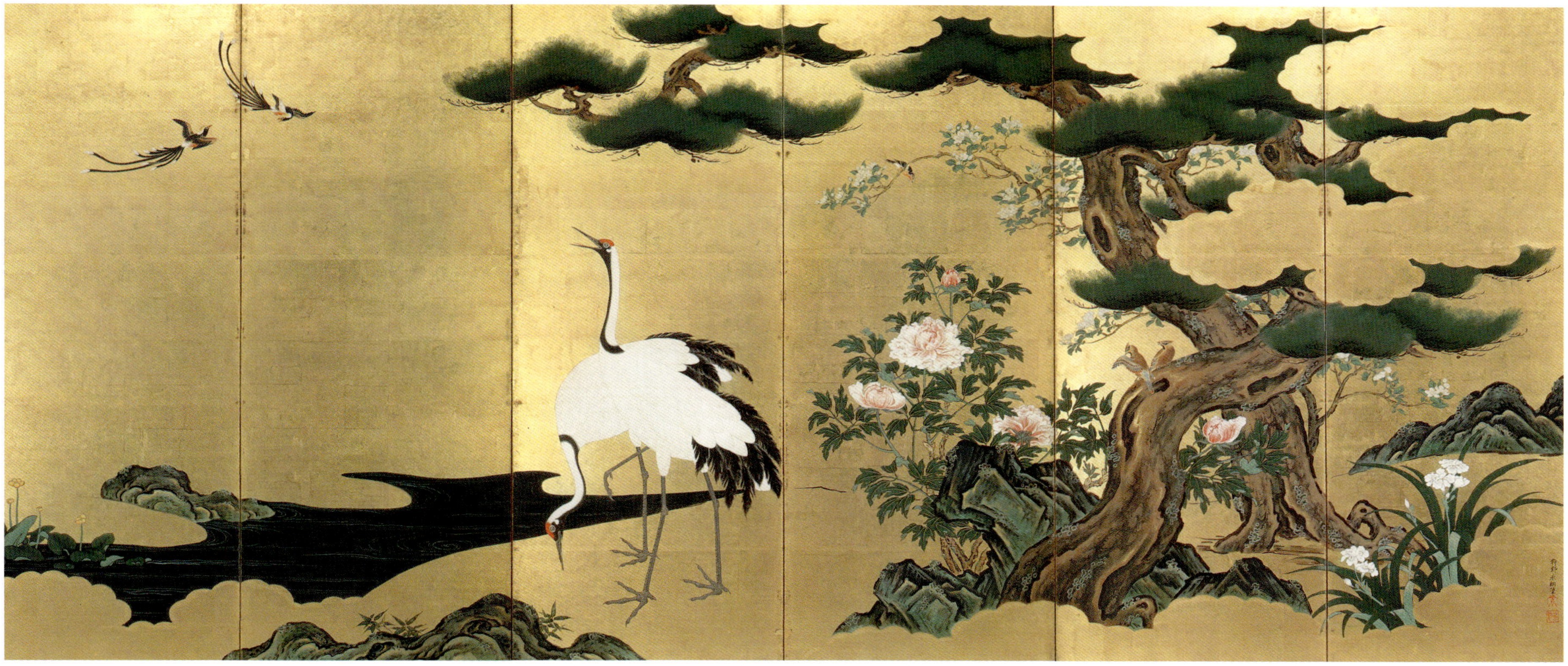

29

SAKAI HŌITSU (1761–1828)

Irises and Eight-Fold Bridge

Edo period, 18th century
Pair of six-panel screens
Color over gold leaf on silk
Each, 70¼ x 163¼ in.
(178.5 x 415 cm)
10607

SAKAI HŌITSU was the second son of the Sakai family, who were feudal lords (*daimyō*) of Himeji, in modern Hyōgo Prefecture, and one of the most trusted families near the Tokugawa shogunate. From his youth Hōitsu loved the literary arts and excelled in comic poetry, *haikai* (long chains of verses), and calligraphy; his particular genius was in painting.

At first Hōitsu studied ukiyo-e and the Kano academy painting style, but increasingly he devoted himself to the painting manner practiced in Kyoto a century earlier by Ogata Kōrin and his circle, which is called *Rinpa*, "school of [Kō]rin." Through his own exquisite, unconstrained, and light-handed style, Hōitsu managed to bring the Rinpa style of Kyoto across time and space to Edo.

In the ninth chapter of the Heian period classic *Tales of Ise*, the hero, Ariwara Narihira, who has left the capital under unpleasant circumstances and is traveling in the eastern regions of Japan, arrives with his companions at the famous Eight-Fold Bridge (*yatsuhashi*) in Mikawa Province. So moved are these men by the beauty of the patch of irises growing in the marsh traversed by the bridge that they spontaneously burst into tears. To commemorate the passing moment, Narihira composes the following poem:

I have a beloved wife,
Familiar as the skirt of a well-worn robe,
And so this distant journeying
Fills my heart with grief.

There remain two sets of folding screens of the ninth chapter of the *Tales of Ise* painted by Ogata Kōrin (1658–1716). One of these, in The Metropolitan Museum of Art, New York, depicts the irises and the eight-sectioned bridge. The other, in the Nezu Museum in Tokyo, simply shows dozens of irises. The Idemitsu Museum's painting could be called Hōitsu's version of the Metropolitan Museum's screens. The painting demonstrates Hōitsu's deep reverence for his predecessor in Kyoto. Indeed, he recorded the Metropolitan Museum's screens and many other of Kōrin's works in *One Hundred Paintings by Kōrin (Kōrin hyakuzu)*, a printed compendium compiled by Hōitsu.

He departed from Kōrin's work, however, by reducing the number of irises and by meticulously painting each leaf and arranging them in rhythmical fashion. This carried on the tradition of copying the painters of the past but also imbued the work with a fresh approach.

Opposite: detail from right screen

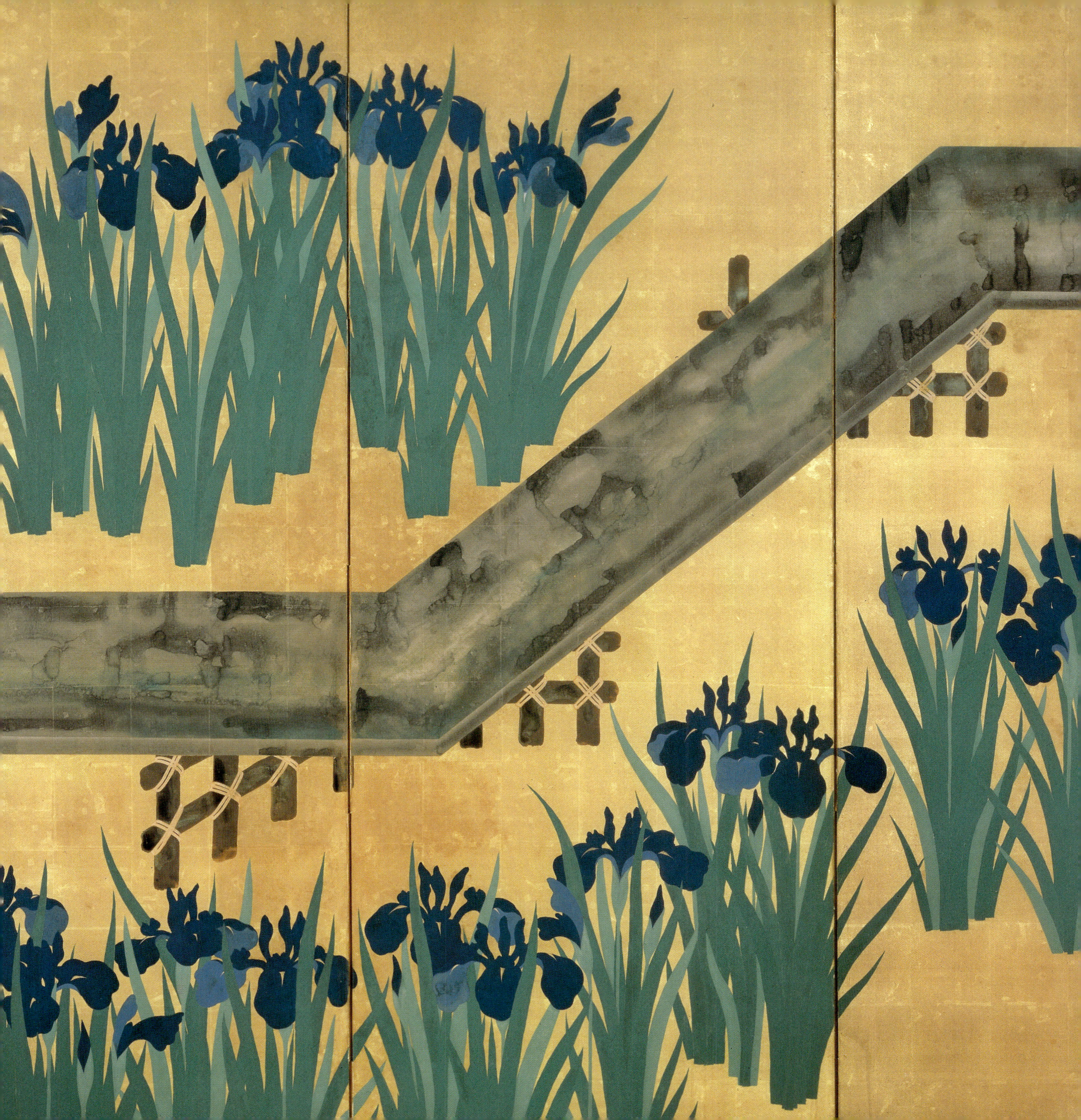

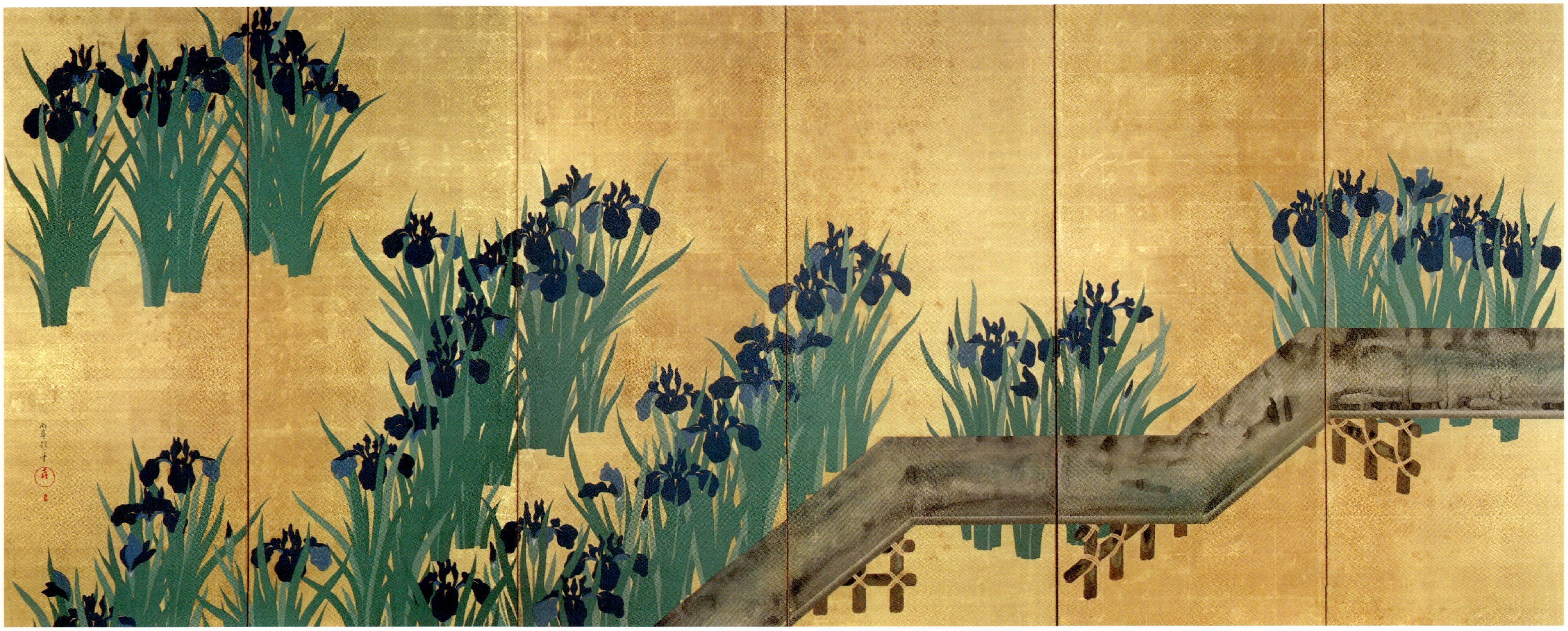

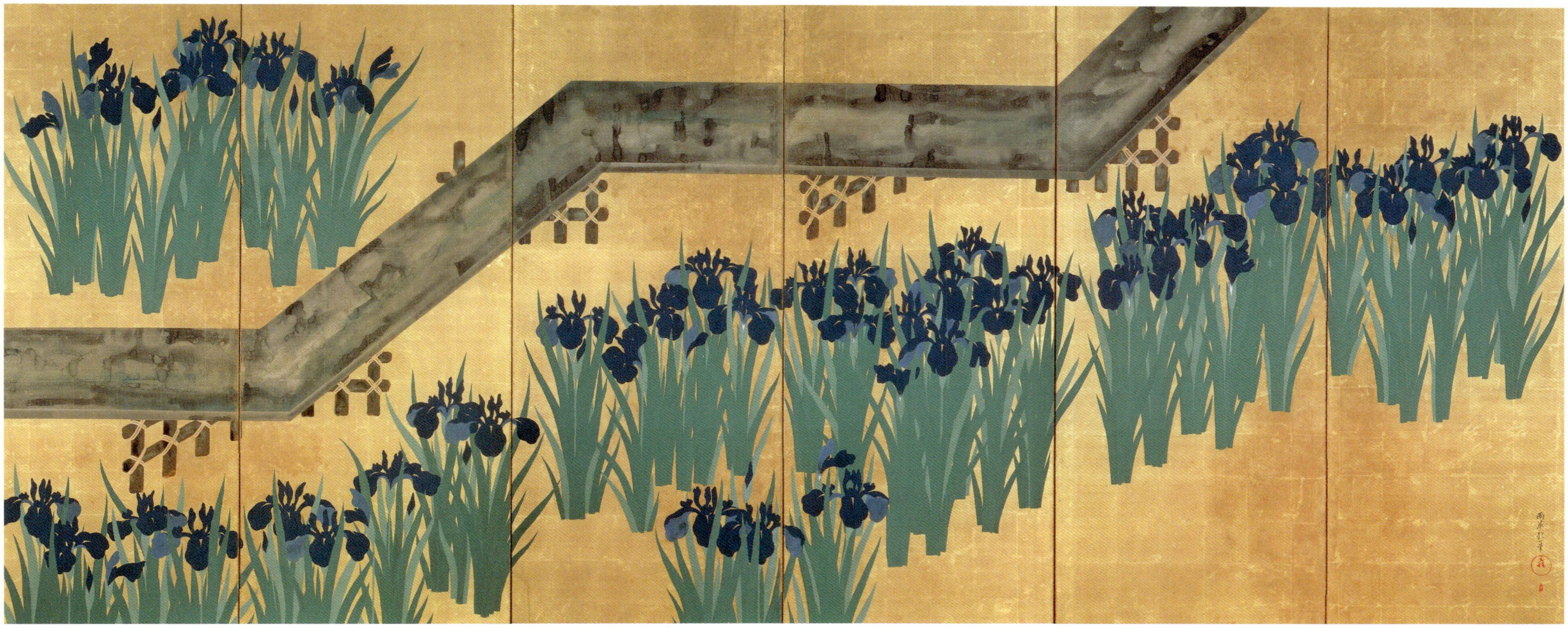

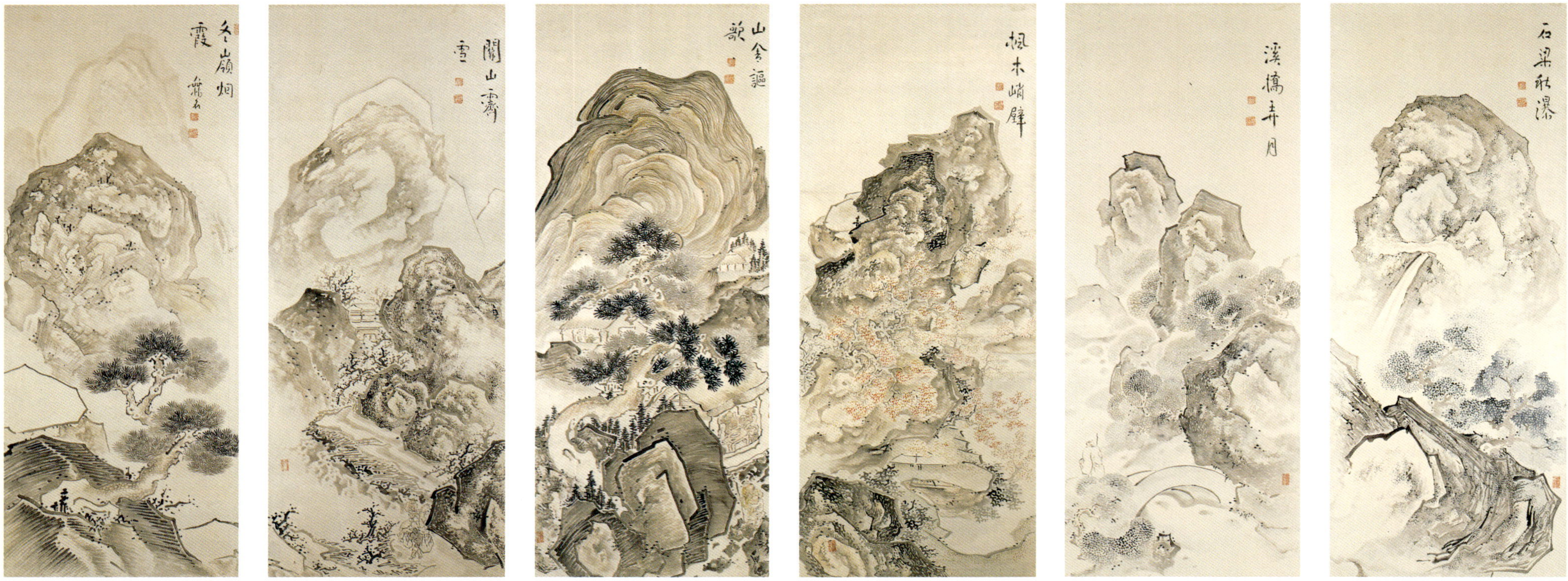

30

IKE TAIGA (1723–1776)

Landscapes of the Twelve Months

Edo period, late 18th century
Pair of six-panel screens
Ink and light color on paper
Each, 69¼ x 136 in.
(176.1 x 345.5 cm)
1871
Important Cultural Property

BY COPYING PRINTED painting manuals imported from China, Ike Taiga mastered traditional Chinese landscape painting. He also drew inspiration from the great early Japanese literati painter Yanagisawa Kien (1706–1758). Taiga incorporated various techniques of both Chinese and Japanese painting into his own unique style.

The screens *Landscapes of the Twelve Months* are composed of twelve separate paintings, each with a distinct title and the artist's seal. Looking at the screens in their entirety, however, makes clear that each landscape forms part of one large composition. Taiga emphasizes the gradual flow of the four seasons across these panels by employing different types of brushstrokes from painting to painting. For example, in the summer scenes (right screen, fourth through sixth panels from right) he uses soft, wet brushstrokes and delicate washes; whereas in the winter panels (left screen, fourth through sixth panels) he resorts to stiffer, more angular, articulated brushstrokes.

The mastery of different styles of brushwork associated with artists of the past was particularly important in the art of the Chinese literati painters of the late Ming (1368–1644) and the Qing (1644–1911) dynasties, such as Dong Qichang (1555–1636). These diverse modes reached Japan in a variety of forms, such as actual paintings and printed manuals like the *Mustard Seed Garden Manual of Painting*. It is possible that Taiga sought to demonstrate his own versatility as a literati painter by incorporating twelve distinct styles of brushwork in this painting.

One of the most impressive of these scenes is the third spring panel (right screen, third panel from right) in which fresh new willow leaves sway gently in the warm spring breeze and seem to glitter in the diffuse sunlight of the season. The screen is an excellent example of Taiga's virtuosity in successfully integrating a number of different styles of landscape painting into a single, large composition.

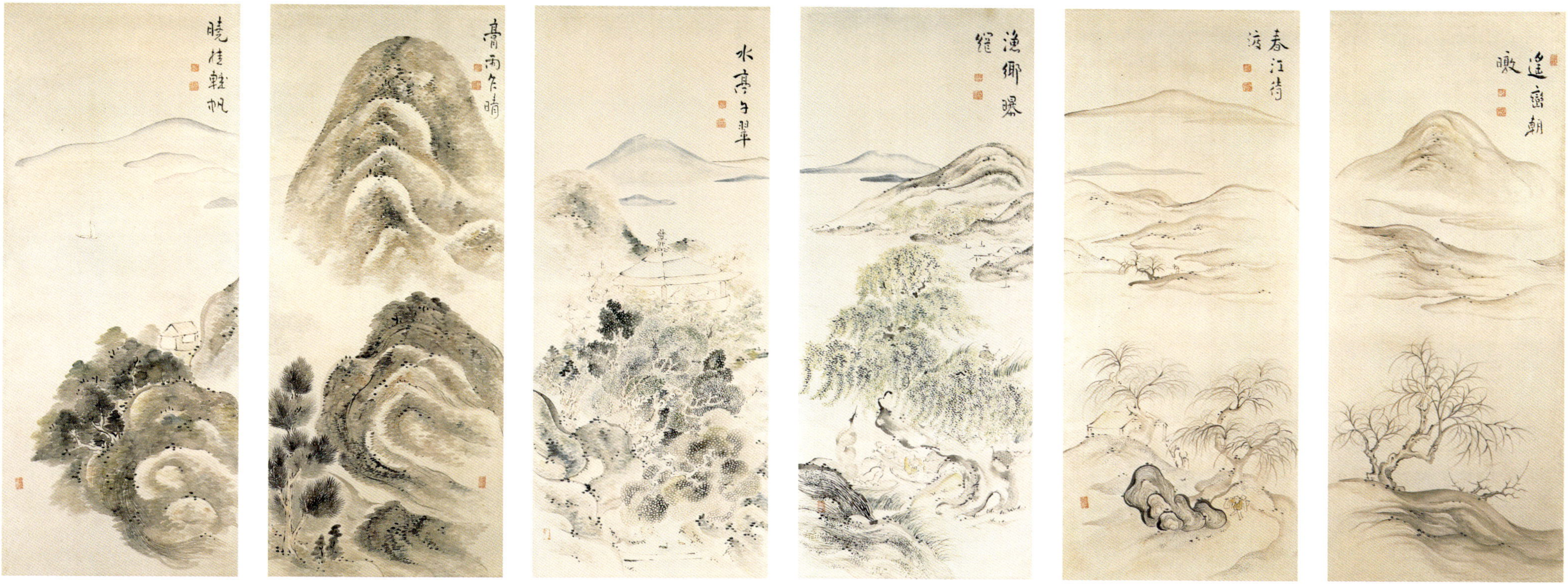

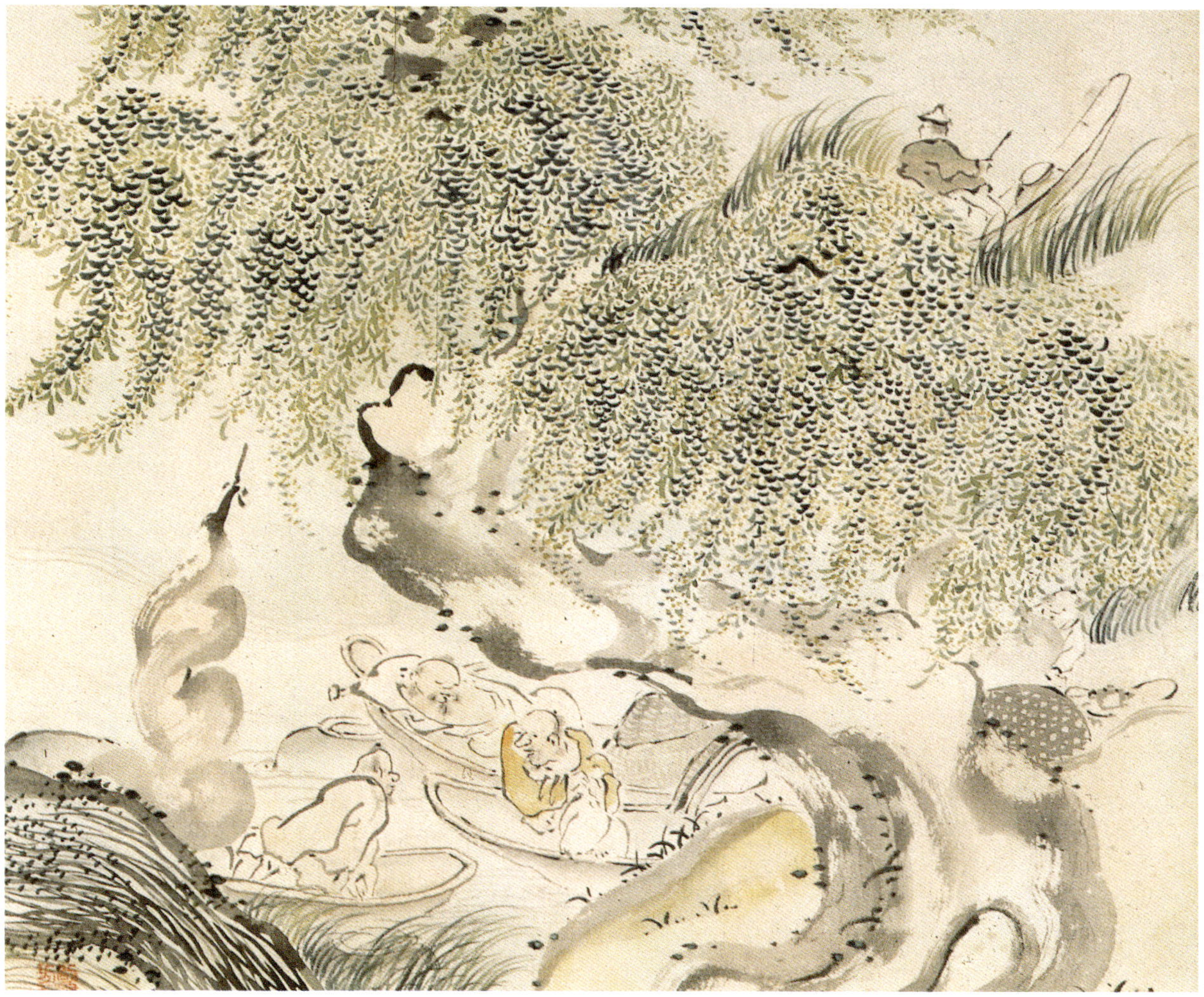

Detail from right screen, third panel from right.

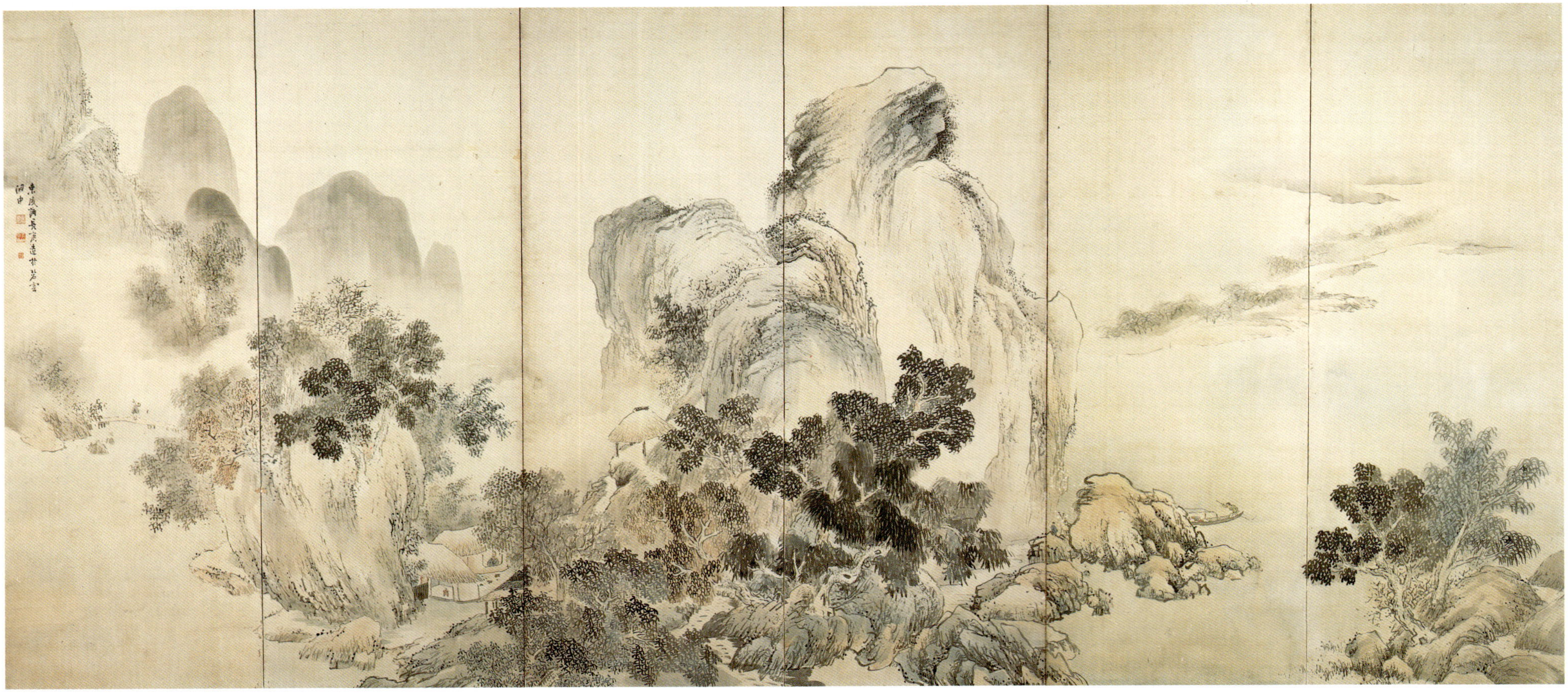

31

YOSA BUSON (1716–1784)

Landscape

Edo period, dated to 1763
Pair of six-panel screens
Ink and light color on satin
Each, 67¼ x 150 in.
(170.8 x 381 cm)
1895
Important Cultural Property

YOSA BUSON STUDIED *haikai* poetry with Hayano Hajin in Edo. Later, on a trip to the northern provinces, he retraced the footsteps of Matsuo Bashō, as recorded in that famed poet's diary, *The Narrow Road to the Deep North*. Buson was celebrated in his own day as a haiku poet, but now he is most highly regarded for his paintings. Imbued with a lyrical quality that could come only from the hand of a poet, his work displays an individualistic style founded upon consummate technical ability. He is therefore known, along with Ike Taiga (1723–1776), as the greatest of Japan's literati painters.

The present work, which is inscribed with a date equivalent to 1763, comes from the period in Buson's career when he is thought to have concentrated on producing paintings on folding screens. The landscape that spreads across these twelve panels extends deep into the distance and is executed with delicate brushwork within a composition of grand scale. The trees arranged rhythmically throughout the landscape unify the painting. The people that appear here and there and the flock of birds in the right screen add a narrative element.

The signature "Sha Chōin" inscribed on this pair of screens appears on other screens by Buson in the Chinese-derived, literati mode of painting. The further inscription "painted at the Blue Cloud Cavern [Buson's studio in Kyoto in the 1760s]" and the misty Chinese landscape of lofty peaks express Buson's identification with the Chinese man of letters (C. *wenren*, J. *bunjin*), who painted as an avocation, unfettered by convention. In this aspect the Idemitsu Museum's screens differ in conception from Buson's *haiga*, paintings inspired by the Japanese poetic form haiku.

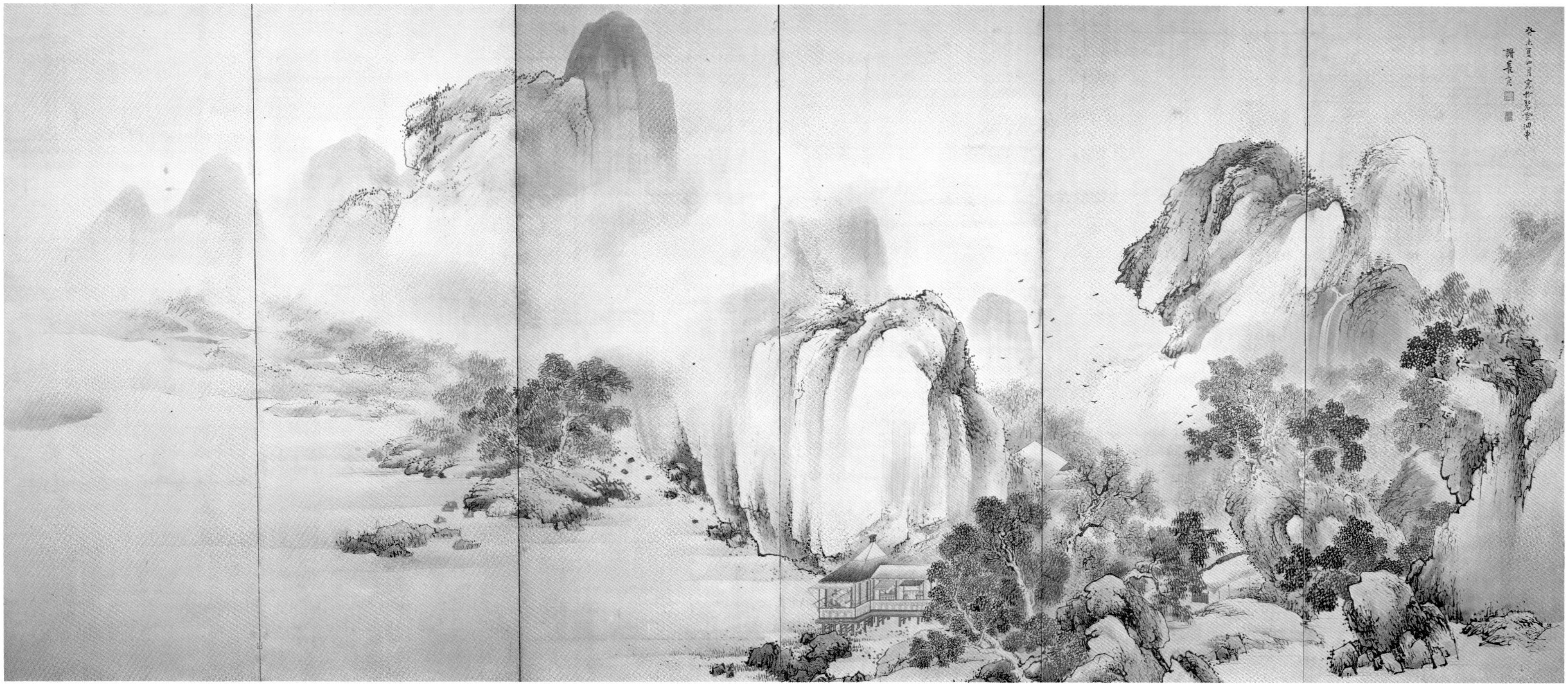

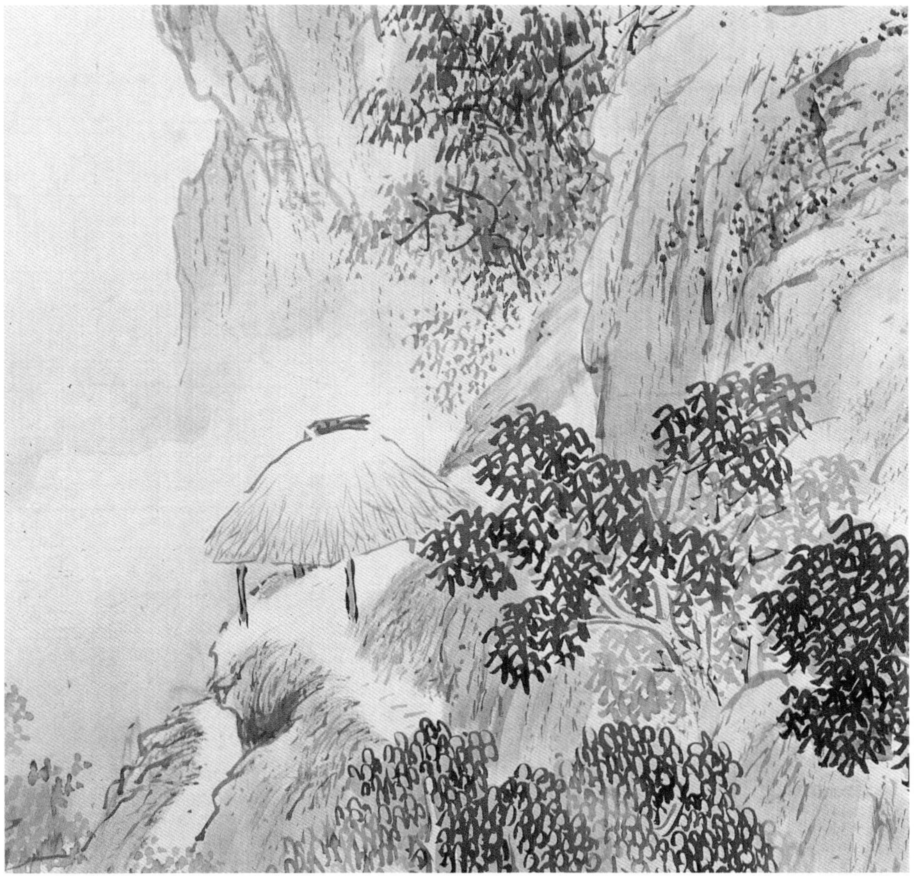

Detail from left screen.

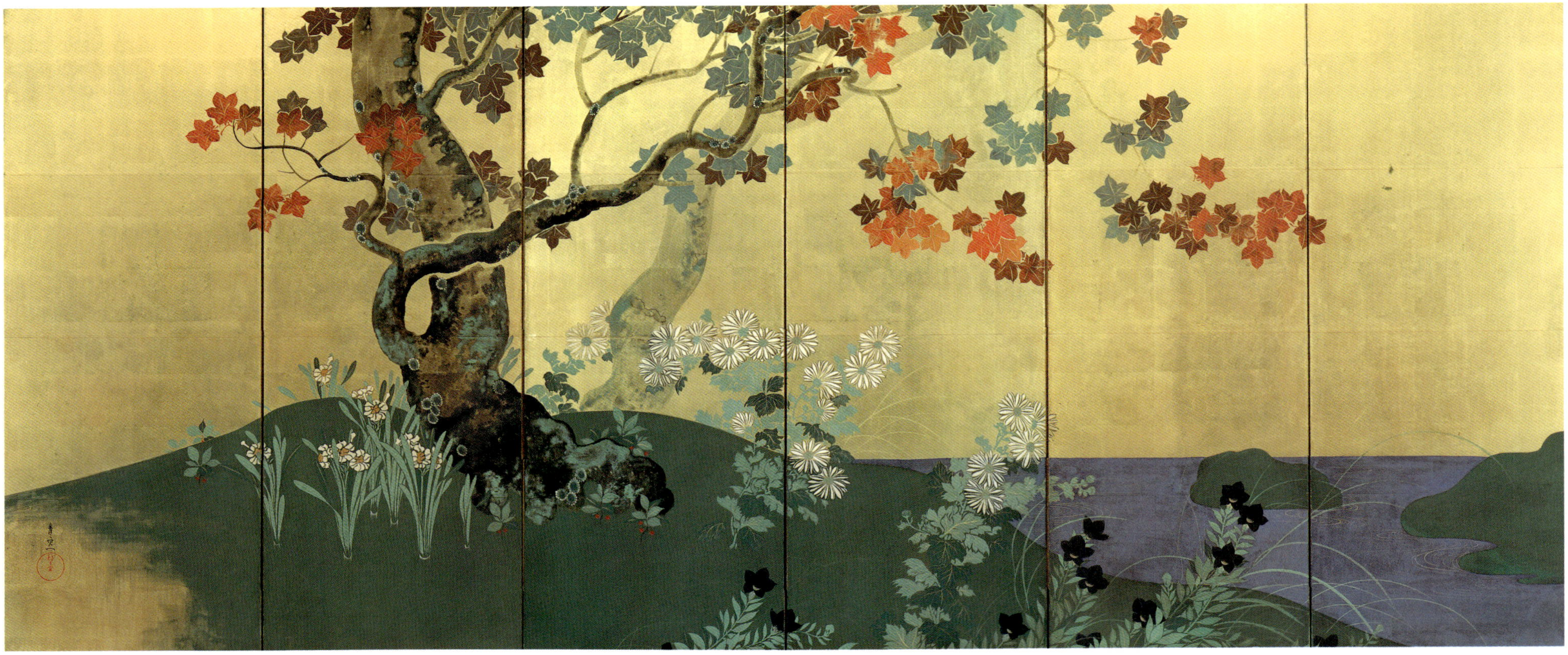

32

SUZUKI KIITSU (1796–1858)

Spring and Autumn Grasses and Flowers

Edo period, early 19th century
Pair of six-panel screens
Color over gold leaf on paper
Each, 54 x 127½ in.
(137.1 x 323.6 cm)
9957

SUZUKI KIITSU WAS the most talented pupil of Sakai Hōitsu (1761–1828), who established the Rinpa style of painting in Edo, and Kiitsu became Hōitsu's successor. Born a commoner, Kiitsu married the sister of Suzuki Reitan, a retainer of the Sakai family. After Reitan's death, Kiitsu headed the Suzuki family.

He so completely mastered the Edo Rinpa style that many paintings with Hōitsu's signature are thought to have actually been painted by Kiitsu. Later in his career Kiitsu's style gradually changed, and he produced works of a highly polished sensuality that have been particularly valued in Europe and North America.

Spring and Autumn Grasses and Flowers is about half the size of standard screens. After gold leaf was applied to the entire surface, Kiitsu painted this dazzling array of flora in vivid colors directly over the gold leaf. The effect is of opaque-colored motifs on a ground with a pervasive sheen. Thus a delicate balance is achieved between the naturalistic subject matter and the abstraction of the even ground of gold leaf. A clear demonstration of his departure from the style of Hōitsu, this work exhibits Kiitsu's mature, individual style.

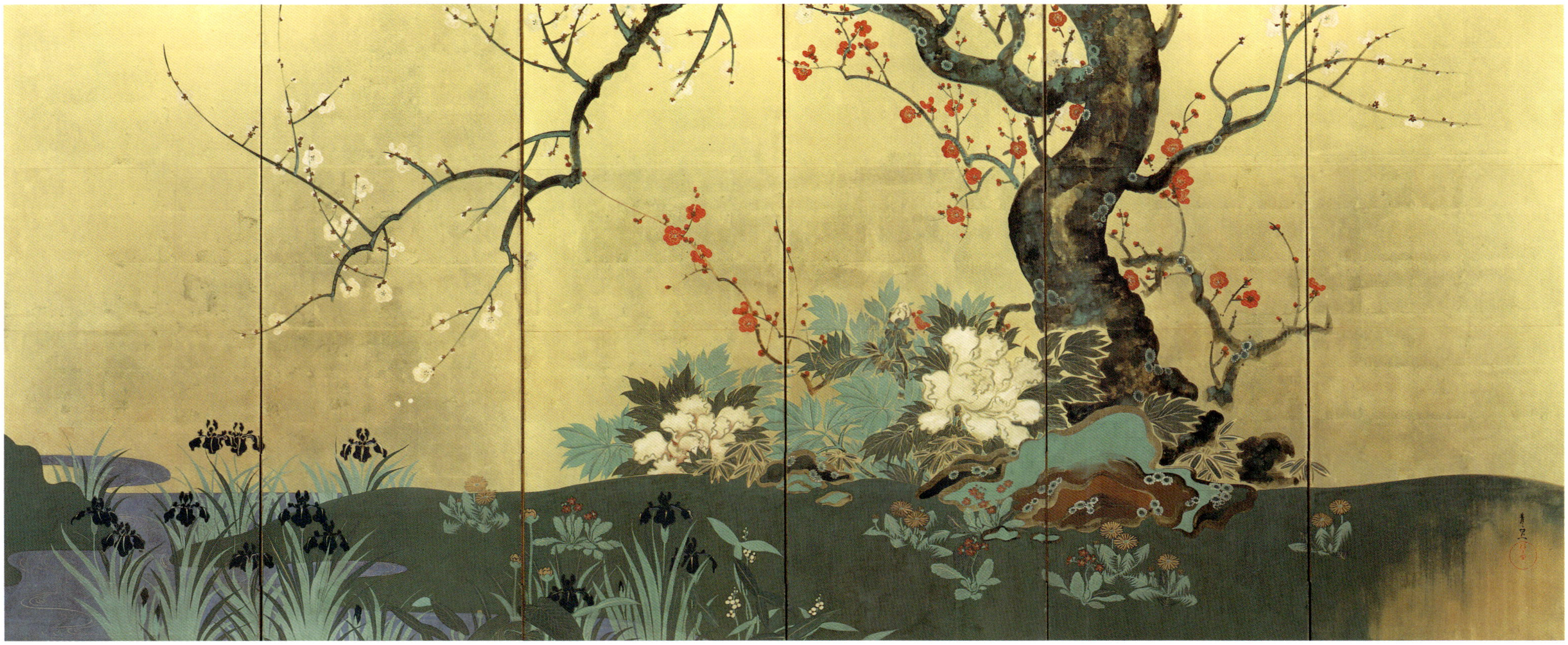

Glossary

JAPANESE HISTORICAL PERIODS MENTIONED

Nara period	710–794
Heian period	794–1185
Kamakura period	1185–1333
Nanbokuchō period	1336–1392
Muromachi period	1392–1573
Momoyama period	1573–1615
Edo period	1615–1868
Meiji period	1868–1912

Amida (Skt. Amithaba): the Buddha who presides over the Pure Land in the West, or Western Paradise. The primary object of veneration in Pure Land Buddhism.

byōbu: see folding screen.

Byōdōin: a Buddhist temple of the Pure Land sect on the bank of the Uji River. Its plan is modeled after descriptions of the Western Paradise of Amida.

chigaidana: see staggered shelves.

Daijōin: a subtemple of Kōfukuji in Nara.

daimyō: provincial feudal lords.

Daitokuji: a large Zen temple complex in Kyoto. Its many notable subtemples possess numerous famous artworks.

deibiki: gold and silver pigment brushed onto paintings.

display platform (*oshiita*): in early *shoin* architecture, a low board—originally portable, then built in—projecting from a wall; used for the display of valuable Chinese objects (*karamono*), often with hanging scrolls above them. Forerunner of the *tokonoma* alcove.

Edo (modern Tokyo): the seat of power of the Tokugawa family. Name given to the period when the Tokugawa ruled as shoguns (1615–1868).

emaki: see narrative handscrolls.

engi: see Legends, Miraculous.

eya: commercial painting shops, which flourished outside official painting lineages and academies.

flower-and-bird painting (J. *kachōga*): a genre popular in both China and Japan; in the latter, sometimes combined with progressions of the four seasons.

folding screen (*byōbu*): a portable, accordian-folded fixture used for the division of space and for decoration in traditional Japanese architecture. The form was originally imported from China, and folding screens became an important painting vehicle in Japan. Along with paintings on sliding panels and fixed walls, screens were incorporated into architectural painting schemes characteristic of the periods represented in this exhibition.

fusuma: see sliding panels.

Genji: *see Tale of Genji.*

gofun: a white, gessolike substance composed of ground seashells used as undercoating and to build up painting surfaces.

haikai: a form of "linked poetry" in which poets alternate supplying verses; progenitor of the three-line haiku form.

Heian (modern Kyoto): the name of the city when it was founded as the imperial capital in C.E. 794 and the name of the period during which it served as the effective capital of the nation (794–1185), a time when courtly culture reached its apogee. It remained the emperor's residence almost continuously until 1868 and is still considered "the old capital."

Heike: *see Tale of Heike.*

Hideyoshi: *see* Toyotomi Hideyoshi.

kachōga: see flower-and-bird painting.

kaisho: see meeting hall.

Kamakura: the city near Tokyo where Minamoto no Yoritomo (1147–1199) established the first shogunate, or military government. The period when Kamakura was the seat of power (1185–1333) is named after it.

Kanga: "Chinese pictures," an Edo period term for a style of painting that began to develop during the Muromachi period based on pictorial styles, materials, and subjects recently imported from China. Two major types of imported models were ink paintings in monochrome or with light colors, usually on paper, by Chan (J. Zen) painters and academic pictures, generally richly colored and on silk. The origins of *Kanga* were in the hanging scroll format, but it was adapted for large-scale architectural commissions. It became associated with the military rulers during the Momoyama and Edo periods.

Kangakuin: a subtemple of Onjōji (also known as Miidera) in Shiga Prefecture, where Kano Mitsunobu's most famous paintings and a significant early *shoin*-style building are found.

Kannon (Skt. Avalokiteshvara; C. Guanyin): the Bodhisattva of Compassion, one of the most revered and the most frequently represented Buddhist deities in East Asia.

Kano: a school of professional painters founded by Kano Masanobu (1434–1530) and headed by his descendants, who formed the most important painting academy during the period covered by this exhibition. Often painters to the shogun, they were the preeminent exponents of *Kanga* (q.v.). The chronology of Kano painters mentioned in this book is as follows: Motonobu (1476–1559), Shōei (1519–1592), Eitoku (1543–1590), Hideyori (d. 1559), Shōshū (1551–1601), Jinnojō (active late sixteenth–early seventeenth century), Naganobu (1577–1654), Sanraku (1559–1635), Mitsunobu (1562/1565–1608), Takanobu (1571–1618), Sansetsu (1590–1651), Tan'yū (1602–1674), Naonobu (1607–1650?), Yasunobu (1613–1685), Einō (1631–1700), Tsunenobu (1636–1713).

keibutsu: "scenic things," set images identified with particular places or seasons and used in literature and the visual arts to evoke them.

kimigakitsuke: "gold burnishing," the adhering, by rubbing, of flakes and small particles of gold to a paper surface.

kinbyōbu: "gold screens," painted folding screens with large expanses of gold paint or gold leaf.

Kokinshū (Kokin wakashū): Anthology of Ancient and Modern Poems [Waka], compiled in the tenth century, the first of twenty-one anthologies assembled by imperial command.

koto (C. *qin*): a long zither with thirteen strings, played with picks.

Legends, Miraculous (*engi*): a genre of "histories," usually of temples, that were often illustrated in multiple handscroll sets.

maki-e: a technique of decorating lacquerware in which metallic powder, usually gold, is sprinkled into damp lacquer.

meeting hall (*kaisho*): a type of building where audiences were held and entertainments presented during the Muromachi period; the place in which the characteristic elements of the *shoin* style were first brought together.

Minamoto: a clan from eastern Japan who trounced the powerful Taira clan at the end of the Heian period and founded the first shogunate in Kamakura. *See also Tale of Heike.*

Momoyama: "Peach Hill," the area near Kyoto where Toyotomi Hideyoshi built his Fushimi Castle. Name given to the period (1573–1615) when several powerful warriors fought to consolidate control of the country.

Munakata Shrine: an ancient Shinto shrine complex in northern Kyushu.

Muromachi: the district in Kyoto that was the primary headquarters of the Ashikaga shoguns, who were in power from 1392 to 1573, and the name given to that historical period.

narrative handscrolls (*emaki*): long, horizontal scrolls in which narrative texts are interspersed with illustrations. Many Yamato-e works from the Heian and Kamakura periods are in this format.

oshiita: see display platform.

Pure Land Buddhism (*Jōdō*): a form of salvationist Buddhism that stresses the adoration and invocation of Amida Buddha to bring about rebirth in the paradisal Pure Land in the West, where one waits to be reborn in an era more propitious for achieving nirvana.

rakuchū-rakugaizu: see Scenes in and around Kyoto.

Rinpa (often Rimpa): "school of [Kō]rin," a style of painting based on the work of Tawaraya Sōtatsu (active first half of 17th century) as formulated by Ogata Kōrin (1658–1716); frequently uses traditional Japanese imagery.

Scenes in and around Kyoto (*rakuchū-rakugaizu*): pictures of famous locales in and on the outskirts of the imperial capital (*raku*); an important subject in early Japanese genre painting.

screen: *see* folding screen.

shamisen: a three-stringed lute, originally associated with the theater and pleasure quarters of the Edo period.

shikishi: pieces of paper, usually square and often decorated, used for calligraphy and paintings.

Shinkokinshū (Shinkokin wakashū): the *New Anthology of Ancient and Modern Poems [Waka],* the eighth imperial anthology, assembled at the beginning of the thirteenth century.

shoin style: a type of residential architecture for the elites that developed during the Muromachi period. New building types reflected changing social patterns, and interiors underwent numerous modifications, some to accommodate the display of artworks imported from China. A variety of features are indicative, but the mature style is generally characterized by the regular appearance in a single room of a *tokonoma* alcove, staggered shelves, and a writing desk, or *tsukeshoin,* the *shoin* of the name (which may be called "study" or "book hall" style). The word *shoin* is sometimes used to denote a building with one or more such rooms, as in Daishoin, "Large Shoin."

sliding panels (*fusuma*): paper-faced partitions that slide in tracks, used to divide interior spaces in *shoin*-style buildings. They provided an important format for painting beginning in the Muromachi period.

staggered shelves (*chigaidana*): built-in shelves on more than one level, used for the display of precious objects.

Taira: *see Tale of Heike.*

Tale of Genji (Genji monogatari): a long work of fiction centered on the life of an emperor's son given the surname Genji. It was written about 1000 by Murasaki Shikibu, a woman at court. The earliest illustrated handscroll dates from the twelfth century, and many paintings in various formats were made through the centuries.

Tale of Heike (Heike monogatari): Japan's most famous war tale, a fourteenth-century account of how the Taira (or Heike) clan fell from a high position at court in a war with the Minamoto (or Genji) clan during the second half of the twelfth century.

Tanabata: a festival on the seventh day of the seventh month celebrating the single yearly meeting of two lovers in a Chinese legend, a princess and a cowherd who live on opposite sides of the River of the Sky (the Milky Way).

Thirty-six Immortal Poets: a group of poets, lionized for their excellence, whose poems are gathered in a famous anthology and who became an important theme in Japanese painting.

tokonoma alcove: in mature *shoin* architecture, a recess for the display of paintings and beautiful objects; variously painted or used for hanging scrolls.

Tosa: A family/school of artists specializing in *Yamato-e* (q.v.). They served the court, and the head often was appointed director of the Imperial Painting Bureau. The chronology of Tosa artists mentioned in this book is as follows: Yukihiro (active 1406–1443), Mitsunobu (1434–about 1525), Hirochika (about 1439–1492), Mitsumoto (active 1530–1569), Ittoku (active early seventeenth century), Mitsuoki (1617–1691), and Mitsunari (1646–1710).

Toyotomi Hideyoshi (1536–1598): a warlord who brought much of Japan under his control during the 1580s. Hideyoshi was the effective ruler of the country until his death in 1598.

tsukeshoin: "built-in *shoin*," called simply *"shoin"* in Muromachi times, when it developed from a functional writing desk adjacent to a window to an alcove where writing implements were displayed.

Uji: a town south of Kyoto (now a suburb) on the Uji River; heart of a picturesque region celebrated in literature.

ukiyo-e: "pictures of the floating world," genre scenes of the entertainment districts popular among commoners during the Edo period, best known in the West through woodblock prints.

waka: a thirty-one syllable poetic form that was preeminent in Japan from about 700 to 1500.

Yamato: the area around the Yamato River, in the vicinity of Nara, where the clan who first unified Japan located their capitals. The archaizing name *Yamato* for the origin and heart of Japanese culture has deep resonance and evokes a particular type of ancient Japaneseness.

Yamato-e: "Japanese pictures," paintings of native subjects, usually portraits and narratives—both historical and literary—typically painted in a detailed style and with bright, often opaque, colors. Many early examples are narrative handscrolls. After the advent of military rule, the style became associated with the imperial court and traditional culture.

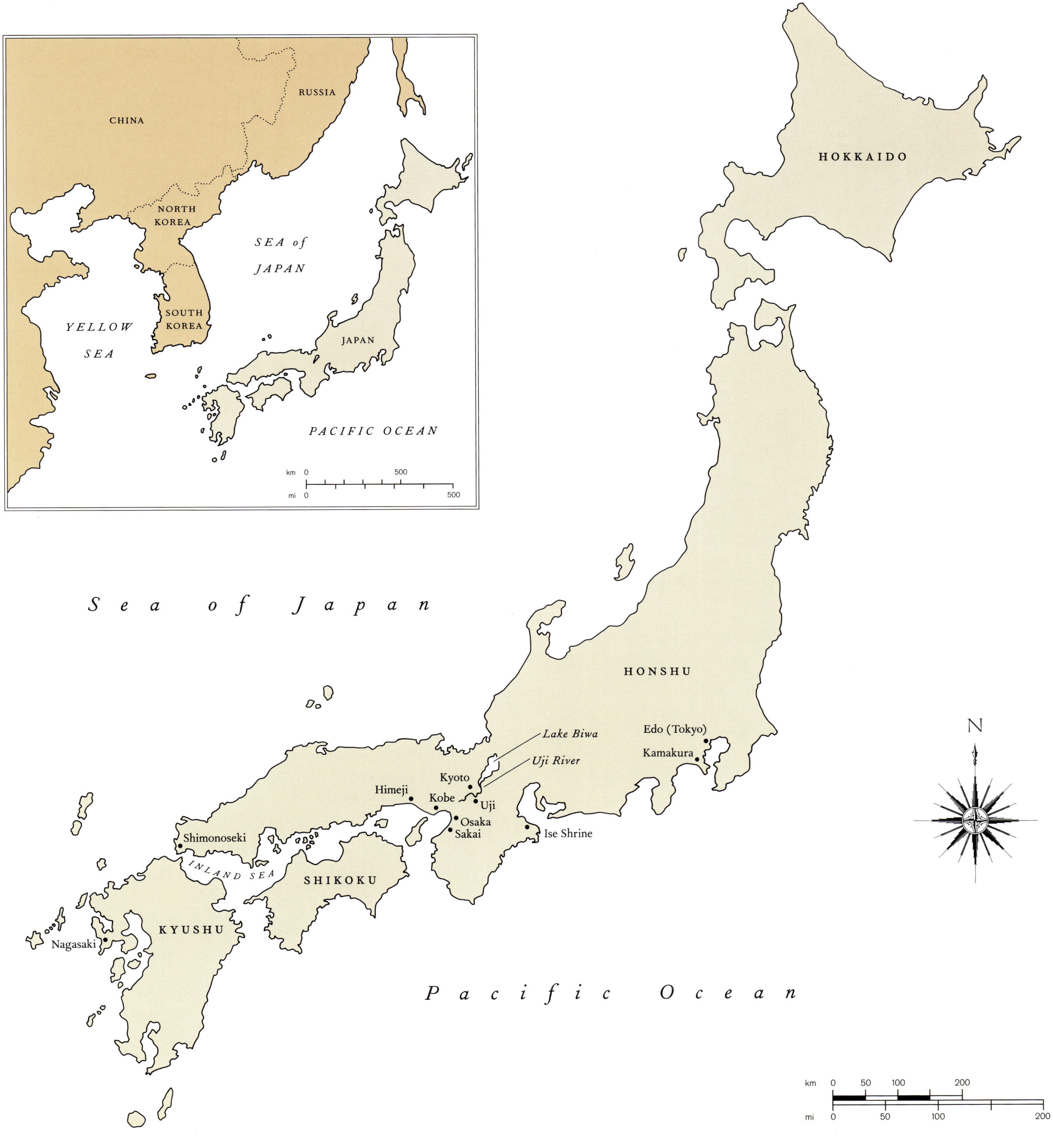
CHINA
RUSSIA
NORTH KOREA
SOUTH KOREA
SEA of JAPAN
YELLOW SEA
JAPAN
PACIFIC OCEAN
km 0 500
mi 0 500
HOKKAIDO
Sea of Japan
HONSHU
Edo (Tokyo)
Kamakura
Lake Biwa
Uji River
Kyoto
Himeji
Kobe
Uji
Osaka
Sakai
Ise Shrine
Shimonoseki
INLAND SEA
SHIKOKU
KYUSHU
Nagasaki
Pacific Ocean
N
km 0 50 100 200
mi 0 50 100 200

Bibliography

SUGGESTED READING

Collcutt, Martin, Marius Jansen, and Isao Kumakura. *Cultural Atlas of Japan.* New York: Facts on File, 1988.

Cunningham, Michael R., et al. *The Triumph of Japanese Style: 16th-Century Art in Japan.* Cleveland: The Cleveland Museum of Art in cooperation with Indiana University Press, 1991.

Grilli, Elise. *The Art of the Japanese Screen.* Tokyo and New York: Weatherhill and Bijutsu Shuppan-sha, 1970.

Hashimoto, Fumio. *Architecture in the Shoin Style.* Trans. and adapt. by H. Mack Horton. Japan Arts Library. Tokyo and New York: Kodansha International, 1981.

Mason, Penelope. *History of Japanese Art.* New York: Harry N. Abrams, 1993.

Murase, Miyeko. *Byōbu: Japanese Screens from New York Collections.* New York: The Asia Society, 1971.

______. *Masterpieces of Japanese Screen Painting: The American Collections.* New York: George Braziller, 1990.

Varley, H. Paul. *Japanese Culture.* Honolulu: University of Hawaii Press, 3rd ed., 1984.

REFERENCES

Adachi Keiko. "Muromachi jidai ebyōbue kō" (Consideration of the picture-screens of the Muromachi period). In *Ōta Dōkan kinen bijutsuten: Muromachi bijutsu to sengoku gadan* (Exhibition commemorating Ōta Dōkan: Muromachi art and the sengoku painting world). Tokyo: Tokyo Metropolitan Teien Art Museum, 1986, pp. 119–124. See also English summary in unpaged section.

______. "Muromachi jidai yamatoe byōbu jitsugetsu kachōzu ni tsuite" (On Muromachi period Yamato-e screens: Sun and Moon, Flowers and Birds). *Kokka* 1083 (May 1985), pp. 13–32.

______. "Nishu no Ryūkyōzu byōbu" (Two kinds of Bridge and Willows Screens). *Kokka* 1135 (June 1990), pp. 7–22.

Akazawa Eiji. "Jūgo seiki ni okeru kinbyōbu ni tsuite" (On the gold folding screens of the fifteenth century). *Kokka* 849 (December 1962), pp. 567–579.

Akiyama, Terukazu. "The Door Paintings in the Phoenix Hall of the Byōdōin as *Yamatoe*." *Artibus Asiae* 53, nos. 1/2 (1993), pp. 144–167.

Autumn Grasses and Water Motifs in Japanese Art from the Suntory Museum of Art. New York: Japan Society, 1983.

Chūsei shōheiga (Medieval screen and mural painting). Kyoto: Kyoto National Museum, 1969.

Cranston, Edwin A. *A Waka Anthology.* Vol. 1, *The Gem-Glistening Cup.* Stanford: Stanford University Press, 1993.

Cunningham, Michael R., et al. *The Triumph of Japanese Style: 16th-Century Art in Japan.* Cleveland: The Cleveland Museum of Art in cooperation with Indiana University Press, 1991.

Furuta Shōkin. "Yanagibashizu—sono Ujibashizu o megutte sono igi o tou" (Paintings of the Willow Bridge: An inquiry about the meaning of the Uji bridge screens). *Idemitsu Bijutsukan kanpō* (Bulletin of the Idemitsu Museum of Arts) 61 (March 1988), pp. 8–23.

Kaikan jūgonen kinenten zuroku (Catalogue celebrating the fifteenth anniversary of the opening [of the Idemitsu Museum]). Tokyo: Idemitsu Museum of Arts, 1981.

Keibutsuga—shiki keibutsu (Scene painting—paintings of the four seasons). Nihon byōbue shūsei, vol. 9. Tokyo: Kōdansha, 1977.

Klein, Bettina. *Japanese Kinbyōbu: The Gold-leafed Folding Screens of the Muromachi Period (1333–1573).* Adapted and expanded by Carolyn Wheelwright. Ascona, Switzerland: Artibus Asiae, 1984.

Kuroda Taizō. "Dattanjin shuryō byōbu no hissha no tegakari" (A Clue to the authorship of the screen of Tartars Hunting on Horseback). In *Idemitsu bijutsukan zōhin zuroku* (Idemitsu Museum catalogue of holdings). *"Fūzokuga" geppō* ("Genre painting" monthly report) (November 1987 supplementum).

_____. "Kōdaiji no sanjūrokkasenzu hengaku" (The *Thirty-six Immortal Poets* on votive plaques in Kōdaiji). *Kokka* 1193 (April 1995), pp. 22–32.

_____. "Munakata taisha no Kuninobu-in sanjūrokkasenzu hengaku" (The *Thirty-six Immortal Poets* on votive plaques with the Kuninobu seal in the Munakata Shrine). *Bijutsushi* 37, vol. 2, no. 124 (April 1988), pp. 166–184.

_____. "Sakura, momo, kaidō-zu byōbu" (A Screen of cherry, peach, and aronia). *Kokka* 1173 (August 1993), pp. 37–39.

_____. "Sōōji byōbu no hissha ni tsuite" (On the painter of the Sōōji screen). *De Arte,* no. 6 (March 1990), pp. 9–32.

Manzies, Jackie, and Edmund Capon. *Japan: Masterpieces from the Idemitsu Collection.* Clayton, Australia: Wilke and Company in conjunction with International Cultural Corporation of Australia, 1982.

Matsushita Takaaki. *Muromachi suibokuga* (Muromachi ink painting). Tokyo: Ōtsuka Kōgeisha, 1960.

Miyajima Shin'ichi. "Shōheiga ni miru kaiga no hen" (Observable transformations in screen painting). *Bijutsushi* 108, vol. 29, no. 2 (March 1980), pp. 119–126.

Mizuo Hiroshi. "Ujigawazu byōbu" (Screens of the Uji River). *Kokka* 873 (December 1964), pp. 23–31.

Murase, Miyeko. *Japanese Art: Selections from the Mary and Jackson Burke Collection.* New York: The Metropolitan Museum of Art, 1975.

_____. *Masterpieces of Japanese Screen Painting: The American Collections.* New York: George Braziller, 1990.

Murashige Yasushi. "Den Tosa Mitsunobu hitsu matsuzu byōbu ni tsuite" (On the screen of pine trees attributed to Tosa Mitsunobu). *Kokka* 1118 (November 1988), pp. 30–41.

Muromachi jidai bijutsuten zuroku (Catalogue of the exhibition of Muromachi period art). Kyoto: Kyoto National Museum, 1967.

Muromachi jidai no byōbue (Screen painting of the Muromachi period). Tokyo: Tokyo National Museum, 1989.

Namiki Seishi. "Kōzu Kobunka Kaikan zō 'Ōgimen shōji' ni tsuite" (On the "screen-mounted fans" in the Kōzu Kobunka Kaikan). *Museum* 452 (November 1988), pp. 25–36.

Narazaki Muneshige. "Sasama kezō ōgimen gachō" (The fan album in the Sasama Collection). *Kokka* 845 (August 1962), pp. 339–380.

_____. "Ujigawazu byōbu" (Screens of the Uji River). *Kobijutsu* 6 (October 1964), pp. 97–98.

Nihon no kaiga hyakusen (One hundred selected Japanese paintings). Tokyo: Idemitsu Museum of Arts, 1983.

Okudaira Shunroku. "Hikone byōbu ni tsuite: Kyōzō kankei to ga-chū-ga no mondai o chūshin ni" (Concerning the Hikone screen: Focusing on the mirror image and the picture within a picture). *Bijutsushi* 37, vol. 2, no. 109 (November 1980), pp. 12–25.

Ōta Dōkan kinen bijutsuten: Muromachi bijutsu to sengoku gadan (Exhibition commemorating Ōta Dōkan: Muromachi art and the sengoku painting world). Tokyo: Tokyo Metropolitan Teien Art Museum, 1986.

Phillips, Quitman E. "Honchō gashi and the Kano Myth." *Archives of Asian Art* 47 (1994), pp. 46–57.

Rosenfield, John M. "Japanese Painting Workshops and the Gardner Museum Collections." *Fenway Court* (1992), pp. 13–16.

Sakazaki Tan, ed. *Nihon Kaigaron taikei* (Overview of Japanese painting treatises), vol. 2. Tokyo: Meichō Fukyūsha, 1979.

Shirahata Yoshi. "Yanagi suishazu (Ujibashi). Meishoe #12" (Willow Bridge and Waterwheel [Uji Bridge]. Famous-place painting no. 12). *Nihon bijutsu kōgei* 459 (December 1976), pp. 64–65.

Suzuki Hiroyuki. "Kisha to kari—Dattanjin shuryōzu byōbu o megutte." (Equestrian archery and hunting—Regarding screens of Tartars Hunting on Horseback). *Kokka* 1077 (October 1984), pp. 13–30.

Takeuchi Misako. "The Meaning of Pattern in Rimpa School Painting: *Mitate* and Visual Imagery." *Apollo* (February 1995), pp. 3–10.

_____. "Ryūkyō suishazu byōbu—Shinshutsubon o shōkai o kanete" (Screen paintings of Willow Bridge and Waterwheel—including the introduction of a newly discovered version). Part 1: *Kokka* 1138 (September 1990), pp. 20–34; Part 2: *Kokka* 1139 (October 1990), pp. 7–18.

Tamamushi Keiko. "'Ryūkyō suishazu' to 'Uji no kawase no suisha'—kayō to fūryū to byōbue no kōkyō" ("Willow Bridge and Waterwheel" and "The Waterwheel at Uji Rapids"—the reverberations between ballads, contemporary chic, and screen painting). In Katano Tatsuro, ed., *Nihon bungei shichchōron* (Trends of thought in Japanese literary art). Tokyo: Ōfūsha, 1991, pp. 859–880.

Tanaka Ichimatsu. "Hamamatsuzu byōbu" (Folding screens with paintings of Pines on a Shore). *Kokka* 783 (September 1953), pp. 244–251.

Toda Teisuke. "Kangakei jinbutsuzu byōbu no rinkaku" (The outlines of Kanga figural screen painting). In *Kangakei jinbutsu* (Kanga figure painting). Nihon byōbue shūsei, vol. 4. Tokyo: Kōdansha, 1980, pp. 37–39.

Tsuji Nobuo. "Ornament (Kazari)—An Approach to Japanese Culture." *Archives of Asian Art* 47 (1994), pp. 35–45.

_____. "Yamatoe byōbu no tenkai" (The development of Yamato-e byōbu). In *Muromachi jidai no byōbue* (Screen painting of the Muromachi period). Tokyo: Tokyo National Museum, 1989, pp. 15–19.

Ueda, Makoto. *Literary and Art Theories in Japan*. Cleveland: Press of Case Western Reserve University, 1967. Reprint, Ann Arbor: Center for Japanese Studies, University of Michigan, 1991.

Yamane Yūzō. "Chūsei Yamatoe byōbu ni tsuite—Jitsugetsu shiki kachōzu o chūshin ni" (Concerning medieval Yamato-e screens—focusing on the *Flowers and Birds of the Four Seasons with the Sun and the Moon*). *Idemitsu Bijutsukan kanpō* (Bulletin of the Idemitsu Museum of Arts) 52 (1986), pp. 9–19.

_____. "Eya ni tsuite" (Concerning painters' shops). *Bijutsushi* 48, vol. 12, no. 4 (March 1963), pp. 107–117.

_____. "Kinpeki shōhekiga no tenkai—kaku ryūha no iwazuru kinchi kōsei o chūshin ni" (The development of gold screen and mural painting—centering on the so-called gold-ground compositions of the various schools). In *Byōbue no seiritsu to tenkai* (The establishment and development of folding screen painting). Nihon byōbue shūsei, vol. 1. Tokyo: Kōdansha, 1981, pp. 114–121.

_____. "'Muromachi jidai no byōbue' gaikan—Wakan haigō no sekai" (Overview of the "Screen Paintings of the Muromachi Period" exhibition: The mixing of Chinese and Japanese styles). In *Muromachi jidai no byōbue* (Screen painting of the Muromachi period). Tokyo: Tokyo National Museum, 1989, pp. 8–14.

_____. *Yūraku fūzokuzu gaikan—Yagai fūzokuzu o chūshin ni* (Survey of amusements and customs: Concerning paintings of outdoor amusements). Kinsei fūzoku zufu, vol. 2. Tokyo: Shogakkan, 1983.

Yamatoe—miyabi no keifu (Japanese painting: The tradition of courtly elegance). Special exhibition commemorating the twenty-fifth anniversary of the Agency for the Protection of Cultural Properties. Tokyo: Tokyo National Museum, 1993.

Yoshida Yūji. *Ishiyamadera engi-e* (Picture scroll of the miraculous legends of Ishiyama Temple). Nihon emaki taisei, vol. 18. Tokyo: Chūōkōron, 1978.

_____. *Tosa Mitsunobu*. Nihon bijutsu kaiga zenshū, vol. 5. Tokyo: Shūeisha, 1979.

Index of Artists and Works in the Exhibition

Numbers indicate catalogue numbers, not page numbers.

Autumn Grasses, attributed to Tawaraya Sōtatsu, 19
Beauties under the Cherry Blossoms, 23
Cranes, Kano Einō, 28
Crows and Pine, Hasegawa Tōhaku, 9
Egrets and Willow, Hasegawa Tōhaku, 9
Famous Views and Entertainment Centers in Edo, 21
Flowers and Birds of Spring and Autumn, Kano School (seal of Motonobu), 13
Flowers and Birds of the Four Seasons, attributed to Sesshū Tōyō, 5
Flowers and Birds of the Four Seasons with the Sun and the Moon, 1
Gion Festival, Kyoto, 14
Hasegawa Tōhaku, 9
Hawk and Pine Tree, Soga Chokuan, 10
Ike Taiga, 30
Irises and Eight-Fold Bridge, Sakai Hōitsu, 29
Kano Einō, 28
Kano Mitsunobu, attributed to, 11
Kano Motonobu, 6
Kano Naonobu, 17
Kano School (seal of Motonobu), 13
Kano Tan'yu, 26
Kano Tsunenobu, 27
Landscape, Yosa Buson, 31
Landscapes of the Twelve Months, Ike Taiga, 30
Map of the World and People of Various Lands, 16
Minamoto no Nakakuni Hearing Kogō Playing the Koto, Kano Naonobu, 17
Ogata Kōrin, attributed to, 20
Pine Tree, 3
Pine Trees and Chinese Black Pines, 7
Queen Mother of the West and Dong Fangshuo, The, attributed to Kano Mitsunobu, 11
Red and White Plum Trees, attributed to Ogata Kōrin, 20
Rolling Waves, Kano Tsunenobu, 27
Sakai Hōitsu, 29
Scenes from the Tale of Genji, 4
Scenes from the Tale of Genji, Kano Tan'yu, 26
Scenes from the Tale of Heike, 25
Scenes in and around Kyoto, 15
Scenes of Tartars Hunting on Horseback, 12
Sesshū Tōyō, attributed to, 5
Soga Chokuan, 10
Spring and Autumn Grasses and Flowers, Suzuki Kiitsu, 32
Suzuki Kiitsu, 32
Tawaraya Sōtatsu, attributed to, 19
Trees and Plants of the Four Seasons, 2
Uji River, 8
Westerners in Japan, 22
West Lake, Kano Motonobu, 6
Whose Sleeves? (Tagasode), 24
Winter Landscape, 18
Yosa Buson, 31
Ziyou Visiting Andao, Kano Naonobu, 17

COLOPHON

Project Director: Joseph N. Newland
Editor: Jacolyn A. Mott, New York
Designer: Sandy Bell, Utah
Publications Associate: Merantine Hens-Nolan
Composition by: Sandy Bell and Chelsea Arts Inc., New York
Printing by: Nissha Printing Co., Inc., Kyoto, Japan
Binding by: Lincoln & Allen, Portland
Text type composed in Fournier
Display type composed in Koch Antiqua
Printed on 127.9 gsm Satin Kinfuji dull paper

PHOTOGRAPH CREDITS

Photographs of works in The Idemitsu Museum of Arts are by Susumu Wakisaka.
Other photographs are courtesy of the owner unless otherwise noted.
Page 34, Otto E. Nelson
Page 43, copied from Yoshida Yūji, *Ishiyamadera engi-e*, vol. 18 of Nihon emaki taisei

LIBRARY OF CONGRESS
CATALOGING-IN-PUBLICATION DATA

Kuroda, Taizō.
Worlds seen and imagined : Japanese screens from the Idemitsu Museum of Arts / Taizō Kuroda, Melinda Takeuchi, Yūzō Yamane.
p. cm.
Exhibition catalog.
Includes bibliographical references and index.
ISBN 0-87848-081-1 (softcover). —ISBN 0-7892-0081-3 (hardcover)
1. Screen painting, Japanese—Kamakura–Momoyama periods, 1185–1600—Exhibitions. 2. Screen painting, Japanese—Edo period, 1600–1868—Exhibitions. 3. Screen painting—Japan—Tokyo—Exhibitions. 4. Idemitsu Bijutsukan—Exhibitions. I. Takeuchi, Melinda. II. Yamane, Yūzō, 1919– . III. Idemitsu Bijutsukan. IV. Asia Society. Galleries. V. Title.
ND1053.4.K87 1995
759.952'074'7471—dc20 95-32833
CIP